The Self and Others

The Self and Others

POSITIONING INDIVIDUALS AND GROUPS
IN PERSONAL, POLITICAL, AND
CULTURAL CONTEXTS

Edited by Rom Harré and
Fathali Moghaddam

Westport, Connecticut
London

Library of Congress Cataloging-in-Publication Data

The self and others : positioning individuals and groups in personal, political, and cultural
  contexts / edited by Rom Harré and Fathali M. Moghaddam.
     p. cm.
    Includes bibliographical references and index.
    ISBN 0-275-97624-6 (alk. paper)—ISBN 0-275-97625-4 (pbk. : alk. paper)
    1. Social psychology. 2. Social perception. 3. Intentionalism. 4. Individuality.
5. Social groups. I. Harré, Rom. II. Moghaddam, Fathali M.
    HM1033.S44   2003
    302—dc21   2003045764

British Library Cataloguing in Publication Data is available.

Library of Congress Catalog Card Number: 2003045764
ISBN: 0-275-97624-6
    0-275-97625-4 (pbk.)

First published in 2003

Praeger Publishers, 88 Post Road West, Westport, CT 06881
An imprint of Greenwood Publishing Group, Inc.
www.praeger.com

Printed in the United States of America

The paper used in this book complies with the
Permanent Paper Standard issued by the National
Information Standards Organization (Z39.48–1984).

10 9 8 7 6 5 4 3 2 1

Contents

CHAPTER 1

Introduction: The Self and Others in Traditional Psychology and in Positioning Theory

Rom Harré and Fathali Moghaddam

THE EMERGENCE OF TWO PSYCHOLOGIES

From its beginnings in the middle of the nineteenth century, modern psychology has been characterized by competition between two main rival visions of the discipline: psychology as a causal science versus psychology as a normative science (Harré, 2002; Moghaddam, 2002). This is first clearly articulated in the scholarship of Wilhelm Wundt (1832–1920), best known as the father of experimental psychology. Students of psychology are typically instructed in their introductory courses that Wundt was the first person to establish a psychology laboratory, and that he trained hundreds of students who went on to assure the dominance of the experimental method in modern psychology. Like all reconstructions of the past, this one is shaped by the particular biases of those writing history at present.

Wundt was one of a number of researchers, including William James (1842–1910), who developed experimental laboratory methods to study psychological phenomena in the late nineteenth century. It is true that Wundt produced a monumental amount of research using the laboratory method (James produced very little by comparison, preferring to invest his time in theoretical writing), but a neglected aspect of Wundt's story is his decades of effort to produce a ten-volume treatise on *Volkerpsychologie*, translated as "folk" or "cultural" psychology. This was not a marginal aspect of Wundt's psychology, but a central feature of the new science as envisaged by him.

In traditional reconstructions of the past, it is neglected that Wundt actually put forward two fundamentally different types of psychology: a laboratory-based experimental science, and a field-based cultural science. Wundt, the father of experimental psychology, recognized that certain types of psychological phenomena, related to language, culture, and collective processes generally, could not be adequately studied using laboratory techniques. The very nature of such collective processes would change when broken into elementary parts to be studied in the laboratory. However, this central feature of Wundt's approach, his "second psychology," did not gain influence immediately.

The story of how Wundt's "second psychology" became neglected, and how the laboratory method and the causal model came to dominate the discipline, is the story of the history of modern psychology. The "competing" schools of psychology that came to dominate academic research throughout the twentieth century, including behaviorism, psychoanalysis, and cognitive psychology, were in agreement on one fundamental assumption: the causal nature of human behavior. That is, each of these schools proposes that every behavior is determined by a cause, and the identification of cause-effect relations must be the goal of psychological science. Thus, behaviorists assume causes to be "stimuli" in the environment, psychoanalysts assume causes to lie in an unconscious, and cognitive psychologists look for causes in "cognitive mechanisms." In one way or another, then, the traditional schools have looked for a "hidden causal hand" that would explain behavior.

The causal model has been translated directly into the details of the laboratory method (see Moghaddam, Walker, & Harré, 2002). Soon after learning about Wundt as the father of experimental psychology in their introductory psychology classes, psychology students are instructed (typically in the first or second chapter of their introductory text, under a title such as "research methods in psychology") that psychologists discover the causes of behavior by manipulating independent variables (assumed causes) to test their impact on dependent variables (assumed effects). Students are of course reminded that tests of association do not demonstrate causation, but this reminder is in practice of little consequence because the theoretical explanations widely used in psychology are causal in nature. Thus, although a researcher might take care not to interpret a specific correlational study in a causal manner, when this study is cited in psychological papers and texts, it typically becomes part of a causal explanation. Also, almost all the major psychology texts affirm that the goal of psychology is to discover the causes of behavior.

The rigid adherence of traditional psychologists to a causal model is worth deeper examination. No doubt this orthodoxy arises in part from the assumption that "real science" is about cause-effect relations, and the discovery of universal laws of "what causes what." But part of the explanation for the pervasiveness of this orthodoxy is also reductionism: the tendency to reduce explanations to the smallest units possible. Again, the major schools of psychology are all in agreement. Just as behaviorists reduce explanations to stimulus-response associations, psychoanalysts reduce behavior to unconscious motives, fears, and so on, and cognitive psychologists reduce behavior to assumed "mental processes."

The traditional reductionist, causal paradigm is inadequate for studying social behavior and the collective processes that Wundt discussed under the topic of "folk" or "cultural" psychology. An important feature of social behavior is the collaborative construction of social reality and the mutual upholding of particular interpretations of the world. By implication, then, psychology should also explore collective processes, rather than only focus on isolated individuals in static situations.

In line with Wundt's original project for psychological science, it is useful to distinguish between two types of psychology: the first concerned with *performance capacity*, how well individual humans do on specific tasks (e.g., auditory perception tasks); the second type of psychology deals with *performance style*, the way people do things and the meanings ascribed to what they do. For example, a psychologist might study individual students one at a time in a laboratory to assess how well they see and distinguish between particular colors (performance capacity). However, in order to understand why the same individual students come to prefer black clothes as a group one particular year, it would be necessary to study the mutually upheld perceptions among students (and others) that black has become "the" fashionable color. The study of performance style requires a more dynamic paradigm, because the individual is part of a network of changing social relationships.

The Dynamic Paradigm and "Positions"

Alongside traditional psychology, which is for the most part concerned with performance capacity, there slowly emerged in the latter part of the twentieth century a stronger "second psychology" concerned with performance style. In this second "dynamic paradigm" psychology, emphasis was placed on the analysis of actual episodes of social interaction as unfolding sequential structures of meanings, ordered in accordance with local rules, conventions, and customs of correct conduct. Studies of the dynamics of social action, for example the *making* of friends, displaced studies of the conditions under which static states, such as *friendship*, were brought about. The methodology characteristic of new paradigm research required the use of the act/action distinction to identify social phenomena as meanings as understood by the participants. Observation of real life episodes replaced experiments. Analysis of participants' justificatory and interpretative accounts was used to identify the projects to the accomplishment of which a social interaction was directed and the rules and conventions in accordance with which it was managed.

The upshot of new paradigm research was a catalogue of situation-specific meanings and sets of context-sensitive rules that explained the pattern of the evolving social episode, as an actual sequence of meaningful social actions. This led to an alliance with the newly emergent field of Discursive Psychology, which was directed to a similar end product. The concept of "rule" stood in for a wide variety of normative constraints that could be seen to be effective in shaping the flow of action.

In his studies of the development of higher cognitive functions, Vygotsky emphasized the way that members of a family or some other well-knit group tend to supplement the actions of someone who is not fully competent in the local skills. In this way the project that person seems to be undertaking is brought to a successful outcome. Vygotsky was influenced in part by Adler's ideas on how individuals strive to compensate for their perceived defects (see Van der Veer & Valsiner, 1991). In a similar vein, Goffman described the way that the substandard performance of a member of a social group is often supplemented or quietly corrected by other members so that the standards of conduct or skill of the whole group are seen to be maintained. The relations Vygotsky emphasized have come to be called "psychological symbiosis," while Goffman called the social processes of mutual redefinition of a social gaffe "face work."

There was an important element missing from the dynamists' point of view, an element that was conspicuously absent from the work of Vygotsky and from Goffman's writings too. Surely, the rights to supplement someone's performance, and even the duties to do so were not uniformly distributed through the group in question. Indeed, in any unfolding social episode, who could perform which actions and so contribute this or that act to the episode structure as a whole depended on subtly varying presuppositions as to right of access to the local repertoire of acceptable conduct and presuppositions as to the distribution of duties to perform the necessary actions. The concept of "position" has been introduced to fill this gap.

"Positions" exist as patterns of beliefs in the members of a relatively coherent speech community. "Positions" are social in the sense that the relevant beliefs of each member are similar to those of every other. Of course, we can assess the similarity of each person's clusters of position-defining beliefs to those of every other only in how each social actor expresses his or her beliefs about positions.

Is there a repertoire of positions to be found in every society? While a case can be made for the universality of certain roles, the close connection between local norms of proper actions and the positions that are recognized in different societies suggests that universally acceptable positions may be hard to find. For example, positioned as simple minded, a person's speech acts are not taken seriously in contemporary Western society. In some places and times the utterances of those we would say were mentally defective or mad have had high status as prophecies.

POSITIONS AS LIMITING ACTION/ACT REPERTOIRES

A fundamental principle of new paradigm psychology was the distinction to be drawn between those actions that were logically possible and those that were socially possible for any social actor at any moment in the flux of social life. There is a certain range of social actions that anybody could perform, if we ignore the presence of other people and the social context in which the action was to be carried out. Within that range is a narrower repertoire of actions that a person could properly perform, engaged with other people, and for which a social context is taken into account.

The boundary between the range of logically possible actions and the repertoire of socially appropriate actions is fuzzy. There are some socially improper actions that one might perform if one had the nerve to do so. Some actions might attract the attention of the police, "streaking at the Presidential Inauguration" for example. Others might lead to one's being condemned as gauche, rude, a show-off, and so on. For example, one does not entertain a causal visitor to a university department with a list of one's major publications, at risk of being branded an egomaniac.

Looked at in terms of what is logically and what is socially possible, a position can be looked at as a loose set of rights and duties that limit the possibilities of action. A position implicitly limits how much of what is logically possible for a given person to say and do and is properly a part of that person's repertoire of actions at a certain moment in a certain context, including other people. This bounds the content of the repertoire of socially possible actions.

This feature of the concept of "position" makes it possible to generalize the concept in studies of discursive interactions between larger units than one-on-one conversations. Institutions and even nations can be positioned in that rights and duties to perform certain categories of speech acts are restricted by the conventions of interaction. The Enron affair in the United States is a good case in point. The "revelations" are a clear example of the restriction of correct actions to a subset of possible actions. Shredding incriminating paper work is a possible action, but it is not among the correct actions that someone positioned as an Enron executive was entitled to do.

Positioning someone, even if it is oneself, affects the repertoire of *acts* one has access to. While *actions*, such as writing as letter to the *Washington Post*, are intended performances, something one does deliberately, acts are what such actions mean socially. One's letter might be a *plea* for the Catholic clergy to marry, for example. Another letter might be a *protest* against nighttime flights from Reagan National Airport. But each of these missives, in the category of actions, could mean something else, in the category of act. To whom is the letter addressed? When was it written? What else was happening at the time it was published by the *Post*? And so on.

THE FINE GRAIN OF LOCAL MORAL ORDERS

The Positioning "Triangle"

1. "Position": a cluster of rights and duties to perform certain actions with a certain significance as acts, but which also may include prohibitions or denials of access

to some of the local repertoire of meaningful acts. In a certain sense in each social milieu there is a kind of Platonic realm of positions, realized in current practices, which people can adopt, strive to locate themselves in, be pushed into, be displaced from or be refused access, recess themselves from and so on, in a highly mobile and dynamics way.

2. Speech and other acts: every socially significant action, intended movement, or speech must be interpreted as an act, a socially meaningful and significant performance. A handshake is an intended action. Does it express a greeting, a farewell, congratulations, seal a bet, or what? It is only significant as far as it is given a meaning in the unfolding episode of which it forms a part. Once interpreted it falls under rules of propriety and standards of correctness, not only in itself but also in what are its proper precursors and consequences.

3. Story line: we have emphasized the enormous importance of the dynamics of social episodes, how they unfold as this or that person contributes to the pattern. Episodes do not unfold in any random way. They tend to follow already established patterns of development, which, for convenience have come to be called story lines. Each story line is expressible in a loose cluster of narrative conventions.

Indirect Positioning

The use of attributions of mental (stupid), characterological (unreliable), or moral (puritanical) traits to position someone, favorably or unfavorably, with respect to oneself and one's interests, or the interests of one's own group, we could call indirect or presumptive positioning.

Positioning someone as stupid is, at the same time, to deny that person the right to correct one's cognitive performances. Positioning someone as unreliable is at the same time to exclude the person from certain duties, such as bringing in the laundry if it starts to rain. Positioning someone as puritanical denies that person the right for their criticisms of one's louche lifestyle to be taken seriously.

This technique of establishing and occupying the moral high ground is evident in larger scale discourses, in which it is nations or cultures that are the beings being positioned. Recently we have noticed the use of indirect positioning of the leader of a nation being used as a device for positioning the nation itself. The current fashion in Europe for using the phrase "The Cowboy President" not only is an indirect positioning of George "Dubbya"[1] Bush but also an indirect positioning of the United States as collectively naïve and ill-informed.

Dynamics

It is important to emphasize that positioning is something that is frequently outside the power of those so positioned to accomplish. Positioning of one person or even a certain category of persons can be brought about deliberately and as a matter of policy by someone else, or by some authority. However, the other actors may thrust it upon someone without explicit intentions. Explicit assent to a certain story line may never have been obtained. Yet, it is evident to an outside observer that a common story line is being maintained by everyone involved. Since positions are always relational, that is by positioning someone in a certain way someone else is thereby positioned relative to that person, the situation may look far more "designed" by those who benefit from the positioning than is justified by an empirical study of the beliefs of the people in question.

We must distinguish two extreme forms of the process of positioning, with many intermediate cases. There are instances in which positioning has been planned and executed deliberately, such as the apartheid laws of the former regime in South Africa. There are also instances in which positioning has been brought about by everyone involved having been brought up in a certain social milieu in which positions were taken for granted almost as if they were just "part of the natural order of things." This seems to have been the situation in Western Europe in medieval times when the social and practical spheres of life of men and women were sharply distinguished. Upheavals such as the Crusades threw these "taken for granted" arrangements into question. Women took on the roles of the men who had gone to the Holy Land. They managed great estates, took up positions in the craft guilds, and so on. However, so strong were the conventions that by the fourteenth century the previous arrangements had been restored, but not by any edict or conscious policy by either church or state.

There is explicit positioning and repositioning. Resisting being positioned or any other way in which positioning is challenged and people are repositioned or reposition themselves is a form of metapositioning. To engage in repositioning oneself or others is to claim a right or a duty to adjust what an actor has taken to be the first order positioning that is dominating the unfolding of events. Those rights may be challenged too. To challenge a position may involve rights at two levels. Since a position is a cluster of rights and duties, to deny someone a right or to refuse a duty is an act of resistance to a certain positioning. However, one might challenge the right of someone to assign positions.

Malignant or Malevolent Positioning

Since acts of positioning create an ephemeral moral order in which a person's rights and duties can be enhanced but also in which they can be reduced, the question arises of whether this reduction is destructive of a person's basic capacities to live a flourishing life, and is thereby immoral. Both Sabat (2001) and Kitwood (1990) have brought to light a pattern of unilateral positioning that is destructive of the possibility of a flourishing life for old people, particularly those with Alzheimer's disease. Minor incapacities become the grounds for positioning an old person as incompetent, in short as suffering from senile dementia. This slide has been called "malignant psychology" or "malevolent positioning." Sometimes it is the result of impatience. Often, we fear it may be malicious, of evil intent, to rid oneself of the nuisance of looking after an aged person. The phenomenon is a special case of indirect positioning. To say that someone cannot quickly bring to mind certain words is to predicate a certain psychological attribute to that person. However, to slide from that attribution to positioning someone as no longer having the right to make life decisions for him or herself is an act of positioning. It is for the practice of making an unjustified slide from attribution to positioning that Kitwood coined the term "malignant psychology."

Context: Its Many Dimensions

The result of the analysis of cognitive practices includes a catalogue of admissible acts. Furthermore one must have access to repertoires of meanings, even to be able, sometimes, to exercise authority as to meanings and norms. Research in social psychology has shown that there are subtle and contextually sensitive moral orders in place that determine in large measure one's rights of access to the materials needed to carry out cognitive projects.

These rights of access to and use of discursive resources differ from person to person, and for any one person, from time to time. The term "position" has been appropriated to refer to those momentary clusters of rights and duties to think, act, and speak in certain ways that are evident in the flux of everyday life (Harré & Van Langenhove, 1999). A position is linked to the kinds of acts that a person in that position can be "seen" or "heard" to perform with any given symbolic device. Both are linked to the story line, the conventional narrative, that the people so positioned are in process of living out. If the story line is a trial in a British court of justice, the various participants are formally positioned with respect to what sorts of speech acts they can legitimately be heard to perform. The judge may refuse to allow a certain speech act to be "heard," requiring that it be struck from the record. This pattern of position/speech act/story line is all but ubiquitous in human affairs.

In one respect our studies of cognitive practices and the tools we use to carry them out are necessarily abstracted from the domain of concrete human activities. We are abstracting from the fluid and shifting positions that people occupy, resist, impose on others, refuse to take up, and so on. Our interest is on what people do and how they do it when they are authorized or take themselves to be authorized to do it. Of course, disputing about whether or not oneself or some other is authorized, that is, positioned in a certain way, is sometimes an exercise in reason, and subject to the conditions of well-grounded and well-rounded thought. But whether a claiming or disclaiming of a position is adequate or not is dependent on the particular content of what is under dispute, the status of the disputants, and the larger social context.

Methodological Procedures

How is research with the dynamic paradigm to be carried out, and what would one regard as an adequate end-product? The "positioning triangle" can be entered empirically at any of the vertices, "position," "speech act," or "story line." For most purposes, entering at "story line" has certain advantages.

As a first step, then, a story line is proposed as a working hypothesis about the principles or conventions that are being followed in the unfolding of the episode that is being studied. Such a story line might be "David and Goliath" or "Doctor and patient." These titles sum up what is to be expected in the episode being studied and comprise the conventions under which to make sense of the events that have been recorded and to express them in a narrative. Actions must be given sense as acts. Is this kiss a betrayal? Is this suicide bomb blast a protest at the injustice of the treatment of the conquered by the conqueror? From the point of view of that story line, tentative meanings for the actions, including speech actions of the participants, can be proposed. Each story line incorporates positions that relate the participants in a definite way. For example, if the narrative unfolding is "Doctor and Patient," then the one positioned as "doctor" has a right to prescribe treatment and the other positioned as "patient" has a duty to follow the "doctor's" orders.

One begins with a hypothesis about the three components of the positioning triangle: story line, positions, and illocutionary forces, and tests it by seeing how far it can be used to make sense of what has happened in some episode. Participants' accounts can be woven into the discussion, but they are never definitive of the nature of the events described at the level of acts. This is for the simple reason that there may be several story lines being lived out, only one of which is expressed in any one actual account.

What can we ascribe to the individuals who take part in an episode that has been made sense of according to some story line hypothesis? Knowledge of possible positions exists in systems of belief that fix shared presuppositions. Unless this had been so, there would never be any situation in which the positions of all the actors made up a coherent pattern. Both mother and child must share knowledge of the positions expressed in "doctor/patient" for the episode of a sick child home from school to evolve smoothly. Maybe the child will reject the positioning his mother has adopted as medically competent and hence with rights to determine what treatment should be administered.

A research report should then include not only an analysis of the episode in question from various points of view, but also a catalogue of what must be tacitly known by the participants. There are shared and unshared beliefs about the story lines unfolding and the rights and duties of participants. It may be quite unrealistic to ascribe motives in the sense of preexisting psychological "forces" that engender action, to people who are trapped in the living out of story lines in which actions are required by the positions those story lines express. As C. Wright Mills and Kenneth Burke have argued, in many cases motives are themselves just part of the content of narrations by which actors give justificatory accounts of their actions in some episode where they have been called to account or think they could be.

PLAN OF THE BOOK

The chapters are organized in three main parts, dealing with: the self and other individuals, the self and social groups, and the self and contexts. A strong theme in the first part is flexibility and plasticity in the ways in which individuals behave: authors point out how things often are, but also how they could become. Apter (chapter 2) views motivational level and style not as a fixed and stable trait, but as varying within the same individual across situations, and sometimes from moment to moment. Emotions are similarly depicted as flexible and "usable" toward positioning goals (Parrott, chapter 3). In chapters 4 (Walton, Coyle, and Lyons), and 5 (Benson), the focus is more on tactics and boundaries of emotions used in positioning. The disparity between what is and what should be is heightened in chapters 6 (Sabat) and 7 (Wetherell), with explorations of how those with more power position others with less power, in this case the minorities being those labeled in some way psychologically abnormal.

The theme of positioning and power is further developed in Part II. In various ways the six chapters in this part deal with the positioning processes involved in minority-majority relations. Specifically, the groups involved are neighborhood groups (Harré and Slocum, chapter 8), world powers (Moghaddam, Hanley, and Harré, chapter 9), men and women (Wilkinson and Kitzinger, chapter 10; Adams and Harré, chapter 11), native people and whites (Aberdeen, chapter 12), and minority-majority groups generally (Taylor, Bougie, & Caouette, chapter 13). In all these cases, positioning theory allows for a more detailed look at dynamic processes over time.

The chapters in Part III extend the theme of dynamic change, but with a focus on different types of contexts, including the European Union (Slocum and Van Langenhove, chapter 14), intellectual property (Moghaddam and Ginsburg, chapter 15), organizations (Boxer, chapter 16), and landscapes (Davies, chapter 17). Finally, in chapter 18 May critically assesses the contribution of positioning theory in the wider context of social theory. In each case, the authors explore how the characteristics of the context influence the kind of positioning that takes place. At the same time, the theme of power continues, because there is often competition to control how the context is interpreted. The chapters in this section also continue the applied theme of the entire book: like all good theories, positioning theory is a very practical tool and can help us navigate the real world.

NOTE

1. Just as our use of the president's nickname also positions him.

REFERENCES

Burke, K. (1945). *A grammar of motives*. New York: Prentice Hall.

Cole, M. (1996). *Cultural psychology: A once and future discipline*. Cambridge, MA: Belknap Press of Harvard University Press.

Harré, R. (2002). *Cognitive science: A philosophical introduction*. London: Sage.

Harré, R., & Van Langenhove, L. (Eds.) (1999). *Positioning theory*. Oxford: Blackwell.

Kitwood, T. (1990). The dialectics of dementia: with particular reference to Alzheimer's disease. *Aging and Society, 10*, pp. 177–196.

Moghaddam, F. M. (2002). *The individual and society: A cultural integration*. New York: Worth.

Moghaddam, F. M., Walker, B. R., & Harré, R. (2002). Cultural distance, levels of abstraction, and the advantages of mixed methods. In A. Tashakkori & C. Teddue (Eds.), *Handbook of mixed methods in social and behavioral research* (pp. 111–134). Thousand Oaks, CA.: Sage.

Sabat, S. R. (2001). *The experience of Alzheimer's disease: Life through a tangled web*. Oxford: Blackwell.

Van der Veer, R., & Valsiner, J. (1991). *Understanding Vygotsky: A quest for synthesis*. Oxford: Blackwell.

PART I

The Self and Other Individuals

CHAPTER 2

Motivational Styles and Positioning Theory

Michael J. Apter

Relatively little attention has been paid to motivation from the positioning theory perspective. In one sense this is not surprising, since most approaches to motivation in traditional experimental psychology have treated motivation, literally or metaphorically, as a form of energy—something that is available to the person in different quantities and that the individual uses in the course of his or her activities. But this is a problematic conception based on an outmoded mechanistic model of human nature. It is, in fact, exactly the kind of hopelessly simplistic model opposed by the discursive approach from which positioning theory has emerged. But there is another way of thinking about motivation, and this is in terms of the *orientation* of individual people to the world about them: what they experience themselves as wanting at a particular time and how their mental life is organized around this. In this respect it is possible to conceive of motivation as a necessary element of positioning, since the ways in which people interact and position each other will depend in part on their orientations in this sense. Such motivational orientations are therefore something that should be included in any version of positioning theory that pretends to completeness.

It is perhaps not without significance that the area where the term "positioning" has been mainly used until now is that of marketing: by positioning a product one is presenting it as a promise to satisfy particular needs in particular groups of people. The marketing concept is therefore essentially motivational (Ries & Trout, 1981). It is also interesting to note that the area in psychology where the term "positioning" has been mainly adopted before the advent of positioning theory is that of object-relations theory. This uses, following Melanie Klein, (1975) such terms as "the depressive position" and the "paranoid-schizoid position." Again, this meaning of "position" has a strong motivational flavor.

It is this idea of motivational orientation and its relationship to positioning that will be explored in the present chapter. More specifically, the aim will be to examine the relevance of a theory that conceptualizes motivation in terms of orientation, or "motivational style" rather than energy. This is the theory of psychological reversals, better known now as "reversal theory" (Apter, 1982, 1989, 2001). Reversal theory is a general theory of motivation, emotion, personality, and stress that provides distinctive accounts of many psychological phenomena from creativity to violence, addiction to risk-taking, leadership to humor. The chapter will start with an outline of some of the key ideas of this theory and then discuss how these relate to the notion of positioning and social relations—self and other. It will then be possible to consider its similarities to, and differences from, positioning theory in the way in which it has been described by Harré, Van Langenhove, and others (e.g., Davies & Harré, 1990; Harré & Van Langenhove, 1991, 1999a, b & c; Van Langenhove & Harré, 1999).

REVERSAL THEORY

The basic proposition of reversal theory is that the way that we see the world and act in it depends on the basic values that we are pursuing at a given time, and that these values are continually changing in the course of everyday life. This means that we are different kinds of people, we have "different personalities" at different moments. For example, if we pursue the value of significant achievement we will adopt a different temporary personality from that which we display when we pursue the value of immediate enjoyment.

There is a further point here, and it relates to the term "reversal." This is that the basic values we pursue come in pairs of opposites, so that we cannot pursue both of them at the same time. We can, however, pursue both at different times by switching back and forth between them. Since they are opposites, such switches are referred to as "reversals." There are four such pairs of states (see below), which means that at any one time we shall be experiencing four states, and four kinds of reversal will be possible from moment to moment. (Of the four active states, however, typically only one or two will be at the focus of attention, the others forming part of the psychological background.)

What are these opposing pairs of values identified in reversal theory, and the motivational styles that go with them? Let us list these. Note that they are also called "metamotivational states" since they are about how we interpret particular motives and motivational variables. In each case below the reversal theory term for the motivational style represented is given in parentheses.

1. The domain of goals and activities.

Achievement. The style that goes with this is a serious style, in which one gains satisfaction from feeling that one is making progress towards some important future goal, even if the current activity is not in itself very pleasant (Telic).

Enjoyment. The style that goes with this is a playful style, in which one gains satisfaction from immediate pleasures (sensory, emotional, intellectual). Here one does things for their own sake, in the here-and-now, rather than because they provide benefits in the future (Paratelic).

2. The domain of rules and conventions.

Duty. The style that goes with this is a conforming style, in which one gains satisfaction from fitting in and adapting. Here one does things because they are right, or because they are expected, or because they are traditional, or because they are laid down, or because they are what one is supposed to be doing (Conformist).

Freedom. The style that goes with this is a rebellious style, in which one gains satisfaction from breaking rules, being unconventional, dissident, and challenging, doing the unexpected, rejecting duties, even being hostile (Negativistic).

3. The domain of transactions.

Power. The style that goes with this is a competitive style, which sees life as a contest. Here one gains satisfaction from feeling tough and in control, looked up to by others, and able to display one's skills and abilities, especially if these are superior to those of others (Mastery).

Love. The style that goes with this is a caring style, which sees life in terms of affection, sensitivity, and intimacy. Here one gains satisfaction from friendship and being close to others (Sympathy).

4. The domain of relationships.

Individuality. The style that goes with this is a self-oriented style, in which it is what happens to oneself primarily that counts. Satisfaction comes from being able to do things on one's own account (Autic).

Transcendence. The style that goes with this is an other-oriented style, in which it is what happens to someone or something else (a child, the team you belong to, the hero you identify with) that counts first. Satisfaction comes from being unselfish, identifying with others, and being "taken out of oneself" by larger causes (Alloic).

These states combine across the pairs. For example, the mastery state can be autic or alloic (primarily desiring control for oneself, or primarily desiring it for others with whom one identifies) and the sympathy state can also be autic or alloic (wanting primarily to be loved, or wanting primarily to do the loving). One of the interesting things that emerges from this is that different state combinations give rise to different ranges of emotions (the particular emotion relating to the outcome of actions), although this is a complicated topic that will not be further pursued here (but see Apter, 2001). (There are also other concepts of reversal theory that we do not need to develop for present purposes, such as the notions of multistability, cognitive synergies, protective frames, and tension-stress versus effort-stress.)

Unlike most other theories of personality, then, reversal theory recognizes—and even celebrates—the inconsistencies and self-contradictions that enter into human psychology. As we go through a normal day, we tend to switch between different combinations of styles, at one time experiencing paratelic mastery, at another autic sympathy, and so on. We also shift between which states are focal—in the foreground of attention—at a given moment (thus someone in the paratelic and mastery states, as in the example just given, might also be in the conformist and autic states simultaneously but not as aware of these as of the paratelic and mastery states). Reversal theory argues that such inconsistencies are needed for healthy living. Otherwise, how could we experience all sides of ourselves and take full advantage of the many qualitatively different situations in which we find ourselves? In this respect, it is not too much to say that mental health is reflected in instability rather than stability. (Reversal theory actually provides an alternative, but systematic, account of the different broad categories of psychopathology that are recognized in modern psychiatry. For a recent review, see Lafreniere, Ledgerwood, & Murgatroyd, 2001.)

These metamotivational states can be seen as different ways of accounting for what one is doing at a given moment, both to oneself and to others. In other words, they are positions in the positioning theory sense. They position one's actions in terms of what one might think of as motivational space by identifying the key motive involved in an action. For example, a father castigates his teenage son for getting in late the night before, and for seeming to be drunk. The son can position himself in terms of narratives of kinds that relate to each of the motivational styles, as shown below. Incidentally, one may suppose that if his father happens to be in the same state as his son when listening to the narrative, his son may "get away with it."

Telic: "I needed to find out what it would be like to get drunk. I thought it would be part of my education, an essential part of growing up."

Paratelic: "What the Hell: I was just having a bit of fun, Dad. Can't you remember just doing something for the heck of it when you were young?"

Conformist: "All my friends were doing it. It was kind of the expected thing to do, you know? Surely you don't want me to be a loner and not to fit in with others?"

Negativistic: "I suddenly felt a need to break free from all the restrictions of being at school. I don't want to always do what others say I should do. Do you want me to be a zombie?"

Autic mastery: "If I had not gone, I would have lost face and been humiliated. You want me to be able to hold my head high among my friends, don't you?"

Autic sympathy: "The people I went with are all good friends. If I don't do things like this with them they won't like me any more. Surely you want me to be popular?"

Alloic mastery: "The people I went out with are a looked up to by others at school, and I did not want to let them down by not drinking. Don't you want me to be loyal?"

Alloic sympathy: "I am very fond of my friends, and I wanted to do something that they would enjoy doing. Besides, it was Bob's birthday, and I did not want to let him down. Don't you agree?"

A number of these explanations could be combined with each other. It is also possible that the son gave different explanations to himself at different times during the course of the evening, thus reversing between different states, and moving the focus of attention between different domains in the course of what has been called "reflexive positioning" (Harré & Van Langenhove, 1999b; Moghaddam, 1999). But the point is that each account implies a story that could be elaborated and expanded, and each is based on a particular motivational style—the meaning of the action is its purpose. Each of the resulting positions could also be renegotiated in the course of a subsequent conversation with his father.

What causes a reversal? Clearly changing situations, events that occur, and encounters that are experienced can lead to reversals. Someone disagreeing with something you have said can induce the negativistic and mastery states, entering a hospital ward to visit a patient can induce the alloic and sympathy states, the arrival of tax forms in the mail can bring about the telic state, hearing a joke can induce the paratelic state, and so on. The resulting reversals are all examples of what have been called contingent reversals. But sometimes people reverse seemingly spontaneously, meaning that the same situation comes to be experienced in a completely different way even though nothing obvious has occurred to bring this about. Reversal theory suggests that there is in fact an underlying satiation process such that the individual becomes increasingly vulnerable to a reversal within a particular pair of states and, if a reversal has not occurred after a period of time, it will happen anyway (like the sleeping-waking cycle). All of a sudden the individual finds himself or herself seeing the world in a different way. Finally, reversal theory proposes that frustration in the attainment of the satisfaction inherent in a particular metamotivational state can itself lead to reversal—as, for example, when failure at something serious leads us to trivialize it or make jokes about it. All three kinds of reversal—contingent, due to satiation, and due to frustration—are deemed to be involuntary. That is, one cannot decide to reverse and then simply do so. But reversals can be brought under indirect voluntary control—for example by deliberately changing situations, or by attempting to reframe the ongoing situation, and so on.

Reversal theory is now supported by evidence of various kinds—psychometric, experimental, psychophysiological. It has also been applied successfully for a number of purposes—in therapy, health counseling, sports coaching, and management consultancy. (For a review of both research and practice, see Apter, 2001.) It should be clear that, although connections can be made between reversal theory and other theoretical ideas—for example, Claude Levi-Strauss's binary oppositions, Norbert Wiener's cybernetic mechanisms, Kurt Lewin's phenomenal fields, Isaiah Berlin's value pluralism, and so on—the theory stands alone as a unique and distinctive framework for understanding psychological processes and for carrying out psychological interventions.

REVERSAL THEORY: SELF AND OTHER

Although the reversal theory analysis starts from an examination of individual experience, it has from the beginning of its development been used to understand personal relationships and the ways in which these can go awry. Indeed, the theory initially emerged from work in a child guidance clinic in which family problems were observed to arise frequently because family members were in different motivational states without realizing it (Apter & Smith, 1979). For instance, one common type of problem arose from children setting parents against each other for the fun of the drama, the children being in the paratelic state and their parents in the telic state. The children were positioning the social situations they created as an entertaining kind of theatre, but their parents were interpreting them as serious and "real." As a result the children were enjoying themselves at the expense of their parents, who were being genuinely upset by what their children were saying and doing.

In personal interactions, people tend to position themselves jointly in terms of the style to be adopted, and they need to do so if successful communication is to take place. We do so in terms of gestures, postures, and also rhetoric. When people are on the "same wavelength" or have "good vibrations," this means that they mutually understand and adopt a conjoint style—they are in the same states at the same time. "Let's be serious," we seem to say to each other. Or "Are we having fun yet?" All the time in our interactions we are asking each other, and telling each other, how we should position ourselves together in the context in which we find ourselves. Is it an adventure, a chore, a routine, a romance, a negotiation, a game? The one exception to the need to share the same state is that of the autic and alloic states, which are compatible when those who are interacting are in opposite states—so that when one wants to give the other wants to receive, and vice versa.

Let us take a simple example of this joint motivational positioning. Suppose a beggar comes up to me in the street and asks for money. I can position our momentary relationship, and my act of giving him something, in a variety of different metamotivational ways, and indeed, I cannot avoid making choices between them. I can see it as a way of helping to keep him alive (telic), a trivial game that we are playing (paratelic), a moral duty I have to perform (conformist), a way of encouraging dissidence in society (negativism), an act of loving charity (alloic sympathy), or as a way of demonstrating superiority to someone and having power over them (autic mastery). If he approached me on different days I might position our interaction in different ways at different times. In each case I would be understanding myself differently. Of course the beggar might reject my positioning. But if he wants to repeat my giving on another day he may feel that he should validate the motivational style that he perceives me as adopting—for example, laughing and smiling if he thinks that my style is playful, being subservient if he thinks I am in the mastery state, and so on (whether or not he is actually in the state that he is representing to me).

This reminds us that the way that we position each other motivationally depends not just on language but on what has been called "body language." Interestingly, the theory of body language also uses the concept of positioning. For example, Scheflen (1964) has defined a position as a gross postural shift involving at least half the body, and has argued that in the course of conversation people combine sequences of positions in order to establish what he calls "presentations."

A further point here is that rather than the reciprocal positions that tend to be emphasized in positioning theory, reversal theory lays stress on the need for jointly adopted, or compatible, stances towards the world. People who have enduringly good relationships, like happily married couples, position the same things as serious, the same moments as intimate, the same situations as funny, and so on. The exception to this, as already noted, is the autic and alloic states. Here, as in a ballroom dance, when one goes forward, the other must go back. That is, people who get on well together know when the other person wants to be giving and when the other person want to be given, when the other person wants to care and when the other person wants to be cared for, and they position themselves appropriately. In this sense, good partners dance well together.

Some people are good in general at correctly sensing the metamotivational states of others. Successful therapists, counselors, teachers, car salesmen, and others with good social skills all are able to "read" people correctly in this way. Professionals who deal with children who have been taken into care adopt different metamotivational states with the children than they do with the adults—they position their interactions differently (Bazex, 2002). Nurses, in interacting with their patients, adopt different metamotivational states for different moments of interaction: they position themselves differently when they give injections from the way that they position themselves when they are being reassuring to patients, or looking for appreciation for themselves (Rhys, 1988). This does not mean that such professionals have to accept the states of those they interact with, and a further essential skill is that of inducing desired states in others—repositioning the situation in a more helpful way by means of postures, emotional expressions, and rhetorical devices.

Things can go wrong. For example, scenarios have been developed by the present author to be acted out in self-development workshops. These mini-scripts represent different kinds of problematic positioning in terms of motivational style and allow participants to discuss what has gone wrong, how it could have been avoided, and what might be done about it. Problems include people being in incompatible states at the same moment but not understanding this, people being unable to reverse into another state when this would be helpful, and people behaving in ways that are counter-productive within a given state.

An interesting example of misunderstanding has been developed from within positioning theory by Davies and Harré (1990) to exemplify the problems that occur when people get at cross purposes in terms of their positions, being in incompatible states. The problem starts out when a man attempts to help a woman acquaintance to find a chemist's shop to buy her some medicine. They fail and the man apologizes for dragging her along when she is not well. She replies with irritation that she chose to come, and things go downhill from there on. In reversal theory terms the origin of the problem is that the man is in the alloic sympathy state—feeling caring and wanting to help—while the woman is in the autic mastery state, feeling her autonomy and self-respect to be under threat. He is also adhering to certain moral principles in the conformist state, while the effect is to push her into a negativistic state in which she feels that her freedom is being attacked.

The same ideas about motivational positioning apply to groups of people in face-to-face situations, such as committees. A committee at a given moment will have an "atmosphere." It might be friendly or solemn, angry or supportive. The point is that, for a group to have psychological cohesion, its members must generally be in the same metamotivational state at the same time. And they must also be able to change as they have to deal with different kinds of problems—logistical, creative, planning, emergency, maintenance, and so on. Again, difficulties can arise in different ways, including when some members of the group are in different states and do not realize this. So what one person takes to be a joke (paratelic) another can take to be deliberately offensive (negativistic), or what one person takes to be helpful advice (alloic sympathy) can be taken by another as an attempt at domination (autic mastery). Such examples demonstrate that effective group functioning can soon be damaged as a result of such misunderstandings.

In a larger context we can begin to understand organizational "atmospheres" (e.g., corporate culture) in terms of the reversal theory framework. What are the values emphasized by a given business company, for example? Are they about getting on well with its customers (alloic sympathy), beating the competition (autic mastery), being innovative (negativism), being far-sighted (telic), or what? It is not without interest that different types of institutional organization tend to provide contexts (including physical contexts) that emphasize different motivational styles. For instance, law courts emphasize the serious telic state, theatres the playful paratelic state, churches the dutiful conformist state, and scientific meetings the controlling mastery state.

REVERSAL THEORY AND POSITIONING THEORY

Positioning theory and reversal theory both represent radical reactions to traditional mainstream psychology. And although these two theories emerge from different intellectual and scientific backgrounds, they would appear to be in essential agreement, and even mutually supportive, in relation to two important basic propositions.

The first is that we cannot understand people unless we understand the *meanings* that they attribute to the situations in which they find themselves (or which they themselves bring about). Indeed, meaning should be the essence of psychology, the key concept, the central term from which all explanation should flow. If people change in their behavior and demeanor, this is because the meaning that they attribute to the situation is changing. If people differ from each other this may be because they are seeing things in different ways. For reversal theory this meaning is largely motivational—what one understands oneself to be "up to" in terms of intentions, purposes, expectations, desired satisfactions, values. For positioning theory it is more about social relationships. That is, it is about the attributes that we assign to each other and ourselves in the course of our interactions and conversations—that we are powerful, stupid, brave, honest, and so on—and the rights and duties that go with such characterizations.

The second basic way in which positioning theory and reversal theory are in fundamental agreement is that they both recognize that people are continually *changing*, sometimes subtly and at other times more dramatically, as their circumstances and contexts change. For reversal theory this is seen as an anti-trait position: to categorize and type people by means of traits is regarded as both over-simple, because static, and unhelpful because limiting. After all, how can you help someone to change after you have told him or her that this is "how they are?" There is a technical term in reversal theory for this kind of error. It is referred to as "chronotyping"—making over-general inferences from how someone is at a given time to how they will always be, and in this respect carrying out a kind of temporal stereotyping. For positioning theory, the opposition is more towards roles and the idea that there are always static sets of rules for how to behave in different situations. From this perspective "the use of 'role' serves to highlight static, formal and ritualistic aspects" (Davies & Harré, 1990, p. 43). Like reversal theory's states, positioning theory sees positions as ephemeral, changing, and open to dispute in the sense that one person can refuse to accept the other's interpretation and attempt to impose his or her own. Another way of putting all this is to say that both reversal theory and positioning theory foreground the temporal aspect of psychological processes. For instance, reversal theory sees personality in terms of patterns of change over time, and positioning theory sees positions as emerging over time from conversations. Tan and Moghaddam (1999) have even emphasized how positioning such as that involved in intergroup processes can only be understood in "historical" terms, the typical "snapshot" social psychology experiment being highly limiting as a way of understanding what is really happening between groups.

How, then, do reversal theory and positioning theory differ? Certainly reversal theory, like positioning theory, is pluralist in the sense that it recognizes that people can make sense of reality in many different ways and in relation to many different evaluative standards. There is no one true interpretation of a given situation, but always multiple possibilities. For reversal theory, however, this does not mean that the possible interpretations that people can make, at least at the motivational level of analysis, are endless, but rather that they relate to a fixed number of metamotivational frames. Just as a finite grammar can underlie the generation of an infinite number of utterances, so the grammar of motivational style can be expressed in an infinite number of different ways, including the different ways typical of different cultures. Consider, for example, the different things that people do when they play—express the paratelic state—in different cultures and at different historical periods. Also, different cultures can encourage different values. For example, Asian countries would appear to encourage more the communal value of the alloic state than Western cultures, while the latter would appear to emphasize more the individualistic value implicit in the autic state. Furthermore, different classes within a culture can, as Bourdieu (e.g., Bourdieu, 1986) has reported in considerable detail, position themselves by means of different tastes in music, food, and so on. But according to reversal theory the basic value set remains the same from culture to culture and class to class. In other words, this motivational grammar is assumed in reversal theory to be (to use an unfashionable terminology) "part of human nature"; but the particular way that the value set plays out will depend highly on particular local circumstances.

Positioning theory tends to be more relativistic than this in its pluralism. This kind of difference between the two approaches would appear to emerge from the fact that meaning for positioning theory is essentially linguistic, culturally relative, socially constructed, and local. For reversal theory, the kinds of meaning that are of prime interest are seen as innate, biologically constructed, and universal, albeit mediated socially and culturally in a variety of interesting ways. The aim of the reversal theory story is to discern an underlying structure to experience and behavior, and in this way to constitute a general psychological theory—what post-modernists such as Lyotard (1979) would dismiss as a "grand narrative." The aim of positioning theory is to provide a careful and sensitive method of analysis and to follow it wherever it might lead: "It is to be treated as a starting point for reflecting on the many different aspects of social life" (Harré & Van Langenhove, 1999c, pp. 9–10). Positioning theorists would no doubt want to demonstrate that motivational styles are themselves socially constructed rather than biological and therefore far from universal. Reversal theory for its part would want to argue that the whole process of positioning is grounded in the biology of motivation, and that positions at some level of analysis are anchored in metamotivational states that determine "what counts," what to be aware of, what is relevant. In this respect reversal theory would see positions of all kinds as being ultimately anchored in the innate values that it identifies.

A second fundamental difference between positioning theory and reversal theory is that the latter allows for both causes and reasons, while positioning theory insists that human action should be understood in terms of reasons alone. Thus reversals are seen in reversal theory as being involuntary and can in this regard be understood in causal fashion, while the actions that people choose within a motivational state are voluntary and can be accounted for in terms of reasons and story lines (as in the example given earlier of the son explaining his night out to his father). Of course people can also choose their metamotivational states. But getting into them is not direct—people have to use certain causal methods for their own purposes—for example by going to a place likely to induce the desired state, or by using ritual actions associated with the state. These "causal moments" can be embedded in an account that cites reasons (e.g., "I knew I needed to have some fun because things were getting on top of me"). On the other hand, reasons can be prompted by prior reversals (e.g., "I don't know why I suddenly had the urge to do something for fun, but this feeling came over me"). The result for reversal theory is an interesting mix of types of process, types of explanation, and a recognition that the complexities of human experience and action can only be fully un-raveled by making reference to both reasons and causes, and their interactions.

Consistent with this, metamotivational states can be examined both phys-iologically and discursively. A classic example here is that of Svebak and Mur-gatroyd (1985). Telic and paratelic dominant participants (people who tend more often to be in the telic and paratelic state respectively) were recruited for a psychophysiology experiment. On the one hand they were shown to have significant psychophysiological differences (for example in terms of elec-tromyographic gradients), and on the other to have different discursive styles when asked to describe their previous day. Telic dominant subjects tended to be precise, chronological, careful, and descriptive, while the accounts of par-atelic dominant subjects tended to be evaluative, global, imprecise, haphazard, impressionistic, non-chronological, and exaggerated.

It will be appreciated that the ways in which the social meanings of central interest to positioning theory and the biological/motivational meanings of reversal theory enter into, and articulate with, each other might deserve much further exploration. The general issue would be that of how one could com-bine the externally imposed rights, duties, and obligations of positioning the-ory with the internally generated wants, purposes, and values of reversal theory. At the very least, the concept of motivational styles is one that could usefully be incorporated within positioning theory as a further type of posi-tioning to add to those discussed by Harré and Van Langenhove (1991). This would lead to a greater recognition in positioning theory of the importance of motivation in giving meaning to people's actions. In turn, the sophisticated notion of positioning is one that should prove fruitful for reversal theory in its attempts to understand all the nuances and subtleties of the ways in which motivational styles play themselves out in complex human interactions such as those involved in conversations, negotiations, arguments, games, seductions, interviews, lessons, rituals, intercessions, and consultations. In conclusion, while emphasizing different aspects of the way in which human relationships are established, develop, and change, positioning theory and reversal theory can be seen as essentially complementary in their emphasis on meaning and on changeability. It seems to the present writer that they could usefully position each other as allies in their attacks on mainstream psychology.

REFERENCES

Apter, M. J. (1982). *The experience of motivation: The theory of psychological reversals.* London and New York: Academic Press.

Apter, M. J. (1989). *Reversal theory: Motivation, emotion and personality.* London: Routledge.

Apter, M. J. (Ed.) (2001). *Motivational styles in everyday life: A guide to reversal theory.* Washington, D.C: American Psychological Association Press.

Apter, M. J., & Smith, K.C.P. (1979). Psychological reversals: Some new perspectives on the family and family communication. *Family Therapy,* 6, 89–100.

Bazex, H. (2002). La maltraitance familiale sur enfant. La specificite des relations entre les co-acteurs de l'intervention: Processus de maitrise et de reparation, mecanismes de defense et etats metamotivationnelles. Ph.D. dissertation, Universite de Toulouse Le Mirail.

Bourdieu, P. (1986). *Distinction.* London and New York: Routledge and Kegan Paul.

Davies, B., & Harré, R. (1990). Positioning: The discursive production of selves. *Journal for the Theory of Social Behaviour,* 20 (1), 43–63.

Harré, R., & Van Langenhove, L. (1991). Varieties of positioning. *Journal for the Theory of Social Behaviour,* 21, 393–407.

Harré, R., & Van Langenhove, L. (Eds.). (1999a). *Positioning theory: Moral contexts of intentional action.* Malden: Blackwell.

Harré, R., & Langenhove, L. (1999b). Reflexive positioning: Autobiography. In R. Harré & L. Van Langenhove (Eds.), *Positioning theory: Moral contexts of intentional action.* Malden: Blackwell.

Harré, R., & Langenhove, L. (1999c). The dynamics of social episodes. In R. Harré & L. Van Langenhove (Eds.), *Positioning theory: Moral contexts of intentional action.* Malden: Blackwell.

Klein, M. (1975). *The writings of Melanie Klein.* Vols. 1 to 4. London: Hogarth Press.

Lafreniere, K. D., Ledgerwood, D. M., & Murgatgroyd, S. J. (2001). Psychopathology, therapy and counseling. In M. J. Apter (Ed.), *Motivational styles in everyday life: A guide to reversal theory.* Washington, DC: American Psychological Association Press.

Lyotard, J.-F. (1979). *La condition postmoderne: Rapport sur le savoir.* Paris: Editions de Minuit.

Moghaddam, F. M. (1999). Reflexive positioning: Culture and private discourse. In R. Harré & L. Van Langenhove (Eds.), *Positioning theory: Moral contexts of intentional action.* Malden: Blackwell.

Rhys, S. (1988). Mastery and sympathy in nursing. In M. J. Apter, J. H. Kerr, & M. P. Cowles (Eds.), *Progress in reversal theory,* pp. 329–338, Amsterdam: Elsevier.

Ries, A., & Trout, J. (1981). *Positioning: The battle for your mind.* New York: McGraw Hill.

Scheflen, A. E. (1964). Significance of posture in communications systems. *Psychiatry,* 27, 4.

Svebak, S., & Murgatroyd, S. J. (1985). Metamotivational dominance: A multimethod validation of reversal theory constructs. *Journal of Personality and Social Psychology,* 48, 107–116.

Tan, Sui Lan, & Moghaddam, F. M. (1999). Positioning in intergroup relations. In R. Harré & L. Van Langenhove (Eds.), *Positioning theory: Moral contexts of intentional action.* Malden: Blackwell.

Van Langenhove, L., & Harré, R. (1999). Introducing positioning theory. In R. Harré & L. Van Langenhove (Eds.), *Positioning theory: Moral contexts of intentional action.* Malden: Blackwell.

CHAPTER 3

Positioning and the Emotions

W. Gerrod Parrott

In the aftermath of the collapse of the giant energy company Enron, one finds a dramatic case of strategic public positioning. As this chapter is being written in the summer of 2002, business executives, employees, auditors, stockholders, and investigators of the Enron Corporation are positioning themselves in a variety of fora for what promises to be a battle of legal, financial, and political consequence. Positioning, defined as the dynamic construction of personal identities relative to those of others, is an essential feature of social interaction (Davies & Harré, 1990). Its strategic and negotiable qualities are especially apparent in situations where there is conflict, such as is occurring with Enron.

One striking feature of this positioning is the central role that is being played by emotions. One way of positioning oneself is to display the emotions that are characteristic of one's position. One way of positioning one's opponents is to state what emotions they ought to be feeling and to characterize as inappropriate the emotions they are feeling. In the example of Enron, we can see the integral role of emotions in positioning. Prior to the company's collapse, the executives of Enron positioned themselves as superior business leaders; expressions of contempt and pride aided this positioning. After the collapse, the employees and stockholders of Enron expressed anger, thereby positioning themselves as victims and characterizing Enron's executives as blameworthy. The employees and stockholders strengthened their position by asserting that Enron executives ought to feel shame at what they did. Some executives attempted to reposition themselves as having made some errors but as having corrected. These executives expressed embarrassment (but not shame), and some expressed pride at their efforts at self-reform.

Thus, emotions play a central role in positioning. This chapter will explore this role in three ways. First, it examines emotions in light of positioning theory. In order for emotions to position actors, emotions must possess the properties that are necessary for positioning to occur, and this section details what these properties are. Thus, the central argument of this first section is that positioning theory can inform us about emotions. Second, the chapter focuses on strategic aspects of positioning. The importance of emotions to positioning is especially apparent when considering the maneuvering of rivals or adversaries. Under such circumstances, one party's emotional expression can be understood strategically as an attempt to establish a superior social identity while assigning an inferior one to the rival. The rival's emotional expression often implies an alternative positioning that refutes the positioning of the first party. In the second section of the chapter, strategic positioning is examined in detail by considering a number of pairs of commonly opposed emotions: in each pair, the first emotion asserts a positioning that is countered by the second emotion. The final section of the chapter takes up the case of Enron in detail. The aim is to analyze the positioning taking place in this current event so as to demonstrate the critical roles played by emotions. The Enron example serves to demonstrate the application to a well-documented, real-life example of the theoretical points made in this chapter.

POSITIONING AND THE NATURE OF EMOTION

In order to play a central role in positioning, emotions must share the properties that theorists have ascribed to positioning. What are these properties? A position has been defined as a place within a moral order (Moghaddam, Hanley, & Harré, in this volume). A position therefore entails a cluster of rights, duties, and obligations (Harré & Slocum, 2001). Emotions can share these properties. Moral accounts of emotions have been offered ever since Aristotle's *Rhetoric*. Central to most such accounts is the idea that emotions involve moral judgments of oneself or of others (Sabini & Silver, 1982). One theoretical perspective, social constructionism, especially emphasizes the ways that emotions embody the moral values and judgments of a culture (Parrott & Harré, 1996). More generally, emotional states are often used to mark the relative status of interpersonal relationships. In fact, Averill (1980) explicitly defined "emotion" as a special kind of social role that includes beliefs about the situation at hand and that entitles the emotional person to behave in ways that otherwise would not be allowed. Much recent theory and research on emotion has emphasized its role in social interaction, relationships, and social control (Parrott, 2001). It is because emotions have these properties that they can establish persons' identities, their places within a moral order.

For emotions to have the functions ascribed to them by these theorists, they cannot consist merely of subjective feelings or "qualia." Emotions have the property of being about something; this is what analytic philosophers call "intentionality" (Harré, 1986). People report being angry *about* something, ashamed *of* something, proud *of* something. Furthermore, the "something" that an emotion is about must be appraised by the emotional person in the way that fits the emotion. To be angry about something is to perceive it as having been the result of wrongdoing by another person; to be ashamed of something is to feel oneself as lowered in stature in someone else's eyes; to be proud of something is to take credit for something of value (Lazarus, 1991; Sabini & Silver, 1982). Some emotions even derive their labels from a sort of metonymy with situations that evoke them. To feel emotionally "hurt," for example, is to feel as if another's actions were intended to cause one pain; to feel "guilt" is to feel as if one were guilty of wrongdoing (Ortony, 1987).

Because emotions entail these intentional and cognitive aspects, their public expression can assert a claim about objective circumstances in the world. If being angry about something entails appraising someone as having engaged in wrongdoing and as being blameworthy, then expressing the anger assigns that person a place within the local moral order and places other people in complementary places of having justifiable complaints. In other words, the intentional and cognitive aspects of emotions permit them to accomplish exactly what is involved in positioning.

Positions are rarely defined in isolation. Rather, positions are usually defined relative to other positions in some complementary or reciprocal fashion, such as the way that being positioned as a nurse makes little sense without others who are positioned as patients (Harré & Slocum, 2001). The same quality exists for many emotions. Angry people must have a target who is guilty of a transgression and blameworthy; the target in turn should feel guilty and ashamed (Averill, 1979). An ashamed person usually has or imagines an audience expressing disapproval or condemnation (Smith, Webster, Parrott, & Eyre, 2002). A proud person typically has or imagines an admiring audience (Lazarus, 1991). Public expression of these emotions can serve to position the emotional person as well as to position the emotion's audience or target. Thus, emotions often establish a position that is defined relative to other persons' positions.

Emotions are also well-suited for yet another aspect of positioning: its strategic aspect. The term "positioning" has its origins in strategic activities. Generals are said to position their forces for battle; chess players position their pieces and study the strengths and weaknesses their opponent's position; marketers position their products to draw away their competitor's customers (Harré & Van Langenhove, 1991). Positioning in discourse retains these connotations. Analyses of positioning typically depict actors as trying to establish for themselves a favorable position; sometimes positive attributes are sought, such as honesty or integrity; sometimes superiority to an opponent is sought (Davies & Harré, 1990; Moghaddam et al., 2001). Emotions contribute to the strategic aspects of positioning in several ways.

One reason why emotions can contribute to strategic positioning is that they are persuasive. As Aristotle said in the *Rhetoric*,

your language will be appropriate if it expresses emotion and character, and if it corresponds to its subject. . . . This aptness of language is one thing that makes people believe in the truth of your story: their minds draw the false conclusion that you are to be trusted from the fact that others behave as you do when things are as you describe them; and therefore they take your story to be true, whether it is so or not. Besides, an emotional speaker always makes his audience feel with him, even when there is nothing in his arguments. (Book III, section 7, W. Rhys Roberts, trans.)

Aristotle's argument suggests that emotions persuasively establish a position because they effectively communicate a point of view. This effectiveness is the result of emotional expressions encouraging an audience to see one's point of view, often to the point of empathetically feeling the emotion themselves (Hatfield, Cacioppo, & Rapson, 1994). Furthermore, because emotions are understood as being passive and at least somewhat uncontrollable, they suggest that the emotional person is strongly committed to the positioning that the emotion entails (Frank, 1988).

In addition to their persuasiveness, emotions are strategic because they can cast an opponent into a weaker position or constrain the opponent's options. Anger can assert blameworthiness. Contempt and scorn can denigrate and assert inferiority. Less directly, excessive self-anger or shame or guilt can prevent excessive attack and even elicit protestations on one's behalf.

Strategic positioning often involves a sequence of moves, with each party angling to achieve its goals. Some of the work of Goffman captures the fluid, negotiated quality of such interactions. His concept of remedial interchanges, for example, involves a sequence of actions that start with an apparent violation of social norms (Goffman, 1971). Interactants "orient to the virtual offense," that is, become aware of the worst possible interpretation of this apparent violation. The person who noticed the infraction may issue a challenge, and the person who broke the norms engages in "face-work" by offering an account of the infraction (Goffman, 1967). This account may range from a denial that any infraction occurred through an excuse or justification for the infraction to an apology or a plea of mitigated guilt. The person challenging the infraction may accept this account or may instead refuse it and insist that the offender accept greater responsibility. The outcome of the exchange determines the future relationship between the two parties and, much like positioning, establishes their place in the local moral order. Offenders may have their former self restored or may have to accept some sort of reduced or probationary status (Goffman, 1971).

Accounts of positioning share Goffman's emphasis on strategic interaction. The positioning concept is generally more dynamic than Goffman's concept of role, extending the range, flexibility, and creativity of self-definitions that are under negotiation. An analysis of a conversation in terms of positioning theory may yield a narrative of mutual accusations, each accusation stimulated by the unintended yet undesired implications of the other person's positioning (Davies & Harré, 1990). Emotions can generate similar narratives. Sympathy from one person to another may be intended as kindly and virtuous, but it can make the sympathized person feel weak and immature and can thereby generate anger rather than gratitude (Clark, 1987). Displaying one's suffering and implying that another is responsible for it may be intended to elicit guilt but may elicit resentment as well or instead (Baumeister, Stillwell, & Heatherton, 1995). The power of positioning theory is that it characterizes both parties in these interactions as active participants. The person receiving sympathy who responds with anger is not passively emitting an anger response to a sympathy stimulus but rather is an active party in the interaction, using anger strategically to avoid the position conferred by the positioning of the sympathizer. The person feeling resentment in response to an attempt to produce guilt is countering an attempt to define their mutual relationship in terms that seem exaggerated and unfair. The emotions in these examples fully exemplify the concept of positioning, thus demonstrating how emotions and positioning are intertwined.

EMOTIONAL MANEUVERING IN STRATEGIC POSITIONING

Emotions' role in strategic positioning is most apparent when one party's emotion is countered by another party's emotion. This maneuvering draws on the subtle cognitive complexity of emotions so that the depiction of the moral order suggested by one person's emotions is contradicted by that depicted by a second person's emotions. There are two principal ways in which emotional maneuvering occurs, which I term "counter-emotions" and "relabeled emotions." Counter-emotions involve two emotions: one expressed by one party, and another expressed by a second party. Relabeled emotions involve only one emotion, which is labeled as one sort of emotion by one party and then is relabeled as another sort by a second party. Each type of emotional maneuvering is described below. Examining a number of pairs of opposing emotions illustrates the strategic aspects of each type of positioning.

Counter-Emotions

Counter-emotions are emotional expressions that contradict the positioning inherent in a previous emotional expression. The subtle variety of counter-emotions may be illustrated by considering the possible responses to an expression of anger.

One person's anger at another construes the other's actions as blameworthy (Averill, 1979). If the second person accepts this positioning, he or she will have to express guilt or shame as part of an apology. But other strategies are possible. For example, the second person can express anger at the accuser for making a false accusation and thereby deny any wrongdoing him- or herself. This type of counter emotion involves a direct counterattack; anger is met with counter-anger. A number of other strategies are possible as well, however.

For example, the second person can accept responsibility for the action but assert that it was justified, not blameworthy (Goffman, 1971). In this case the person might express pride rather than guilt. The expression of pride contradicts the picture of the moral order implicit in the first person's anger, but it does so by asserting a justification, not by construing the anger as blameworthy.

Alternatively, the second person can assert that a third person actually performed the blameworthy act. Someone else did it. With this tactic the second person joins with the first person in being angry at the truly guilty party rather than blaming or refuting the angry person.

A fourth variation of counter-emotion involves admitting a lesser type of wrongdoing by expressing embarrassment rather than shame. The distinction between shame and embarrassment allows for a counter-emotion that repositions while acknowledging the appearance of wrongdoing. Shame is more strongly linked with morality, embarrassment more with poise and appearances (Parrott & Harré, 1996). It has been argued that the two words refer to essentially the same emotional experience, with "embarrassment" suggesting the appearance of defect or wrongdoing is false and with "shame" suggesting it is correct (Sabini, Garvey, & Hall, 2001). The display of embarrassment in the face of anger thus involves a more subtle type of counter-emotion than the previous types. To announce that one is embarrassed rather than ashamed is to deny the stronger moral connotations of shame. The focus is more on the awkwardness of one's position and on the anxiety one feels about how others will perceive oneself (Parrott & Smith, 1991). Like shame, embarrassment announces an awareness of social norms and displeasure at having upset them. But unlike shame, embarrassment makes no admission that public scorn is justified, that one possesses a serious defect or feels self-contempt. The emotion is linked to the present situation, not to one's enduring self or character. Embarrassment therefore counters the force of anger by pleading guilty to a lesser charge. One has muffed the present situation, but one is not a bad person.

These four forms of counter-emotion do not exhaust the possibilities, but they are examples of the ways that the positioning of one emotion can be countered by that of another emotion. These four strategies—denial and counterattack, asserting a justification, joining in the anger, and admitting to a lesser charge—challenge the moral order proposed by another person's anger. In all four of these remedial interchanges the emotion expressed—counter-anger, pride, joint-anger, or embarrassment—conveys an alternative construal of events that positions the person in a more favorable manner than that implicit in the first person's display of anger. By using a counter-emotion rather than unemotional words, a person can counter the emotional force of the first person's anger and thereby increase the rhetorical effectiveness of the positioning, as Aristotle suggested.

Relabeled Emotions

Another tactic for countering the positioning of an expressed emotion involves relabeling that emotion. Rather than expressing a counter-emotion that contradicts the first one, this tactic involves reinterpreting that initial emotion.

One illustration of this tactic is found in political discourse where the anger expressed by one political group is discounted or belittled by another political group, which relabels the anger as "envy." Suppose that one political group expresses anger over a benefit enjoyed by another group; for example, suppose that the first group is angry that the inheritance tax is so small that the children of the wealthy inherit large fortunes and thereby enjoy unearned advantages that are unfair to others from less privileged backgrounds. The second group, rather than responding with a counter-emotion, might instead try to relabel the righteous anger of the first group. If they were to announce that there was no basis for anger, and that the hostility of the first group was a symptom of envy, they would be employing this second strategic use of emotions. This tactic relies on there being some similarity in the symptoms of anger and envy, which in fact is the case (Parrott, 1991; Smith, Parrott, Ozer, & Moniz, 1994). The same hostility that is characteristic of anger is also characteristic of malicious envy. The difference between the emotions is moral, not phenomenological. Labeling this hostility as envy completely undercuts its moral force. Anger construes the angry party as a victim and the target of the anger as blameworthy. It asserts that a moral wrong exists. Envy, in contrast, casts the hostile party as the moral inferior. That hostility is understood as a symptom of inferiority, as a pathetic attempt to protect self-esteem and public reputation by belittling the apparent superiority of others (Sabini & Silver, 1982). The power of this strategy was understood by the moral philosopher John Rawls (1971), who devoted a chapter in his *Theory of Justice* to defending the righteousness of justice-based hostility by distinguishing envy from "resentment proper."

A related tactic involves relabeling one's own emotion after another person has labeled it in an unwanted way. One example involves the pair, "anger" and "irritation." As has been shown by Averill (1979), the word "irritation" conveys much of the feeling and motivation of "anger" without implying the existence of an objective moral transgression. If one person labels another person's emotion as "irritation," that labeling positions the irritated person as lacking a legitimate target for his or her feelings. Perhaps that person is tired, frustrated, or grouchy, but that person does not have a blameworthy target for anger. The counter-positioning of that person might consist of the statement, "I'm not irritated—I'm *angry!*", thereby asserting an objective and socially sanctioned basis for hostility. This pair of emotions could just as easily be used in the opposite direction: A person might be asked why he or she is acting so angry. If he or she did not feel that the evidence of blameworthiness was strong enough, or did not feel that the issue was important enough to press, or simply did not want to air the moral accusation inherent in anger at the present time, he or she might reposition by stating, "I'm not angry—it just irritates me when this happens." The positioning of irritation construes the situation as one of personal idiosyncrasy rather than of objective wrongdoing.

Thus, whether an emotion is first labeled by the person having the emotion or by the person witnessing it, relabeling can be used as a tactic of emotional maneuvering. Relabeling and counter-emotions demonstrate the strategic way that positioning can be accomplished with emotions.

In the final section of this chapter the approach shifts from theory to real-life application. The rise and fall of the Enron Corporation presents a rich narrative on emotions and positioning, one that presents a suitable test of the claim that the properties of emotions allow them to accomplish all the social, moral, and strategic aspects of positioning.

THE CASE OF ENRON

Enron Corporation was once the seventh largest company in the United States and one of the world's largest traders of electricity and natural gas. For much of the 1990s this company was the darling of investors and financial journalists due to its continuous innovation and expansion into new markets and businesses. Founded in 1985 as a natural gas pipeline company, Enron transformed itself to an energy trading company in 1989. Later, it expanded into electricity trading, moved its trading operations online, and further expanded its businesses to include commodities, Internet broadband, and financial derivatives. For six continuous years in the 1990s Enron was ranked as the most innovative company in the United States by *Fortune* magazine. Between 1998 and 2000 the price of its stock tripled, peaking above $90 per share in the autumn of 2000 (Behr & Witt, July 28, 2002; "Enron," 2002; "Timeline," 2002).

Then, in less than a year, the company collapsed with little warning from analysts and with no warning from the management or from the company's auditors, the respected accounting firm Arthur Anderson. The company had been reporting profits continuously for the previous four years. Although a number of officials at Enron and Arthur Anderson wrote internal memoranda that questioned the viability and legality of the company's business and accounting practices in 2000 and 2001, there were no public signs of problems until the summer of 2001, when several Enron executives resigned for "per-

sonal reasons." These resignations led to large drops in share prices as investors wondered whether something was amiss.

Something most certainly was. In August 2001, an Enron finance executive
contacted the company's president, Kenneth Lay, and the company's auditor,
Arthur Anderson, to raise questions about the riskiness and legality of the
company's complex accounting practices. During this period Lay publicly re-
assured the financial markets that all was well, but privately he and other
Enron executives began to sell large numbers of their own shares in the company. At Arthur Anderson it was realized that it had approved aggressive accounting tricks that were viable only if the company's stock was rising, and
the stock was falling, fast, dropping below $30 per share (one-third their peak
price) by September 2001. The accounting would have to be revised, but
revising the accounting would mean that the company would have to announce enormous losses that previously had been concealed from the public.
Soon afterward, employees at Arthur Anderson began shredding thousands
of documents related to Enron.

Because Enron's pension plan consisted primarily of company stock, employees had strong reasons to be concerned about how Enron stock was performing and wondered whether they should try to sell some of this stock to
diversify what for many of them was their life's savings. Employees watching
their retirement savings evaporate were assured by management that nothing
was wrong. For a time Enron executives actually barred employees from selling their shares while these same executives continued selling their own
shares. Over the next two months the company's stock dropped to pennies
per share, realizing the employees' worst fears.

In late October 2001 it was revealed that Enron's chief financial officer,
Andrew Fastow, had set up the schemes that hid the company's losses in a
way that created conflicts of interest and that benefited himself financially.
He was fired, the Securities and Exchange Commission announced an investigation, and the stock price plummeted to $15 per share. Enron then had to
restate its earnings for the past four years, admitting that instead of the large
profits it had reported, it had actually lost large amounts of money the whole
time. On December 2, 2001, with its stock now below $1, its credit rating
lowered to junk status, and unable to pay its debts, the Enron Corporation
filed for bankruptcy protection.

In terms of positioning theory, the story of Enron's demise unfolds over
time and involves the positioning of two principal parties, one being the executives at Enron and Arthur Anderson and the other being the employees
and stockholders of the company, plus the general public. I shall refer to the
first of these groups as "the Executives" and to the second as "the Public,"
although both groups can and occasionally must be further subdivided. In the
years preceding the summer of 2001 the Executives positioned themselves as
being on the cutting edge of what was called "the New Economy," as a radical
break from traditional ways of doing business. They hired the smartest

people, they encouraged innovation and gave executives unheard of freedom to pursue new ideas (Gladwell, 2002). As one of the top executives, Jeffrey Skilling, told a group of business school professors, "We're the world's coolest company" (Behr & Witt, July 28, 2002). Or, as an executive who left the company put it more critically, "We were creating a very arrogant management team. . . . We were trying to project a figure of Super Human" (Witt & Behr, July 29, 2002). Whether cool or arrogant, the Executives reinforced their positioning by projecting a set of congruent emotions. They acted proud of their company (the world's coolest) and of their achievements. They also expressed contempt for their competitors. Jeffrey Skilling was known for denouncing traditional business practices and for mocking competitors as "foundering clipper ships" (Witt & Behr, July 29, 2002). They projected complete confidence in the superiority of their methods. This pride, contempt, and confidence played a role in persuading others to accept the positioning it expressed. As one "high-ranking executive" at Enron put it, "Bells and whistles go off, but then you say it's Jeff and Ken and Andy and everybody is supporting it . . . so maybe if I don't get it, maybe I'm wrong. . . . You got lulled. You got seduced. If you didn't jump on the bandwagon, maybe you just weren't smart" (Behr & Witt, August 1, 2002).

For years the Public largely accepted the Executives' positioning. Energy trading was congruent with several popular ideas of the time, namely deregulation in the late 1980s and early 1990s and the use of the Internet to facilitate transactions between companies ("B2B") in the late 1990s. As long as the company was profitable and the price of the stock continued upward, the financial press and the general public were happy to accept the company's positioning.

This complicity came to an abrupt halt in 2001 as evidence emerged first of trouble and then of outright deception. The positioning of the Public then became one of moral outrage and victimization. Moral outrage and public indignation were expressed over what appeared to have been particularly exploitative and immoral behavior by the Executives. Enron's executives, it was claimed, had intentionally enriched themselves not only by engaging in fraudulent practices but also by preventing 20,000 Enron employees from protecting their retirement savings. Essentially, they had grabbed millions of dollars for themselves by ensuring that thousands of much lower-salaried employees would lack economic security in their old age. Investors were deceived as well. Enron insiders sold over $1 billion worth of stock to others, knowing it would drop in value. The auditors at Arthur Anderson, a "reputable" firm whose approval of Enron's accounting practices gave many the confidence to invest, had cooperated in deceiving financial markets about the company's profitability and then knowingly destroying the evidence.

Enron investors counter-positioned themselves as the victims of wrongdoing and characterized the Executives as heartless, greedy criminals. Enron employees especially took this position. The public in general claimed this position as well, although the claim to victimhood and thus the standing for moral reproach had to be justified on different grounds (Sabini & Silver, 1982). The position was claimed on grounds that the entire economic system depended on trusting public statements made by corporations and auditors; that government supervision was undermined by Enron's undue influence of the White House and Congress (the company contributed heavily to the campaigns of many politicians); and that the corruption at Enron was only an example of a more pervasive problem in American corporations (several other business scandals became public about the same time).

The role that emotions played in this positioning is striking. Supporting the Public's new positioning was a different emotion, anger. Employees, shareholders, government officials, and others expressed anger at the Executives for the harm they had caused. Examples abound, but to document the phenomenon, representative expressions of anger may be found in records of U.S. Congressional hearings conducted into Enron's collapse (e.g., 107th Congress House Hearings, 2002, which refer to employee's anger and describe the shredding of documents by Arthur Anderson as "brazen, outrageous, and completely unacceptable"). These expressions of anger not only assert a position of outrage and victimhood, but also partially constitute this positioning.

This positioning by the Public also implies that certain emotions ought to be felt by the targets of this anger. In particular, the Public's new positioning involves the claim that the Executives ought to experience the emotions of shame and remorse. For example, in the Congressional hearings the representative from Florida, Michael Bilirakis, repeatedly asserted that the firm of Arthur Anderson "should be ashamed" of its actions and their repercussions (107th Congress House Hearings, 2002).

Finally, the commentary on the collapse of Enron included exhortations about what emotions people should *not* feel. Although the Public should feel anger, which is consistent with blaming the Executives, they should not feel embarrassment or self-anger, which would contradict the desired positioning by directing some blame toward themselves. An example is provided by a newspaper column on the topic of stock market investing. Journalist James Glassman consoled investors who had lost money from owning Enron stock with the following words:

But could the average investor have seen through this story and determined that the company was in trouble? Absolutely not. Investing decisions, even those made by professionals, are built on trust. . . . and small investors can't be expected to understand the intricacies of SPEs [Special Purpose Entities] or complex trading contracts. . . . They have to trust Enron to give them a clear picture of the company's health. This Enron did not do. . . . If you had Enron in your portfolio and didn't sell it at $90 or even at $10, *don't feel embarrassed* [italics added]. (Glassman, 2001, p. H1)

This change in the Public's positioning directly challenged the prior positioning by the Executives. The leaders of the World's Coolest Company stood accused of being the World's Most Fraudulent Company. The Executives' reactions varied. The most senior Enron executives tended to say nothing at all, obviously on advice from legal counsel. Even so, strategizing about positioning continued. For example, the highest ranking executive of all, Enron chief executive Kenneth Lay, received a memo from an assistant shortly before the bankruptcy suggesting that he blame his subordinates, the lawyers, and the accountants (Witt & Behr, July 31, 2002), essentially positioning himself on the side of the Public and joining them in their anger.

For the Executives less central to Enron, the more common strategy was to position themselves by acknowledging having erred but not to the extent it seemed. For example, executives from Arthur Anderson, when testifying before Congressional investigations, stressed that they had voluntarily disclosed that their office had shredded documents, that they had cooperated with investigations, that the firm had realized its error and fired the employee most responsible for it and would freely disclose further mistakes if they were discovered (107th Congress House Hearings, 2002). The chief executive of Arthur Anderson, Joseph Berardino, asserted before Congress that his firm has been deceived by Enron, and he proposed new laws criminalizing lying to an accounting firm (Capitol Bound, 2002).

Again, emotions played an important role in the positioning, in this case quite a shrewd role. In the face of the Public's position that the Executives ought to feel ashamed of themselves, Arthur Anderson's counterposition involved a mix of embarrassment and even pride for having (belatedly) done some things right. Chief executive Barardino stated "I'm embarrassed by what happened at my firm" (Capitol Bound, 2002). Several of the directors and partners at Arthur Anderson who testified before the House Energy and Commerce Committee asserted that "We certainly are not proud of the document destruction, but we are proud of our decision to step forward and accept responsibility" (107th Congress House Hearings, 2002).

As this chapter is being written, an Enron executive has been convicted of money laundering and wire fraud. A variety of other misdeeds are being investigated as well, including manipulation of electricity prices in California and undue influence with politicians. Arthur Anderson's lead Enron auditor has been convicted of obstruction of justice. Although this story will doubtless continue to unfold, the positioning described so far will suffice to demonstrate the important place of emotions in positioning.

CODA

It has been the premise of this chapter that emotions play important functions in strategic social interactions. These functions are nicely described in terms of positioning theory, and they demonstrate some of the social qualities of emotions. Expressions of emotion project a claim about social reality because of the cognitive appraisals that ground emotions in the objective world. These claims often involve moral qualities and thereby serve to position actors within a moral order. The opposition of emotion and counter-emotion, along with the relabeling of emotions, are basic ingredients of strategic positioning.

The focus of this chapter has been positioning as a social action. The emphasis therefore has been on interaction, self-presentation, persuasion, and interpersonal strategy. Emotions have been shown to contribute to public positioning by merit of their communicative expression, their cognitive appraisals, and their rhetorical force.

For some readers, this emphasis may be surprisingly "exterior." Emotions, after all, are frequently understood as private experiences, as states of consciousness, as feelings. Pursuing the role of emotions in interpersonal positioning has led to an emphasis on those aspects of emotions that are most relevant to interpersonal behavior. Although experiences and feelings can be understood as aspects of the thought and motivation that influence public positioning, they have not been central to this chapter.

Yet, it is worth noting that theorists have extended positioning theory from the realm of the interpersonal to that of the intrapersonal. The concept of "reflexive positioning" has been introduced to describe how positioning theory can explain internal discourse that is constitutive of a self-concept and personal identity (Tan & Moghaddam, 1995). Reflexive positioning is the process by which one positions oneself in personal narratives that are told *to oneself.* If the role of emotions in reflexive positioning were to be examined, the more intrapsychic aspects of emotions would surely be more salient to the analysis. But full development of that idea would be the topic of a different chapter.

REFERENCES

107th Congress House Hearings. (2002, January 24). The destruction of Enron-related documents by Andersen personnel [Electronic version]. (DOCID: f:77569.wais) Washington, DC: U.S. Government Printing Office.

Averill, J. R. (1979). Anger. In H. Howe & R. Dienstbier (Eds.), *Nebraska Symposium on Motivation* (Vol. 26, pp. 1–80). Lincoln: University of Nebraska Press.

Averill, J. R. (1980). A constructivist view of emotion. In R. Plutchik & H. Kellerman (Eds.), *Emotion: Theory, research and experience*, Vol. 1 (pp. 305–339). New York: Academic Press.

Baumeister, R. F., Stillwell, A. M., & Heatherton, T. F. (1995). Personal narratives about guilt: Role in action control and interpersonal relationships. *Basic and Applied Social Psychology*, 17, 173–198.

Behr, P., & Witt, A. (2002, July 28). Visionary's dream led to risky business: Opaque deals, accounting sleight of hand built an energy giant and ensured its demise. *The Washington Post*, p. A01.

Behr, P., & Witt, A. (2002, August 1). Hidden debts, deals scuttle last chance. *The Washington Post*, p. A01.

Capitol bound: Lawyer says ex-enron chief will appear; Lawmakers rip accountant. (2002, February 5). *ABCNEWS.com*. Retrieved from http://abcnews.go.com/sections/business/DailyNews/enron_lay_hearings020205.html.

Clark, C. (1987). Sympathy biography and sympathy margin. *American Journal of Sociology*, 93, 290–321.

Davies, B., & Harré, R. (1990). Positioning: The discursive production of selves. *Journal for the Theory of Social Behaviour*, 20, 43–63.

Enron: The rise and fall. (2002). *BBC News Online*. Retreived August 24, 2002 from http://news.bbc.co.uk/hi/english/static/in_depth/business/2002/enron/time line/default.stm.

Frank, R. H. (1988). *Passions within reason: The strategic role of the emotions*. New York: Norton.

Gladwell, M. (2002, July 22). The talent myth. *The New Yorker*, pp. 28–33.

Glassman, J. K. (2001, December 9). When trust collides with risk. *The Washington Post*, p. H1.

Goffman, E. (1967). *Interaction ritual: Essays on face-to-face behavior*. Garden City, NY: Anchor Books.

Goffman, E. (1971). *Relations in public*. New York: Harper & Row.

Harré, R. (1986). An outline of the social constructionist viewpoint. In R. Harré (Ed.), *The social construction of emotions* (pp. 2–14). Oxford: Basil Blackwell.

Harré, R., & Van Langenhove, L. (1991). Varieties of positioning. *Journal for the Theory of Social Behaviour*, 21, 393–407.

Harré, R., & Slocum, N. (2001). Disputes as complex social events: On the uses of positioning theory. Unpublished manuscript.

Hatfield, E., Cacioppo, J. T., & Rapson, R. L. (1994). *Emotional contagion*. Cambridge, England: Cambridge University Press.

Lazarus, R. S. (1991). *Emotion and adaptation*. New York: Oxford University Press.

Moghaddam, F. M., Hanley, E., & Harré, R. (2003). A social psychological analysis of the Kissinger papers through positioning theory. In this volume.

Ortony, A. (1987). Is guilt an emotion? *Cognition and Emotion*, 1, 283–298.

Parrott, W. G. (1991). The emotional experiences of envy and jealousy. In P. Salovey (Ed.), *The psychology of jealousy and envy* (pp. 3–30). New York: Guilford.

Parrott, W. G. (2001). *Emotions in social psychology*. Philadelphia: Psychology Press.

Parrott, W. G., & Harré, R. (1996). Embarrassment and the threat to character. In R. Harré & W. G. Parrott (Eds.), *The emotions: Social, cultural and biological dimensions* (pp. 39–56). London: Sage Publications.

Parrott, W. G., & Smith, S. F. (1991). Embarrassment: Actual vs. typical cases, classical vs. prototypical representations. *Cognition and Emotion*, 5, 467–488.

Rawls, J. (1971). *A theory of justice*. Cambridge, MA: Harvard University Press.

Sabini, J., Garvey, B., & Hall, A. (2001). Shame and embarrassment revisited. *Personality and Social Psychology Bulletin*, 27, 104–117.

Sabini, J., & Silver, M. (1982). *Moralities of everyday life*. Oxford: Oxford University Press.

Smith, R. H., Parrott, W. G., Ozer, D., & Moniz, A. (1994). Subjective injustice and inferiority as predictors of hostile and depressive feelings in envy. *Personality and Social Psychology Bulletin*, 20, 705–711.

Smith, R. H., Webster, J. M., Parrott, W. G., & Eyre, H. L. (2002). The role of public exposure in moral and nonmoral shame and guilt. *Journal of Personality and Social Psychology*, 83, 138–159.

Tan, S.-L., & Moghaddam, F. M. (1995). Reflexive positioning and culture. *Journal for the Theory of Social Behaviour*, 25, 387–400.

Timeline of Enron's collapse. (2002, February 25). Retrieved from http://www.washingtonpost.com/wp-dyn/articles/A25624-2002Jan10.html.

Witt, A., & Behr, P. (2002, July 29). Dream job turns into a nightmare: Skilling's success came at high price. *The Washington Post*, p. A01.

Witt, A., & Behr, P. (2002, July 31). Losses, conflicts threaten survival: CFO Fastow ousted in probe of profits. *The Washington Post*, p. A01.

CHAPTER 4

"There You Are Man": Men's Use of Emotion Discourses and Their Negotiation of Emotional Subject Positions

Chris Walton, Adrian Coyle, and Evanthia Lyons

POSITIONING THEORY

Davies and Harré clearly outlined the relationship between discursive practices and subject positions:

We shall argue that the constitutive force of each discursive practice lies in its provision of subject positions. A subject position incorporates both a conceptual repertoire and a location for persons within the structure of rights and duties for those who use that repertoire. (1990: 46)

Various modes of positioning were later categorized by Van Langenhove and Harré (1999). Of particular importance to this analysis are the concepts of first and second order, tacit, and intentional positioning. First order positioning was defined as "the way persons locate themselves and others within an essentially moral space by using several categories and storylines," while second order positioning is said to occur when "the first order positioning is questioned and has to be negotiated" (1999, p. 20). Van Lagenhove and Harré contend that most first order positioning is of a tacit kind: "the people involved will not position themselves or others in an intentional or even conscious way" (1999, p. 22), while second order positioning is always necessarily intentional. Within the category of intentional positioning, van Lagenhove and Harré identify four distinct forms, one of which—"deliberate self-positioning"—is of particular relevance to our analysis. Van Langenhove and Harré state that "deliberate self-positioning occurs in every conversation where one wants to express his/her personal identity" and that one of the ways in which this can be accomplished is "by referring to events in one's biography" (1999, p. 24). Leaving aside discussions of the ontological assumptions implied by the use of words such as "conscious," "deliberate," "wants," and "identity," positioning theory and the concepts outlined above provide a useful theoretical framework for an analysis of the functions served by emotion discourses in interpersonal relations.

EMOTIONS

From the outset, it should be clearly stated that this chapter and the analysis within it take a strongly social constructionist approach to the concept of emotions. Therefore, this introduction, while drawing upon existing literature on emotions, is also necessarily critical of the ways in which emotions have typically been conceptualized. As Harré put it, "Psychologists have always had to struggle against a persistent illusion that in such studies as those of the emotions there is something *there*, the emotion, of which the emotion word is a mere representation" (1986, p. 4; emphasis in original). The "persistent illusion" of an ontologically existent emotion is important because it frames both the analytic inquiries of psychologists and the functions served by emotion discourses in social interactions.

The theoretical framework for a social constructionist, discursive approach to emotions has been exhaustively elaborated by Edwards (1997). Our approach draws upon this work and the social constructionist approaches of Averill (1980) and Harré (1986). Averill (1980) conceptualized emotions as "behavioral syndromes" and as "transitory social roles" (1980, p. 307). Emotions as syndromes were "defined as a *set* of responses that covary in a *systematic* fashion" (1980, p. 307; emphasis in original). The conceptualization of emotions as discourses draws upon the definition of a discourse as "a systematic, coherent set of images, metaphors and so on that construct an object in a particular way" (Burr, 1995, p. 184). Hence, the two approaches are roughly analogous except for the fact that the emphasis in the discursive approach is placed squarely upon the construction of the emotions through language. Within this approach, discourses that construct emotions—emotion discourses—can be identified in talk and their social functions can be discerned.

The "persistent illusion" that Harré spoke of—of something ontological underlying emotion words—is of importance to an analysis of the functions served by emotion discourses. The prevalence of the assumption that there *is something there*, led Edwards to conclude:

It is because people's emotion displays (thus categorized) can be treated either as involuntary reactions, or as under agentive control or rational accountability, as internal states or public displays, reactions or dispositions, that emotion discourse can perform flexible, accountability-oriented, indexically sensitive, rhetorical work. (1999: 288)

The work performed by emotion discourses is not only rhetorical. Through the subject positions that they make available, emotion discourses are also capable of performing social functions—an idea that can be persuasively traced back to Aristotle. In the *Rhetoric*, he provided an analysis of male displays of anger, which highlights the determinant relationship between the social context, the emotional display, and the social functions performed (*Rhetoric*, 1378[a]-1379[a]). More recent work by the likes of Armon-Jones (1986), Averill (1992) and Keltner and Haidt (1999) has led to the development of social-functional approaches to the study of emotions. In their review of the literature, Keltner and Haidt (1999) identify four levels at which the social functions of emotions have been examined; briefly they are the individual, the dyadic, the group, and the cultural. At the dyadic level—the level that most closely resembles our data—Keltner and Haidt describe previous research as identifying three primary social functions of emotions: they help "individuals know others' emotions, beliefs and intentions," evoke "complementary and reciprocal emotions in others," and serve "as incentives or deterrents for other individuals' social behavior" (1999, p. 511). In positioning terms, these functions can be constructed as sequences of first and potentially second order tacit and intentional positioning. From a social constructionist perspective, the four levels of analysis—individual, dyadic, group, and cultural—are of course linked through language (Gergen, 1985). That is to say, emotion discourses in any particular language are potentially operative across all four levels. Consequently, drawing on the work of Hochschild (1990) and Lutz (1990), the use of emotions discourses has been argued to function in the reification and perpetuation of "cultural ideologies and power structures" (Keltner & Haidt, 1999, p. 514).

Perhaps the most salient cultural ideology and power structure of which emotion discourses are a part is that of gender. Emotion discourses, at any level of use, have been argued to function in the maintenance of gender differences and hierarchies. As Catherine Lutz clearly stated, "any discourse on emotion is also, at least implicitly, a discourse on gender" (1990, p. 151). Within our analysis, we are specifically concerned with the relationship between emotion discourses and one half of the constructed gender dichotomy—the masculine.

MASCULINITIES

In essentialist terms, men are typically reported as—and indeed report themselves to be—less emotionally expressive than women (Balswick, 1988; Brody & Hall, 1993; Fabes & Martin, 1991; Fischer, 1993; LaFrance & Banaji, 1992; Shields, 1991). Such "findings" have led some researchers to talk of "comparative male unemotionality" (Larsen & Pleck, 1999, p. 32) or of men's "restrictive emotionality" (Jansz, 2000; Levant, 1995). The problematization of men's reported lower levels of emotional expressiveness has been identified as a central feature of the "crisis in masculinity" discourse (Coyle & Morgan-

Sykes, 1998). Though the contemporary "crisis in masculinity" discourse has been identified as only the most recent in a long line of such constructions (Kimmel, 1987), this has not prevented it from being reproduced in discussions of political and social policy on such topics as health, education, and crime (Whitehead, 2002).

A particular way of doing or, perhaps more appositely, not doing emotions is consistently constructed as problematic and as typical of men. Consequently, explanations are constructed in support of this "fact"; these explanations range from the evolutionary to the psychoanalytic to theories of sex-roles. The dominant explanations for the "fact" of men's comparative inexpressiveness are those derived from sex-role theory (Brannon, 1976; Pleck, 1981) and from broader sociological theories (Carrigan, Connell & Lee, 1985; Connell, 1995). These theories construct "masculinity" or "masculinities" as culturally available resources, as a set of normative roles, or as parts of a structure of social practices respectively. Within both approaches, "masculinities" are constrained, as normative roles or social practices, and one of these constraints appears to be the proscription of overt emotional expression.

More recently there has been a turn to discursive approaches to masculinity, in which "masculinities" are viewed as discursive accomplishments (Edley & Wetherell, 1997, 1999, 2001; Gough, 1998, 2001; Speer, 2001; Wetherell & Edley, 1999). These approaches have sought to identify the discourses and discursive strategies that construct "masculinities," and which consequently afford individuals "masculine" subject positions. Up until now, these discursive approaches have been concerned with identifying those discourses which explicitly construct objects as "masculine," that is, they have been concerned only with talk about "men," "masculinity," or "gender."

Men's self-reported lower levels of general emotional expression in studies such as that of Feldman Barrett, Robin, Pietromonaco, and Eyssell (1998) are, however, typically open to the social constructionist criticism that the participants' responses constitute performative acts: that is to say, the reporting of low levels of general emotional expression can be interpreted as men "positioning" themselves as "men" in accordance with socio-cultural expectations of gender and emotions. Consequently, we tentatively contend that there may be some systematic organization to men's use of emotion discourses. The ways that men use emotion discourses, the 'emotional' subject positions that they occupy, negotiate, and refute may therefore constitute one of the ways by which men do being "men." It is this possibility that our research is intended to explore, and the analysis presented here represents the first tentative steps towards the meeting of that aim.

METHOD

The two data excerpts presented in this chapter are taken from two different group discussions. The men in the group from which excerpt 1 is taken were aged between 19 and 23 years, all self-identified as gay and as White British. All were engaged in undergraduate or postgraduate study at a university in the south of England. The men in the group from which the excerpt 2 is taken were aged between 21 and 54 years and all self-identified as gay. Four of these men self-identified as White British, one as White Irish, one as White European, and one as Asian (Indian) British. The educational levels of the men in this group ranged between National Vocational Qualification (NVQ) and post-doctorate. Though the men in both groups self-identified as gay, they did not consistently speak from this position in the discussions and consequently should not be interpreted as having done so. The first author and researcher—Chris—is present in both excerpts.

Both these groups of men participated in a group discussion on the subject of "men and emotions," in a discursive task and in a reflective discussion. In each case, the discursive task consisted of the group being split in two and each subgroup being assigned a position (for or against) on a particular statement. The statements were selected on the likelihood that they would evoke the use of emotion discourses. The subgroups were given ten minutes to generate arguments in support of their position. At the end of this time, they were asked to present their arguments to the group as a whole and to a concealed (but in truth nonexistent) panel of judges. The group as a whole was then informed as to which subgroup's arguments had been rated the most persuasive. The winners received a reward of wine or chocolate. The whole group was then invited to reflect on the task in which they had just participated. Excerpt 1 is taken from one group's reflective discussion of that group. Excerpt 2 is taken from one of the subgroup discussions in which the participants were attempting to generate arguments in support of their position.

All these discussions were audio- and video-recorded and were transcribed by the first author, using the transcription system outlined by Jefferson (1985). The texts were analyzed using a discourse analytic approach of the type outlined by Coyle (2000) and Wetherell (1998). This involved reading and re-reading the transcripts several times, searching for patterns of language use in the men's constructions of emotions. Throughout this process, we monitored the texts to assess what functions were being fulfilled by the language used: particularly we were concerned with identifying the subject positions that were afforded to the participants. This sometimes involved a micro-level consideration of particular features of language use. The analysis recursively moved between, on the one hand, a global consideration of the constructions that the texts were offering and the rhetorical functions to which the texts were oriented and, on the other hand, a more micro-level focus on textual detail (although not as micro-level as in conversation analysis), with the former being grounded in the latter. Throughout the analysis we were mindful of both the discursive resources that were being drawn upon in the construction emotions and the subject positions that these discursive practices afforded the participants.

ANALYSIS

This first excerpt is taken from a discussion in which the men were reflecting on the discursive task in which they had just participated. In this task, the contentious statement had been "The United States of America should cease involvement in Afghanistan." The statement had been selected because of its temporal significance—this group discussion took place on November 14, 2001—and because it was thought likely that the arguments constructed by the participants might involve the use of emotion discourses.

Excerpt 1

92. Ben: hmm (5) really I think it was a good choice a good choice for er what we were
93. sort of discussing this afternoon =
94. Paul: = hmm =
95. Ben: = i.e. 'cause it is it's very fresh it's very emotional I (.) *personally* lost a a
96. family friend [in erm New York] erm so for me particularly it's quite an emotional
97. Chris: oh dear I apologize
98. Ben: issue =
99. Chris: = mhmm =
100. Ben: = erm you know had you have asked about something else you know sort of I
101. don't know (.) whatever er it wouldn't have had that er impact so to speak =
102. Chris: = ok =
103. Ben: = but yeah (4) it does need you to sort of take a step back and look at the
104. whole picture =
105. Chris: = ok =
106. Ben: = °without being reactionary =
107. Chris: = Lawrence =
108. Lawrence: = I don't know I'm er >what was the question?< ((*group laughs*)) did I
109. find it difficult? erm *no:* I like contentious issues and I and that issue er I don't know
110. when I go home and stuff my dad's a great one for starting debates like that at the
111. dinner table which my mum loves↑ ((*others laugh*)) erm and it's just kind of things
112. like that trying to distance (.) kind of a loss of life (.) >and I'm not trying to say
113. anything nasty< I'm [(inaudible)]
114. Ben: yeah yeah that's yeah don't worry =
115. Lawrence: = trying to distance that from the actions of both sides you know and
116. look at it from a kind of completely objective point of view so I'm not usually very
117. good at it but I was then 'cause I like having an opinion and then just kind of let
118. loose but I like things like that yeah =
119. Chris: = ok right [ ]

Ben begins the excerpt at line 92 with what is constructed as a personal reflection on the emotive quality of the discussion topic and its consequent appropriateness for a discussion group concerned with men and emotions. Through first order intentional positioning—"I think"—Ben positions himself as someone who is able to evaluate the appropriateness of the topic in terms of its emotive qualities. Between lines 95 and 96, Ben is then able to warrant this initial position, as one who is aware of the emotional significance of the discussion topic, through his first order positioning as someone who was emotionally affected by the events in "New York" (line 96). Ben's reference, only to "New York," was heard and is interpreted here as a reference to the destruction of the World Trade Center on September 11, 2001, the event that precipitated the United States military involvement in Afghanistan. Consequently the listener and reader must assume that Ben's "family friend" was killed in that attack.

Of particular interest are the specific features of Ben's construction of the emotional significance of the discussion topic. The topic and its emotive quality are constructed in the present tense, as ongoing (lines 96 and 98). Consequently, his subsequent disclosure regarding the "family friend" and the constructed high level of personal relevance, in lines 95–96, function to create a first order, intentional, emotional subject position that is contemporarily significant. Ben is exclusively and intentionally positioned within this interactional context as someone with both the contemporary knowledge- and emotion-based right to talk on this subject.

Chris's initial response, in line 97, can be interpreted as an acknowledgement of and orientation to Ben's contemporary emotional subject position. Chris's "apology" functions to position him as in some way responsible for Ben's emotional subject position. Chris, as the researcher and provider of the discussion topic, takes up the position of the individual responsible for both the interactional and rhetorical context that gave rise to Ben's contemporary emotional subject position. Ben's comments at lines 100–101 therefore constitute a reiteration of the constructed effectiveness of the discussion topic as an emotive subject and its consequent appropriateness within the interactional context. They also function as second order positioning. Ben orients to Chris's first order positioning as the responsible agent and, in doing so, tacitly accepts the subject position afforded to him, as someone whose emotional subject position resulted from Chris's actions (lines 100–101). Ben's comments are, however, couched in uncertainty and do not explicitly position Chris as blameworthy. The vague generality of Ben's construction of an alternative discussion topic are implicitly contrasted with the singularly exceptional emotive quality of this topic. The worked-up exceptional quality of the discussion topic functions as second order positioning. Chris retains the position as the agent responsible for Ben's contemporary emotional position, but his actions and their consequence are constructed as not deliberate. Ben's subject position is constructed as the product of a unique set of circumstances.

Chris's response at line 102 can therefore be interpreted as both an acceptance of his own renegotiated position and an attempt to close down what is a potentially personally problematic interactional avenue. At lines 103–104, Ben shifts the focus of the discussion from the personal affective subject positions of the participants, including himself, to the intellectual requirements of the task. He implicitly contrasts his own constructed emotional reaction to the topic with a requirement for rational evaluation. With respect to effective participation in the discursive task, distanced rational evaluation of the "whole picture" is privileged over his own proximate emotional reaction. This contribution can be interpreted as the playing out of an ideological dilemma concerning the relative merits of the rational and the emotional. This interpretation is reinforced by Ben's completion of his turn at line 106. "Reactionary" is interpreted here as pejorative and as describing a hypothetical and resisted position based on an emotional rather than rational appraisal and response. Ben minimizes the importance of his own previous emotional subject position in favor of a first order position as someone who appreciates the need to privilege rational evaluation over emotional reaction.

At line 107, having previously failed to end Ben's turn with two "ok" utterances (lines 102 and 105), Chris explicitly directs the turn to one of the other participants. Lawrence, through first order intentional positioning, positions himself as someone who enjoys tasks of the type in which he had just participated and warrants this construction with an autobiographical narrative (lines 109–111). He then orients to Ben's earlier construction of the requirement to privilege rational appraisals over emotional reactions (lines 111–112). However, inherent in this construction, privileging as it does rational "distance" over emotional proximity to an event, is a potential first order position for Ben, in which his previously constructed emotional subject position is potentially devalued. Lawrence's subsequent repair, in lines 112–113, can therefore be read as a preemptive counter to this potentially problematic rhetorical and interactional possibility. The repair contains an implicit acknowledgement of this possibility and, as such, functions as first order positioning. Lawrence positions himself as someone who would not be deliberately "nasty."

Ben's response, overlapping Lawrence's repair, therefore functions as both permission to Lawrence to continue his turn and discursive construction and as an acknowledgement of the validity of the construction of rationality as privileged over emotionality. Ben's response also functions to deflect the intimated possibility that his own emotional position is being devalued. Consequently, Lawrence is able to complete his turn and his construction and positioning within the previously negotiated rational position or, as he puts it, to "look at it from a kind of completely objective point of view" (line 116).

The second excerpt is taken from a small group discussion in which the participants had been asked to formulate an argument in opposition to the statement "A man should be faithful to his partner." This statement was selected because a discussion of relationships and (in)fidelity was thought likely to involve the use of emotion discourses. It should also be made clear that the men in this discussion all self-identified as "gay" on the demographic information sheets that they completed beforehand. Indeed, in the excerpt, Eric can be seen to position himself as someone who is involved in a same-sex relationship.

Excerpt 2

36. Alex: = oh we can argue whatever we want to argue the whole point about this is
37. winning erm ((*Jeff laughs*)) for *me* the important thing is emotional fidelity (.) and I
38. don't *care* if there is physical infidelity = [ ]
46. Eric: = yeah because that's sort of what I thought we had in our relationship but but
47. but I didn't really want it that way I was sort of pushed into that position and now
48. I've had some doubts that maybe maybe my partner has had some things and it's
49. really upset me (.) a lot and he's said well it's something you can't it's really hard to
50. discuss it's better just to like leave it =
51. Alex: = hmhm = [ ]
61. Eric: = it's not the act so much it's just the other person feels rejected though that's
62. the problem is you still feel rejected and =
63. Alex: = you *can* feel rejected = [ ]
280. Eric: = I think afterwards though they might the session after is going to be talking
281. about this personally maybe =
282. Alex: = possibly or they will be analyzing how we have spoken to each other and
283. how we've responded to what is a very emotional subject =
284. Eric: = ye::ah =
285. Alex: = which I think you've not been totally happy with =
286. Eric: = well well well =
287. Alex: = but it's [also it's] an emotional thing for all of us =
288. Eric: it's it's   = well no normally like
289. six months ago I would have said 'yeah yeah whatever it's no big deal why should
290. we conform to like these societal stereotypes why shouldn't we have more sexual
291. freedom' but but just within like the last two months I've been dealing with this issue
292. really on erm =
293. Alex: = and if you'd had a gun at home God help you you'd be locked up by now =
294. Eric: = no but it wasn't anger though that's just it no hmm (10) yeah anyway so it's
295. very topical I suppose in my head ((*laughs*))

There are three features of this excerpt that are of specific interest to a discussion of the functions served by emotion discourse in interpersonal relations. Briefly, they are Eric's construction of an emotional subject position in
lines 46–50, Alex's orientations to that position in lines 51–63 and again in
lines 282–293, and the functions served by Eric's emotional subject position
throughout the interaction as a whole. It should be noted that there are obvious excisions from this excerpt. These in no way represent an attempt to
distort the data. Rather they are an attempt to make the process of the construction and negotiation of the subject positions easier to track through what
would otherwise be a very long excerpt (the full excerpt is available from the
authors).

The excerpt begins with Alex's construction of a difference between the
relative importance of "emotional" (line 37) and "physical" (line 38)—presumably sexual—infidelity. He explicitly positions himself as someone for

whom physical infidelity is of relatively lower importance than emotional infidelity. It is to this construction that Eric's contribution between lines 46 and
50 is oriented. We contend that, through this turn, Eric constructs and occupies an emotional subject position that has immediate impact on the discussion and the interactional context as a whole. There are a number of
features of Eric's turn that make this subject position available and this argument persuasive.

The first feature is Eric's use of an autobiographical narrative. Within the
narrative, Eric constructs himself as unwillingly and emotionally affected and
positioned by the actions of his partner. This narrative provides the rhetorical
context for Eric's occupation of an emotional subject position within the contemporary interactional context. This simultaneous occupation of emotional
subject positions within the rhetorical and contemporary interactional context
is worked up through subtle shifts in tense. At the outset, the narrative is
clearly constructed in the past tense. However, by the end of line 47, the
narrative is constructed in the present perfect tense—"and now I've had some
doubts"—and can be interpreted as contemporarily operative. The use of the
present tense continues in lines 49–50. This shift in tense functions to make
Eric's autobiographical narrative the basis of an ongoing emotional subject
position, which is effective within the contemporary interactional context.

The particular emotion category invoked by Eric—"upset" (line 49)—is,
owing to its negative implications for the individual, a rhetorically powerful
one. Consequently, Eric's closing comments in lines 49–50 can be read as
both a construction of ongoing communication difficulties within his relationship and as a reflection on the relative emotional difficulty of his participation in the group discussion. That is to say, Eric occupies an emotional
subject position that compounds the relative ease with which he can contribute to the ongoing discussion.

When Eric takes the turn at line 61, he offers a construction of the cause
of the "upset" subject position. Physical infidelity is constructed as secondary
in importance to its affective consequence (lines 61–62). This construction is
offered entirely in the present tense and there is a subtle shift in the focus of
the constructed affective response. In line 61, the object of the affective response is constructed in the third person. However, in line 62, the definition
of the object is narrowed through the use of the potentially self-inclusive
second person pronoun "you." These shifts in object construction and in tense
tacitly function to position Eric as someone who *does* feel rejected. Consequently Alex's response at line 63, with emphasis, can be read as a simultaneous
affirmation of both Eric's discursive construction and his negotiated ongoing
emotional subject position.

Following his contribution at lines 61–62, Eric makes no further contribution to the development of arguments, leaving the task to Alex and Jeff.
Eric only significantly contributes to the interaction again at line 268 with a
construction of the possibility that the task in which they are participating

might not be what it seems. It is within this discursive context that Eric takes the turn at line 280. He constructs the possibility that after the task they will be asked to speak about the topic "personally" (line 281). Alex offers a tentative agreement with Eric and offers his own construction of the likely interests of the researchers (lines 282–283). He constructs the possibility that the researchers might be concerned with the affective reactions of the participants to the discussion topic. This construction, and Eric's affirmative response, affords Alex an opportunity to orient explicitly to Eric's emotional subject position within the interactional context. He does so in quite a subtle and minimal way, constructing Eric's position only as not "totally happy" (line 285). In doing so, Alex tacitly positions himself as someone who is sensitive to the emotional subject positions of others. In line 287, Alex constructs Eric's position as warranted within a discursive context that is constructed as universally emotional. These rhetorical strategies function to construct Eric's emotional subject position as reasonable and proportional, appropriate and acceptable.

However, Eric challenges and rejects—"well no" (line 288)—both Alex's construction of this discursive topic as a universally emotional context and the consequent appropriateness of his own emotional subject position. Eric attempts to minimize the importance of the interactional context as a determinant of his position. He constructs his emotional subject position as contrary to his own reported ideological beliefs—persuasively worked up through the use of reported speech—and his normalized biography. Hence, Eric's position is subtly renegotiated as the exceptional product of the coincidence between his constructed lived reality and the discussion topic. Consequently, the cause of his emotional subject position is located somewhere between the two and, importantly, is not wholly constructed as a product of the contemporary emotional context.

In line 293, Alex can be seen to respond to this shift in the location of Eric's subject position through his potentially joking construction of violent aggression as one possible emotional response to infidelity. Eric rejects this afforded possibility, as an emotional position that he had been unable to occupy. However, Eric is unable—evidenced by the subsequent ten second pause—to offer any construction of the (emotional) position that he did occupy. Instead he settles for a construction of the general topicality of the subject of (in)fidelity and, by locating it internally—"I suppose in my head" (line 295)— is finally able to construct his emotional subject position as separate from the current interactional context.

CONCLUSIONS

Throughout the analysis, we have argued that in both excerpts certain individuals occupied subject positions that could be categorized as *emotional* and that in both excerpts the other participants oriented to these positions as *emotional.* However, despite or perhaps because of this, in both excerpts the individual occupying the emotional subject positions did considerable rhetorical work to minimize the importance of their position within the interactional context. Eric was careful to relocate the cause of his emotional subject position beyond the bounds of the group discussion on infidelity. Similarly, Ben constructed an emotional subject position as secondary, in terms of importance, to a rational one. He also implicitly constructed his emotional subject position as exceptional. Also, both Ben and Eric constructed their emotional subject positions in non-specific terms. Ben categorized his only as "emotional" while Eric categorized his as "upset," albeit "a lot." Both these categorizations are not what psychologists would recognize as discrete emotion categories. The questions that we must ask are: why did Ben and Eric do this and what functions are served by these actions?

We contend that these actions constitute the negotiation of an ideological dilemma. Ben and Eric take up subject positions, through the use of emotion discourses, that potentially conflict with discourses and subject positions of masculinity. The simultaneous occupation of subject positions as emotional and as masculine, while not impossible, is potentially problematic and requires careful negotiation. Rhetorical strategies, such as minimization and distancing, represent the management and policing of this dilemma. The function and perlocutionary force of any emotion discourse is in part dependent upon the constructed qualities of the emotion. From a discursive perspective, emotion discourses are inherently descriptive of the "status" of the individual and "a description formulates some object or event as something; it constitutes it as a thing and a thing with specific qualities" (Potter, 1996, p. 111). Of the various qualities that an emotion might be constructed as possessing, "intensity" is of paramount importance. The constructed intensity of an emotion has the potential to determine the rhetorical power of a discursive formulation and therefore its perlocutionary force. The quality of intensity is implicit within emotion words (Frijda, Ortony, Sonnemans, & Clore, 1992). Thus the functions served in terms of positioning are likely to differ depending upon the intensity implicit within any emotion discourse. It is not difficult to appreciate that "I'm annoyed," "I'm angry," and "I'm furious"—three discursive formulations grouped within the "anger" category—may differ in the first and second order subject positions that they make available.

In these excerpts then, the intensity and relevance of the emotional subject position is downplayed, so that the individual does not appear *too* emotional. The occupation of such a position would implicitly conflict with a masculine subject position and the discourses upon which that position is based. Typically, as noted in the introduction, traditional or hegemonic discourses of masculinity proscribe overt emotionality. We do, of course, accept that discourses of masculinity and the explicit occupation of masculine subject positions are absent from these excerpts. However, the individuals in these discussions were male and were participating in a social psychological study concerned with what men had to say on the subject of "men and emotions." Consequently, their contributions can be interpreted as, in some part, oriented towards meeting the requirements of the study and warranting their right, as "men," to participate.

Though the men in these excerpts do position themselves in minimal emotional terms, according with typical social constructions of masculinity, they do so through an active process of construction and negotiation. Similarly, the other participants, Alex and Lawrence, and the researcher, Chris, can be seen to orient to the emotional subject positions. Further, though they may do so in a minimal manner, they are sensitive to potentially problematic rhetorical and interactional possibilities related to the emotional subject positions of Eric and Ben respectively. Though Ben and Eric are not explicitly invited to expound on their emotional subject position, neither are their positions challenged or ridiculed. Eric's position even excuses him from participating in the discursive task and his lack of involvement is not questioned. What emerges from these two excerpts and their analysis is a picture of these men as emotional beings, as skilful and subtle in their use of emotion discourses, as sensitive to their emotional subject positions, and as negotiating the fine line between doing "emotions" and doing "being a man."

We acknowledge that this analysis is concerned only with the talk of a small number of men in a particular and circumscribed context and that, as such, these conclusions may not be generalizable to other men and other contexts. However, the above analysis does demonstrate how emotion discourses can function in the construction and negotiation of subject positions within an interactional context and, as such, it is invaluable. Further analyses with a similar focus on the effects of context may elaborate the functions served by emotion discourses in the negotiation of subject positions. However, while some general themes for the functions served by emotion discourses in interpersonal relationships may appear across analyses—such as men's minimization of emotional subject positions—it should be appreciated that these do not constitute rules: the number of possible permutations of interlocutors, discourses, subject positions, interactional contexts, and ideological dilemmas is too great. Further, the dynamic nature of the relationship between subject positions and discourses should be remembered. Languages, in terms of the words used, their social meanings, and their functions are in a constant state of change. Thus, the functions served by emotion discourses in interpersonal relationships are not only contextually but temporally determined.

This said, emotion discourses represent one—but the most accessible—mode by which emotional subject positions are constructed and negotiated. Non-verbal, facial, and vocal modes of expression cannot be ignored in analyses of the functions served by emotions in interpersonal relations. Each mode of communication is amenable to analysis in terms of the functions served in interactional contexts. Future analyses must also be similarly attentive to the relationship between interactional context and the subject positions afforded by emotion discourses. Only then, with analyses that are attentive to the peculiar implicit qualities of emotion discourses, their modes of communication, and their relationship with interactional contexts, will we be better informed about the positions they afford.

REFERENCES

Armon-Jones, C. (1986). The social functions of emotion. In R. Harré (Ed.), *The social construction of emotions* (pp. 57–82). Oxford: Blackwell.

Averill, J. R. (1980). A constructivist view of emotion. In R. Plutchik & H. Kellerman (Eds.), *Emotion: Theory, research, and experience* (Vol. 1). *Theories of emotion* (pp. 305–339). New York: Academic Press.

Averill, J. R. (1992). The structural bases of emotional behaviour: A metatheoretical analysis. In M. S. Clark (Ed.), *Review of personality and social psychology* (Vol. 13). *Emotion.* (pp. 1–24) Newbury Park, CA: Sage.

Balswick, J. O. (1988). *The inexpressive male.* Lexington, MA: Lexington.

Brannon, R. (1976). The male sex-role: Our culture's blueprint for manhood, what it's done for us lately. In D. David & R. Brannon, (Eds.), *The forty-nine percent majority: The male sex role* (pp. 1–49). Reading, MA: Addison-Wesley.

Brody, L. R., & Hall, J. A. (1993). Gender and emotion. In M. Lewis & J. Haviland (Eds.), *Handbook of emotions* (pp. 447–460). New York: Guildford Press.

Burr, V. (1995). *An introduction to social constructionism.* London: Routledge.

Carrigan, T., Connell, R. W., & Lee, J. (1985). Towards a new sociology of masculinity. *Theory & Society,* 14, 551–604.

Connell. R. W. (1995). *Masculinities.* Cambridge: Polity.

Coyle, A., & Morgan-Sykes, C. (1998). Troubled men and threatening women: The construction of "crisis" in male mental health. *Feminism & Psychology,* 8(3), 262–284.

Coyle, A. (2000). Discourse analysis. In G. M. Breakwell, S. Hammond, & C. Fife-Schaw (Eds.). *Research methods in psychology* (2nd ed.) (pp. 251–268). London: Sage.

Davies, B., & Harré, R. (1999). Positioning and personhood. In R. Harré & L. Van Langenhove (Eds.) *Positioning theory* (pp. 32–52). Oxford: Blackwell.

Edley, N., & Wetherell, M. (1997). Jockeying for position: The construction of masculine identities. *Discourse & Society,* 8(2), 203–217.

Edley, N., & Wetherell, M. (1999). Imagined futures: Young men's talk about fatherhood and domestic life. *British Journal of Social Psychology,* 38, 181–194.

Edley, N., & Wetherell, M. (2001). Jekyll and Hyde: Men's constructions of feminism and feminists. *Feminism & Psychology,* 11(4), 439–457.

Edwards, D. (1997). *Discourse and cognition.* London: Sage.

Edwards, D. (1999). Emotion discourse. *Culture & Psychology,* 5(3), 271–291.

Fabes, R. A., & Martin, C. L. (1991). Gender and age stereotypes of emotionality. *Personality and Social Psychology Bulletin,* 17(5), 532–540.

Feldman Barrett, L., Robin, L., Pietromonaco, P. R., & Eyssell, K. M. (1998). Are women the "more emotional" sex? Evidence from emotional experiences in social context. *Cognition and Emotion,* 12(4), 555–578.

Fischer, A. (1993). Sex differences in emotionality: Fact or stereotypes? *Feminism & Psychology,* 3(3), 303–318.

Frijda, N. H., Ortony, A., Sonnemans, J., & Clore, G. L. (1992). The complexity of intensity: Issues concerning the structure of emotion intensity. In M. S. Clark (Ed.), *Review of personality and social psychology* (Vol.13). *Emotion* (pp. 60–89). Newbury Park, CA: Sage.

Gergen, K. (1985). The social constructionist movement in modern psychology. *American Psychologist*, 40, 266–275.

Gough, B. (1998). Men and the discursive reproduction of sexism: Repertoires of difference and equality. *Feminism & Psychology*, 8(1), 25–49.

Gough, B. (2001). "Biting your tongue": Negotiating masculinities in contemporary Britain. *Journal of Gender Studies*, 10(2), 169–185.

Harré, R. (1986). An outline of the social constructionist viewpoint. In R. Harré (Ed.), *The social construction of emotions* (pp. 2–14). Oxford: Blackwell.

Hochschild, A. R. (1990). Ideology and emotion management. In T. D. Kemper (Ed.), *Research agendas in the sociology of emotions* (pp. 117–142). Albany: State University of New York Press.

Jansz, J. (2000). Masculine identity and restrictive emotionality. In A. H. Fischer (Ed.), *Gender and emotion: Social psychological perspectives* (pp. 166–186). Cambridge: University Press.

Jefferson, G. (1985). An exercise in the transcription and analysis of laughter. In T. A. van Dijk (Ed.), *Handbook of discourse analysis* (Vol. 3) (pp. 25–34). London: Academic Press.

Keltner, D., & Haidt, J. (1999). Social functions of emotions at four levels of analysis. *Cognition and Emotion*, 13(5), 505–521.

Kimmel, M. S. (1987). The contemporary "crisis" of masculinity in historical perspective. In H. Brod (Ed.), *The making of masculinities: The new men's studies* (pp. 121–153). Boston: Allen & Unwin.

LaFrance, M., & Banaji, M. (1992). Toward a reconsideration of the gender-emotion relationship. In M. S. Clark (Ed.), *Review of personality and social psychology* (Vol. 14). *Emotion and social behaviour* (pp. 178–201). Newbury Park, CA: Sage.

Larsen, R., & Pleck, J. (1999). Hidden feelings: Emotionality in boys and men. *Nebraska Symposium on Motivation*, 45, 25–74.

Levant, R. F. (1995). Toward the reconstruction of masculinity. In R. F. Levant & W. S. Pollack (Eds.), *A new psychology of men* (pp. 229–252). New York: Harper Collins.

Lutz, C. A. (1990). Engendered emotion: Gender, power, and the rhetoric of emotional control in American discourse. In C. A. Lutz & L. Abu-Lughod (Eds.), *Language and the politics of emotion* (pp. 151–170). Cambridge: Cambridge University Press.

Pleck, J. H. (1981). *The myth of masculinity*. Cambridge, MA: MIT Press.

Potter, J. (1996). *Representing reality: Discourse, rhetoric and social construction*. London: Sage.

Shields, S. A. (1991). Gender in the psychology of emotion: A selective research review. In K. T. Strongman (Ed.), *International review of studies on emotion* (Vol. 1) (pp. 227–245). New York: Wiley.

Speer, S. (2001). Reconsidering the concept of hegemonic masculinity: Discursive psychology, conversation analysis and participants' orientations. *Feminism & Psychology*, 11(1), 107–135.

Van Langenhove, L., & Harré, R. (1999). Introducing positioning theory. In R. Harré
    & L. Van Langenhove (Eds.), *Positioning theory* (pp. 14–31). Oxford: Blackwell.
Wetherell, M., & Edley, N. (1999). Negotiating hegemonic masculinity: Imaginary
    positions and psycho-discursive practices. *Feminism & Psychology*, 9(3), 335–356.
Wetherell, M. (1998). Positioning and interpretative repertoires: Conversation analysis
    and post-structuralism in dialogue. *Discourse & Society*, 9(3), 387–412.
Whitehead, S. M. (2002). *Men and masculinities*. Cambridge: Polity.

CHAPTER 5

The Unthinkable Boundaries of Self: The Role of Negative Emotional Boundaries in the Formation, Maintenance, and Transformation of Identities

Ciarán Benson

> Disgust, along with contempt, as well as other emotions in various settings, recognizes and maintains difference. Disgust helps define boundaries between us and them and me and you. It helps prevent our way from being subsumed into their way. Disgust, along with desire, locates the bounds of the other, either as something to be avoided, repelled or attacked, or, in other settings, as something to be emulated, imitated, or married.
>
> W. I. Miller, 1997, p. 50

INTRODUCTORY COMMENTS ON KINDS OF DEFINITION OF SELF, IDENTITY, AND BOUNDARIES

The aim of this chapter is to suggest some ideas that can be used to describe what I am calling the "boundary conditions" of identities. I want to argue that these "identity-defining boundaries" are substantially constituted by negative feelings. This description, if defensible, promises to enhance the analysis of specific instances where personal and group identities can be identified as having changed *in kind*, as having been transformed from being one type of self or identity into another sort of self or identity. In more general terms, the focus is on how to better describe the connection between feelings, identities, and change.

"Self" is shorthand for extremely complex, multi-layered processes that are capable of being stabilized as continuities while remaining open to great variation and change. "Self" is, as I have argued elsewhere, the adaptive outcome of the requirements of reflexive location, the abiding requirement to know where you are if you are to function adaptively (Benson, 2001). These "locative demands" are a constitutive part of every moment of a person's life. They are what underpin the idea that who you are is a function of where you are, of where you have been, and of where you want to be. The processes involved, and their respective fields of functioning, begin with the incessant mapping by the brain of body states, themselves a function of what happens to the body (Damasio, 1996, 1999). They extend to the formative ideals and meanings that can only exist as part of the immeasurably complex intersubjective worlds that we call "cultures." These latter phenomena come into sharp focus in the fields currently contributing to "cultural psychology" (Taylor, 1989; Stigler, Shweder, & Herdt, 1990; Harré, 1993; Bruner, 1996; Cole, 1996; Shore, 1996; Tomasello, 1999; Shweder, 2000; Benson, 2001; Valsiner, 2001).

In this chapter, my focus is on the role of negative emotions in stabilizing and maintaining any "self" as *this* sort of self and not as *that* sort. The *outer* "boundaries" between being this sort rather than that sort of self are comprised of thoughts of acting that a person, or members of a group with a strong identity, might call "unthinkable." These thoughts, I will argue, are actively composed of very strong negative feelings such as shame, guilt, fear, disgust, and so on (Nussbaum, 2001).

In the most general sense, how are we to think about ways of defining identity and self? We can think of what things *are* in two related ways. The first way of defining what a thing is is to say how it is formed, how parts are organized into the whole that it is. The second way of defining what a thing is is in terms of what it *does*, how it functions, the *uses* to which its organized parts are put. The identity of a person, defined in terms of *form*, concerns the ways in which that person can be picked out as unique from among the array of all other persons by such formal aspects as appearance, finger-prints, eyes, personal historical identifiers, DNA, and so on. The identity of a person defined in terms of *function* derives from observations that lead to judgments that in any given situation this person is likely to act in distinctive and predictable ways because he or she *is* that *sort of person*.[1]

There is an underplayed dimension in psychological studies of self, though not in many artistic and literary explorations, that recognizes the importance of fine-grained, micro-temporal analyses of the subtleties of experience. This would take seriously the idea, for example, that there is a sense in which you *are* what you see *while* you are seeing it, or that you are the music while you are listening to it, and so on (Benson, 1993, 2001). In more abstract terms, subjectivity and intentionality co-constitute conscious experience. The investigative implication of this is that neither the subject nor the object should be the primary term of analysis in the first descriptions of phenomena of experience, but rather the relationship that constitutes them as *this* subject and *that* object at *this* time. The intentional object shapes the qualities of subjective experience, particularly during the period when it is an object of attention

(Wollheim, 1984). For example, to the extent that I am in sympathy with a character in a play or novel, then to that extent will I feel good when good things happen to her, and bad when tragedy comes her way. This is similar in real life when I strongly care about what happens to certain people. The qualities of my feelings—my subjectivity—are causally tied to the fate of what I attend to and care about—my intentional objects.[2] Conscious experience plays out these duets in exquisitely complex choreographies.

If we take a functional view of self and identity, then the question of how to take an equally functional view of their boundaries also arises. In what follows, my suggestion is that negative emotions play a foundational role in the dynamics of those boundaries that constitute identities, be they personal identities or social identities. I will use the adjective "negative" as applied to emotion in a rather distinctive way. To rage at someone and to do so because I am a bad-tempered person is to display a negative emotion. But this is not primarily what I intend negative to mean. We are what we are largely because of the things that we simply will *not* countenance doing voluntarily. This is the sense I want "negative" to have in the argument that follows. As it happens, negative emotions in the first sense do play a central role in this second sense of "negative." More of that later. Seeing whether there is substance to this idea will now take us on a somewhat circuitous but necessary journey through a variety of contemporary psychological and philosophical territories.

FIVE KEY CONCEPTS FOR UNDERSTANDING THE EMOTIONAL BASES OF IDENTITIES

The five concepts which I want to introduce and connect, when exploring the emotional bases of identities, are identity-boundaries, body-boundaries, action boundaries, feelings of ownership, and unthinkability. The metaphor of self as a "container" depends upon the associated idea of a "boundary" (Lakoff and Johnson, 1999). Self's integrity or oneness, its unity or type, is a function of the kinds of boundary that, it is assumed, "contain" the system that is self. Qualities of a self's integrity are a function of the nature of the boundaries containing and structuring it. Integrity—in the senses both of coherence and of "moral fiber"—and boundaries are thus mutually constitutive. A person's integrity is intimately bound up with what they will *not* do.

There are, I think, at least two general kinds of identity boundary. There are *bodily boundaries* and there are *psychological boundaries of extension*. Psychological boundaries of extension are tied up with acts of possessing or of owning. They include *what belongs to me* (things, people, ideas, skills, rights, reputation, privileges, and so on that I control and can call "my own"). They also encompass the *ways in which I belong to others* (forms of solidarity, group identity, obligation, and so forth that control and have claims on me). In this sense, what people own, and how people are themselves owned, helps make them the sort of people they are. Less tangible, but perhaps more significant for their being the sorts of people they are, are the dynamics of what they will and will not do.

In this sense, self's psychological boundaries of extension can be further analyzed into members of the class of *action boundaries* that define the limits of a person's behavior. I am using the term "action boundary" as a metaphor for the improbability of performing some type of action or other. The boundaries of identity, especially in Rom Harré's senses of Self 1 & 2 (Harré, 1998), are most usefully conceived as *the limits of the reach of the set of action-skills that constitute a self*. Simply put, I am what I can and will do, but also, of neglected significance, what I cannot do and will resist doing.

Let me outline an example of what I mean by a *self-constituting action-skill*. Consider a high-level skill like responsibility-taking, by which I mean the disposition to actively accept or reject responsibility for actions directly or indirectly connected to the person. This is a learned skill, I believe, inculcated according to the accepted practices of the culture that had the dominant role in shaping the person (Benson, 2001, Chapter 8). The skill has to do with what the person feels emotionally connected to. The reach of this connection signifies the reach of that person's self as a responsibility-taker. So, if that person feels a connection to the well-being of, say asylum-seekers, then they are likely to feel that they have some responsibility for acting in the best interests of that group. The ways in which they act towards that end, the skills that constitute those ways of acting, determine boundaries of their selves. In related terms, they determine the nature of the fields of significance that form the person's *world*. I will expand this below when I speculate on the tragic case of Fahime and Rahmi Sahindal.

The primary question posed by the present chapter is whether the "containing" boundaries of selves and identities are possibilities for acting in ways that their subjects might describe as *unthinkable* for them?[3] "The unthinkable," in my elaboration of the term, marks the boundary between my being one sort of a person as against my being another—currently undesirable—type of person. What are the implications if acts, previously unthinkable for the person, become thinkable and desirable, possibly under new conditions of opportunity without external sanction or cost? Would we say that such a person has ceased to be one type of person/self and has become another type? Or would we say that such a person has now "shown their true colors," colors that had previously been masked or inhibited from appearance by stronger forces of restraint such as local law enforcement or the power of local opinion? The answer, I think, depends on differences between the meanings of "could not" and "would not unless."

In one case the person, irrespective of the demands of external forces, might continue to regard certain acts as unthinkable for themselves, they being the sort of person who simply "could not" do that sort of thing. On the other hand, they might be the sort of person who "would not" do that sort of thing "unless," that is, they could get away with it. In the former case the unthinkable continues to bind self whereas in the latter the unthinkable is actually quite thinkable but is simply inhibited by ambient conditions. The distinction between "could not" and "would not unless" is critical to assessing the claim that unthinkability can be a potent descriptor of self-boundaries.

A "true" rebel against a hated regime who simply could not conceive of betraying his comrades under any circumstances, for example, despite his disapproval of what they may be doing, would fit the "could not" category. However, other comrades may not be made of such sterling stuff. Given opportunities to betray their comrades without their knowing, they might well do so. This is what marks the "true" follower of the cause from the potential "traitors" or "informers." If, however, they betrayed for reasons of conscience, then their allegiance would be to a stronger ideal than "The Cause." For such people it would be more unthinkable to betray the ideal constituting their conscience than it would be to betray the subsidiary ideal for which they are fighting. All this is, of course, a function of which point of view is adopted, but the point is simply that the felt identity of those who remain "true to the cause" is shaped by the unthinkability of acting traitorously.

"Could not," as the strong case of unthinkability, is my focus of interest here. In the "could not" case, one might say that in being this sort of self— that is, the type of self for whom this kind of act is unthinkable—there is an absence of volitional power of the kind that would make acting in this way feasible and desirable (Frankfurt, 1993). I will return to this below.

In the weaker "would not unless" case of unthinkability, there is the probable presence of such power to desire and act in this way. It is inhibited and controlled, however, by another type of power. This other kind of power may derive from a cost-benefit analysis of betraying to personal advantage and of getting away with it; or it may derive from balancing the doing of this act against an estimation of how badly one might feel afterwards in terms of guilt, shame, remorse, self-disgust, or self-contempt. Or as mentioned above, betrayal may result from conscientiously following an ideal that is taken to be higher than the one demanding comradely loyalty. This last person would more properly fall into the "could not" category.

The next question of the present chapter is this: What is it that guards these "unthinkable" borderlands of self and identity? What actively maintains them and threatens counter-attack if they are attacked or threatened? The answer, I suggest, is coalitions of conscious and self-conscious negative feelings such as feelings of revulsion and repulsion, feelings linked to the contempt, anger, or disgust of others and subjectively transformed into feelings of self-contempt, fear, embarrassment, shame, or guilt (Lewis, 1993; Oatley & Jenkins, 1996; Kagan, 1984).

Such feelings can combine in various distinctive ways depending on the culture. How they combine depends upon the nature of the local moral order. Moral orders differ in their prevailing *conditions of regard*, which are shaped by the tacit felt rules and ways for judging actions and evaluating actors that distinguish them. Different moral orders also have their own local practices for forming the psychology of their members. Given this context, it is to a significant degree the potential presence of these negative feelings that promotes the unlikelihood of individuals acting in certain ways. This suggests the need for an analysis of the emotional dynamics governing the maintenance or transformation of unthinkable boundaries and their consequences for transformations of selves and identities. What, to continue the example above, are the active boundaries between an identity characterized by a tendency to act in a steadfastly loyal way, and an identity characterized by a tendency to betrayal?

The answer is connected to a further and central aspect of selfhood and identity, namely the dynamics of possession. *Feelings of ownership* and *feelings of control* are intimately connected. Both types of feeling are foundational for selfhood. Being mistaken about the facts of control is connected to being mistaken about the facts of ownership. This is of great significance for what I judge to be me, mine or part of *my*-self. If the operative boundaries of identity are, as I am suggesting, the boundaries specified by thinkable and unthinkable actions and dispositions to act, then the controls—and hence the varieties of ownership and the varieties of identity—are *feelings of various kinds*.

The boundaries of unthinkability, in my specific sense of the term, can be visualized as the very outer perimeters of identity. They "contain" further boundaries that define more proximate aspects of selfhood and identity. There are, for example, boundaries relating to the possibility and ease of *consciously knowing* what it is that structures, maintains, orients, and motivates the self that I feel myself uniquely to be. These are epistemic boundaries such as might exist between conscious and unconscious "levels" of self and identity. This is the territory of psychoanalysis, and indeed much contemporary cognitive science, and is not a primary concern here. I will, however, return below to certain emotional aspects that broadly constitute identity's psychological boundaries of extension.

First, let me offer some examples that support the assertion that feelings are of primary importance when it comes to understanding the relationship between possession—facts and acts of owning—and the body's own boundaries. If feelings of possession play a primary role in specifying the physical boundaries of identity, then how much more potent is the role they play in specifying the psychological boundaries of selfhood and identity?

THE PRIMACY OF FEELINGS IN THE CONSTITUTION AND MAINTENANCE OF BODY BOUNDARIES

Although what follows can be extended to the analysis of large-scale group identities, for reasons of brevity my focus here is on personal identity rather than on kinds of social and group identity. The body and its boundaries are central to the processes of selfhood and identity. In common-sense dualism, the physical boundaries of the body—"the body envelope"—are often taken uncritically to be limits of the self "contained by" it. My limits, it might be said, are the limits of "my reach." Some implications of this for understanding how processes of feeling constitute self have been theoretically advanced by recent thinking in neurology (Damasio 1996, 1999).

In Damasio's thinking—as with Merleau-Ponty (1981) or Susanne Langer (1970)—the "world" is what happens to, what is registered by, and what the brain maps of the responding body. The brain is to be understood as a wetly integral part of the living, moving, feeling body rather than as some dry, remote detached computer distantly representing what is happening to it. The body must also be understood as being part of the world. The brain incessantly maps as percepts that which stimulates its body using, for comparison, maps already formed. The brain is also simultaneously and constantly mapping how the body is responding to what is stimulating it, again utilizing maps already formed. Furthermore, if Antonio Damasio is correct, the brain is incessantly mapping, as an ongoing third type of representation that unifies stimulus and response, the *relationship* of the body in the very act of responding to what is happening to it.

The intuitive sense of feeling oneself *as a subject* of impact and action, it is speculated, is engendered by these particular representations of the organism in the act of feeling what is happening to it. At the highest levels of human cognitive functioning supporting the construction of self, the brain enables the symbolic articulation and integration of these various kinds of neural map and "neural narrative" into the ongoing, more or less coherent, narrative that is autobiographical self (Damasio, 1999). Brain, body, world, and society are thus, from this perspective, co-constitutive (Benson, 2001; Harré, 1998; Bruner, 1996). This, once again, is the field of cultural psychology.

Given this context, there is one particular aspect to be emphasized. This is the primacy and centrality of *feeling* for knowing who and what I am, for knowing where I end and the "rest of" the world begins. Specifically, I want to highlight the idea that, in fundamental ways, people intuitively trust their feelings *before* they trust their conceptual understanding, even when the evidence from expert others as presented to a person is, apparently, incontrovertible.

Examples from pathologies that disrupt the mapping of body boundaries supply evidence supportive of this. I have in mind the sorts of anosognosia whose theoretical significance for the role of the body in selfhood has been particularly well elaborated by Antonio Damasio. These are "diseases of knowledge" where, despite manifest evidence to the contrary, people who have suffered specific forms of brain damage do not feel themselves to be paralyzed or blind, for instance. In time they may come to accept the judgements of others that they are, but in doing so they must come to doubt and distrust that which, in the first instance, they show most signs of trusting and accepting, namely their own feelings about how they are.

Take the following examples from transcripts recently published by Todd Feinberg (Feinberg, 2001). The interpretations that follow are mine and are offered to reinforce the suggestion that feelings of ownership depend substantially on *feelings of control*. Sonya suffers from damage to the right parietal lobe and is asomatognosic.

FEINBERG: What is this?

SONYA: A hand.

FEINBERG: A hand? Whose hand is it?

SONYA: Not mine!

FEINBERG: It's not yours? How do you know?

SONYA: Well, it's just not mine.

FEINBERG: Are you positive?

SONYA: Yeah . . .

FEINBERG: Well, whose could it be? This hand here. [Her hand is held before her eyes. No response.] Does it have another name? What would you call it?

SONYA: A strange. (Feinberg, 2001, p.14)

Obviously the sense of no longer acknowledging that one possesses parts of one's body, such as one's hand, is an intriguing phenomenon for any theory of the relationship of boundaries to integrity of self. The *feeling* that a part of the body is "mine/not mine," just as the feeling that some other attribute (a belief, a value, an impulse, etc.) is or is not part of "me," appears to be foundational to the felt integrity of self. Sonya has lost control of her hand, presumably no longer has any neurally supplied "feelings of control," and consequently has lost "feelings of ownership" for her hand.

In contrast, take the example of Patsy, who is anosognosic and whose left side is paralyzed:

FEINBERG: OK. What are you doing here?

PATSY: You all tell me I have a weak left side.

FEINBERG: I'm sorry?

PATSY: You all say I have a weak left side.

FEINBERG: We all say you have a weak left side?

PATSY: And I don't agree!

FEINBERG: And you don't agree?

PATSY: No.

FEINBERG: Why?

PATSY: Because I know I don't!

FEINBERG: It feels fine?

PATSY: Yes.

FEINBERG: There's no weakness over there . . .

PATSY: No. [She is asked to raise her right arm, which she does.]

FEINBERG: Now raise the other arm for me. Raise your left arm for me. Can't you do that for me? [Pause.] Did you do it? Did you raise it?

PATSY: I did now.

FEINBERG: You did now? Did you have any difficulty raising it?

PATSY: No.

FEINBERG: OK then. Why don't you touch your nose? [Touches nose with right hand.]

FEINBERG: Why don't you touch it with the other hand? Can you touch it with the other hand?

PATSY: Yes. (Feinberg, 2001, p. 24)

How does Patsy "know" that she is not paralyzed? She knows because she does not "feel" paralyzed. All the evidence presented to her by the medical team, both visually and discursively, emphasizes that she is, but at this stage post-injury she relies first and foremost on her own feelings in making (erroneous) judgements about her body and its boundaries. Her internally supplied feelings about her bodily self present her, for the moment, with more compelling evidence about herself than do the externally supplied observations, demonstrations, and arguments of others.

The problem is that her feelings are out of date and derive from neural maps that were valid prior to her brain damage but, though still apparently supplying information, are now invalid. My interpretation is that Patsy, unlike Sonya, continues to have "feelings of control" neurally supplied to her, albeit from representations of her body that are now out of date. These feelings of control underpin her continuing feelings of ownership of a normally active left arm. From the observer's point of view, she is mistaken and now possesses a paralyzed arm; from her viewpoint what she still feels herself to possess is a motorically responsive one.

Both Patsy and Sonya, I suggest, exemplify *the primary role of feelings in the formation of our convictions and certainties,* even concerning facts of body boundaries that are demonstrably wrong. Each of these cases exemplifies a contrasting pole of possession, Sonya a phenomenon of dispossession, Patsy one of mistaken possession.

Such examples can be multiplied (Feinberg, 2001). All are adequately summed up in an observation offered by C.W. Olson in 1937 as quoted by Feinberg (2001, p. 11):

She denied that the affected limbs were hers and said that "yours" or another's were in bed with her. When she was shown that they were attached to her and that the arm in question merged with her shoulder and that it must be hers, she said: "But my eyes and my feelings don't agree, and I *must believe my feelings* (my emphasis). I know they look like mine, but I can feel they are not, and I can't believe my eyes."

I now want to generalize the possible significance of these phenomena of feeling and possession. The subjectivity of body boundaries—how they seem to me—*reveals the evidential premium placed by people on internally supplied feelings*. If this is the case in terms of the bodily dimensions of selfhood, is it also the case for the feelings of selfhood that rely on the sorts of boundaries of extension that are created, as I argue, by those skills in acting and not acting that comprise selfhood? I propose that it is, and that the concept of "unthinkability" is a useful tool for exploring this proposition.

NEGATIVE BOUNDARIES AND CONCEPTS OF THE "UNTHINKABLE"

For most of us there are things we could never envisage ourselves doing because "We *are not* that sort of person." It would be unthinkable for the Pope to become a Protestant because he *is not* that kind of person. What kind? In this example, a heretic or an apostate. Yet many people undergo such transformations of religion and identity. It would be unthinkable for most fathers or mothers to have sex with their children. Why? Because to do so would be to abuse the very core of parenthood and to break the incest taboo. Yet some parents do this, as the courts amply attest. It is unthinkable for most of us to mutilate and murder defenseless, innocent people, or anyone else for that matter. Why? Because we *are not* brutal murderers. Yet in every century tens of thousands of "ordinary" people do just this (Browning, 1992; Goldhagen, 1998; Staub, 1989; Benson, 2001). The social and historical sciences are keenly interested in the crossing of such boundaries and in the implications of such crossings for the dynamics of identity change.

These are some examples of the sorts of meaning that I want my use of "unthinkability" to have. The *nature* of my identity—both personal in the sense of how I am to and for myself, and social in the sense of how I am to and for others—is directly connected to the sorts of action I am likely or unlikely to perform. These are actions that flow unhindered from my being the sort of person I am (Frankfurt, 1993). The sorts of actions that normally would be classed as "unthinkable" or as "unspeakable" would also tend to be categorized as "criminal," "perverse," "treacherous," "treasonable," "heretical," "cruel," "inhumane," "disgusting," or, at their more benign pole, "totally out of character" or "disreputable."

I now want to refine my use of the "unthinkable" to have a very specific meaning. There are many things that I cannot envisage myself doing because I do not have sufficient imagination, intellectual ability, ambition, or simply opportunity. I therefore exclude from my use of the "unthinkable," as it applies to the boundaries of identity, all thoughts about acting that derive from an imaginative or intellectual incapacity, or from the inhibitions and constraints that arise from lack of opportunity. Nor am I talking about an inability arising from forms of reticence or gentility to imagine all sorts of unpleasant actions *in general*.

What I have in mind is *an inability to vividly and realistically imagine my doing certain "extreme" things without, at the same time, having inhibitory negative feelings.* To borrow a phrase from Richard Wollheim, this sense of the unthinkable involves a dynamic, emotional inhibition of the ability to *experientially imagine* acting in certain ways (Wollheim, 1984). The strong negative feelings *that are constitutive of the unthinkable* ensure that these sorts of possible action tend to be actively "unthought." This further implies, as psychoanalysts might suggest, that these constituting boundaries of identity tend to be actively non-conscious. They are closely connected to processes of inhibition. We know that these processes are especially dependent on the prefrontal lobes, which mature after birth, and most actively between the ages of two and five. They are shaped by the dynamics of the developing child's relationships with its parents and other emotionally significant people in its life. In this sense, these highly important neural processes are social-cultural products.

As Solms and Turnbull (2002, p. 281) put it:

From the neuroscientific point of view, ironically perhaps, the essence of "free will" appears to be the capacity for *inhibition*—the capacity to choose *not* to do something. What distinguishes human beings more than anything else from their nearest primate relatives is the development of a higher-level "self" system which is organized fundamentally on *inhibitory* mechanisms. These mechanisms, which have their physical locus in the *pre-frontal lobes* (the crowning glory of the human brain), bestow on us the capacity to *suppress* the primitive, stereotyped compulsions that are encoded in our inherited and emotional memory systems. On this basis, the inhibitory prefrontal lobes may be regarded, with some justification, as the very tissue of our humanity.

The actions that constitute the category of the "unthinkable" are substantially socially constructed. The boundaries that "contain" them—which may well have been built up using positive feelings such as pride and affectionate approval mixed, perhaps, with fear—are primarily boundaries of strong negative emotion. The functioning of "that which they contain" depends on strong positive feelings like "self-righteousness," "feelings of familiarity," "pride," and so on (Benson, 2001, chap. 7).

My use of the unthinkable denotes thoughts about acting that will arouse in me such strong negative feelings as to make even the imaginative enactment of those thoughts highly aversive. I also want it to indicate that, should anyone suggest that I would do something that to me is unthinkable in this sense of the word, I would feel genuine indignation and perhaps outrage at being misidentified in this way. This emotionally aversive character might be theorized in psychoanalytic terms of repression or suppression (Laplanche & Pontalis, 1980) or in learning theoretical terms as forms of inhibition (Bandura, 1985). I want to focus instead on some recent work in the psychology of emotion, and specifically on that of Paul Rozin and his colleagues (Rozin et al., 1993, 1999) on the nature of disgust and its extensions.

These aversive thoughts about acting in certain ways—such that I might say that it is unthinkable that I would do something like this or that—are exactly those dimensions of acting that most make me what I am. In other words, these personal "unthinkabilities" are what most define and maintain my identity. They are the boundaries of action that make my integrity just the sort of integrity that it is. This is as true for group identities as it is for personal ones. The feelings determining the unthinkable are core constituents of self and, as is the case with the anosognosics and others above, they are load-bearing walls in the architecture of identities. Of course, they are complemented in this supporting role by all sorts of positive emotions, emotions that shape what a person will do (Oatley & Jenkins, 1996). To pursue that complementarity is, however, a bigger task than can be attempted here.

We should note in passing that there are individuals whose very *ability* to act in ways that would be unthinkable for most other people place them in a category of their own. "Psychopaths" are consistently described as having, amongst other characteristics, a "shallowness" of emotions, an impulsiveness that contrasts with normal inhibitory skills, an incapacity for remorse, guilt, empathy, and so on (Hare, 1993). As so described, clinically diagnosed psychopaths seem to offer an example of people whose boundaries of identity are *not* unthinkable thoughts. Given the absence of identity-stability entailed by this, it is not surprising that experts in psychopathy identify further related aspects of psychopaths' selves. They exhibit "a truly astounding egocentricity and sense of entitlement," which, coupled with their emotional incapacities, impulsivity, and lack of forethought, make for a dangerously inchoate type of person who can be witty and articulate on the one hand but deceitful and manipulative on the other. And many do terrible things (Hare, 1993, p. 38).

To summarize this part of the argument, the "unthinkable," in the sense developed above, marks the boundary between my being one kind of person as against my being another, currently highly undesirable, type of person. The implication of this is that if the feelings constituting unthinkable actions can be changed into feelings supportive of acting in these ways, then the very nature of a person's, or of a group's, identity will have been changed. What then is the connection between identity and the sorts of *necessity* associated with easily thinkable or aversively unthinkable acts?

IDENTITY BOUNDARIES, UNTHINKABLE ACTS AND NEGATIVE FEELINGS

When the philosopher Harry Frankfurt speaks of "the necessity" of ideals he means not only that they are desirable but also that they are necessary conditions for an identity to have integrity at all (Frankfurt, 1988, 1993). Total freedom of choice, unrestrained by an identity that is defined in terms of what the person loves and cares about would imply, Frankfurt argues convincingly, the actual absence of an individual identity. Freedom and individuality constrain each other. For any individual to be free there must be limits to that freedom for the individual to have his or her particular identity. He writes:

Unless a person makes choices within restrictions from which he cannot escape by merely choosing to do so, the notion of self-direction, of autonomy, cannot find a grip. Someone free of all such restrictions is so vacant of identifiable and stable volitional tendencies and constraints that he cannot deliberate or make decisions in any conscientious way. If he nonetheless does remain in some way capable of choice, the decisions and choices he makes will be altogether arbitrary. (Frankfurt, 1993, p. 19)

The constraints of caring about something mean that you are adversely affected if something damaging happens to who or what you care about, just as you would be positively affected if good things happened to them. It also means that there are actions that you simply cannot bring yourself to do, actions that are unthinkable. This is not a question of lack of power or opportunity but is rather because you have a powerful aversion to acting in this way, and this limits your conduct.

Furthermore, it is important to you to endorse this aversion, to think of yourself as being the sort of person for whom it matters to have such aversions. It is this endorsement, in Frankfurt's view, that marks the difference between situations in which you would find such an action *unthinkable*, and those in which inability to act is due to addiction, terror, or some other kind of compulsion. You consider that your inability to do something is an important and defining part of who you are, of your identity. Addicts may wish to act differently than they do but find themselves unable to be that sort of person precisely because of their addiction. You may find that your incapacity to do unthinkable things flows effortlessly from being the sort of person you are, whereas if you are an addict you will find yourself in conflict with yourself when you wish to act against the urges of your addiction.

We can summarize the conclusion of this argument as follows.

Integrity of identity = f (Quality of Boundaries)

What I want to add, and elaborate in what follows, can be summarized as follows.

Potency of boundaries = f (Negative feelings constitutive of unthinkability)

The moral basis of personal and social identity has been outlined by philosophers like Charles Taylor (Taylor, 1989).[4] For Taylor, identity is defined by "the horizon within which I am capable of taking a stand" (p. 27). The formation and maintenance of such moral horizons is a task of culture. It varies from one to another just as it does from one cultural-historical period to another. Cultural psychologists like Richard Shweder and his colleagues have proposed a taxonomy of the types of ethic that cultures use to constitute and resolve moral issues (Shweder et al., 1997). These sorts of cultural ethic define the horizons within which their members' identities are bounded and their integrity structured.

The three broad categories proposed are ethics of community, autonomy, and divinity. An ethic of community stresses the primacy of the group and of where a person is located in its hierarchical structures. The wrongness of an action within such an ethic will tend to concern infringements of duty, respect for authority, loyalty, the honor of the group, and so on. Ethics of autonomy, in contrast, stress the importance of individual rights and freedoms. Here wrongness has to do with violations of rights, issues of justice and fairness, and in general a disrespect for individual freedom and choice. An ethic of divinity will conceive of a person as being in some way an instance of God or the Divine. Here the stress will be on preserving purity, guarding against contamination, sinfulness, and recognizing and respecting the divinely or-dained order of things.

It makes a huge difference to the sort of person you are which ethic con-stitutes your identity. It shapes the sort of turbulence you will experience if you try to change the moral horizons that constitute the sort of integrity you desire for yourself. It influences how you will feel if compelled to adapt to a new moral order as, for instance, an immigrant and parent in a new society. The reasons for this have to do with the ways in which these different ethics shape the emotional architecture of their members and adherents.

NEGATIVE FEELINGS, DOMINANT ETHICS, AND DESIRABLE IDENTITIES

In psychological life, strong negative feelings play a role in defending the boundaries of a particular ethic's desirable identity similar to that of the Tal-iban's "Virtue Police." Paul Rozin and his colleagues have begun to explore how different moral emotions like contempt, anger, and disgust (referred to as CAD) tend to be differentially recruited by the ethics identified by Shweder and his colleagues (Rozin et al., 1999). Incidentally, the initials of the com-munity, autonomy, and divinity ethics are also CAD, and this gives rise to what Rozin et al. call "The CAD Triad Hypothesis." This can be economically presented as follows (Rozin et al., p. 576).

Emotion	Shweder ethic	Principal Virtues
Contempt	Community	Respect, duty, hierarchy
Anger	Autonomy	Individual freedom, rights
Disgust	Divinity	Divinity, purity

Contempt has a particular prominence in a community ethic since it is an emotion linked to social hierarchies. People embedded in such hierarchies will avoid incurring the contempt of their fellows by not violating social norms. If they do break these rules a range of negative, self-conscious moral emotions such as shame, embarrassment, and guilt come into play (Lewis, 1993). Upholding the norms of the ethic, and being seen to do so, gives rise to positive self-conscious emotions like pride. These are emotions that facilitate fitting in with others, behaving in ways that are acceptable, and avoiding causing harm to fellow members of the community.

Anger in human beings is mainly a moral emotion. A person whose rights are infringed or who is insulted will, in a predominantly autonomy ethic, feel angry. They will also feel angry if those close to them (bound to them by extension) have their rights infringed or are attacked or insulted. Anger, then, is prominently tied to ethics of autonomy. Avoiding incurring the anger of others by insulting them, or by infringing their rights, would be a goal of a member of an autonomy ethic. They could anticipate feeling guilty, embarrassed, or ashamed at the thought of acting like this.

Disgust—a topic of particular interest to Paul Rozin—has its phylogenetic roots in "distaste" (Rozin et al., 1993; Calder et al., 2000). Rozin and his colleagues distinguish *core disgust* from *sociomoral disgust* (Rozin et al., 1999). Core disgust is "a guardian of the mouth against potential contaminants" (p. 575). It elaborates in human worlds to regulate sex, eating, hygiene, and defecation. Its regulatory role further generalizes and can become a key constituent of responses to such diverse actions of others as cruelty, abject subservience, and betrayal (Miller, 1997). Disgust, it is hypothesized, plays a particularly important role in divinity ethics where purity and protection against the indignity of contamination is of central importance.

This is, of course, a schematic simplification. However, early studies to test the CAD Triad Hypothesis suggest that the relative prominence of particular negative feelings with particular types of ethic has validity (Rozin et al., 1999). These hypothesized connections can now be integrated into the general form of the present argument about the ways in which negative emotions shape and guard the boundaries of self/identity, and hence the type of identity it is. This can be most economically presented as follows. Here I have split CAD and incorporated vectoral dimensions of possession ("belonging to me" and "my belonging to others"). I have also included the hypothesized emotions typical of differently positioned players (the emotions of those who breach a significant ethical rule and also the emotions of those committed to the ethic who observe the breaking of such a rule).

Boundary of Self	Shweder Ethic	Feelings of Others After Violations of Core Norms or Ideals	Feelings of Self After Violating Core Norms or Ideals
Belonging to me	Autonomy	Anger, etc.	Fear, anxiety, guilt, etc.
My belonging to others	Community	Contempt, etc.	Shame, guilt, embarrassment etc.
	Divinity	Disgust, etc.	Self-disgust, shame, etc.

If these emotions (contempt, anger, disgust and shame, embarrassment, guilt) function as perimeters, or boundaries, which shape different types of ethic, then do they also shape the emotional boundaries of individuals whose identities are predominantly formed by one or the other ethic? Is this a useful way to think about the "unthinkable" emotional boundaries of individual selves? We can test the utility of this analytic framework by applying it to a recent example involving the mutually constitutive identities "daughter-father." The specific emotions involved in this example are anger and fear locked with contempt and shame. Their associated ethics, in the example I will now elaborate, are those of autonomy and community, as outlined above.

AN EXAMPLE OF IDENTITY CONFLICT FOUNDED ON CONTRASTING ALLEGIANCES TO COMMUNITY AND AUTONOMY ETHICS: THE CASE OF FADIME AND RAHMI SAHINDAL

Fadime Sahindal was a 26-year-old Kurdish-Swedish woman murdered in Sweden in January 2002 by her father Rahmi Sahindal in an apparent "honor" killing (*The Irish Times*, February 9, 2002).

Fadime grew up in two cultures at odds with each other. She was reared within the patriarchal Turkish/Kurdish culture of her family, which was itself contained by the liberal democratic Swedish culture of her schooling, friends, and recreational world. Her father and male relatives, while living within Swedish society, appear to have withheld allegiance from it when it came to important issues like responsibility in arranging the marriages of female family members. Their identities were primarily Kurdish/Turkish, and they actively resisted certain specific transformations of their identities into those of liberal democratic Swedes.

How are we to understand the murder of Fadime by her father Rahmi? Of course there will be uniquely individual aspects of this tragedy. Only a tiny number of Turkish/Kurdish fathers would go to such extremes of murderously enforcing "family honor" in a European country as did Rahmi Sahindal. Not-withstanding that, and knowing no details of the case other than what the newspapers reported, we can nonetheless make certain general points about the dynamics of identity-maintenance and their emotional "boundaries."

Here are some of the ingredients that may have constituted Fadime's and Rahmi's interrelated dilemmas. Fadime *felt* it was "her right" to fall in love with her Swedish boyfriend Patrik Lindesjö. Her father *felt* she had no such rights in this sphere of her life and that the rights to choose whom she should marry were "his" (again note what must be involved in believing/feeling that a right is "yours"). Fadime's *feeling* of her own freedoms, and her entitlements to them, were radically and insurmountably at odds with those of her father.

In all likelihood, Fadime's *feelings* on this would have been very different had she grown to womanhood in her native village in Turkey. The odds are that the gap between father's wishes and daughter's would have been much smaller, that her opportunities to make partner-choices would have been immeasurably less, and that the accepted precedence of her father's wishes over hers would have been taken for granted within her ambient community. And likely as not, she would be still alive.

Fadime exercised "her own sense of autonomy" and followed her feelings by opting to be with her boyfriend and by rejecting her father's wishes regarding an arranged marriage back in Turkey to a cousin. Presumably she felt distressed at the consequences of, as she would have seen it, being forced into this conflict-ridden dilemma. But, we imagine, her feelings for Patrik were *hers* and the choice in going to him was a choice in line with the inclinations of her being the sort of person she then was. The distress she felt was, we might surmise, an amalgam of grief at being estranged from her family (particularly her female relatives), fear of her father coupled with anger at his attempts to subordinate her wishes to his, and love for Patrik. Presumably she also felt, given the sort of person she was, that she was right to opt for this course of action, which involved exercising her own right to choose a partner rather than feeling it was right to subordinate her own feelings to those of her father. In other words, Fadime's *hierarchy of feelings with respect to identity-relevant decision-making did not synchronize with that of her father.*

Confronted with the evidence that Fadime had assumed an authority over decisions about her own life which he felt was his prerogative and not hers, and that she did this very publicly, Rahmi Sahindal reportedly experienced the sort of anger that is called rage. His opposition to his daughter became total. His sense of "honor," derived from the patriarchal structure of *his* family and communal world, was radically threatened. The equilibrium of "honor relations" could only be restored, and righteous anger fulfilled, by killing his daughter. This he did. Given the emotional dynamic of a community ethic sketched above, Rahmi's feelings for Fadime were likely to have been a mixture of self-righteous anger and contempt for the "errant" Fadime evolving into hate. Again we can only speculate on his feelings now that he has killed Fadime, but *feelings of satisfaction* must form or have formed some part of his affective world in the immediate aftermath of his murderous actions. The word "hate" seems justified in describing his eventual feelings for his daughter (Beck, 1999). It should be added that Rahmi killed Fadime long after another tragedy had marked her life when her boyfriend Patrik had been killed in a car accident. At the time of her murder she was single but campaigning on behalf of other young women caught in her predicament in Sweden.

Remembering Fritz Heider's "fundamental attribution error," we can see how the subjective dimensions of individual psychology in this case are contingent on the structural dimensions of the respective cultures (Heider, 1958). The origin of the *feelings of possessing, or not possessing, "rights"* lies in the intersubjective worlds of the protagonists. These "worlds," which preexist their members, help to construct those feelings, which in time come to assume their executive roles in the individual or personal psychology of their members. (Moghaddam, 2002).

From a liberal democratic European perspective, it is not part of the dynamics of fatherly identity to feel a "right" to murder a noncompliant daughter. To do so would be, as we say, unthinkable. A liberal democratic European identity, as it has evolved thus far, is founded on notions of gender equality (however inequitable the base from which it works and however patchy its implementation). Daughters as much as sons are reared to become the sorts of people who endorse and feel this equality. Their identities in this regard have very similar emotional dynamics. They get angry when rights that they feel to be an intrinsic part of themselves are infringed and they expect agreement across gender divides that they are right to do so.

It would now (that is in 2003) be unthinkable for most young European daughters to submerge their wishes and reject someone they love because their father had other plans for them. Faced with such an "unreasonable" father, they might angrily reject him as much as he might reject them, and they would expect that the consensus of right-minded people would support their stance rather than that of their father. Even liberal Swedish society changed significantly during Fadime's lifetime as far as gender equalities are concerned. The male line of succession to the throne, for example, ceased to be exclusive about twenty years ago and Victoria, the Princess Royal, became first in line to the throne ahead of her younger brother. This equalization of gender rights is, of course, a recent historical development, but one that forms a linchpin of the modern identity. So here, in schematic form, is one interpretation of the dilemma of Fadime and Rahmi Sahindal.

For Fadime's identity as, primarily, a young Swedish woman of Turkish origin shaped mostly by an autonomy ethic, it was unthinkable not to follow her own feelings in love. Her father's infringement of her rights as she understood them would have produced feelings that included, one might speculate, a grieving anger towards him. For Rahmi, whose identity as a Turkish/Kurdish father was presumably shaped by a community-type ethic, but who happened to be occupying an economic place in Swedish society, his allegiance was to traditional Kurdish family dynamics. His daughter's public rejection of his authority would have produced feelings that included, one surmises, humiliated anger turning dangerously into the sort of contemptuous hate that sees the annihilation of the object of these feelings as the only course of action consistent with being the sort of self he felt himself to be.

For Fadime, the course of action entailed by her feelings was rejection of her father accompanied, one imagines, by grief at having to do this, and a moving away towards her boyfriend. For Rahmi, the course of action enrolled by his humiliated anger, and attendant hate, was a rectification of an imbalance in his world. It was, however, a murderous course of action involving the annihilation of the object of anger/hate, Fadime. She would have been the cause of his humiliation, both in his own eyes and in those of his culture, which, developmentally, amounts to the same thing.

Underlying both Fadime's and Rahmi's crises were those boundaries of identity that have to do with possession, and which I have called *the action boundaries of identities*, with the emotional dynamics that both constitute and maintain them as what they are. Rahmi believed that the determination of his daughter's rights to action in the erotic domain belonged to him, as confirmed by the governing belief systems of his traditional Kurdish culture with its predominantly community-type ethic. Fadime believed they belonged to her as confirmed by the Swedish culture within which she was educated with its informing autonomy ethic. The focus in this example has been on structural determinants of identity and identity maintenance, on the ways in which intersubjectivity structures the emotional dynamics of, in this case, contending subjectivities.

POSITIONING THEORY AND THE NEGATIVE EMOTIONAL BOUNDARIES OF IDENTITY

In the terms of "Positioning Theory" (Harré & Van Langenhove, 1999), Fadime and Rahmi's fatal relationship can be redescribed as follows. Fadime Sahindal would have found that her *self-positioning* as a modern young Swedish woman of Kurdish extraction conflicted with her father's forced self-positioning of her as a to-be-obedient Kurdish daughter. Her strategy of coping with this dilemma would have been to engage in *second-order positioning* whereby she refused the legitimacy of her father's positioning of her and, in so doing, denied his legitimacy to position himself as her master in matters of love. This was a double de-legitimizing of the self-positioning of her father, whose story line for his moral actions was one of traditional honor derived from his identity-forming moral order.

But Fadime went further. She engaged in *third order positioning* by making her troubled relationship with her father, over the issue of the right to choose whomsoever she wished to love, a public and political issue. Her argument here, on behalf of young immigrant women like herself, was that women's rights to choose their partners should have precedence over family and paternal rights to choose marriage partners for them. By publicly challenging the very idea that Rahmi had any legitimate claim to his felt right, she undermined publicly the very moral order that was a foundation of his identity as a Kurdish father and thereby delegitimized his identity on a third and profound level. The emotions involved were, as we know, murderous in their conclusion. The previous illustration of the difference between "belonging to me" and "belonging to others" again suggests how we might reconstruct how they both felt and why.

The moral good that constituted Fadime's identity, derived from a moral order stressing the desirability of egalitarian autonomy typical of Western democracies, irreconcilably confronted the moral good that constituted Rahmi's identity, which was derived from a moral order that stressed a patriarchal authoritarian communalism. Fadime felt herself right in claiming that the boundaries of her self included the limits of those actions of erotic desire, which constituted her love for Patrik and her desire to be with him. In her eyes, her father violated the norms of her constituting moral order—Swedish egalitarianism. Anger at his stance would have been part of her emotional response combined, in all likelihood, with some combination of fear, anxiety, and guilt, at least in the early stages of defying her father.

For Rahmi's part, he would have felt the boundaries of himself to be the boundaries of his community's regard for himself as he imagined it. He is likely to have felt contempt for Fadime for violating the moral order he intended her to have made part of herself, and to have himself felt some mix of shame, guilt, and embarrassment for her actions' effect in shaping how he imagined his community now regarded him. Given the sorts of selves we assume them to have been, it was unthinkable for Fadime to subordinate her choice of a lover to the arranged choice of her father. It was equally unthinkable for Rahmi not to act to restore his sense of honor, and that of his imagined community, by punishing her. In each case, the boundaries of their identities were strong negative emotions.

I give this as an example involving the specific negative emotions of shame and blame. In this same category of shame and blame, I could just as readily have offered other examples involving the violation of codes of honor, or examples involving religious or political apostasy. Were we to take disgust and contempt as the focus of our analyses, we could develop examples involving, say, cannibalism, inter-caste relationships, or homophobia. If guilt and its related anger were our focus then we might look at different examples of murder and betrayal.

In each case, the pertinent question would be: what makes actions in any of these categories unthinkable? Is it the strong negative emotions that restrain the agent of these potential actions? Included here would be those negative emotions s/he feels when s/he imagines doing the action, but also the feelings s/he imagines others having upon knowing that s/he is imagining doing those actions. If the answers are in the affirmative, then the claim that boundaries of identities are strong negative emotions of the kind to make the action "unthinkable" in the way I have defined it, is further strengthened.

CONCLUSION

People's identities are shaped to a large degree by the quality of the emotional relationships they have had with others since infancy. The maturing prefrontal lobes are significantly shaped by what those who most matter to the young child do and say. People's current feelings about themselves are also deeply influenced by the ways in which what they now most care about synchronizes with what those, among whom they live, most care about. People's feelings when someone else violates some norm, which they think very important, tells them something highly significant about themselves. The circumscription of their own behavior, caused by their anticipation of others' emotional responses—were they themselves to violate a deep, identity-forming moral injunction—is another key indication of their own emotional construction. Finally, their anticipations of how they themselves would feel if they were to break a highly important local moral rule again signifies what sort of person they most truly *are*.

The architecture of individual and group identities is, therefore, fundamentally emotional. The concept of unthinkable boundaries, as argued in this chapter, is a useful analytic tool for comparing and contrasting types of identity. It has both analytic and synthetic power. It bears a close relationship to the concept of *an ideal* (Frankfurt, 1993). These abstractions are particularly useful to the sorts of psychology utilized by historians, biographers, and autobiographers. Such histories are narratives of the kind that would help validate, and elaborate, the argument about the structure of identities presented here. Analyses of particular identity-constituting ideals, and of their unthinkable boundaries, are ideas that psychology might usefully borrow from other human sciences, integrate with contemporary psychological research and understanding, and then return to such disciplines as history and biography, confident that value has been added.

I began this chapter with an epigraph from W. I. Miller, which claimed that "Disgust, along with contempt, as well as other emotions in various settings, recognizes and maintains difference. Disgust helps define boundaries between us and them and me and you" (Miller, 1997, p. 50). I have gone on to argue that these negative emotions define differences not just *between* persons and groups but *within* the very identities of persons and groups. "Within" identities these emotions define the "outer boundaries" between being one type of self and being another. To think about "the unthinkable" in this sense is to confront what most protects or constrains the nature of human identities, both individual and group.

NOTES

1. This has similarities to the functionalist position, which holds "that the condition for being in a mental state should be given by the functional role of that state, that is, in terms of its standard causal relationships, rather than by supposed intrinsic features of the state" (Honderich, 1995).

2. In studying aesthetic experiences of art, I think that the micro-temporal focus is particularly relevant. I expect that in a relatively short time the emerging field of social cognitive neuroscience will go some way towards remedying this deficit in empirical psychological understanding (Azar, 2002).

3. I am indebted to the philosopher Harry Frankfurt for a use of this idea of the

unthinkable, which prompts me to speculate on its theoretical utility for descriptions of the essential limits of particular selves and identities (Frankfurt, 1993). It is an idea that I have introduced in a recent book on the cultural psychology of self, but that I want to explore in more detail here (Benson, 2001).

4. For an introduction to Charles Taylor's work on identity from a cultural psychological perspective see Benson (2001), chapter 4.

REFERENCES

Azar, B. (2000). At the frontier of science: Social cognitive neuroscience merges three disciplines in the hope of deciphering the process behind behavior, *Monitor on Psychology*, January, 40–43.

Bandura, A. (1985). *Social foundations of thought and action*. Englewood Cliffs, NJ: Prentice Hall.

Beck, A. (1999). *Prisoners of hate: The cognitive basis of anger, hostility and violence*. New York: Harper Collins.

Benson, C. (1993). *The absorbed self: Pragmatism, psychology, and aesthetic experience*. Hemel Hempstead: Harvester Wheatsheaf.

Benson, C. (2001). *The cultural psychology of self: Place, morality and art in human worlds*. London: Routledge.

Browning, C. R. (1992). *Ordinary men: Reserve police battalion 101 and the Final Solution in Poland*. New York: Harper Perennial.

Bruner, J. (1996). *The culture of education*, Cambridge, MA: Harvard University Press.

Calder, A. J., Keane, J., Manes, F., Antoun, N. & Young, A. M. (2000). Impaired recognition and experience of disgust following brain injury. *Nature Neuroscience*, 3, 11, 1077–78.

Cole, M. (1996). *Cultural psychology: A once and future discipline*. Cambridge, MA: Harvard University Press.

Damasio, A. (1996). *Descartes' error: Emotion, reason and the human brain*. London: Papermac.

Damasio, A. (1999). *The feeling of what happens: Body and emotion in the making of consciousness*. New York: Harcourt Brace.

Feinberg, T. (2001). *Altered egos: How the brain causes the self*. Oxford: Oxford University Press.

Frankfurt, H. (1988). *The importance of what we care about*. New York: Cambridge University Press.

Frankfurt, H. (1993). On the necessity of ideals. In G. G. Noam & T. E. Wren (Eds.), *The moral self*. Cambridge, MA: MIT Press.

Goldhagen, D. (1998). *Hitler's willing executioners: Ordinary Germans and the Holocaust*. London: Abacus.

Hare, R. D. (1993). *Without conscience: The disturbing world of the psychopaths among us*. London: Guilford Press.

Harré, R. (1993). *Social being* (2nd ed.). Oxford: Basil Blackwell.

Harré, R. (1998). *The singular self*. London: Sage.

Harré, R., & Van Langenhove, L. (Eds.). (1999). *Positioning theory: Moral contexts of intentional action*. Oxford: Blackwell.

Heider, F. (1958). *The psychology of interpersonal relations*. New York: Wiley.

Honderich, T. (Ed.). (1995). *The Oxford companion to philosophy.* Oxford: Oxford University Press.

Kagan, J. (1984). *The nature of the child.* New York: Basic Books.

Lakoff, G., & Johnson, M. (1999). *Philosophy in the flesh: The embodied mind and its challenge to Western thought.* New York: Basic Books.

Langer, S. (1970). *Mind: An essay on human feeling* (vol. 1). Baltimore: Johns Hopkins University Press.

Laplanche, J., & Pontalis, B., (1980). *The language of psycho-analysis.* Trans. D. Nicholson-Smith. London: Hogarth Press and the Institute of Psycho-Analysis.

Lewis, M. (1993). Self-conscious emotions: Embarrassment, pride, shame and guilt. In M. Lewis & J. M. Haviland (Eds.). *Handbook of emotions.* New York: Guilford Press.

Merleau-Ponty, M. (1981). *Phenomenology of perception.* Trans. C. Smith. London: Routledge & Kegan Paul.

Miller, W. I. (1997). *The anatomy of disgust.* Cambridge, MA: Harvard University Press.

Moghaddam, F. (2000). Toward a cultural theory of human rights. *Theory & Psychology,* 10, 3, 291–312.

Moghaddam, F. (2002). *The individual and society: A cultural integration.* New York: Worth.

Nussbaum, M. (2001). *Upheavals of Thought: The intelligence of emotions.* Cambridge: Cambridge University Press.

Oatley, K., & Jenkins, J. M. (1996). *Understanding emotions.* Oxford: Blackwell.

Rozin, P., Haidt, J., and McCauley, C. R. (1993). Disgust. In M. Lewis & J. M. Haviland (Eds.), *Handbook of emotions.* New York: Guilford Press.

Rozin, P., Lowery, L., Haidt, J., & Imada, S. (1999). The CAD triad hypothesis: A mapping between three moral emotions (contempt, anger, disgust) and three moral codes (community, autonomy, divinity). *Journal of Personality and Social Psychology,* 76, 4, 574–586.

Shore, B. (1996). *Culture in mind: Cognition, culture, and the problem of meaning.* Oxford: Oxford University Press.

Shweder, R. A., Much, N.C., Mahapatra, M., & Park, L. (1997). The "Big three" of morality (autonomy, community, divinity) and the "Big Three" explanation of suffering. In A. Brandt & P. Rozin (Eds.), *Morality and health.* New York: Routledge.

Shweder, R. A. (2000). The psychology of practice and the practice of psychology. *Asian Journal of Social Psychology,* 3, 207–222.

Solms, M., & Turnbull, O. (2002). *The brain and the inner world: An introduction to the neuroscience of subjective experience.* New York: Other Press.

Staub, E. (1989). *The roots of evil: The origins of genocide and other group violence.* New York: Cambridge University Press.

Stigler, J. W., Shweder, R. A., & Herdt, G. (Eds.). (1990). *Cultural psychology: Essays on comparative human development.* Cambridge: Cambridge University Press.

Taylor, C. (1989). *Sources of the self: The making of the modern identity.* Cambridge, MA: Harvard University Press.

The Irish Times, February 9, 2002, 11.

Tomasello, M. (1999). *The cultural origins of human cognition.* Cambridge, MA: Harvard University Press.

Tugendhat, E. (1993). The role of identity in the constitution of morality. In G. G.
    Noam and T. E. Wren (Eds.), *The moral self.* Cambridge, MA: MIT Press.
Valsiner, J. (2001). Cultural developmental psychology of affective processes. Paper
    delivered to the 15th Tagung der Fachgruppe Entwicklungspsychologie der
    Deutschen Gesellschaft für Psychologie, Potsdam. September 5.
Wollheim, R. (1984). *The thread of life.* Cambridge: Cambridge University Press.

CHAPTER 6

Malignant Positioning and the Predicament of People with Alzheimer's Disease

Steven R. Sabat

In the dynamic conversational interactions occurring between people in the course of everyday life, it can be seen that persons at various times take for themselves, impose on others, accept, and sometimes reject, the positions that make their behavior intelligible as social acts (Van Langenhove & Harré, 1999). It is through such positions that a person's moral and personal attributes can be defined, strengthened, and diluted, and through which story lines or narratives about that person can be developed and acted upon by others in the person's social world. Likewise, positioning can be understood as a way by which people explain their own behavior as well as that of others in their social interactions. Among the types of positioning that have been delineated, two are especially germane to the issues in this chapter: (a) interactive positioning, wherein what one person says positions another person, and (b) reflexive positioning, wherein one positions him or herself (Davies & Harré, 1999). In the various social exchanges that occur in everyday life, one person might attempt to position another in a particular way (interactive positioning), but the second person, for a variety of reasons, might not desire to be positioned as such and not only rejects that position, but attempts to position him or herself in what he or she sees to be a more desirable way (reflexive positioning). Although it is quite common for individuals to accept as well as to reject positions vis à vis others, the social situations that are confronted by people with Alzheimer's disease (AD) are quite different, and as a result people with AD can become extremely vulnerable as regards aspects of their personhood.

In order to appreciate more fully the meaning of what follows in this chapter, it is important to understand what AD means at the level of the individual as well as at the level of society. At the present time, more than four million people have been diagnosed with probable AD in the United States alone, with nineteen million family members working as caregivers. Recent projections are that by the middle of this century, barring a cure or preventive measures, the numbers will more than triple, owing to the growing proportion of those in the "baby boom" generation who will become senior citizens, and the costs involved in caring for people with AD will reach $375 billion (Alzheimer's Association, 2000). The disease is a progressive, irreversible, neuropathological disorder that destroys brain cells and depletes neurotransmitter systems (Sabat, 2001) and reduces life expectancy by fifty percent (Katzman, 1976). The disease disrupts the ability to employ explicit memory (especially the ability to recall recent events), coherent and skilled movement (praxis), and selective attention, and it affects emotion as well. Many researchers have concluded that AD can have profound effects on language (Sabat, 2001). Appell et al. (1982) observed that language disturbances are an "almost universal finding" among dementia sufferers.

In this chapter, I should like to explore various aspects of positioning as they apply to people with AD and how some forms of positioning can be "malignant," that is to say dangerous, insofar as they can have negative effects not only upon the ways in which the person with AD is seen by others, but upon the ways in which the person with AD is subsequently treated and may come to see him or herself to one or another degree. Furthermore, as the person with AD is positioned in malignant ways, the ability to reposition him or herself can, to some extent, be vitiated by (1) the extant story lines created about him or her by healthy others, and (2) the compromised ability of the person with AD to reject the initial positioning due to such things as word-finding problems and the ever-growing sense of a loss of control in social situations. Taking this line of thinking a step further, and using the lenses of Social Construction Theory (Harré, 1983, 1991) we will appreciate that when a person with AD is positioned negatively by others, that person's ability to construct valued, worthy, social personae (Self 3 personae) is likewise compromised such that the person with AD will receive cooperation from others only in the construction of a Self 3 that can be called the "burdensome/dysfunctional patient." A persona such as this is anathema to that person, serves to compound the sense of loss that he or she has already experienced, and can serve as a source of further embarrassment and humiliation.

TYPES AND SOURCES OF INTERACTIVE MALIGNANT POSITIONING

The sources of malignant positioning of the interactive type are many and varied. Before delving into some of the most common, it is important first to appreciate some blatant examples of such positioning as can be seen in samples of public discourse.

Explicit Positioning

They don't know anything anymore

This statement was made by a caregiver for a person with AD during a caregivers' education lecture that I was giving at a local adult day care center. He was talking about people with AD, to whom the "they" in his comment refers. His wife, who had AD, still lived at home and despite his daily interaction with her, he was somehow convinced that she as well as other people with AD "don't know anything anymore." Interestingly enough, the speaker had relatively little experience with people with AD beyond his experience with his wife. Thus, we see that the caregiver was engaging not only in malignant interactive positioning insofar as his wife was concerned but was positioning all people with AD in that manner. In this case, it might be appreciated that the mere presence of the diagnosis and some obvious symptoms such as problems with recalling recent facts and experiences can result in a type of positioning that is negative, because the speaker, without having met a host of people with AD, had come to the conclusion that "they don't know anything anymore."

Now, it might occur to the reader that this man, a lay person, was revealing a certain ignorance in making such a stereotypic statement as a result of the fact that he was not highly educated (which he was not) or terribly observant. One should not assume, however, that higher education exempts a person from making such inaccurate generalizations, as we can see by the following comment, made by a physician who was the internist for a person with AD:

Treating an Alzheimer's patient is like doing veterinary medicine

In this statement, the physician is indicating that, because of his own inability to engage in effective communication with his patient, he sees the task of treating such a person as being akin to that of trying to treat an animal who, by nature, cannot communicate via language. It is not my intention to imply that all lay people and all physicians are represented by these comments, but, at the same time, it is the case that a variety of people, including professionals, see people with AD primarily in terms of a host of negative, dysfunctional attributes and position them accordingly.

In large segments of the professional literature, there has been a predominance of defectological descriptions of people with AD; that is, people with AD are characterized most often in terms that highlight their deficits in a variety of ways. For example, terms such as confusion, emotional lability, disorientation, neuroticism, hostility (Chatterjee et al., 1992), agitation, disturbances in abstract thinking and judgment (DSM-IV; American Psychiatric Association, 1994), loss of interest in usual activities, paranoia, phobias, hallucinations, delusions, anxiety (Reisberg et al., 1987), uncooperativeness, apathy (Bozzola et al., 1992), and personality alterations (Hamel et al., 1990) have been applied to persons with AD in the moderate to severe stages.

In a sense, it is not surprising to discover such a powerful focus on the dysfunctions found among people with AD, for such a focus is an important part of a medically oriented approach to understanding a disease. The "signs and symptoms" of the disease are catalogued and compared to other diseases so as to come to a better understanding of AD's similarity to and differences from other neurological disorders, as well as to isolate symptoms such that they might be treated pharmacologically. As a result, AD has come to be understood in terms of its presumed symptomatic defects. Although this approach is consonant with attempts at understanding a disease and may prove in some ways to be revealing of the nature of the disease as well as a means of developing possible drug-based interventions, it is not necessarily revealing of the person who is afflicted, for one's personhood extends far beyond the attributes connected to the disease process. Indeed, the person with AD in the moderate to severe stages may be seen to manifest a host of intact, healthy attributes (Sabat, 1991, 2001; Sabat & Harré, 1994; Sabat & Cagigas, 1997; Sabat et al., 1999). Nonetheless, persons with AD come to be positioned as being defective quite often.

Yet, malignant interactive positioning is found as well among professionals who are not physicians. A few examples are illustrative.

Patients with Alzheimer's disease experience fear throughout their disease course. As they decline and lose capacities, part of what is also lost is the ability to articulate their fears and cope with them. Essentially, what is lost is the person's ability to self-soothe if fears become overwhelming. This is akin to the behavior seen in infants who do not have the neurological and cognitive capacities to overcome their unrealistic fears. (Raia, 1999 p. 33)

Although the author, who is the director of patient care and family support at the Alzheimer's Association of Eastern Massachusetts, may not have intended it, the person with AD is here being positioned as being akin to an infant and burdened by unrealistic fears. The implication that such fears as the person with AD experiences are "unrealistic" is questionable at the very least (Laing, 1965). Such an interpretation is challenged further by the author's earlier comment that a person with AD "loses the ability to articulate" his or her fears. If a person cannot articulate his or her fears, it is difficult indeed for another individual to be able to assess those fears as being "unrealistic." Yet, logic seems not to stand in the way of the story line or narrative being woven here, given the malignant positioning of the person with AD as being as incapable of communicating, of "self-soothing," as is an infant. Furthermore, although the person with AD may have difficulty in articulating his or her fears, among other things, this in itself does not mean that the same person cannot communicate effectively when provided with facilitation, such as through the use of indirect repair, from healthy others (Sabat, 1991).

Implicit Malignant Positioning

In the next example we see evidence of what we may call "implicit" malignant positioning. In this case, the author is referring to the practice of staff members keeping track of the moods of people with AD and their caregivers while the former were involved in a program that included different types of work for AD-afflicted veterans.

Staff members are amazed at the relaxed manner and sometimes candor with which the men talk to each other about their forgetfulness and difficulty with their everyday problems. (Maddox and Burns, 1999, p. 69)

That the staff members were "amazed" at the behavior in question implies that the behavior did not conform to their expectations. What those expectations were can be hypothesized to be something verging on the opposite of what actually happened. That is, the staff members expected that the men with AD would not speak with one another about their problems in a relaxed and candid way, the assumption being that men with AD would not be able to communicate or commiserate with one another about their problems as they did, or if they were capable of doing so, they would not be desirous of doing so.

Thus, the initial expectation involves positioning the men with AD in a way that would preclude the very behavior in question. What was it that fueled such an expectation? Perhaps it was the fact that the men had a diagnosis of AD and that the staff members' previous experience of people with AD did not include such behavior. Perhaps it was a combination of these along with the possibility that the staff had never encountered a group of AD sufferers who had the opportunity to interact with one another in a social setting such as this one. In any case, the staff members had positioned these particular men in such a way as to include a story line about them that did not include the ability or desire to discuss their problems with other men who had AD as well. If the staff members had engaged in explicit malignant positioning, they would have said directly that the men with AD could not or would not engage in the discussion in question. Instead, they admitted to being "amazed" at the discussion that occurred, and so they have implicitly positioned these men with AD.

Implicit malignant positioning clearly exists before the moment in which it is revealed in such comments as being "amazed that . . . ", and it can have a negative effect on the ways in which those who engage in such positioning behave toward those whom they are positioning. Such behavior can be seen to inspire what Kitwood (1990) called "malignant social psychology," which itself can (1) compromise the personhood of those with AD and (2) inspire in such persons negative reactions ranging from hostility to learned helplessness to depression (Seligman, 1975). It is not too far afield, I think, to envision a scenario in which a staff member engages in implicit malignant positioning and then quite innocently treats the person with AD in ways that might be described as patronizing. The person with AD reacts negatively, perhaps aggressively, and this reaction is then viewed as "irrational" by the staff member. Perhaps the staff member's report of the AD sufferer's behavior is brought to the attention of a staff psychiatrist who then prescribes medication to treat the behavior in question. The characterization of "irrational" is itself irrational but is nonetheless incorporated into story lines about the person with AD in such a way as to validate the initial implicit malignant positioning.

Malignant Positioning and the Creation of Validating Story Lines

Some of the examples cited in the previous section, as well as the following examples of malignant positioning, have been drawn from professional literature devoted, ironically, to enhancing the quality of life in late-stage dementia and AD. Authors include a speech and language pathologist specializing in geriatrics (Benjamin) whose commentary is addressed below, as well as occupational therapists (Burns, cited in the previous section) a director of patient care and family support, a clinical nurse specialist (Maddox, cited in the previous section) and other professionals.

That malignant positioning leads to the creation of story lines that confirm the initial positioning about the person in question can be seen more clearly in the following commentary about a study (Toseland et al., 1997) of the effectiveness of validation therapy:

. . . nurses reported that patients receiving validation therapy were less physically and verbally aggressive, less depressed, but more nonphysically aggressive in terms of increased wandering, pacing, and repetitive movement. (Benjamin, 1999 p. 124)

Here, we see that the authors have interpreted behaviors such as wandering, pacing, and repetitive movement as being "nonphysically aggressive" as if it is a fact that such behaviors constitute a species of aggression. A person might walk about or pace back and forth because he or she has nothing to do or is anxious about something. There may be a variety of reasons for engaging in such behavior. The loving and devoted relatives and friends of a person who is undergoing major surgery may pace about the waiting room and walk up and down hallways, due to a combination of being anxious and not wanting to remain sitting in one place for hour after hour. This behavior would hardly be labeled "nonphysically aggressive." Therefore, it is the context of the behavior and who is engaging in the behavior that seems to have been critical in determining the label used. The persons described in the quotation above were people who had a diagnosis of dementia and who lived in a nursing home. The diagnosis ("dementia patients") and the location of the people in question turn out to lead to malignant positioning and the "needs" of the staff (having difficulty, or experiencing stress and frustration in dealing with people who walk about in the halls and such and wanting to minimize these "problem" behaviors) lead to the resulting story lines in which the behavior is characterized as being "aggressive" as if the behavior in question is, in fact, an expression of aggression purposefully being "inflicted" on the staff members. That such a story line is not a reflection of fact but is, rather, an interpretation, is clear.

Yet another story line is exemplary of how initial malignant positioning serves as the basis for subsequent story lines that are consonant with the original positioning.

To deny the feelings of increasing confusion and to alleviate fears of losing control of their mental facilities, these patients adopt a rigid set of social standards. Often, they do not want to associate with persons who display confusion or disorientation; they do not want to be touched nor do they want to touch others. (Benjamin, 1999, p. 112)

The behaviors in question, not wanting to associate with other people who display behavior that is disturbing, not wanting to be touched, and not wanting to touch others, are here interpreted as being a function of dementia. People with dementia are thus said to adopt rigid social standards for purposes of denial. Thus the behaviors in question are interpreted as being forms of pathology stemming from the disease. I use the term, "interpreted" because there is nothing in the behaviors themselves that is objectively pathological, yet the flavor of the author's discussion clearly indicates that there is something pathological involved. What alternative interpretations might be applied?

From the perspective of William Stern, "The person seeks in the world that which he lacks, and reacts against the world with the force of *counteraction*, whenever his own being must be asserted in opposition to the process of assimilation" (1938, p. 91). Stern used the term, "assimilation" to refer to the process by which a person becomes a homogeneous member of the human order (much like becoming a mere "number") and thereby losing his or her own individuality. In terms of the situation confronted by the person with dementia, the notion of being assimilated into a homogeneous group such as "AD sufferers" or "patients" or "demented" means that the person in question is at risk of others not honoring or attending to his or her own individuality and whatever admirable qualities he or she possesses. To react with "counteraction" against such a threat is hardly pathological. Indeed, it might alternately be construed as a type of goal-directed behavior of a high order, the goal being one of self-maintenance or self-development (an autotelic goal in Stern's terms).

Likewise, from a Social Constructionist point of view (Harré, 1983, 1991) to be positioned primarily as a "demented" person, an AD patient as stereotypically conceived, a person will not be able to gain the necessary cooperation needed in order to construct a social persona in which he or she can take pride. To reject being in the company of other "patients" can be understood as an attempt to differentiate oneself from others thus positioned. Instances of people with AD in the moderate to severe stages who have behaved in similar ways have been reported in the literature (Sabat, 2001). The main point here is that behavior such as avoiding the presence of people who display overt symptoms that are troubling to oneself is not ipso facto an indication of pathology, but might instead be understood as a form of the intact ability to evaluate a situation, understand its meaning, and working to avoid it for worthy reasons. In other words, we have here a form of "semiotic" or "meaning driven" behavior (Shweder & Sullivan, 1989). Indeed, it may even be interpreted as being an indirect way for a person with dementia to reject the way in which others are positioning him or her—in a sense, trying to avoid "guilt by association."

The other behavior discussed above, not wanting to be touched and not wanting to touch others, also need not be understood as being pathological. Indeed, this is well known in research on culture and personal space as described in "basic" texts on social behavior and culture (Moghaddam, 1998). In order to evaluate the meaning of such behavior, one must first understand something about the person who is behaving in these ways. To wit, if that person, throughout the course of his or her life in healthier times, has been one who has not enjoyed being touched by people who are not close friends or relatives, or who has not enjoyed such contact even with close friends or relatives, then the persistence of the same behavior even in the presence of AD or some other form of dementia could hardly be construed as the adopting of a "rigid set of social standards" that itself is founded in the person's denial of confusion or need to alleviate fears. It is, rather, the continuation of a long-standing way of interacting with others, which itself has not been compromised by the neuropathology of AD. Behavior in and of itself is not necessarily understandable outside of the context of the life, the abiding inclinations, needs, and wants of the person engaging in that behavior. In other words, the behavior must be seen in the context of the individual him or herself in order to understand its meaning. When a person with AD is positioned in a malignant way, the only context in which his or her behavior is interpreted is the context of having been diagnosed with a form of neuropathology, and the balance of that person's behavior and inclinations and dispositions in healthier days is tacitly consigned to the realm of the inconsequential. Thus are the labelers, the positioners, lacking insight into the individuality and the motives and, more broadly, the culture of the person whom they are positioning—solely on the basis of the diagnosis.

The aforementioned examples of malignant positioning have been drawn from professional literature devoted, ironically, to enhancing the quality of life in late-stage dementia and AD. It is, however, the case that forms of malignant positioning have also entered the realm of the lay public press, thereby contributing further to the predicament of people with AD, for the lay press reaches far and wide into the lives of the general public. I should like to call the reader's attention to a few examples of this recent tendency in the following section.

Malignant Positioning in the Popular Press

"Here's an intimate and unhappy fact of senile dementia: They become unappetizing" (Cooney, 2001, p. 47). The author's comment is part of an article about her mother's Alzheimer's and the ways in which the author experienced turmoil in her life as a result. Although the article is about her mother, the author has positioned all people with dementia as being "unappetizing" (whatever that actually means aside from being a literary device). The author claims this quality to be a "fact" about people with dementia, as opposed to her own singular point of view.

"It was bad enough that she had to lose her mind ... " (Cooney, 2001, p. 48). Here, the author has concluded, as a result of some of her mother's problems with explicit recall and such, that her mother had lost her mind. In recalling her mother's behavior years ago and comparing it to the present time, the author says, "She didn't cry often when I was a child. Now she'd cry three or four times an hour, suddenly and with no warning. God, the perversity of her disease. Everything that made her a whole person was going or gone, but the memory of Mike and his death grew steadily sharper and newer every day" (Cooney, 2001, p. 54). Mike was the mother's third husband, the love of her life, to whom she was married for more than twenty years, and who had died in 1989.

One can see how the malignant positioning and related story lines create a lack of logical coherence here. According to the author, "it was bad enough" that her mother "had to lose her mind," but the same person who had "lost her mind" also had memories of her late husband that "grew steadily sharper and newer each day." It is difficult, indeed, to imagine how a person who had lost her mind already could simultaneously have stronger and sharper memories of a loved one. If there is no mind, there can be no such higher level memory system. It is likewise difficult to understand how someone could be bereft of "everything that made her a whole person" and still mourn the loss of the love of her life. Even further, it is difficult to understand how a person who had lost her mind could be simultaneously depressed and also "always puts together a jaunty outfit every morning" (p. 56). Interestingly enough, the mother was always a "snappy dresser," but the fact that she remains as such does not indicate to the author that her mother has a mind—a mind that would be required to make the necessary evaluation of clothes that would result in putting together a jaunty outfit each morning. The fact that the mother would cry three or four times an hour when in earlier, healthy times, she rarely did so is not necessarily a direct result of neuropathology, but it is easily understood as being the mother's reaction to the situations in which she finds herself at present—having lost a great measure of her independence, being moved from her home in the east to a new unfamiliar location across the country, and trying desperately to come to grips with the losses that are due to neuropathology and the loss of control that she has experienced in many areas of her life. The author's mother had a great deal at present about which to cry!

In a final example of the relationship between malignant positioning and the incoherence of the story lines created about the person with AD, we learn that the author placed her mother in an assisted living residence, a decision in which the mother had no input. "The day after we took her there, she cried and begged to come home" (p. 58). It is difficult once again to understand how a person with no mind would respond in such an appropriate manner and also show that she knows the difference between where she is and where she is not but wants to be. The mother must have had at least some memory function in order to behave in this way, so on what basis can the author declare, about her mother, that "she has no memory at all of the past seventeen months" (p. 58)?

A second instance of malignant positioning drawn from the popular press reveals how an author's misunderstanding of how cognitive function is affected by AD can lead to malignant positioning of persons with AD.

Caring for an Alzheimer's patient is gruelingly repetitious precisely because the patient himself has lost the cerebral equipment to experience anything as a repetition . . . if your short-term memory is shot, you don't remember, as you stoop to smell a rose, that you've been stooping to smell the same rose all morning . . . Hence, the ghost-like apparition of the middle-stage patient who continues to walk and feed herself even as she remembers nothing from hour to hour. The inner child isn't inner anymore. Neurologically speaking, we're looking at a one-year old. (Franzen, 2001, p. 86)

Taking the author's comments in reverse order, we see the author positioning a person (a generic person, all persons) with AD in the middle stages as akin to a one-year-old, albeit, the author qualifies this by saying, "neurologically speaking." Of course, the author is blissfully unaware (should I say "in denial"?) of a large and growing literature in which people with AD in the middle stages have been shown to exhibit the ability to act meaningfully, to attempt to avoid humiliation, to seek ways to maintain their pride and self-worth, to set logical and meaningful goals for themselves, and the like (Sabat, 2001). To my knowledge there are no one-year-old children, "neurologically speaking," who can behave in these ways.

Indeed, the author seems to ignore the evidence apparent in his father's own case. The author and his wife took his father out for dinner and then brought the father back to the nursing home where he lived. As they were about to reenter the nursing home, the father said, "Better not to leave, than to have to come back." Clearly, the father recalled having been in the nursing home before being taken out to dinner and recalled the feeling of not wanting to live in the nursing home, which flies in the face of the author's allegation that a person with AD "remembers nothing from hour to hour." The father also shows a level of cognitive ability that he has been alleged not to possess, when he comments rather philosophically that he'd rather just stay in the nursing home than go out and have to return—that it is more painful to have a brief pleasant glimpse of the outside world and then have to be re-institutionalized than it is simply to remain in the painful world of the nursing home. I am not aware of any one-year-old children who could think in these terms. The author is likewise unaware of the literature showing that people with AD can and do develop new long-term memories and can demonstrate the existence of these memories in explicit (recall and recognition) as well as in implicit ways (Grosse et al., 1990; Heindel et al., 1989; Knopman & Nissen, 1987; Sabat, 2001). Although I would not expect the author to be conversant with the scientific literature I have cited, it remains that the author, in describing his father's own behavior and quoting his father's comments, seems not to understand that what his father was doing and saying was providing evidence that negated the author's previously stated beliefs about people with AD in general and his father in particular. Thus, the author's malignant positioning of his father has contributed to his rather striking lack of appreciation of the meaning of his father's behavior—so that he can avoid disturbing the negative story line already in place—for the author comments that, " . . . a change in venue no more impressed my father than it does a one-year-old" (Franzen, 2001, p. 89). According to the author, his father was not aware of the difference between the restaurant and the nursing home in spite of the fact that his father's words indicate the opposite.

When the author finally turns to a brief discussion of his father's "self," he says that he believes it is "mostly right" that the person with AD loses his or her "self" long before the body dies, and although he believes that in his father there was a "bodily remnant of his self discipline . . . when he pulled himself together for the statement he made . . . outside the nursing home" (p. 89), he seems again to ignore the effects on his father's behavior of the way he positioned his father in the first place. Indeed, the title of the article, "My Father's Brain: What Alzheimer's Takes Away" is the ultimate commentary. The author seems to believe that his father's behavior was a result of the neuro-pathology of the disease alone and not a whit affected by the ways in which his father was positioned and treated by others. Sadly, it was this belief that formed the basis for the malignant positioning and related, illogical, dysfunctional story lines he wove about his father in order to validate the initial malignant positioning. It wasn't his father's mind, or "remnant" thereof that authored the comment outside the nursing home, it was some "bodily remnant" akin, perhaps, to a spinal reflex. Even here, the story line is such that the father, in a profoundly sad way, still receives no credit for mentation per se, not to mention meaning-driven behavior of a high order.

SUMMARY AND CONCLUSION

People with AD can be profoundly affected by malignant positioning. Most people who are deemed healthy can reject being positioned in ways they find objectionable and can work successfully to reposition themselves. For a number of reasons, however, people with AD are at a severe disadvantage in such situations. As a result of word-finding and/or syntactic problems, along with the anxiety and distress that they feel in reaction to their own disease-produced losses, people with AD often cannot summon efficiently the necessary resources to reposition themselves in ways they would find more desirable. So at the very outset, people with AD are vulnerable in the very social settings in which positioning occurs.

As a result of the inability to reposition themselves efficiently and coherently, people with AD can be and often are the targets of negative story lines, which characterize in dysfunctional ways their very attempts to reposition themselves. Thus, people with AD who do not want to take part in activities they find boring and always have found boring or unappealing in other ways are characterized as being "reclusive," "adopting a set of rigid social standards," "uncooperative," and the like. Indeed, there is precious little that such a person, on his or her own, can do to be seen as anything but dysfunctional and burdensome. If the person cries a great deal, the person is characterized as being "emotionally labile"; if the same person were not to cry at all, but instead, "put on a happy face" so as not to trouble others, he or she is characterized as being "in denial" of his or her problems, or as "lacking insight" into those problems. If the person cried occasionally, as a result of thinking about what the disease has done to his or her life, such a person can easily be described as "crying for no apparent reason." If the person is on edge, or bored, and needs walk about or tap his or her foot while sitting down, the person is engaging in "nonphysically aggressive" behavior, rather than just doing what most normal people do when they're tense, anxious, and the like. The cycle of negative story lines never ends, having an inertia all its own in the minds of "healthy" others who malignantly position the person with AD.

Often it is those very "healthy" others who, at the same time as they position people with AD in malignant ways and observe the resultant behavior, feel burdened by the effects of that behavior while being blind to their contribution to its origin. In addition, many caregivers are seemingly oblivious to the many instances of remaining intact and coherent behavior and thoughts of those with AD, for dysfunctional story lines do not allow for the possibility that the person with AD can engage in functional and meaningful intentions and actions. Thus are many people with AD doubly imprisoned: they are imprisoned by the effects of neuropathology, which no one can control or reverse at this time, and they are also imprisoned by the effects of malignant positioning and all that follows in its wake. It is malignant positioning that can be reversed by caregivers, but before caregivers can reduce the effects of such positioning, they must first recognize the existence of malignant positioning in their own thoughts and actions. This chapter is an attempt to help facilitate such recognition and thereby eliminate the walls of the social prison in which many people with AD dwell.

REFERENCES

Alzheimer's and Related Disorders Association. (2000). *A race against time*. Chicago, IL: ADRDA.

American Psychiatric Association. (1994). *Diagnostic and Statistical Manual of Mental Disorders*. Washington, DC: APA.

Appell, J., Kertesz, A., and Fisman, M. (1982). A study of language functioning in Alzheimer patients. *Brain and Language*, 17, 73–91.

Benjamin, B. (1999). Validation: A communication alternative. In L. Volicer & L. Bloom Charette (Eds.). *Enhancing quality of life in advanced dementia* (pp. 107–125). Philadelphia: Brunner/Mazel.

Bozzola, F., Gorelick, P., & Freels, S. (1992). Personality changes in Alzheimer's disease. *Archives of Neurology*, 49, 297–300.

Chatterjee, A., Strauss, M., Smyth, K, & Whitehouse, P. J. (1992). Personality changes in Alzheimer's disease. *Archives of Neurology*, 49, 486–491.

Cooney, E. (2001). Death in slow motion: A descent into Alzheimer's. *Harper's Magazine*, October, pp. 43–58.

Davies, B., & Harré, R. (1999). Positioning and personhood. In R. Harré & L. Van Langenhove (Eds.), *Positioning theory* (pp. 32–52). Oxford: Blackwell.

Franzen, J. (2001). My father's brain: What Alzheimer's takes away. *The New Yorker*, Sept. 10, 2001, pp. 81–91.

Grosse, D. A., Wilson, R. S., & Fox, J. H. (1990). Preserved word-stem completion priming of semantically encoded information in Alzheimer's disease. *Psychology and Aging*, 5, 304–306.

Hamel, M., Pushkar, D., Andres, D., Reis, M., Dastoor, D., Grauer, H., & Bergman, H. (1990). Predictors and consequences of aggressive behavior by community-based dementia patients. *The Gerontologist*, 30, 206–211.

Harré, R. (1983). *Personal being*. Oxford: Blackwell.

Harré, R. (1991). The discursive production of selves. *Theory and Psychology*, 1, 51–63.

Heindel, W. C., Salmon, D. P., Shults, C. W., Walicke, P. A., & Butters, N. (1989). Neuropsychological evidence for multiple implicit memory systems: A comparison of Alzheimer's, Huntington's, and Parkinson's disease patients. *Journal of Neuroscience*, 9, 582–587.

Katzman, R. (1976). The prevalence and malignancy of Alzheimer's disease: A major killer. *Archives of Neurology*, 33, 217–218.

Kitwood, T. (1990). The dialectics of dementia: With particular reference to Alzheimer's disease. *Aging and Society*, 10, 177–196.

Knopman, D. S., & Nissen, M. J. (1987). Implicit learning in patients with probable Alzheimer's disease. *Neurology*, 37, 784–788.

Laing, R. D. (1965). *The divided self.* Baltimore, MD: Penguin.

Maddox, M. K., & Burns, T. (1999). Adapted work program: A sheltered workshop for patients with dementia. In L. Volicer & L. Bloom-Charette (Eds.), *Enhancing quality of life in advanced dementia* (pp. 56–79). Philadelphia: Brunner/Mazel.

Moghaddam, F. M. (1998). *Social psychology: Exploring universals in social behavior.* New York: Freeman.

Raia, P. (1999). Habilitation therapy: A new starscape. In: L. Volicer & L. Bloom-Charette (Eds.), *Enhancing Quality of Life in Advanced Dementia.* Philadelphia: Brunner/Mazel.

Reisberg, B., Borenstein, J., Salob, S., & Ferris, S. (1987). Behavioral symptoms in Alzheimer's disease: Phenomenology and treatment. *Journal of Clinical Psychiatry,* 48 (Suppl.), 9–15.

Sabat, S. R. (1991). Facilitating conversation via indirect repair: A case study of Alzheimer's disease. *Georgetown Journal of Languages and Linguistics,* 2, 284–296.

Sabat, S. R. (2001). *The experience of Alzheimer's disease: Life through a tangled veil.* Oxford: Blackwell.

Sabat, S. R., & Cagigas, X. E. (1997). Extralinguistic communication compensates for the loss of verbal fluency: A case study of Alzheimer's disease. *Language and Communication,* 17, 341–351.

Sabat, S. R., Fath, H., Moghaddam, F. M., & Harré, R. (1999). The maintenance of self-esteem: Lessons from the culture of Alzheimer's sufferers. *Culture and Psychology,* 5, 5–31.

Sabat, S. R., & Harré, R. (1992). The construction and deconstruction of self in Alzheimer's disease. *Aging and Society,* 12, 443–461.

Sabat, S. R., & Harré, R. (1994). The Alzheimer's disease sufferer as a semiotic subject. *Philosophy, Psychiatry, and Psychology,* 1, 145–160.

Seligman, M. (1975). *Helplessness: On depression, development, and death.* San Francisco: Freeman.

Shweder, R. A., & Sullivan, M. (1989). The semiotic subject of cultural psychology. In L. Previn (Ed.), *Handbook of personality theory and research.* New York: Guilford.

Stern, W. (1938). *General psychology from the personalistic standpoint.* Translated by H. D. Spoerl. New York: Macmillan. (Original work published 1935.)

Toseland, R. W., Diehl, M., Freeman, K., Manzanares, T., Naleppa, M., & McCallion, P. (1997). The impact of validation group therapy on nursing home residents with dementia. *Journal of Applied Gerontology,* 16, 31–50.

Van Langenhove, L., & Harré, R. (1999). *Introducing positioning theory.* In R. Harré & L. Van Langenhove (Eds.), *Positioning theory* (pp. 14–31). Oxford: Blackwell.

CHAPTER 7

Paranoia, Ambivalence, and Discursive Practices: Concepts of Position and Positioning in Psychoanalysis and Discursive Psychology

Margaret Wetherell

In social psychology we have become familiar with analyzing positioning as a discursive phenomenon. We are used to the idea that people become located as they speak and write. Indeed, as Harré argued in 1983, this is an inevitable consequence of the grammar of personal pronouns. As *I* describe my actions and thoughts and account for these, *I* construct myself. The *I* acquires content. And, usually, a set of moral responsibilities, rights, and duties are evoked by the positions taken up (Davies & Harré, 1990). Certain story lines become more likely depending on the particular flavor of the describing. A possible, albeit temporary, social order may emerge for the subsequent flow of meaning making over the next set of turns in the conversation. Positions are specified for others who might then go on to assimilate, resist, or reinflect these in their own discourse in reply.

In other words, as Donald Carbaugh elegantly puts it:

Every social interaction presupposes and creatively invokes culture, intelligible forms of action and identity. Interacting through symbolic forms carries with it claims, tacitly or consciously, about the kind(s) of person one (and other) is, how one is (currently being) related to others, and what feelings are to be associated with the social arrangement. (1999, p. 160)

We are also increasingly familiar with the intellectual trajectories of these ideas. This history includes Foucault's work on "subject positions" at the level of "big discourse" (see Hall, 1997), and his claims about the ways in which discourses "subject" people as they realize themselves in the speaking positions different epistemic regimes and institutional discursive complexes offer. It includes Van Langenhove and Harré's (1999) conceptual mapping of the various (almost logical) possibilities for positioning in everyday interaction. Related notions such as Bakhtin's concepts of "voice" and the "dialogical" are also becoming standard reference points (cf. Maybin, 2001), along with Goffman's (1981) original work on footing and participation frameworks. But that is only part of the story. What is much less familiar is the alternative but no less interesting intellectual history of the concept of "position" in psychoanalysis. In psychoanalytic theory (originating with the work of Melanie Klein in the 1930s), "position" carries a whole other set of theoretical associations and commitments. It evokes the internal psychic world. Typically this is seen in psychoanalysis as a contrasting form of reality to the external public world of discourse with its own laws, processes, and dynamics. It evokes the unconscious. And it evokes the long-term developmental history of the individual and their psychobiography.

My aim in this chapter is to put these two senses of position and positioning side by side in engagement with each other to see what we might learn. This engagement picks up on the current debate in social psychology between discursive psychology and psychoanalysis (Billig, 1999, 2002a, 2002b; Frosh, 2002a, 2002b; Frosh, Pheonix & Pateman, in press; Gough, in press; Hollway & Jefferson, 2000; Wetherell, 1999, 2001). But it is also a fruitful way of bringing discursive work on positioning into sharper focus. As someone more embedded in discourse theory than psychoanalysis, I am intrigued by the challenges and questions the psychoanalytic version of positioning poses for discourse theory. These are issues about understanding the nature of personal habitus, about discourse as "diagnostic" as well as "performative," and concerning the continuity of identity and repetition of patterns over the course of a life. Criticisms of my own and other discursive work for neglecting these aspects (Frosh, 1999, 2002a; Madill & Doherty, 1994; Rattansi, 1995) are longstanding now. Equally, I feel that discursive work on positioning raises some profoundly uncomfortable issues for psychoanalysis. How can that split between a "public social outside" and a "private psychological inside" be maintained? How can the postmodern fragmentation of identity increasingly emphasized by psychoanalytic writers (e.g. Bollas, 1993; Chodorow, 1999; Flax, 1993) be understood through a set of concepts in many ways so resolutely modernist?

I want to first present some discursive data as a stimulus for thinking these issues through. Then I shall try and construct a psychoanalytic reading of the positioning work evident in the extracts, which I trust will also review some key Kleinian concepts (or at least as these have been interpreted in recent object relations theory) without doing undue violence to these. I hope this reading will show both what psychoanalysis can offer and begin to indicate where discourse theory might balk at psychoanalytic assumptions. Finally, I want to reflect on the differences between discourse theory and psychoanalytic readings of position and suggest some ways in which both enterprises might be influenced by this engagement.

SOME DISCURSIVE DATA

The following extracts come from a research project I conducted with Nigel Edley on men and masculinity (cf. Edley & Wetherell, 1997; Wetherell & Edley, 1999). I have taken material from interviews with two men socially positioned in very similar ways and who share a range of experiences, but who represent those experiences very differently. I am interested in the contrasts and how they might be explained, and what might be called from a psycho-analytic perspective the "emotional flavor" or "patterns of investment" (Holl-way, 1984) evident in the discourse.

Of the two men, John Eales was interviewed once by Nigel Edley (NE in the transcript) while Phillip Jones was interviewed on several different occa-sions. Some of the material below comes from Phillip's first interview with Nigel, which was a group interview (two other interview participants were present), and some of it comes from later "life history" interviews I (MW in the transcript) conducted with him about his biography. Both men have been given pseudonyms.

The two men were 26 years old at the time of the interviews. Both were recently married with one child, and both were or had been serving as soldiers in the British army. John Eales was still in the army and working in an intel-ligence support unit. Phillip Jones had left the army a year before to take up a career in the police. Phillip had seen a great deal of active and troubling service in Northern Ireland, while John's army career had been less imme-diately threatening. Both men were currently studying for a university degree but had rather different educational histories. Phillip left school at 16 (as soon as he was able) with few qualifications and joined the army at that point, while John had been in the army cadets at school, did attend the sixth form, and got one A level before joining the army. He described his entry into the army as a choice for a certain kind of career, while Phillip described joining as a matter of chance (attracted by the ad in the shop window of a local recruiting center) and rebellion against school. Both men were raised in mixed-class environments by mothers who were single parents with various inputs from grandfathers and stepfathers at different points. In both cases neither knew or had any contact with their biological fathers. Below I have counter-posed extracts from Phillip and then John in relation to three main topics—their experiences of basic army training, friendships, and sexual relationships with women in their army days.

Extract One

MW: Yeah—and how did you take to the kind of—the lifestyle, in terms of discipline and sort of stuff like that? Was that difficult to (.)

PHILLIP: Er, basic training, a lot of the stuff was fairly petty er, (*MW:* Mm) but having said that, I used to get quite a buzz out of it er, you know. You'd be getting such a hard time it would be a battle of wills—er, "I'm a rubber duck and you won't break me". (*MW:* Mm) Er,—"No matter what you attempt to do to me, you will not succeed" and I will—you know, I didn't take [inaudible]. (*MW:* Hm m) Er, and how some servicemen, you know, they hate getting beasted, you know, forced to march and do weapons, drill whole weapons, for a period of time. I used to get a real sort of buzz out of it and think it was great which annoyed the instructors even more.

Extract Two

JOHN: They wanna see you just be naturally aggressive and they want to see you driven by your aggression and (.). I mean our training was only 10 weeks but you sort of (.) you go for these long runs. I mean they put, they (.) they (.) you have what's called Battle PT and that's sort of really mindless things, running round with logs and stuff like that. (*NE:* Hm m) And I can remember once we went for a run. I mean there was like a (.) I think it was a generator shed or something. We all had to climb on the roof and it was, you know just to see who could be the last man standing on top of this roof. You just like [laughs] you know sort of punch your way and see who was left standing and we played this Murder Ball with a *rock* [laughs] and it was just, you know, they were looking for the blokes who were sort of getting stuck in I suppose. But I mean it's not (.)

NE: How well did you do, at Murder Ball and (.) and punching people on the roof?

JOHN: I mean I'll be completely honest and say it wasn't really my (.) it wasn't my scene. I mean I think I had as much determination as everyone else to get through. I think, because they sort of present you with all these really difficult things and you're all *there*, then you wanna be (.) you don't wanna be the one that (.) that fails at any of it (*NE:* Sure) these things so. (.) But I mean I (.) certainly in my mind I didn't think this is really ace and I liked it and you know.

Extract Three

This extract from Phillip consists of two fragments. The first comes from the group interview conducted by NE and the second from a life history interview conducted by MW.

(Discussing male friendship)

PHILLIP: Not so much er in the job I'm in now but when I was in the Army, there, there was blokes there that I sort of like literally loved, you know, I'd die for them. And, if, you know, anybody sort of *slagged* any of my mates then they'd be going for a right hiding. Because we were, you know, sort of true friends, and even now you know I still keep in contact, er with them blokes.

(Telling a story about an episode when on leave in Spain with his army buddies.)

MW: Right. So you were all fairly similar blokes, er, the blokes that you were with?

PHILLIP: We were all fairly similar. Er, I can recall one incident [on holiday]. I was in a night club one night, been drinking all day er. I was in a bar. I drank that much that I couldn't drink anymore but I was aware of everything that was going on and two civilians er, blonde hair and stuff sort of were, you know, really taking the mickey out of me. And in the meantime one of my mates who had drunk a considerable amount took offence that they were taking the mickey out of me. Sort of crashed on this bar er, sort of walked across and gave them words of advice. And his actual words of advice were, after he'd sort of slapped them about or whatever it was, you know, "what have you ever done with your life except dye your hair and pierce your ears?" You know? And threw them out the actual night club, you know. "Don't speak to this bloke like this. In the last three months he's been shot at twice and blown up once and you have a go at him for being drunk," you know. Er, they sort of threw them out the bar and in the meantime a southerner, the ex-pat who was saying he'd buy me champagne and stuff which was great. We drank in that pub for quite a few days and he was sort of buying me champagne and I was the center of attraction.

Extract Four

NE: (. . .) what sort of things do people get the piss taken out of themselves for in the Army? What sort of ribbing goes on?

JOHN: Well, as I said I suppose it would be things that would be considered, erm, perhaps not macho. I mean things like (.) you always hear words like mach (.) not macho but *wimp* and words like that. It's a sort of when you're in basic training it's just (.) like the ultimate insult. If you can't manage something then you're a wimp. And it's (.) it's like one of these pathetic words but it's (.) erm. I dare say (.) I mean to say if you don't wanna (.) if you're not interested in going down the bar one night and you'd perhaps rather sit in and read a book (*NE:* Hm m) then you know, that sort of thing. And, er, I dunno. If (.) I mean a lot of blokes'll play a lot of football and a lot of rugby and things like that. And I don't like football and I don't like rugby, maybe something like that (.). I mean it's not happened to me personally, but those sort of things might be, erm, sort of frowned upon, I suppose. Erm, I don't know. I mean I (.) one thing I always (.) that always sticks in my mind (.). I was *here* on a course in (.) about 2 years ago and a friend of mine was at the Art College doing furniture design (*NE:* Hmm). And I went out one night with some lads from camp and I said, "well, I'll be in this night club, meet me there". And (.) and some of the blokes I was with actually got quite aggressive. I mean they were drunk (.). With him because, you know, he had long hair and round specks and to them this was (.) I don't know (.) he was a poof. (*NE:* laughs) And I felt really embarrassed because I was just there with friends from the Army and a civilian friend and there was (.) you know it wasn't very nice.

Extract Five

(Discussing typical patterns in relationships with women)

PHILLIP: *Yeah*, from my perspective, yeah. Erm, I did, I must confess, you know as I said earlier, I used and abused women. I just, after a couple of nights, you know. I think the longest I ever went out with a woman was about a week. And then, "cor that was nice!" And I was off to the next one. Yeah, a different, a couple of different women in a night, you know.

(. . .)

PHILLIP: Mine was the total opposite. I just sort of finish with women (*NE:* Yeah?). Yeah. The fun was in the chase, so to speak, as soon as they were bedded, well, great. And, if sex was available—fabulous. Then as soon as they got serious, sort of a bit over-emotional (*NE:* Right). Sort of like, "I love you" type of stuff, phff, a hot potato. You're binned, on to the next one.

NE: Was that the goal? The explicit goal of it then was then to get them in bed? (*PHILLIP:* Yeah) Right and then, and then they would (.) would you keep them as long as they were interested in sleeping with you? Or, or, was it almost like a trophy?

PHILLIP: A lot of it was sort of get both. The sort of (.) a bit of a competition. I had to get my sort of quota in a month and (.).

NE: Right, so you actually scored?

PHILLIP: If I had a bad month, I'd be pretty depressed, yeah.

NE: Right

PHILLIP: And then as I say, so long as sort of, you know, there was sex at the end of it, yeah I'd be happy enough. As soon as they displayed any sort of emotion, you know, it would be sort of, because I was a bit of a male slag, you know, didn't want all these sort of hugs and cuddles, all of this sort of emotional stuff.

Extract Six

JOHN: Erm (.), well really as I say at 6th form (.). I started going out with someone when I was 17 but she was sort of from home and then I remember she chucked me because she said I wasn't affectionate enough [laughs]. (*NE:* Hm m) And then I went out with someone else. And, er, I think she finished with me because I was joining the Army and then that sort of put a spanner in the works (.). I sort of did my basic training and then I came here. And then, er (.), I suppose that was like (.) the Army had an influence on me then. Because, I mean, I thought nothing of say going to a night club here and getting off with someone and sort of perhaps seeing them. And then going home at weekends and doing the same in London. (*NE:* Hm m) I thought, you know, I didn't think there was anything morally wrong with that, you know, even to sort of sleep with people in two different places. (*NE:* Hm m) And I *think* (.) I'd go as far as to say that was because, you know, that sort of behavior was really (.) you know, it was really ace in the Army, that's what you (.) that's what you'd gotta do.

(. . .)

JOHN: (. . .) You'd, sort of, go home for your weekend. And, you know, you were sort of (.) not (.) *expected* that you came back and everyone sort of discussed their exploits. As if, you know, as you say this sort of counting (.) sexual counting and if you got to number 15 with this girl, you'd have was just (.) just nothing (.). It was just like a notch, I suppose. (*NE:* Hm m) And, you know, I can remember (.). Well, when I got to Germany, I started going out with a German girl. And I sort of thought, "well, you know, I'm going out with this girl, you know, I started sleeping with her". And I thought, "well, you know, I'm sleeping with her and that's (.) that's it (.) I'm sort of (.)". And, er, even *that* you're sort of ridiculed. I mean if (.), you know, if you sort of display any signs of being serious say with a girl, then you were sort of ridiculed a bit. I mean every (.) every (.) I mean, you know. I'd say a lot of blokes do sort of (.), at some stage they'll meet someone and think, "right," you know, "this is the girl for me." But (.) you know, no one sort of openly admits it. And, if you're sort of seen to be going, you know, seriously—"great big poof!" [laughs] If you're serious with a woman. (*NE:* Hm) Things like that (.) erm, and that's why I stopped (.). A lot of things I think in the Army is because you just all join at 16 and 18. You're sort of carried along with the flow and it's not (.). I mean certainly with me I sort of (.) sort of got to 19 or 20, 21. I'd sort of think, "right, I don't wanna get on the bottle tonight and drink with them and I'm not gonna." And, you know, "I'm not gonna sleep with loads of women, and if I do I'm not gonna discuss it with anyone because I don't want to." It's sort of like becoming your own man if you like. (*NE:* Right) But I think, you know, you are sort of carried along and it's just (.) it's just the case of really deciding to step off and be yourself.

A PSYCHOANALYTIC READING

In developing this reading I have drawn on the entire range of material I have available from Phillip and John. However, the features of their discourse I wish to highlight should also be evident in just the brief extracts above. I have drawn on accounts of Kleinian and object relations thinking presented by Ogden (1994), Steiner (1993), Chodorow (1999), Klein (1959, reprinted 1984) and Hinshelwood (1998) and most particularly the creative and lucid account of cultural psychoanalysis developed by Dawson (1994). Dawson's work on "soldier heroes" is especially relevant as an obvious point of interest in the extracts above in the different ways in which Phillip and John "do being a soldier."

Self-Compose, Psychic Reality, and Phantasy

In different ways both discourse theory and psychoanalysis offer construc-tionist theories of meaning, although in the case of psychoanalytic object relations theories this is usually a partial constructionism. Both note how our access to reality (whatever that might be) is indirect and mediated. Both point to the ways in which stimuli and events are standardly worked up in some way. Psychoanalysis, unlike relativist discourse theories, suggests limits on this constructionism and often combines it with a realist or critical realist episte-mology. Thus it is argued that it may be difficult, but it is possible to work out a "straight" view of reality, and indeed part of the method of psychoan-alytic psychotherapy is identifying when clients are dealing with reality and when their impressions have been unconsciously distorted. Freud argued that much of the time reality testing fails and we see the world and other people through the screen of unconscious preoccupations and desires, but it is none-theless the ego's task to strive to form an accurate picture. Later psychoana-lysts have become more qualified and hesitant about the reality-testing process, but some notion of legislating between what is really the case and people's phantastic constructions tends to persist in psychoanalytic readings of people's discourse (c.f. Chodorow, 1999; Hollway & Jefferson, 2000).

These epistemological questions aside, both psychoanalysts and discourse analysts would be interested in what John and Phillip *make* of their experiences in the extracts above. Both perspectives would argue that in the interviews, John and Phillip are engaged in what Dawson (1994) calls "self-composure." Phillip and John are composing themselves for a particular audience and this is especially evident in narratives such as, for example, Phillip's more extended account about events on holiday in Spain in Extract Three, with its plot line, heroes, villains, and denouement. The metaphor of "composing" suggests the artful bringing together of diverse elements into a new gestalt. Discourse analysts are alert to the possibility that John and Phillip will compose themselves quite differently in different contexts. Psychoanalysts assume more continuity and that varying modes of self-composure will be psychologically linked in some way across contexts. Discursive psychologists interested in positioning focus primarily on the cultural resources through which intelligible selves are constructed. These resources are evident in the interaction practices and routines used to accomplish different activities and the intertwining of these with socially figured forms of interpretation and representation. Consensual representations of the "soldier hero" are a good example of the latter, while the procedures and rhetorical devices involved in presenting oneself as "just neutrally describing what happened next with no stake or self-interest" (Potter, 1996) are a good example of the former. For discursive psychologists, how John and Phillip *make* themselves is diagnostic of culture and people's uses of what is culturally available. Psychoanalysts, however, see modes of making self as diagnostic of "psychic structures" and "psychic reality."

What is psychic reality, then? In psychoanalytic terms, John and Phillip's discourse express the organization of their particular individual internal worlds. It is revealing about their unconscious phantasies. Their talk might tell us a few things about veridical reality, about, for example, a sequence of events and the order in which they happened, but it is mostly revealing about reality as it appears to them—how they summon up the world and "imagine" it. Klein adopted the term "phantasy" (and the unusual spelling) to indicate this more pervasive and mundane process of "imagining" in contrast to the conventional meaning of fantasy as brief "off-duty" moments of wish fulfilling daydreams. Phantasy is seen as the medium through which experience is assimilated. Silverman (1992) argues, for example, that it is only things that resonate within psychic reality that we can truly believe in—this space, she suggests, is the one that is most real for us. Psychic reality thus forms the texture of subjective experience. It is informed by actual events, but it is not isomorphic with those; something is added from the unconscious.

Laplanche and Pontalis (1986) similarly present psychic reality as a new kind of place, locality, or scene between perception (actual stimuli) and consciousness (worked, through accounts). The status of discourse is rather unclear here and indeed, as Billig (1999) has argued, this is one of the major problems with psychoanalysis as a social psychology. It has no elaborated theory of language as a practical activity, and its implicit model of language practice (how language works and its social and psychological significance) has not been adequately rethought in light of recent theoretical and empirical advances. But here I assume that from a psychoanalytic perspective discourse will be seen as a further site where the private internal world of psychic reality will be expressed and revealed. (See Bollas, 1993, on how the everyday world of objects and cultural forms is used to express what he calls "private idioms.")

In terms of this approach, the real social world, Phillip and John's real experiences in the army, in Northern Ireland, in Germany, and elsewhere have become the raw material they are, so to speak, "dreaming" (cf. the "dream work of the social," Pile, 1998). Their accounts have been filtered through their internal world, the unconscious and their imaginative constructs. Objects and people move in and out of salience, become configured and reconfigured, and made personally and symbolically significant, some links and connections are made, other links are denied or falter, and the emotional climate of the telling waxes and wanes. More coherent than dreams, these accounts nonetheless could potentially reveal some distinctive principles for ordering meaning such as condensation, displacement, and repression (Pile, 1998). But how, more precisely, is psychic reality organized? How is it patterned and how might that pattern appear in the extracts above?

Imagos and Object Relations

Dawson, drawing on Klein's work, describes inner worlds or psychic reality as a constant stream of meaning making, often organized as ongoing narrative. Internal narratives are organized around the relations between "objects" or imagos. "Phantasy, then, is an ongoing process, a kind of narrative in which the self is imagined doing and being-done-to, as taking in and investing psychic material" (Dawson, 1994, p. 33). Relational scenes, in other words, are constantly being staged internally and are being worked over, rehearsed, modified, dropped, returned to, and so on. These relational scenes are organized around and operate on "imagos" or "internal objects." What an internal object is and how it is defined remains mysterious and loosely conceptualized, perhaps necessarily so (see Hinshelwood, 1994, pp. 68–84). However, here is Dawson's account as a working definition.

Klein describes this inner world as being made up of internal phantasy figures or "imagos" (also known as the "inner" or "internal" object, as distinct from the "external object" or real person). These are imaginative constructs which mediate the psychic and the social: the product of continual interaction between elemental psychic impulses and wishes, and social reality. They are derived partly from the various qualities and aspects of the social world (and prototypically, from the parents and their bodies, experienced in infancy as, for example, benevolent or punitive, and felt to be alive and

active within the psyche), partly from conflicting internal impulses of aggression and
libido, hate and love. The self registers, relates to and handles these impulses through
omnipotent phantasies in which it does things, both beneficial and harmful, to its
imagos, and invests them with the capacity to do things back. (1994, p. 33)

Extrapolating back to the extracts above, we can now ask the standard discursive psychological question about positioning with these Kleinian concepts
in view—how is self and other constructed on a moment-to-moment basis in
this talk?

Phillip constructed a number of interesting positions. One recurrent theme
for him in his various narratives (evident across the range of his interview
material) was that of a conflict where he gets the better of someone else. There
is an example in Extract One. He gets the better of his instructors in basic
training because he wouldn't be broken and indeed he relished and won the
"battle of wills." Similarly, in Extract Three, although he is not the active
agent (a mate acts on his behalf giving "words of advice" to the civilians),
Phillip gets the better of these persecutors with their dyed hair and pierced
ears. Others in these narratives tended to be positioned as strong and worthy
opponents (such as the instructors) or, alternatively, as weak and unworthy
(the civilians). Phillip also frequently positioned himself as aligned with a band
of brothers (his friends and mates) (see Extract Three) where both self and
others are strong and idealized. Phillip's more general positioning of self
tended to be narcissistic in the sense that he often positioned himself as the
center of admiring attention (Extract Three again) or with an admiring stance
towards his own actions.

Sometimes, humor was used to introduce what could be read as potential
moments of critical self-reflection. In Extract Five, for example, Phillip "con-
fesses" to "using and abusing women" and, later, to being a "male slag." Possibly because this behavior is constructed as part of a wild past and not current
(something he used to do but no longer, as the rest of the interview made
clear), these evaluations do not seem perturbing but rather are presented in
a more neutral and matter-of-fact manner. It is a remarkably "untroubled"
confession. Finally, one other positioning feature of Extract Five worth noting
is the construction of women and Phillip as a man in relation to women.
Women want emotional stuff and Phillip doesn't. He is the powerful agent
who judges their actions and "bins" them if necessary. Women are constructed
as dependent and reactive. They remain a homogeneous category, an interchangeable series, defined through their use value for Phillip without a complex individuality.

In contrast, in the extracts from his interviews, John constructs a self that
is more detached from and less identified with the flow of activity. He stands
to one side and evaluates and puzzles over the motives of others. Others for
Phillip in his narratives are often caricature sketches, possessing a few salient
attributes that explain his reactions to them, but with no other features to

be curious about. Others tend not to be constructed as "psychological individuals" in Phillip's narratives, and as a consequence their motives and the reasons for their actions are sometimes left rather enigmatic. In contrast John tends to contextualise others. Thus in Extract Two, the instructors in basic training are constructed as having reasons for what they do—"they want to see you driven by your aggression." The instructors have a general strategy John describes in the turn immediately preceding Extract Two as producing soldiers who will obey orders unthinkingly when necessary. Extract Four, like Phillip's story in Extract Three, tells a tale of an instance of being teased or persecuted, although now the evaluations and the protagonists are reversed. Here again John's accounting for the behavior of his army peers who give his friend from Art College a bad time locates that behavior in its broader cultural context of army values and beliefs and in terms of their drunkenness. (Although this stance is, of course, made possible by the tenor of the interview question and the frames it makes appropriate, including a more "sociological" or "documentary" style of reporting.)

John also constructs himself in less narcissistic and more self-reflexive ways. Thus, in Extract Two, having "confessed" that basic training was not "his scene" he presents himself as determined ("I had as much determination as everyone else"). But he goes on to account for this as a reasonable characteristic in the situation ("you don't wanna be the one that fails at any of it"). John's identification with the cultural position of soldier hero, which Phillip enthusiastically embraces, is mixed but incomplete. In his next turn not reproduced in Extract Two he goes on to say that he felt "uncomfortable" with basic training because he thought it was "silly." So what positive identity position does he construct as an alternative to the soldier hero? In effect, it is the person who is independent and non-conformist, who is "his own man," who at the end of Extract Six "steps off" the conveyor belt of social expectations and becomes an individual. This, of course, is also a familiar cultural subject position—the liberal, post-Enlightenment, independent, and rational masculine agent. We have argued elsewhere that although this identity position is very frequently presented as a counterpoint or contrast to "being macho," it is in many ways a no less effective way of "doing hegemonic masculinity" (Wetherell & Edley, 1999). In Extract Six, John describes some of the same sexual patterns as Phillip in Extract Five, but in line with his self-reflexive positioning these are constructed as indeed perturbing and as a basis for personal change. Further, in line with his general positioning of others, women are presented as having reasons for their actions and being potentially matched with him in terms of emotional investment.

To explain the difference in the positioning work evident in the extracts from these two men, psychoanalysis would now move "behind" the text, seeing these positions as indicative of the relational landscape characteristic of each man's internal world. The hypothesis might be that Phillip's internal world is made up of battles, power struggles, and conflicts between relatively undifferentiated idealized and denigrated competitors, with Phillip as the hero in these battles, and his friends aligned and strongly identified with him as helper figures. In contrast, the hypothesis for John might be that his relational landscape of imagos and internal objects mobilizes more complex protagonists in his internal scenarios and narratives with differentiated reasons for their actions. What further insights might Kleinian analysis offer?

Paranoid and Depressive Positions

In the rudimentary analysis of the extracts above, I used "position" in its usual discursive senses. For example, what position or stance is this person constructing to describe events from? What broader discourses and cultural subject positions are evident? And, what kinds of characters are being formulated from moment to moment in the narratives told in the interviews? (However, unlike more usual forms of discursive analysis I paid little attention to the context constructed by the interviewer's questions or the forms of activity made relevant as turn followed turn.) In Kleinian psychoanalysis, however, "position" has a different and more global set of connotations.

Hinshelwood (1991) defines position as a "constellation of anxieties, defenses, object relations and impulses" (p. 393). It is "the characteristic posture that the ego takes up in relation to its objects" (p. 394). In a similar vein, Ogden (1994) suggests that positions are "psychological organizations that determine the ways in which meaning is attributed to experience. (. . .) Associated with each of the positions is a particular quality of anxiety, forms of defense and object relatedness, a type of symbolization, and a quality of subjectivity. Together these qualities of experience constitute a state of being that characterizes each of the positions" (pp. 34–35). Klein argued that there are two basic positions or psychological patterns in the sense defined above. These result from the typical organization of the infant's experience and from the tasks the infant has to accomplish as part of maturation, such as sorting out the source and origins of good and bad feeling states.

The paranoid-schizoid position is a posture towards objects that is shot through with strongly polarized binaries (hence schizoid). Thus, some objects become constructed in highly idealized terms while others become constructed as destructive, aggressive, and full of malign influences. Typically a complex object, like the mother or the primary care-taking environment, becomes represented as both good and bad depending on the infant's somatic state (satisfied or in discomfort). Klein argued that healthy development depends on the infant being able to introject or incorporate inside the self idealized, loved, and loving objects as a foundation for personal psychic reality. Equally, experiences feared because they are full of pain and discomfort are projected outward and seen as belonging outside the self and as "not self," as some bad state done to the self by a bad persecuting object (hence paranoid).

The developmental task for the child is to produce a more integrated view.

To move, that is, from a mental organization splitting the mother, producing a good mother (good breast) and bad mother (bad breast), to a psychological state where good and bad are seen as mixed in the same object. Klein argued that this more ambivalent and complex view of others, which is more responsive to their actual nature, allows the child new kinds of emotional experiences such as guilt, gratitude, and mourning. The child can feel guilt for his or her own hostile impulses towards this mixed good and bad mother object and anxious about the effects of these hostile impulses on her. As Dawson argues, "if the internal landscape in the paranoid-schizoid position resembles a battlefield at the height of the struggle, in the depressive position we inhabit a psychic landscape of broken ruins, mutilated bodies and other fragmentary figures of the aftermath" (1994, p. 39).

In Kleinian psychoanalysis, positions seem to be seen as both developmental stages and as much more fluid and recurring psychological states. They are developmental stages in the simple sense that it is assumed that for the infant the paranoid-schizoid position precedes the depressive position and the depressive position is to some extent a resolution or psychological movement forward. However, recent commentaries also stress the ways in which adults cycle backward and forward between paranoid-schizoid interpretations of the external world and depressive readings. Ogden (1994), for example, discusses what he posits as a "dialectical relationship" between the two positions. He characterizes subjective life as a continual movement backward and forward between the more chaotic and unintegrated emotional states typical of the paranoid-schizoid position and more integrated moments of emotional closure typical of the depressive position. Both moments of integration and deintegration are unavoidable, however (see also Steiner, 1993).

Are we moving, then, in this psychoanalytic reading of John's and Phillip's discourses to the claim that while John inhabits the depressive position evident in his more mixed and ambivalent puzzling over people, their motives and his own motives, Phillip shows more evidence of the paranoid-schizoid position? One could argue that there is more evidence of the defense mechanisms of splitting and projection in Phillip's discourse than in John's. Other people, for example, as noted, seem to be split by Phillip into two rigidly separated and polarized categories that don't mix. Either others are very good (his mates) or very unworthy (the civilians) and this "splitting" was a strong feature of many of Phillip's narratives of army life. In terms of projection, it could be argued that in line with many popular claims about the psychology of masculinity (Hollway, 1984), Phillip projects what he perhaps finds to be uncomfortable feeling states such as vulnerability and loving emotions for others onto women (Extract Five). Women experience these things and he does not. In comparison, John in Extract Six does not seem to project any particular feeling states or qualities onto the women he discusses. They are left blank rather than emotionally colored in by his feelings projected on to them. This reader at least is left with the sense that the individual qualities of each one and John's particular reaction to those qualities could be fleshed out in more detail if the conversation had taken that turn.

Although a plausible argument can be mounted for some paranoid-schizoid features in Phillip's discourse, he also doesn't quite fit this scenario in the sense that he is not full of fear of the objects defined as "bad." They don't seem frightening or persecutory. Indeed, Phillip doesn't seem to award them much power at all. In Extract One he is confident that the instructors will not break him. The civilians and emotional women are easily dispatched in Extracts Three and Five. Accordingly, one could argue that Phillip's discourse is more characteristic of what Klein described as the "manic defence" against the anxieties of the depressive position. Dawson provides an accessible description of this hypothesized subjective state or internal relational scenario. The manic defence is seen in Kleinian terms as not another full-blown position in itself but as a mode (a response to anxiety) that is part of the more global depressive position.

One possible response to this situation [the tasks demanded by the depressive position] is for the self to abandon the difficult efforts towards integration and to reassert its omnipotent control over the internal world. Depressive anxiety, loss, guilt and despair may be countered by a series of denials: that the self's own impulses are at all ambivalent; that its internal world is in any sense dependent on a separate social world beyond its control; and that the destroyed imagos are indeed of any value to it. [. . .] Phantasies of contempt render the latter into a safely deserving recipient of destructive attacks, for "an object of contempt is not an object worthy of guilt, and the contempt that is experienced in relation to such an object becomes a justification for further attacks on it." (Segal, 1973, p. 84)

In these so-called "manic" phantasies of uplifting triumph over the omnipotently defeated and worthless "bad object," the self is enabled to own, justify and enjoy the aggressive and destructive aspects of its own nature, without arousing feelings of loss, guilt and mourning on behalf of the destroyed imagos. (1994, p. 39)

In psychoanalytic terms then, this might be a more satisfactory account of the internal world producing the emotional flavor and pattern of self and other categorizations evident in Phillip's discourse.

REFLECTIONS FROM DISCURSIVE PSYCHOLOGY

A psychoanalytic account, then, is rich in suppositions about John and Phillip's different narrative styles. Patterns in discourse are related back to the global positions each might typically take in relation to self and others. While attentive to the specific personal psychic realities each man displays, a psychoanalytic reading also relates these to universal forms of subjectivity or to universal tasks such as dealing with perceptions of good and bad, sorting out others' motives, and the mixed and complex nature of social reality. Representational strategies articulated in the present are seen as the further acting out of modes of psychic functioning laid down early in life. A psychoanalytic reading in this way diagnoses character and tries to describe the "flavor" of each man. Some continuity and repetition would be expected in John and Phillip across situations.

From a discursive psychological point of view, there is an enormous amount that could be said in response to such a reading (cf. Wetherell, 1999, 2001a for a limited exploration; and Billig, 1999, for an extended account of some of these issues; and see in reply, Frosh, 2002). It raises questions around method and the theories of language implicitly assumed in the interpretative process, along with questions about the kinds of knowledge claims a psycho-analytic reading entails and the justification for these. The notion of "psychic reality" highlights many epistemological and ontological queries. There are issues, too, regarding the status of psychoanalysis as a regulative discursive regime in itself, caught up in particular institutionalized orders of discourse (e.g., Parker, 1997). And, crucially, there are the problematic ethics of diag-nosing "character" (Phillip's real nature, for example) and the potential voy-euristic violence of research as diagnosis. Is this more problematic than critically evaluating the cultural resources available to speakers to make sense of their situations? What kind of analyst (discursive or psychodynamic) as-sumes more omnipotent authority and how is that authority justified as aca-demic expertise?

Here, however, I want to focus more positively on what can be learned by discursive psychology from this exercise of focusing on individual difference and identifying what could be called "personal style" in positioning work. And, in turn, I want to challenge psychoanalysis to re-formulate its *psychology* in what I think are more useful and less opaque ways. I take a broad definition of discursive psychology (see Wetherell, 1998, 2001b) to include finer-grain research on cognition, rhetoric, emotion, and identity management (e.g., An-taki & Widdicombe, 1998; Edwards, 1997; Edwards and Potter, 1992; Horton-Salway, 2001; Potter, 1996), and to include also more critical discur-sive work on interpretative repertoires, ideological dilemmas, narrative, and cultural identity positioning (e.g., Burman & Parker, 1993; Edley, 2001; Phoe-nix & Frosh, 2001; Wetherell & Potter, 1992).

First, what can discursive psychologists take from this? The activity of gen-erating a psychoanalytic reading encourages an emphasis on forms of order and pattern in John and Phillip's discourse often neglected in discursive work. All discourse theories study what Hodge and Kress (1988) call semiosis or the flow of meaning making. Our interest is in the patterning of this flow, what shapes it, how is it organized. Order is evident at different levels and in dif-ferent ways in different domains or sites. Social interaction, for example, is one obvious domain where the flow of meaning making gets organized into routine social activities. Thus there are procedures for acts such as inviting, apologizing, agreeing, disagreeing, asserting, turn-taking, and so on. In these ways potentially chaotic flows of meaning are organized as mundane culture and as recognizable intersubjective communication. Institutions are another obvious domain where meaning is organized. A university, for instance, defines itself through the regular ways in which flows of meaning and action are arranged as knowledge, pedagogy, bureaucracy, management, and so on.

With the exception of some forms of narrative analysis (cf. Edley, 2002; Mishler, 1995; Riessman, 1993), discourse analysts rarely sample the discourse of one particular individual. We need to do more to examine the person as yet a further site where meaning gets organized, displaying specific and recurring devices, procedures, and modes of practice. This is where critical and feminist psychologists working from a psychoanalytic perspective have made a major contribution (e.g., Hollway & Jefferson, 2000; Walkerdine, 1990, 1997). In effect, this takes up Chodorow's (1999) challenge to social and cultural theory to deal with *personal* as well as *cultural* meaning. But while acknowledging that "individual style" and individual psychobiography are neglected areas in discursive research, I also want to question just how "personal" or "purely psychological" this ordering of meaning making is and the apparatus psychoanalysis provides for making sense of personal meaning making.

As we have seen, a psychoanalytic reading of discourse moves behind the text to find some distinctive psychological processes at work. Such processes include splitting and projection and the processes involved in feeling states towards self and others such as idealization, manic contempt, or narcissism. In Klein's work there is also an account of how internal psychological structure forms through the developmental tasks of infancy as the child reconciles what Klein theorized as the innate or instinctual urges of love and aggression with the environmental situation. The actual psychology, however, remains in very many respects rather mysterious and ambiguous. What are these processes and structures, how exactly do they arise, and how do they work?

Many psychoanalytic accounts of these psychological processes and structures rest on a core but often tacit distinction between the social and the psychological as two different kinds of ontological stuff. This is often expressed in terms of a form/content distinction. Thus the social world provides the contents on which the mind works, but psychological processes provide the form. Social relations provide the raw material, the things we think about, mull over, work on, and customize for our own purposes—ideologies of the soldier hero, for instance—while the organizing form, the shaping principles are provided by psychological processes that stand outside the social domain. In many ways this division of labor is appealing to cultural studies theorists who are happy to acknowledge there might be a realm outside their particular sphere of expertise that usefully "humanizes" the post-structuralist subject. However, it is less appealing for any social psychologist having to explain what this psychology is.

The consequence of a form/content distinction is to create enigma and to render subjectivity or psychic reality almost beyond further empirical investigation. We are left with autonomous and deep psychological properties like repression, splitting, the paranoid-schizoid position posited as properties of human minds and used as explanatory principles. These processes stand outside social relations and social action and in some unspecified way act on social and cultural material to add a psychological twist to our utterances and accounts. Kleinian psychology in particular also seems rather frozen and static, confined to the very earliest moments of life, with repetition thereafter. Psychological structures (the paranoid and depressive positions) are laid down very early in this model. There is no account of how internal mental contents might be transformed, added to, and fundamentally re-written through socialization except on a more-of-the-same basis as the child who has attained the depressive position assimilates more and more "reality."

What is an alternative way, then, of thinking through "personal order"? In many respects, discursive psychology takes an agnostic line on mental contents and mental structures (e.g., Edwards, 1997). It is not the role of discursive psychologists to tell cognitive neuroscientists, for example, about how the brain is organized and the psychological competencies and states brain chemistry might enable. The Kleinian analysis of how early experience is laid down may be a perfectly valid and "good enough" account of the emergence of a patterned internal emotional world, particularly from a therapeutic perspective. What discursive psychology can offer, in contrast, is an exploration of these ideas from the standpoint of research on discourse practices. How does what we now know about discourse and its operation change or inform psychological theory? I want to suggest that discourse theory and empirical work suggest that the boundaries between the social and the psychic may be more porous than the Kleinian framework presupposes. It has something to offer too concerning what might be internalized, how the "external" becomes "internal" through the growing child's various discursive apprenticeships, and an argument to make about the lifelong nature of this socialization.

This contribution would draw, for example, on the Bakhtin/Voloshinov writings on "voice" and the "authoring of self" (see Maybin, 1993, 2001) and on social constructivist and Vygotskian work in developmental psychology (see Wertsch, 1990). This work studies the ways in which stories, dialogues, and others' voices are carried "inward" to form mental life so that internal modes of representation, while differing discursively in some important respects from external performances, bear the marks of those public and cultural performances along with the contexts of acquisition. These lines of work are becoming familiar components of social constructionist thinking in psychology and in psychological anthropology (Gergen, 1991; Holland et al., 1998; Shotter, 1993; Wetherell and Maybin, 1996).

I want to suggest on the basis of this and related bodies of research that the relational scenarios evident in John's and Phillip's interviews (ambivalence and complexity versus manic omnipotence, for example) could be usefully reformulated as discursive styles or routines. These styles are part of the discursive "habitus" or "cultural capital" available to the child (to borrow Bourdieu's (1992) formulation in his sociology of lived practices). In a sense, they are part of what we have called elsewhere the psycho-discursive practices (Wetherell & Edley, 1999), which make up what could be described as "psychological capital." Children learn how to model and become expert in reproducing as appropriate certain psychological languages for representing self and other.

This suggests that the performance of relational scenarios could be more flexible and fragmented and less rigid than the notion of one or two primary modes of self-composure, such as the paranoid-schizoid or depressive positions. Indeed, several styles might be overlaid together, and people might cycle rapidly as appropriate through different modes of positioning self and other as the broader social and immediate context of social interaction changes. Examination of other parts of John's and Phillip's interviews suggests, for example, that in some discursive contexts Phillip does act out a complex ambivalence resembling that displayed by John, and at times John performs what from a psychoanalytic perspective could be read as "manic defence." Psychoanalysis stresses the ways in which people might be unconsciously impelled to act out certain relational scenarios. On the other hand, discursive psychology pays more attention to familiarity and availability of different relational styles as part of people's customary discursive repertoires and everyday forms of knowledge. Psychoanalysis is interested in how patterns repeat over the course of a life, and in the internal momentum to repeat. Discursive psychology has been much more interested in social context and immediate inter-subjectivity. What kinds of utterance become plausible, relevant, and occasioned by the preceding utterances in an interaction? What discursive styles do they evoke and what frames are constructed for the next utterance?

The discursive habitus is likely to be a complex mix of cultural discursive styles and the working of those by parents, caretakers, and other family members as their own personal voices. With John and Phillip, for instance, it would be interesting to explore not just early home environments and prevalent modes of discursive relating within these, but educational and academic history. I suspect that the complexity and ambivalence seen as characteristic of the depressive position is closely related to certain genres of "educated discourse" where reportage in terms of immediate identification is replaced with the more "sociological" or explanatory documentary style noted above for John. Relational scenarios, in other words, are likely to bear the marks of class and other forms of cultural capital. An anthropological study by Miller and Sperry (1987) is instructive in this regard.

Miller and Sperry studied the communicative practices between mothers and their two- to three-year-old daughters in a working class area of South Baltimore. They were particularly interested in emotional talk, specifically, expressions of anger and aggression. They examined the ways in which the young girls not only were socialized into their mothers' and other caretakers' expectations for how to be angry but also modeled vocabularies and entire dialogues and discursive routines characteristic of this community and culture. In effect, children were acquiring strategies and procedures for how to be heard as "angry." They were learning what situations deserved this response and what it was like to take up not only the position of the "angry subject" but also what was appropriate when one was the object of someone else's anger. They were learning the flexible forms of talk and modes of self and other representation through which uncomfortable internal states could be expressed.

Although this opens up fascinating potential new avenues to explore with John and Phillip in terms of their discursive and cultural communities of origin, it doesn't address the particular focus of psychoanalysis on individual difference. People may be socialized in the same broad discursive and cultural community and yet they are not interchangeable in their positioning work. The discursive habitus of the child includes many complex and intertwining local and global social contexts (see Capps & Ochs, 1995 for a sketch of these for one agoraphobic woman). One key task is to develop concepts for understanding and describing those individual repetitions in meaning making in emotional and relational contexts that become defined as "character" or "personality" or as "symptoms" in conventional psychological terms.

Personality, in my view, represents an ongoing process of discursive settlement, ossification, and transformation in relation to the provisional and ever-changing settlements of culture and the linked settlements of those influential "voices" with whom we were engaged in earlier positioning work. And this is where I hope the engagement between psychoanalytic and discursive approaches to positioning, which I have tried to foster in this chapter, might prove most stimulating and thought-provoking for future work. In the end the goal is the same, to try and study further this "settlement process" and to become more sophisticated in the concepts we mobilize as social psychologists for explaining pattern and order.

ACKNOWLEDGMENTS

Initial versions of this chapter were presented as keynote addresses at various conferences. I am especially grateful to the Critical Psychology Group at the University of Western Sydney, the Psychology of Women Section of the British Psychological Society, and the Pavis Centre in Cultural Studies at the Open University for their invitations. I owe a particular intellectual debt to Ann Phoenix, John Oates, Janet Maybin, Wendy Hollway, Peter Redman, Michael Billig, Nigel Edley, and Stephanie Taylor, and to the discourse and psychosocial research groups at the Open University for their comments. Wendy Hollway also directed me to the Kleinian sources I needed and generously shared her knowledge of psychoanalysis with me.

REFERENCES

Antaki, C., & Widdicombe, S. (1998). *Identities in talk*. London: Sage.

Billig, M. (1999). *Freudian repression: Conversation creating the unconscious*. Cambridge: Cambridge University Press.

Billig, M. (2002a). Henri Tajfel's "Cognitive aspects of prejudice" and the psychology of bigotry. *British Journal of Social Psychology*, 41 (2), 171–189.

Billig, M. (2002b). Response to Brown and Frosh. *British Journal of Social Psychology*, 41 (2), 199–203.

Bollas, C. (1993). *Being a character: Psychoanalysis and self experience*. London: Routledge.

Bourdieu, P. (1992). *The logic of practice*. Cambridge: Polity.

Burman, E. & Parker, I. (Eds.) (1993). *Discourse analytic research*. London: Routledge.

Capps, L., & Ochs, E. (1995). *Constructing panic: The discourse of agoraphobia*. Cambridge, MA: Harvard University Press.

Carbaugh, D. (1999). Positioning as display of cultural identity. In R. Harre & L. Van Langenhove (Eds.), *Positioning theory*. Oxford: Blackwell.

Chodorow, N. (1999). *The power of feelings*. New Haven: Yale University Press.

Davies, B., & Harre, R. (1990). Positioning: The discursive production of selves. *Journal for the Theory of Social Behaviour*, 20 (1), 43–63.

Dawson, G. (1994). *Soldier heros: British adventure, empire and the imagining of masculinities*. London: Routledge.

Edley, N. (2001). Analyzing masculinity: Interpretative repertoires, subject positions and ideological dilemmas. In M. Wetherell, S. Taylor, & S. J. Yates (Eds.), *Discourse as data: A guide to analysis*. London: Sage.

Edley, N. (2002). The loner, the walk and the beast within: Narrative fragments in the construction of masculinity. In W. Patterson (Ed.), *Strategic narrative: New perspectives on the power of personal and cultural stories*. Oxford: Lexington.

Edley, N., & Wetherell, M. (1997). Jockeying for position: The construction of masculine identities. *Discourse and Society*, 8, 203–217.

Edwards, D. (1997). *Discourse and cognition*. London: Sage.

Edwards, D., & Potter, J. (1992). *Discursive psychology*. London: Sage.

Flax, J. (1993). *Disputed subjects: Essays on psychoanalysis, politics and philosophy*. New York: Routledge.

Frosh, S. (1999). What is outside discourse? *Psychoanalytic Studies*, 1 (4), 381–390.

Frosh, S. (2002a). *Afterwords: The personal in gender, culture and psychotherapy*. London: Palgrave.

Frosh, S. (2002b). Commentary—Enjoyment, bigotry, discourse and cognition. *British Journal of Social Psychology*, 41 (2), 189–195.

Frosh, S., Phoenix, A., & Pattman, R. (in press). Taking a stand: Using psychoanalysis to explore the positioning of subjects in discourse. *British Journal of Social Psychology*.

Gergen, K. (1991). *The saturated self*. New York: Basic Books.

Goffman, E. (1981). *Forms of talk*. Oxford: Blackwell.

Gough, B. (in press). Psychoanalysis as resource for understanding emotional ruptures in text: The case of defensive masculinities. *British Journal of Social Psychology*.

Hall, S. (1997). The work of representation. In S. Hall (Ed.), *Representation*. London: Sage.

Harré, R. (1983). *Personal being*. Oxford: Blackwell.

Hinshelwood, R. D. (1991). *A dictionary of Kleinian thought.* (2nd ed.). London: Free Association.

Hodge, R., & Kress, G. (1988). *Social semiotics.* Cambridge: Polity Press.

Holland, D., Lachicotte Jr., W., Skinner, D., & Cain, C. (1998). *Identity and agency in cultural worlds.* Cambridge, MA: Harvard University Press.

Hollway, W. (1984). Gender difference and the production of subjectivity. In J. Henriques, W. Hollway, C. Urwin, C. Venn, & V. Walkerdine (Eds.), *Changing the subject.* London: Methuen.

Hollway, W., & Jefferson, T. (2000). *Doing qualitative research differently: Free association, narrative and the interview method.* London: Sage.

Horton-Salway, M. (2001). The discursive action model: The case of ME. In M. Wetherell, S. Taylor, & S. J. Yates (Eds.) *Discourse as data: A guide to analysis.* London: Sage.

Klein, M. (1959 and 1984). Our adult world and its roots in infancy. *Human Relations,* 12 (4), 291–303. Reprinted in P. Barnes, J. Oates, J. Chapman, V. Lee, & P. Czerniewska (Eds.), *Personality, development and learning: A reader.* London: Hodder and Stoughton.

Laplanche, J., & Pontalis, J-B. (1986). Fantasy and the origins of sexuality. In V. Burgin, J. Donald, & C. Kaplan (Eds.), *Formations of fantasy.* London: Methuen.

Madill, A., & Doherty, K. (1994). Personal agency in discursive psychology. *Journal of Community and Applied Psychology,* 4, 261–273.

Maybin, J. (1993). Children's voices: Talk, knowledge and identity. In D. Graddol, J. Maybin, & B. Stierer (Eds.), *Researching language and literacy in social context.* Clevedon: Multilingual Matters.

Maybin, J. (2001). Language, struggle and voice: The Bakhtin/Volosinov writings. In M. Wetherell, S. Taylor, & S. J. Yates (Eds.), *Discourse theory and practice: A reader.* London: Sage.

Miller, P. J., & Sperry, L. L. (1987). The socialization of anger and aggression. *Merrill Palmer Quarterly,* 33, 1–31.

Mishler, E. (1995). Models of narrative analysis: A typology. *Journal of Narrative and Life History,* 5, 87–123.

Ogden, T. (1994). *Subjects of analysis.* Northvale, NJ: Jason Aronson.

Parker, I. (1997). *Psychoanalytic culture: Psychoanalytic discourse in western society.* London: Sage.

Phoenix, A., & Frosh, S. (2001). Positioned by "hegemonic" masculinities: A study of London boys' narratives of identity. *Australian Psychologist,* 36 (1), 1–9.

Pile, S. (1998). Freud, dreams and imaginative geographies. In A. Elliott (Ed.), *Freud 2000.* Cambridge: Polity Press.

Potter, J. (1996). *Representing reality: Discourse, rhetoric and social construction.* London: Sage.

Rattansi, A. (1995). Just framing: Ethnicities and racisms in a "postmodern" framework. In L. Nicholson & S. Seidman (Eds.), *Social postmodernism: Beyond identity politics.* Cambridge: Cambridge University Press.

Riessman, C. K. (1993). *Narrative analysis.* Newbury Park, CA: Sage.

Segal, H. (1973). *Introduction to the work of Melanie Klein.* London: Hogarth.

Shotter, J. (1993). *Conversational realities.* London: Sage.

Silverman, K. (1992). *Male subjectivity at the margins.* New York: Routledge.

Steiner, J. (1993). *Psychic retreats: Pathological organizations in psychotic, neurotic and borderline patients.* London: Routledge.

Van Langenhove, L., & Harre, R. (1999). Introducing positioning theory. In R. Harré & L. Van Langenhove (Eds.), *Positioning theory.* Oxford: Blackwell.

Walkerdine, V. (1990). *Schoolgirl fictions.* London: Verso.

Walkerdine, V. (1997). *Daddy's girl: Young girls and popular culture.* London: Macmillan.

Wertsch, J. (1990). *Voices of the mind: A socio-cultural approach to mediated action.* London: Harvester Wheatsheaf.

Wetherell, M. (1998). Positioning and interpretative repertoires: Conversation analysis and post-structuralism in dialogue. *Discourse and Society, 9,* 431–456.

Wetherell, M. (1999). Discursive psychology and psychoanalysis. Paper presented at the Millennium World Conference of Critical Psychology, University of Western Sydney.

Wetherell, M. (2001a). Gendered subjectivity: Identity, the unconscious and imaginary positions. Paper presented at the British Psychological Society Annual Conference, Glasgow.

Wetherell, M. (2001b). Introduction to minds, selves and sense making. In M. Wetherell, S. Taylor, & S. J. Yates (Eds.), *Discourse theory and practice: A reader.* London: Sage.

Wetherell, M., & Edley, N. (1999). Negotiating hegemonic masculinity: Imaginary positions and psycho-discursive practices. *Feminism and Psychology, 9,* 335–356.

Wetherell, M., & Maybin, J. (1996). The distributed self. In R. Stevens (Ed.), *Understanding the self.* London: Sage.

Wetherell, M., & Potter, J. (1992). *Mapping the language of racism: Discourse and the legitimation of exploitation.* London: Harvester Wheatsheaf.

PART II

The Self and Groups

CHAPTER 8

Disputes as Complex Social Events: On the Uses of Positioning Theory

Rom Harré and Nikki Slocum

INTRODUCTION

An assumption shared by all styles of the "new psychology" is that psychology is the scientific study of the creation and management of meanings. Positioning theory is one of the systems of concepts through which research in this mode in the domain of social psychology can be controlled and its results interpreted.

Once one turns one's attention toward the psychology of the unfolding of social episodes, one is struck by how complex yet orderly most stretches of social life turn out to be. Not only that, but one is also struck by the rapidity with which the action occurs, and the speed with which the patterns of dominance and influence among the participants change. Psychologists have rarely attempted to study the flux of social life. Instead most social psychology has been based on the search for correlations between contrived conditions or "stimuli" and people's responses, so constrained as to be very simple in meaning and structure. These are presumed to be permanent and ubiquitous. For example, it is said that the degree to which someone comes to like another person is a function of the frequency with which they meet.

The inspiration for the development of positioning theory came partly from longstanding dissatisfactions with this essentially static conception of social interactions. For example it has been claimed that friendships are formed in certain conditions, without a close study of the flux or process of evolving interactions by which a stable relationship is finally arrived at. The other major influence has come from feminist studies, highlighting the differences between what women and men feel themselves entitled to say and do in social episodes of various sorts. These are differences in presuppositions about rights and duties not of their own choosing nor necessarily assented to. Social psychology seemed to stand in need of a new approach that combined attention to the small-scale and very rapid dynamics of social interactions with insights into the local moral orders of rights and duties that were invoked, explicitly or implicitly by the actors. In many cases these moral orders were happily lived out. In other cases they can be challenged. The simple protest "It's not fair!" can frequently be heard as such a challenge. "Why should she be allowed to do this when I am not?"

PEOPLE IN ACTION

According to the point of view of discursive psychology, the topic of social psychology must be the creation and management of joint meanings by participants in unfolding episodes. There are some causal relations to be discerned in this domain. However, we must be on our guard not to mistake one kind of social regularity for another. Causes require mechanisms to engender their effects. Meanings require rules and conventions to influence the pattern of subsequent meaningful acts that people perform. Meaning relations can easily be misinterpreted as causal interactions. Both appear regular and necessary, but these necessities are quite differently grounded. The fact that people are happy when Scottish dancing may look like a causal relation. However, realistically, it is a presentation of one of the semantic criteria for using the word "happy." If one denied one was happy while doing this vigorous but enjoyable exercise one would not know what the word "happy" meant.

The phenomena to be identified and classified in the preliminary taxonomic studies required for this, as for any scientific field, are the repertoire of meanings available to an actor. Together with these we need a catalogue of the norms within which they are properly deployed in the forwarding of social projects of many kinds. How are meaning making and episode forwarding activities to be distributed among the participants? Does everyone have equal access to the local repertoire of meaningful actions? Surely not. Some are more advantageously positioned than others are.

To find the right level of analysis one must be careful to maintain the distinction between intended actions and the acts performed by carrying out those actions. The criteria of sameness and difference are quite distinct. Two actions that come under the same material description, say shaking hands with someone, may serve for the performance of different acts in differently developing episodes. One may be a greeting and another congratulations. Positioning theory is concerned exclusively with analysis at the level of acts, that is of the meanings of actions. It will rarely be necessary to take account of the vehicles by which acts are performed.

WHAT ONE SAYS AND DOES, WHAT ONE MAY SAY AND DO, AND WHAT ONE CAN SAY AND DO

People in real life do not have an infinite reservoir of possible actions from which to choose. What people are permitted or licensed to do on any occasion is drawn from surprisingly narrow repertoires of categories and subcategories of actions. Among these are the actions that, in those circumstances, they are taken or take themselves to have the right or the duty to do. These are the actions one *may* do. They are drawn from the wider range of general possibilities, the actions that are physically or physiologically possible. Immanuel Kant remarked that one could only be required to do what it is in one's power to do.

We now have three categories of actions: those one has done, is doing or will do; those which one is permitted, allowed or encouraged to do; and those which one is physically and temperamentally capable of doing. Sometimes the second and third categories coincide. Someone who is excessively conscientious may not be able temperamentally to do what he or she knows not to be permitted.

Positioning theory is concerned with the relations between these three domains. The focus, however, is on the relation between what one has or believes one has or lacks a right to perform and what one does, in the light of that belief.

RIGHTS AND DUTIES IN THE CONTEXT OF POSITIONING

Since a position is to be understood as a cluster of rights and duties with respect to the acts one is enabled to accomplish as an occupant of a position, the place of rights and duties in social action needs to be examined. Rights are expressed as anticipatory or retrospective justifications for the propriety of demands or requests for action by someone else. Duties are expressed as anticipatory or retrospective expressions of demands for action by oneself.

Claims to have certain rights and the acceptance or undertaking of certain duties are basic active self-positioning moves. For the most part the acknowledged possession of a right requires the acceptance by a person or institution of a correlative duty. So the rights implicit in one's positioning oneself in a certain way serve to position someone else or some institution in the correlative position. But this position is so far wholly defined by duties.

One might include obligations under duties. The fulfillment of an obligation, since it is something undertaken explicitly, is mandatory. However, not all duties are. For example there are many duties that an individual may feel they should fulfil that are not mandatory. These are the supererogatory duties. They are of great importance in the moral development of societies, since new domains of morality open out as supererogatory duties come to be taken as mandatory. A good contemporary example is the spread of environmental consciousness with its emphasis on duties to the planet, to unborn generations, and so on, duties that a bare generation ago would have been thought to be supererogatory.

Do positions include supererogatory duties? We think there is an asymmetry in this matter between adopted and ascribed positions. I may well adopt a position that includes supererogatory duties and be thought something of a prig if I do so. Positioning oneself by undertaking certain duties does not automatically engender a correlative position defined in terms of the rights of others to demand the fulfillment of those duties. When I position you, I can saddle you with what I regard as supererogatory duties. If you do not go along with the position I have put you in, and even if you resent it, I may thereby impose duties on you that are supererogatory for me. They must be mandatory for you, fulfilled by you by virtue of the power that my acts of positioning and your inability to resist them effectively give me over you.

Another matter of considerable philosophical and historical/practical interest is the question of the possibility of a moral order constructed wholly on the basis of duties, and without the acknowledgement of rights, tacit or explicit. In the medieval feudal system we seem to have a moral order that could be expressed wholly in terms of reciprocal duties. Those in the lower ranks owed fealty to those above them, while those above owed maintenance and protection to those below. A document like the Magna Carta can be read in terms of rights. However, it seems to me more plausible to interpret it as a reminder to King John of the duties he owed to those who were his vassals. Are there positions recognizable in contemporary life that are built on a moral order of duties alone?

It seems at first sight to be somewhat the other way round. We hear a great deal about the "client society," and the abusive exercise of rights without any attention to or acknowledgement of duties. People say "I know my rights!" but we rarely hear them say "I know my duties." Since the point of positioning theory is to enable us to look closely at small-scale interactions, family life is an obvious domain to explore in search of a duty morality. We do find that in many families there is just such a positioning system in place. Each member is assigned "jobs." I had to bring in the kindling, fetch the milk from the neighboring farm, feed the calves, and help with the dishes. My mother, father, and siblings had their proper share of duties. There was never any mention of rights. What could they possibly have been? From time to time my brothers and I deeply resented the call to duty, especially if we had our noses in a good book.

THE CONTRAST WITH ROLE THEORY

Role theory provided analytical tools not unlike those developed within positioning theory. But they were too coarse-grained and static for the analytical tasks for which the concept of "position" was introduced. It will be useful to bring out the contrast.

A role represents a set of constraints and requirements that is rather pervasive in someone's life. There are official roles, like "Vice President." There are semi-official roles like "family doctor," and there are informal roles like "dutiful son." Each is, or is assumed to be, the dominant long-term influence on a large part of the affairs of someone's life.

Roles dominate the possibilities of action over substantial stretches of a person's lifetime. This is a reflection of how static a role specification usually is, and how tightly one is required by official and unofficial forces to conform to it. The notions of "role" and "job" are closely linked. Even after retirement one sees people who fulfilled a role for a lifetime still adopting some of the performance styles of the role, which has by now become second nature.

We tend to take for granted that there are socially important actions that are "out of role." Often, as Goffman (1969) has pointed out, one may deliberately distance oneself from the repertoire of role-appropriate actions that normally fall to one to perform. Superior competence in a role may be displayed by seeming to take the performance lightly. Goffman called this "role-distance," but it seems more appropriate to subsume it as a category of self-positioning. Furthermore even for the most dedicated federal prosecutor, bus driver, or coal miner there must be "time out." Role compliance may, on occasion, be both constraining and irksome. Identifying a role serves to mark out a subdomain of someone's life, but that subdomain may be long lasting and extensive.

In contrast, positions, as we understand them, are characterized by the following attributes: Positions tend to be situation specific. Someone may be positioned as "pathfinder" for just this journey, or "host" for just this lunch party. There are short-term consequential assumptions of relevant rights and the acceptance of relevant duties.

Unlike roles, acts of positioning are always defeasible. Sometimes they are disputed then and there, or, in time, they may become matters for dispute. Feminist analyses of oppressive and contestable social relations have been one of the sources of the concept of positioning. Research reveals how often and how passionately the positioning of women in such positions as "family nurse" or "helpless but charming companion" is disputed and challenged. Either, it may be remarked, may be willingly adopted and defended.

Positions are ephemeral. One's rights and duties in the microworld of small-scale episodes are always changing and shifting focus. For example, contrast the way speech-act rights are distributed in an official meeting with how they are distributed in informal socializing after the meeting is over.

THE POSITIONING TRIAD

Positions, we claim, constrain what one may meaningfully do. In this way positioning may diminish the domain of what one does as a subdomain of what one can do. To specify more closely the nature of the actions that are so constrained we need two further concepts.

Actions, intended movement, or utterances can be used to perform social acts. Such acts as promising, abusing, thanking, and so on can have profound and fateful consequences in one's life. The very same utterance can be heard as the performing of all sorts of social acts. "Why don't we get going?" could be an invitation to start off on some journey; it could be a question in search of a factual answer "The horses have not yet arrived." It could be a rebuke or even an insult. These are speech acts. They are performances that John Austin (1959) first clearly identified as having a distinctive character. In saying "I am sorry I'm late" I am using a standard form of words to express contrition. I am not describing my state of mind. What that might be is irrelevant to the force of the apology. The speech act expresses the illocutionary force of an utterance.[1] By apologizing I am turning aside your wrath. That is the perlocutionary force of a speech act. This distinction between utterance and speech act is one species of the generic action/act distinction introduced at the beginning of this chapter.

Presumed, adopted, or ascribed positions have an important role in fixing the meaning of the speech acts through which a certain strip of life is being carried forward. Thus a husband may properly remark on the state of his wife's slip and be heard as giving a friendly warning. The same remark on the lips of a relative stranger may be heard as a somewhat forward or even unacceptably intimate remark.

The third component in the positioning triangle is the story line. Depending on how one is positioned, a person may be fairly tightly constrained as to what storyline it is possible, proper, or even necessary to be living out. Positioned as the class dunce, one may be "required" to perform also as the class clown. One has an ascribed duty to play the fool. A university student positioned as a child to whom the university is *in loco parentis* may take this as a license for unruly and irresponsible behavior. Taking charge after an accident positions one as "the leader." So positioned, one may be called on to perform heroic feats and to display effortless mastery with becoming modesty.

MULTIPLICITY OF LAYERS (IMBRICATION)

Positions are relative to one another. If one is positioned as "nurse," the expectation will be that someone else is positioned as patient. Even taking on the nurse position oneself may serve to position someone else as patient whether he or she did or did not want it. Often, too, someone positioning him or herself as patient drives someone else into the nurse position. It is easy to see that these "positions" are nothing but clusters of rights, duties, and obligations to perform or to require the performance of certain kinds of acts. In psychological reality they exist as expectations, beliefs, and presuppositions.

It is also true that at any moment each of two or more people might simultaneously be occupying more than one position. This may be because each adopts and ascribes a different position-pair from that which the other does. Uriah Hemp is positioned as a lowly and humble assistant by Mr. Pecksniff. However, he also positions himself as dominant in relation to his employer. For a while both story lines run simultaneously.

Any one utterance may be used and understood as a performance of more than one speech act. For example one member of a pair may take him or herself to be positioned in a different pattern of rights and duties from the positioning taken for granted by the other. The same utterance may be heard as a different speech act by each of them. A parent may mean a just rebuke, while a child so castigated may hear an act of discrimination or oppression.

Several story lines may be unfolding simultaneously. "Nursing a patient" can go along with "challenging male condescension" carried by the same pattern of utterances, or speech actions (Davies & Harré, 1991).

STRATEGIC POSITIONING

In carrying on disputes it is an enormous advantage to be occupying the "moral high ground." Positioning one's opponent(s) in various disadvantageous ways can reduce the scope of their actions markedly. Furthermore it has the advantage of making sure that what they say or do is interpreted according to a story line and as a speech act that suits one's own case. This is a familiar tactic in the law courts. It has an equally important place in meetings of the faculty, in disputes between scientific research groups, in the coach's admonitions to a sports team, and so on. Gilbert and Mulkay (1982, p. 390) report an excellent example of strategic positioning in which the leader of one research team positioned the leader of the rival group as reckless and scientifically untrustworthy, before the scientific debate proper ever began. In this kind of positioning the preliminary "work" is done by ascribing derogatory or admirable psychological, characterological, and moral attributes to the person or group that is being positioned. The inference from attributes to rights and duties to perform certain categories of acts is usually implicit. If someone is prepositioned as stupid, that person will not be accorded either the right or the duty to decide what it would be best to do. If someone is prepositioned as trustworthy, that person is likely to be positioned as the keeper of the common purse, and so on.

This illustrates the point that a position not only delimits the speech acts available to the person so positioned, but it also serves to preinterpret what that person says or does. Actions must be made sense of within story lines. The close relation between positions adopted and/or ascribed and the story lines that are taken to be or even deemed to be unfolding is responsible for this preinterpreting that is so important in understanding real life episodes.

THE ONTOLOGY OF POSITIONS

What exactly is a position? We think there are three aspects that need to be taken into account case by case.

Sometime it seems that in describing a position I am doing no more than giving a summary account of the pattern of actions and acts to be discerned in a meaning-oriented analysis of a certain type of episode. Some descriptions of political debates have this character.

Sometimes we seem to be setting out the shared presuppositions of some orderly slice of life, as when someone positions him/herself as the expert on Limoges ceramics and we all stand around amazed at his erudition. We share the presuppositions of the "classroom" story line even if we are grown-up members of a cultural tour.

Sometimes we seem to be describing systems of beliefs, that is of cognitive dispositions, to reason, to respond, and to act in certain ways.

All three of these aspects are involved in what it is for someone to be put into or to deliberately occupy a position, in the sense in which the advocates of positioning theory make use of this rich and multifaceted notion.

APPLICATION TO THE ANALYSIS OF DISPUTES AND DISAGREEMENTS

The application by Georgetown University to increase the number of students in the coming years has led to a sharp and acrimonious conflict between the university and certain people in the neighboring Georgetown community. This dispute appears, at first sight, to be chaotic, with the ground shifting in almost every encounter. Positioning theory provides the right level of analysis and the right detail with which to reach a more subtle analysis of the dispute.

People's narratives are always part of a broad discourse and vary depending upon many contextual factors. One of the most important contextual factors is the nature of the audience for a person's discourse. Therefore, when collecting data for a narrative analysis, it is important to collect narratives that were presented to a variety of audiences. One must always be aware not only of the specific character of the audience, but also of other aspects of the context and the general discursive frame in which particular interventions and contributions are set. The study, some aspects of which we report in this chapter, is an attempt to capture as much as possible of the broad public discourse surrounding the conflict, as well as the more private discourse.

There are usually a plethora of explicit and implicit story lines in any extended discourse in a situation of dispute and disagreement. Indeed the existence of multiple story lines is the core of many conflicts. The individual story lines in a typical cluster are often interrelated. At times making distinctions between versions of a generic story line and distinctive narrative forms is a matter of the thrust of the analysis. Since the analysis is also a cluster of story lines, positioning analysts are themselves positioned.

Furthermore, a judgment must be made as to the location of the "boundaries" of the discourse on a given topic. The circumference of the discursive content will necessarily shrink as the specificity of the topic being addressed increases. Are we disputing about the role of universities in the management of student behavior? Are we disputing about exactly how many new student places Georgetown should create? The boundaries of conflicts are always more or less diffuse, in part because the parties often differ even in their definition of what the conflict is about. In most cases, it is probably most prudent and illuminating to begin with a broad approach and then to narrow in on specific issues once they have been placed within a broader context. Topics around which conflicts emerge are based upon certain premises that narrative analysis and positioning theory help to reveal. When these premises are challenged, so too is the legitimacy of the issue, or the way the problem is approached.

In accordance with these insights, the plethora of narratives extracted from the diverse sources were read and analyzed many times, each time incorporating new insights and information from new materials.

The analytical procedure can be routinized somewhat as follows: People's perceptions of the nature of the conflict must be identified. To do this the first step is to try to discern from each person's point of view what the conflict is "about." What are the main issues? What is/are the central short-term and long-term goal(s)?

The answers to these questions can be gleaned from the following clues: the starting and ending points of people's free narratives, the events contained in each narrative, the qualitative character of the measures used to categorize and evaluate the parties involved, and the issue(s) around which the narrative revolves.

We also need to know who/what groups appear in the narratives as the main actors in the conflict. How is each of the relevant groups defined? Who is included/excluded as a (non-) member of each group? These are the beings who will be adopting and defending positions, or themselves being positioned by others.

The next step consists of a detailed analysis of people's perceptions of the conflict. The goal here is not to ascertain what "really" happened or who is "right" or "wrong." Rather, the researcher attempts to paint a picture of each participant's subjective reality. This includes not only the events that occur (actions), but the meaning that these are given (acts). The goal of this phase of the analysis is to identify:

a. the various story lines that constitute the collection of narratives,

b. the positionings of others and oneself in each story line,

c. the illocutionary forces of utterances in the story lines.

The final step in the analysis comes about because in commenting upon the positionings of others in the debate, any of those involved can take a step back and adopt a position with respect to the positionings already accomplished. This is to adopt a position, namely one that includes rights to comment on first order positioning triads. Some people even believe that they have a duty to do so.

This fulfills the main features of positioning dynamics as it was set out in the "Positioning Triad" of positions/speech acts/story lines.

We are now able to set out a catalogue of positions, story lines, and available speech acts relative to each of the persons or institutions engaged in the various episodes through which the dispute has evolved. This enables us to make comparisons between participants' positionings and story lines, group or shared positions and story lines, and what the various participants are doing, that is what illocutionary and perlocutionary forces of the speech acts are engendered.

Finally, we should be able to discern who does and does not possess positioning power. On what basis is this power allocated? What role do differences in positioning power play in the conflict?

The results of this analysis provide a view of the full palette of discourse to which various participants might be responding (and thus make them understandable). We may also be able to reveal why some of the story lines are more dominant (though not necessarily more pervasive) than others.

The above analyses enable the comparison between the professed goals of each person/group, the broader goal of resolving the conflict,[2] and what is actually being achieved through the interaction of positionings and illocutionary (and perlocutionary) forces. Also, how are the story lines and positionings related to people's professed short-term goals and conclusions/demands? Are these short-term goals/conclusions/demands likely to facilitate the realization of the long-term goals?

ANALYSIS

Six story lines were distinguished in the discourse that revolved around the Georgetown town-gown conflict. Some of the story lines were challenged by dissenting opinions that were a direct negation of the story line. However, a negation does not constitute a new story line.

Story Lines Offered Mostly by Community Residents:

1. *The Students as Savages Story Line:* students are ravaging and violating the affluent and prestigious Georgetown community.

2. *The Aggressive University Story Line:* GU[3] is encroaching upon the Georgetown neighborhood's territory. GU is arrogant and hypocritical in that it cares only for its students and neglects the interests of the community.

3. *The Parent/Children Story Line:* GU is a negligent parent, and the students are unruly children.

The story lines are sometimes woven together in some of the actual discourses of the activists on the community side.

The positionings and speech act types that form positioning triads with these story lines are not hard to envisage.

Story Lines Expressed Mostly by GU Students or Administration:

4. *The Malicious Residents Story Line:* Neighborhood activists are hostile extremists who discriminate against students. They are jealous of the students and wish them harm. They are hindering GU development.

5. *The Benevolent University Story Line:* GU has been responsible and cooperative. Its students are responsible members of the community, and, in general they are idealists and leaders.

6. *The Historical Rights Story Line:* GU and its students were here first.

The disputes and disagreements that fuel the conflict are, we contend, maintained and made orderly and attractive by virtue of the story lines with which the discourse of disputants is controlled.

STORY LINES AND THE ASSOCIATED POSITIONS

In the dominant discourse of the Georgetown Community activists, the Students as Savages and GU as Neglectful Parent story lines are embedded within an "American Dream" story line. Coming to live in Georgetown is the ultimate realization of the American Dream and is not supposed to end surrounded by drunken, dirty, and noisy savages. This lends a strong sense of injustice to the portrayed outcome. In this story line, rights (including the right to position) are acquired to the extent that one pays taxes, owns property, and steps into the drama of the "American Dream" game. Indeed one so positioned also acquires the duty to "do something about it."

The activists' speech acts are to be classified, from their positions, as protests, righteous indignation, doing one's duty by society, reprimands to the unruly, and so on.

In the discourses of GU administrators, the Georgetown Community activists are positioned as devoid of rights to interfere with the progression of GU's development and particularly with the campus plan. An anonymous administrator positions herself as spokesperson for the institution as having rights and duties as "partner" and "neighbor" to the surrounding community, engendering the reciprocal position in the Georgetown Community. The failure of the community to accept this benevolent positioning is culpable. Positioned as rejected suitor, GU has the right to issue utterances that have the illocutionary force of rebuke, chastisement, and accusation. In rejecting the positionings of GU, the Georgetown activists appear in the story line as morally defective, for example "stubborn" and "uncooperative."

Just as the American Dream story line underlies the story lines of Students as Savages and GU as Neglectful Parent, so there is a common underlying story line in the discourses both of the activists and of the GU administration. Displayed in seemingly antithetical narratives is the almost universal story line of "Students are Children and the University is their Parent." This story line is associated with a certain positioning of the University and indeed of the students. The position in which the university has been put involves both rights and duties to manage the students' behavior (in loco parentis). At the same time, that position reciprocally positions the students as without civil rights, for example to drink in bars, and as having the duty of obedience to the university, positioned as having the rights and duties of a parent.

Ironically, this leads both contending parties to conclude, for example, that students should be housed on campus and controlled by the university as much as possible. By assuming the position of "parent," GU entrenches the positioning of students as "children" and thus perpetuates the problem. This covertly confirms the very story line that is overtly the locus of the conflict.

INSIGHTS FOR CONFLICT RESOLUTION AND REALIZING GOALS

A narrative analysis of the Georgetown town-gown conflict highlights certain aspects of the discourse that contribute to a perpetuation of the conflict. First, it is important to note that the vast majority of residents' complaints concern students' behavior. A large portion of the residents' expressed dissatisfaction with GU, for example the entire Negligent Parent story line, positions the university as responsible for the actions of persons matriculated there. This engenders the reciprocal position for students to occupy, namely that of Unruly Children devoid of rights and enmeshed in duties.

Ironically, the essence of this part of the conflict is that residents do not want students to act like children, but to conform to the social norms of their neighborhood. Of course, it might be argued that students are treated like children, because they act like children. However, implementing measures that are based upon this metaphor only perpetuates it. It is interesting to note that the Students are Children story line was one of the few aspects that people from all groups agreed upon. In fact, a majority of the narratives from every group, except the students themselves, presumed the logic of this premise. Ironically, precisely these positionings (e.g. the positioning of students as children and GU as a parent) have proven problematic. A transformation of these positionings and the associated story lines presents a possibly viable and durable resolution to this conflict. The illocutionary and perlocutionary forces of the speech acts of the participants in discussions thereafter would themselves be transformed.

However, all this is easier said than done. We are convinced that positioning theory is a powerful tool for diagnosing the roots of disputes and disagreements in the social domain. It is quite another matter to provide recipes for remaking the local moral orders. This kind of transformation requires not merely a denunciation of the currently dominant positionings, but the creation of new positions. Positions are interwoven with story lines. It is our belief that of the three components of the positioning triad, the story line offers the best chance of successful intervention. The creation of new positions is best facilitated by beginning to live a story line that entails these new positions. In this particular case, a story line is needed in which students are positioned as mature, responsible adults that are an integral part of the Georgetown community. The old story line of students as exclusively members of the university as family has to be dropped, but dropped by both sides! As members of the community, persons of whatever provenance are positioned as having duties to display mutual respect and consideration. Along with this must go a redistribution of rights. For example the setting of the "drinking age" at twenty-one is not only barbarous, but also counterproductive. It is the surest way to encourage irresponsible drinking, since where there are no rights there are no duties either.

This does not mean to suggest that existing problems should be ignored, but rather that a discursive space be created that can become the new social norm. Alternatively, the logical consequence of wholehearted adoption of the Children/Parent story line would be a Draconian implementation and enforcement of complete segregation, curfews, a considerable expansion of the university's ironically ill-named Public Safety Officers,[4] and various other measures doomed to failure.

CONCLUSION

The new discipline of Positioning Theory offers an analytical tool for getting inside situations that otherwise have proved opaque to the efforts of social psychologists and intractable to the efforts of the social institutions charged with resolving conflicts, disputes, and disagreements. We believe that most such irresolvable situations have their roots in the tightly bound triad of positions, story line, and speech acts. While these components of the micro-ordering of social interaction remain invisible, the situation offers no grip for resolution. Opening up the tightly woven fabric of positioning may not be a panacea, but it does offer us some hope of finding a place where interventions might have some chance of succeeding.

NOTES

1. Austin used the expression "illocutionary force" for the social meaning of a speech act, and "perlocutionary force" for what was brought about by an utterance being taken to have a certain illocutionary force.

2. In some conflicts, it emerges that one or more parties have an interest in extending the conflict itself.

3. We will use the abbreviation "GU" for Georgetown University throughout.

4. It is amusing to recall that Robespierre's notorious institution that sent so many to the guillotine was called the Committee for Public Safety.

REFERENCES

Austin, J. L. (1959). *How to do things with words.* Oxford: Oxford University Press.

Bruner, J. S. (1990). *Acts of meaning.* Cambridge, MA: Harvard University Press.

Davies, B., & Harré, R. (1991). Positioning. *Journal for the Theory of Social Behaviour,* 21: 1–18.

Gilbert, G. N., & Mulkay, M. (1982). Warranting scientific beliefs. *Social Studies of Science,* 12, 383–408.

Goffman, E. (1969). Role distance. In *Where the Action Is.* London: Allen Lane.

Van Langenhove L., & Harré, R. (Eds.). (1999), *Positioning Theory.* Oxford: Blackwell.

CHAPTER 9

Sustaining Intergroup Harmony: An Analysis of the Kissinger Papers Through Positioning Theory

Fathali Moghaddam, Elizabeth Hanley, and Rom Harré

The last few decades of the twentieth century witnessed an impressive mobilization of social psychological research efforts focused on intergroup relations (Brewer & Miller, 1997; Worchel & Austin, 1986). Since the 1970s, much of this research has been particularly influenced by Tajfel (1982) and his students (Abrams & Hogg, 1990; Billig, 1976; Breakwell, 1991; Brown, 2000; Giles & Coupland, 1991; Turner, Hogg, Oakes, Reicher, & Wetherell, 1987), but North Americans have also been major contributors (Gaertner & Dovidio, 2000; Worchel, 1999). Among the most important achievements of this research movement has been the development of a variety of theories, including social identity theory, realistic conflict theory, relative deprivation theory, and equity theories (for a review, see Taylor & Moghaddam, 1994).

In the first part of this chapter we review a number of major intergroup theories to identify an important gap in the literature concerning small-scale dynamic interactions between representatives of very large groups, and particularly the strategies used in such situations to sustain intergroup harmony. There are usually a very small number of people engaged in such interactions. National leaders, for example, may interact repeatedly in face-to-face encounters, over a period of years. These interactions between group leaders can have enormous consequences for world peace, and even the survival of humankind. It is essential that students of intergroup relations come to a better understanding of the processes involved in such interactions, but available theories need to be supplemented by theories that give more attention to dynamic social processes. With a brief description of positioning theory (Harré & Van Langenhove, 1999) we introduce one proposal for filling the gap. In the second part of the chapter we show the usefulness of positioning theory in the analysis of the social processes and harmony-sustaining strategies that occur among the members of such a long-term sequence of short-term, small-scale encounters. At a certain level groups interact via the interactions of their leaders. The mode of group interactions of this sort will be seen in the dynamics of a sequence of interactions between a small group of leaders.

THE ANALYSIS OF PATTERNS OF SMALL-SCALE INTERACTIONS

Existing Theoretical Perspectives

Many important interactions between very large groups of people, such as nation states, actually takes place in the form of small scale interactions between a very few people, those who serve as representatives of their "constituencies." Such people sometimes come to form a longstanding group meeting in a long-term sequences of small-scale encounters. Existing theories of intergroup relations are not well suited to the study of the dynamic social processes of this important social phenomenon. The empirical foundations of most influential intergroup theories have been brief episodes, typically involving strangers who meet in a laboratory, or, in the case of Tajfel's (1982) minimal group paradigm, do not meet at all. They leave the study without expectations of interacting again with the other participants. Thus, the research basis for the major intergroup theories has not included studies of realistic long-term, intimate encounters, comprising many short-term episodes involving the same people.

Interestingly, the few studies that have attended to longer-term processes have had tremendous influence. Two examples are studies by Sherif (1966) and Zimbardo (1972), respectively, of boys at a summer camp over several weeks and students in a prison simulation for five days. These studies are discussed in all major social psychology texts and are often cited, even though neither adheres to the strict protocol of experimentation. Also, both the Sherif (1966) and Zimbardo (1972) studies involved discrete episodes in situations that were largely controlled, in comparison to the influence of mostly tacit conventions in real life.

Most social psychological intergroup studies have looked at the relation between certain features of the interaction and/or the participants and outcome measures rather than at the fine details of the interactional *process*. Detailed analyses of the *processes* of social interaction have been the province of conversational analysts (CA) or ethnomethodologists. For the most part these analysts have studied patterns that are discernible in the forms of utterances, such as the grammatical forms of adjacency pairs. Positioning theory allows the analyst to look at other constraints on interaction possibilities by attending to common assumptions of differentiated rights and duties with respect to the social meanings of what can be said. With transcripts of actual conversations made available one can examine the details of real-life interaction within a closed format and follow how personal relations are established and maintained, reanimated or modified, moment by moment and encounter by encounter.

Positioning theory is precisely designed to take into account the constantly shifting, evaluating aspect of human interaction over time, in just the kind of sequence of small-scale encounters that are recorded in the Kissinger transcripts. It thus provides a method for analysis of discourse between individuals as they establish, maintain, and transform their relationships (Tan & Moghaddam, 1999).

The Project of this Study

Throughout the material to be analyzed we see leaders not only as representatives of the groups of which they are the leaders but also as protagonists of national ideologies and points of view. The point of this distinction is that generally a protagonist is assumed to be offering opinions and so on that are derived more or less faithfully from those of his or her constituents. A representative, on the other hand, though in many ways a member of a group and seen as its leader, has a much greater freedom to maintain the interests of the group in ways that he or she sees fit in situations such as those we analyze. In these studies it soon became clear that none of the three major figures, Kissinger, Brezhnev, and Mao Zedong, presented himself primarily as merely the protagonist of national interests or ideological positions.

Our study concerns the relations between established leaders as these are created, maintained, and mediated discursively in a long-running sequence of small-scale and intimate encounters. We focus on such a sequence as revealed by transcripts of conversations between Dr. Henry Kissinger (Assistant to the United States President for National Security Affairs and later also Secretary of State) and Mao Zedong (Chairman of the Communist Party of the People's Republic of China), and between Dr. Kissinger and Leonid I. Brezhnev (General Secretary of the Central Committee of the CPSU). The appearance in print of these declassified transcripts (Burr, 1999) affords social psychologists a valuable opportunity to study the behavior of an international elite group as their interactions unfold ostensibly in a world context, interactions that were presented to the public as fateful negotiations. These conversations took place during 1971–1976, a turbulent era in United States and world history, and they had as background the Vietnam War and the ongoing cold war, as well as the Watergate episode, which eventually led to the end of the Nixon administration.

Positioning Theory

Positioning theory derives from studies by feminist social and developmental psychologists, particularly Hollway (1990) and Davies (1991), of the kind of small-scale interactions in which there seem to be different possibilities for types of social action assigned to men and to women. In any social interaction there is an understood framework of rights, duties, and obligations, in short a moral order. Certain kinds of acts are possible and other kinds are ruled out for the participants in the interaction insofar as they are seen as having one set of rights and duties rather than another. In many cases this framework is preestablished by virtue of the actors' shared knowledge of the range of proper and improper actions, which define the situation in which the interaction occurs. However, in some important cases the participants enter into a social interaction in which the pattern of possible actions for each of them is not preestablished. For example, when the representatives of two corporations meet to discuss a merger it is not always certain that everything that constrains the topics and the rights of individuals as speakers is settled in advance. Yet it is also evident that a moral order is shortly established. Positioning theory is concerned with the process by which short-term and small scale moral orders are established and maintained, and with the way the actions of participants are constrained to flow in accordance with sharply delimited schemata or conventions.

The basis of positioning theory is a triad of interlinked concepts that serve to define the character of constraints and possibilities for each category of actor recognized by the participants in the informally established moral order of some specific episode. As Goffman (1959), Bruner (1990) and others have shown, an interaction episode tends to follow a certain pattern, the story line, which is drawn from a culturally relative repertoire of commonly understood narrative conventions. Positioning theory is based on the thesis that the type of participation that is open to any given member of the social group involved in the ongoing story line that is unfolding in some episode is limited by a loosely defined set of rights, duties, and obligations. Each such set, as explicitly or implicitly recognized by the actors, is a position. Taken together, the current story line and the related positions determine the social meanings of what is said and done by the actors, for this particular episode.

The distinction between correlation and causation is frequently made by psychologists in interpreting empirical studies. In many cases of small-scale, close-order social interaction, neither concept seems appropriate. A certain measure of voluntarism, of deliberate choice of strategy, must be acknowledged. In studying the means by which participants position one another in the process of creating ephemeral moral orders, there seems to be a spectrum of cases between a deliberate Machiavellian management of positions and an implicit acknowledgment of positioning that can be seen in the way the actions in an episode are patterned. In the study reported in this chapter, the positioning acts undertaken by the protagonists of the three national points of view seem to be deliberate and to fall towards the fully voluntarist end of the spectrum described above.

Positions are ephemeral, disputable, and changeable. By positioning oneself with respect to the others in an encounter, a certain range of interpretations of one's actions is preestablished, provided the others adopt or are pushed into reciprocal positions. Indeed, among interactional strategies there are the techniques of positioning others in "moral" locations that one wishes them to be in, thus predetermining the social meaning of what they do. It may be very difficult to disentangle oneself from a position into which one has been cast by the dominant speaker, who thereby *is* dominant by his or her own self-positioning. Positions in a close encounter can be challenged and sometimes revised, altering the whole tenor of the episode. They may or not be successfully mutually established, nor may all the actors understand the positions from which they each act in the same way.

The social force of the actions that anyone has done is a function of the positions of all concerned, so there is a mutuality of meanings between the social forces of what has been said and done and the relative positions from which the actors take themselves and others to be acting. There is an important difference between the sentence, that is the utterance considered as a verbal formula, and the uses to which a sentence can be put. The same verbal formula can be used to perform a variety of social acts, depending on who is using it and the context in which it is used. For example, someone might be invited out for the evening with the verbal formula "Why don't we go to the movies?" The social force of the utterance is "invitation" not "question." There are also many cases in which the same social act is performed by the use of different verbal formulae. For example, "Were you born in a tent?" and "Close the door" have the same social force, that of a command or request. From the point of view of studies of social interactions borne by verbal exchanges, the social force is the crucial matter. In the context of positioning theory acting from a position by the use of a sentence is to be interpreted as the social act performed, in which we understand the utterance as having a certain social force—reprimand, advice, request, apology, and so on.

These ways of using language were first studied systematically by Austin (1961). He used the term "illocutionary force" to refer to the social force of an utterance. We prefer to use the less technical term "social force" for the context-dependent act that anyone performs by uttering a certain sentence. It should also be remarked that "social force" only exists insofar as the listener is willing or able to interpret the speaker's utterance as having a certain force, that is as the performance of a certain social act. For instance if one proclaims one's honesty, this is not so much a description of one's moral character as a social act, the force of which is to set oneself up in a superior position to the less scrupulous of one's interlocutors, who may in turn make a complementary declaration of honesty.

Furthermore, the story line that unfolds in any given small-scale episode will itself be a function both of the positions adopted or imposed and the social force given to what has been said. This pattern of mutual influence can be expressed diagrammatically in the "positioning triangle":

$$\text{Position}_1 \, (\text{Position}_{2, \, 3} \dots)$$

$$\text{Social force}_1 \, (\text{Social force}_{2, \, 3} \dots) \qquad\qquad \text{Story-line}_1 \, (\text{Story-line}_{2, \, 3} \dots)$$

In principle, every positioning triangle is shadowed by representations of other possible patterns of relationships between positions, social forces, and story lines (Davies & Harré, 1990). Using this triad of concepts it is possible to explain and even to anticipate other ways that the very same words and actions can be interpreted as socially meaningful acts. It may well be that positions as seen from the point of view of the occupant of one speaking position are different from those as seen by the occupant of another. In short, several simultaneous conversations can be occurring during the same verbal exchanges, to everyone's satisfaction at the time. The results of such a situation can sometimes be disastrous, since each actor, enveloped in his or her own interpretation, may not realize how differently others have understood the very same words. In positioning theory we have a means for understanding how seeming agreements can be sincerely interpreted in radically different ways by the different parties to the apparent concord. Insofar as positions differ, so too do the interpretations of what has been said and done, as well as the sense that participants have of the unfolding story line that shapes their encounter. One party interprets the conversational acts according to one pattern of position/story line/social forces, while the other interprets the same words according to another (Davies & Harré, 1991).

It is evident that the concepts provided by positioning theory are particularly well adapted to the analysis of the social psychological aspects of such sequences of small-scale encounters among a group of people who meet again and again. Examples of such encounters are found in the episodes recorded in the Kissinger transcripts, between the three major figures of Kissinger himself, Secretary Brezhnev, and Chairman Mao Zedong.

Motives for Acts of Positioning

Looking over the shoulders of statesmen at confidential meetings, as we are able to do in this case, one has the impression of a unique micro-culture. We suggest that the best research strategy is to view these records as the display of a micro-social-world with its own rules, conventions, and aims. What are the aims? At a first level, simply to keep the conversation going, to maintain that micro-world in existence. When the conversation breaks down as it did between Reagan and Gorbachev in Iceland, a micro-world is fractured and disappears. In some such situations, nothing else may happen. There may be no large-scale consequences. In other cases the results of the deletion of such a micro-world may be catastrophic, such as the "breakdown of talks" at certain junctures in the Middle East or in the Northern Irish peace processes.

Our contention is that each side represented in the Kissinger papers needs the cooperation of the other in order to sustain intergroup harmony, and to prevent/postpone Soviet invasion for the Chinese and nuclear war for the Soviets and Americans. But the leaders can only hope to influence this broad goal by keeping the dialogue moving forward, even if nothing other than talk is achieved. Interestingly, the proposition that elite leaders interact in distinct ways and often "keep the conversation moving" without any actual connection with the rest of the world is brought up by General Secretary Brezhnev, when he tries to mock the "professional" diplomats, such as Kissinger and Gromyko. Brezhnev explains that he has observed foreign ministers and noticed that they speak a special language. He also remarks: "foreign Ministers speak in such an interesting way but resolve nothing" (p. 246).

As we shall show, priority in the small-scale episodes is given to the maintenance of balance within the social patterns of the conference room itself. Since any change in the status quo is potentially threatening, the safest strategy is often to ensure that nothing happens. In this way the balance of forces and interests in the outside world and on a grander scale may also be maintained, or at least so the three leaders whose interactions we have analyzed seem to believe.

What is the relationship between what happens in the meetings between elite leaders and what happens in the wider world? In some instances the discussions have little influence on the way things are in the world outside the conference chamber. Those involved, who have dedicated their lives to politics and to representing and leading their respective nations, certainly mention the importance of these talks frequently—if nothing else, positioning themselves not only as intimate, honest, and trustworthy, but also as responsible, engaged in serious events, and essential for the success and happiness of each nation involved, as well as the world. One could look on this act of positioning as a way of vindicating themselves as the right persons to take the talks seriously. But this is not always realistic. Rather, it is itself just part of the rhetoric, needed to keep things going and maintain the smooth flow of interaction, so that nothing untoward will occur.

Closely tied up with this is the issue of power. What can these people really do? What sort of power do they have? Our contention is not that they have power in terms of getting their own decisions acted on and brought to fruition. (See Bullock's 1992 study of the loose lines of communication in Hitler's Third Reich.) Rather, these national leaders, through successions of meetings, can develop relationships in their small groups that increase the probability of peaceful intergroup relationships being sustained at the international level.

In summary, positioning theory leads us to explore the discussions of leaders as an ongoing activity in itself, without assuming that this activity must necessarily have an impact on the world outside the elite group of leaders. Thus, at one level the major project seems to be oiling the machinery so that the conversations can proceed smoothly. Acts of positioning are intended to maintain the cohesion and functioning of the group of elite leaders. At a second level, when conversations do move forward, or at least do not collapse, leaders may also enjoy opportunities to positively impact the world outside, so increasing the possibility that intergroup harmony is sustained.

AN ASSESSMENT OF THE KISSINGER PAPERS

The Positioning Patterns and Their Dynamics

In this second part of the chapter we demonstrate the usefulness of positioning theory by examining positioning by elite leaders in the role of members of a longstanding group of people who have come to adopt certain styles of behavior amongst themselves. By maintaining their ongoing relationships, these leaders can also help sustain harmony at the intergroup level.

Our analysis is based on the hypothesis that there are three interrelated positions that are created and maintained in the conversations as recorded in the transcripts. Our study will be concerned with bring out how these positions are discursively maintained in the course of the interactions. The positions are "intimate", "honest man," and "trustworthy partner." Since a position is a set of obligations and rights we present our positioning hypotheses in the form of a table.

The First Positioning Act

By positioning each other as friends or *intimates*, each member of the threesome joins in laying the groundwork for the possibility of agreement on the political and practical issues to which the business of the meeting is ostensibly addressed. In the course of the conversations further coherent positioning acts are accomplished, those of "honest man" and "trustworthy partner."

The majority of overt positioning acts are used to establish the position of "honest man." So positioned, the actor is committed to a set of duties, obligations, and rights. One must be truthful in one's words and behavior, and one has the right to expect the same from the others so positioned.

Position	Major Obligation	Major Right
Intimate	Willingness to make disclosures	Confidences to be respected.
Honest man	Tell the truth and all the truth.	To be told the truth and all the truth.
Trustworthy partner	To fulfill commitments.	Not to be exploited.

Regardless of the power differential between these three nations due to their respective nuclear capabilities, all three leaders position themselves as "trustworthy partners," of comparable standing, engaged in a common task. Disparities in power are thereby relegated to the background. Specifically, depending on whom they are meeting, the Americans position themselves as trustworthy partners of the Soviets or of the Chinese on the issues that arise as the most important.

How is partnership established with "working together" as the associated story line? As we shall show, this seems to have been accomplished by positioning of themselves over and over again in the associated position, that of "honest men." This is achieved through the *unchallenged* use of expressions such *honest, frank, clear, straightforward, open, correct, true*, and derivatives of these terms. Though *honesty* was the term most often used in acts of self-positioning, each member also questions or affirms the honesty of each of the others at some point, thus threatening or confirming the original positioning act.

Although the words of the Chinese and Russians appear here in translation, according to the text, there is no difference in the choice of words among the three sides, all most frequently using the terms "honest" and "frank." The difference between these words is important. "To be honest" is to be prone to tell the truth, but "to be frank" is to be ready to tell all the truth. Though there are some cultural differences in how these terms are used, the Americans (in almost all cases Kissinger himself) employ the device of honesty positioning much more often than the representatives from either China or the Soviet Union. Out of 56 comments or exchanges about honesty, over 30 are made by Kissinger. While the Russians took part in at least 12 such exchanges throughout the talks, the 10 comments by the Chinese were largely made later in the talks, when Deng Xioping, Vice Premier of the People's Republic of China, rather than Chairman Mao Zedong and Premier Zhou Enlai, acted as the Chinese representative.

"Honesty" in Positioning Acts in Conversations with the Chinese

The different participants in this international triangle employed the honesty device at different times and seemingly for establishing subtly different positions. In the first example, Kissinger positions himself as an honest man and a trustworthy partner, thus establishing the third position, that of an intimate with the Chinese. It becomes clear in the conversation that these three interlocked positions not only include frankness among their obligation/rights patterns, but there is a commitment to mutual secrecy as well. This is part of the "intimacy" position. In doing so Kissinger performs the social act of aligning with the Chinese and with them against the Soviets:

Dr. Kissinger: I have told the Prime Minister [of China] that we speak to no other country as frankly and as openly as we do to you.

Chairman Mao responds with similar concerns and comments further on about why these talks and the mention of honesty is so important:

Chairman Mao: But let us not speak false words or engage in trickery. We don't steal your documents. You can deliberately leave them somewhere and try us out. Nor do we engage in eavesdropping and bugging. There is no use in those small tricks. And some of the big maneuvering, there is no use to them too. I said that to your correspondent, Mr. Edgar Snow. I said that your CIA is no good for major events.

Dr. Kissinger: That's absolutely true. That's been our experience.

Here Kissinger, as an intimate of Mao Zedong, distances himself from the CIA, a prominent American intelligence agency. Thus he undertakes an act of secondary positioning of himself as an independent agent. He continues:

Dr. Kissinger: We may have to use different methods sometimes but for the same objectives.

Chairman Mao: That would be good. So long as the objectives are the same, we would not harm you nor would you harm us. And we can work together to commonly deal with a bastard.

Both sides have begun a story line, a framework in which a common project is defined. The positions established so far ensure that it is possible to continue the story line without disruption (a disruption that would be uncomfortable, potentially dangerous, and certainly harmful to their other efforts). It is understood that under the rules of diplomacy, the mutual positioning of each as "honest man" must be maintained indefinitely for any part of the conversational project to progress smoothly. Knowing whether the initial threefold positioning is maintained or challenged is central to understand the sequence of acts in which the story line of these conversations is unfolded.

Dr. Kissinger: Let me explain to you . . . we tell you about our conversations with the Soviets; we do not tell the Soviets about our conversations with you.

Premier Zhou Enlai: Why do you want to continue to talk so much?

Dr. Kissinger: Because it is very important that you and we understand what we are going to do and to coordinate our actions, and therefore we always tell the Prime Minister what our plans are in various areas of the world so that you can understand the individual moves when they are made.

Repositioning himself as honest, frank, and an intimate, Kissinger stresses the outline pattern of the story line realized in these conversations.

Dr. Kissinger: I have set up a very secret group of four or five of the best officers I can find to see what the U.S. could do if such an event occurred. This will never be publicly known. I tell it to you in the strictest confidence.

Here Kissinger positions himself again as an independent agent, *and as an intimate of Chairman Mao*, with a common project in which they are partners. Here the episode has unfolded to the point where the maintenance of the positions established in the micro-world of the conversations overrides what common sense would see as the normal moral framework within which a national representative would be expected to work. With the framework of positions so far established, the Chinese are given the right to know what is kept secret from others, even, perhaps especially, other Americans.

We propose that overall all three leaders are keen to continue the flow of conversation by minimizing the chance of argument or distrust. In this case positioning the Chinese as intimates would ensure their compliance when he proposes ideas and policies that they might not easily accept. Positioned as partners, a position Mao Zedong has accepted, outright rejection is not a conversational option.

The next exchange is interesting. "Why would I lie to you today?" Kissinger asks (p. 105). With this speech act he not only emphasizes his own position as "honest man" but maintains a degree of tension. He might have reason to lie to the Chinese on other days, and the reminder of this prevents the Chinese from feeling too cozy in the mutual positioning of intimate and trusted partner. Though this is an opportunity for the Chinese to challenge the story line, and Kissinger's position, they do not.

Such comments are initially made in the early conversations with Zhou, Mao and Ambassador Huang Hua, but Kissinger reiterates the sentiment later on in the relationship.

Secretary Kissinger: And also we have an understanding with you not to do anything with the Soviet Union without informing you. And so we inform you of things with them whether you attach significance to them or not. And we are not asking you to do anything about it.

Kissinger reiterates his positioning of himself as "honest man" but adds a rider, disclosing a motive, namely that adopting this position this has more to do with the United States's own interests than simply a wish to help the Chinese.

Dr. Kissinger: I tell you this, Mr. Prime Minister, not out of altruism, but because I believe the destruction of China by the Soviet Union, or even a massive attack . . . would have unforeseeable consequence for the entire international situation. I don't tell this out of abstract altruism because I believe it is in our interest to prevent such an attack.

Reiterating the partnership that the intimacy positioning has led to, the conversation continues.

Dr. Kissinger: But on our fundamental objectives we will act very decisively and without regard to public opinion. So if a real danger develops or hegemonial intentions become active, we will certainly resist them wherever they appear. And as the president said to the Chairman, in our own interest, not as a kindness to anyone else.

Chairman Mao: Those are honest words.

Dr. Kissinger: This is our position.

To further reassure the Chinese members of the intimate circle, and later the Soviet members of the other, intersecting circle, Kissinger positions himself as "honest man" when he admits that he is working for the interests of the United States rather than "out of abstract altruism." In tacitly accepting Kissinger's act of self-positioning all three position themselves not as charitable or exploitative powers but as equal partners engaged in the same project, and above all as "open," that is "frank." These comments have a use beyond truth telling in that they work to convince the other side of Kissinger's trustworthiness and dedication to the talks. Thus the storyline of honest partners is continued and furthered with an emphasis on a type of honesty that is in line with American ideals. These comments take the form of confessions, or statements affirming bravery and independence, which are strong American values, and are perhaps meant to imply to the Chinese that the United States, a being in the macro-world, is not only on their side but sure of its values even in the face of risk. This continues the United States's superior position, by positioning American values as the correct ones, at the same time it provides a balance of sorts in that the United States needs/prefers to have China on its side almost as much as China needs the United States.

Kissinger addresses this dichotomy directly:

Dr. Kissinger: We have no interest in maintaining tension in the West, but we have an interest in maintaining our position in the West.

The referent of the first person plural in the above quotation is of some interest as itself an act of positioning. Kissinger has set himself against factions back in the United States in his assertions affirming secrecy and displaying trustworthiness, positioning himself more as a protagonist for a certain point of view rather than as a representative of some other body. This suggests that he is presenting himself as more committed to this diplomacy and so to the members of this micro-society, in that he emphasizes his "intimate friend" position, than to members of his own government. Among many other comments he says:

Dr. Kissinger: This is very confidential, obviously, and we are not eager for it to be known. At least not until congress gets out of town tomorrow.

It is worth quoting some of the exchanges between President Nixon and the Chinese leadership to illustrate the difference between the standard devices of diplomacy and the techniques of discursive positioning.

President Richard Nixon, in his talk with Chairman Mao, deploys a quite different rhetoric, for which positioning theory is an unsuitable analytical tool. He uses the device of personifying the nation-state in his own assurances to the Chinese that the *United States* rather than *Richard Nixon* is a trustworthy friend with whom the Chinese should work to get along. Though he makes a perfunctory move to position himself as "honest man" his talk is directed to the *national* United States's position of dominance. He speaks as an authority not only on the American but the Chinese collective goals and minimizes the importance of the two sides' differences in light of a greater similarity—not wanting to dominate the world. But this is a collectivist metaphor, not an act of positioning oneself as a peace-person. Here is what he said:

> *President Richard Nixon:* That is why—this point I think can be said to be honest—we have differences . . . It also should be said—looking at the two great powers, the United States and China—we know China doesn't threaten the territory of the United States; I think you know the U.S. has no territorial designs on China . . . Also—maybe you don't believe this, but I do—Neither China nor the United States, both great nations, want to dominate the world. Because our attitudes are the same on these two issues, we don't threaten each other's territories. Therefore, we can find common ground, despite our differences, to build a world structure in which both can be safe to develop in our own ways on our own roads.

Here Nixon's language is that of diplomacy and the referents are nation states with all the metaphorical language of "wants" and "threats." He knows that he must address the concerns of the Chinese in the same sentence that he dismisses them. Mao suggests a recurrent concern of the Chinese, that the United States is not trustworthy and despite its claims would be pleased if the Soviet Union invaded China. Due to the varying degrees of nuclear power among the troika members and the very real threat of Soviet invasion, the Chinese did indeed have reason to worry that the United States would act against them, directly or indirectly.

On a later occasion, quoted earlier from page 88, Mao brings up the same concern but within the framework of a position structure. Mao seems to be testing the story line, the positioning framework in which both he himself and Kissinger have been maneuvering. He challenges the plausibility of the story line in a way that is subtle but has the potential to lead to a conversational breakdown. Kissinger once again assures Mao of *his* honesty, positioned as a trustworthy partner, even to the point of devaluing his own government's agency.

The Chinese also bring up honesty when speaking of other topics that might lead to conflict, such as when they offer a criticism or disagree with the Americans. In these examples, bringing up the topics of honesty or frankness works to avoid a confrontation by reemphasizing the positioning of the two leaders as honest and frank. The smoothness of the conversation is maintained by virtue of the maintenance of the framework.

It is evident that the use of declarations of frankness is central to the United

States's plan for diplomacy with the Chinese. As part of their rules of diplomacy, the essential nature of the positioning framework that we have described is continually reinforced. Kissinger expresses this twice, first in discussions of tactics with his staff:

Secretary Kissinger: My experience with the Chinese is to tell them exactly what our position is. Be frank with them.

Then instructing Mr. Vance, the incoming Secretary of State for the Carter administration:

Secretary Kissinger: Cy, I've always found that I could tell our Chinese friends the main lines of our policy—I cannot say they always agreed to every last step. It was helpful to our mutual understanding to have this kind of frank dialogue.

Mr. Vance: Well, I would hope very much that we could continue this kind of frank dialogue.

Secretary Kissinger: And of course it [the first talk with Ambassador Huang] was my first acquaintance with the Chinese style of diplomacy, in which I learned, as I have said publicly, that the Chinese word counts, that one can rely on what our Chinese friends say.

With these statements in his final conversations with the Chinese, Kissinger reinforces the honesty ideal that expresses the three-fold position structure that has been built up, for one last time. He reemphasizes the positioning of the protagonists as "intimate friends," "honest men," and "trustworthy partners," which has been maintained throughout the encounters, enabling a consistent story line to be maintained and guaranteeing a common interpretation of the social force of what has been said.

Positioning Acts in Conversation with the Russians

With the Soviets, issues of friendship and working on the same side come up from both sides:

Secretary Kissinger: In the 7 or 8 times I have been here there has developed a relationship of confidence that enables us to speak frankly.

Secretary Kissinger: Since we speak here as friends, I can tell you . . .

Minister Gromyko: That's what we do from friendship.

General Secretary Brezhnev: We have no secrets from each other.

Here we have the three familiar positions, "friend [intimate]," "honest man," and "trustworthy partner," which necessarily sets up a positioning triangle with the story line of common projects as the framework which provides the discursive structure for the conversations to come. Kissinger engages in a rather subtle act of positioning. To create intimacy he positions himself as open and vulnerable. Brezhnev responds by accepting the position of well-intentioned friend, thus beginning a story line of an honest partnership.

Secretary Kissinger: I had lost 2 kilos before I came.

General Secretary Brezhnev: You look well, honestly.

These comments have the same motives and effects as those made during conversations with the Chinese—the establishment of a sense of intimacy that allows for easy conversation, encourages compliance with cross positioning and discourages conflict. Each leader voluntarily takes up a position of "honest man" and the obligations and rights that define it. By establishing a sense of intimacy they are acknowledging their shared situation as elite leaders in a small-scale setting. Here they are more than individual protagonists of antagonistic worldviews and conflicting ideologies. They are friends, more than they are representatives of competing superpowers. In this situation as so positioned they take certain obligations as well as acquiring certain rights. Positioned as an "intimate friend" one must follow certain rules, such as the necessity to be honest at all times. Because any challenges to the initial story line will take place within the friendship framework, they will be dealt with as smoothly as possible.

We have pointed out that this threefold pattern of positions involves some derivative features. One of these is frankness, leaving nothing hidden or unclear. Each leader positions himself (Kissinger still is the most common user of honesty language, but the Soviets use it fairly often) as looking for the truth, the facts, and in doing each positions himself as a reliable source of accurate information. This is the trustworthiness component under another name. Frankness, in this form as in any other, is greatly valued and considered essential for the continuation of the story line and so of the talks.

Secretary Kissinger: Wait a minute. Let me get this straight.

General Secretary Brezhnev: Dr. Kissinger, I listen to you and I hear the exact words of our general staff when they report to me. But vice versa. Our people say the Americans have more [nuclear warheads] than we do.

Secretary Kissinger: True.

General Secretary Brezhnev: The fact that in the U.S. about 500 land-based launchers have been covered up. And we have made two representations about that.

Secretary Kissinger: But we have stopped that.

General Secretary Brezhnev: That is still going on.

Secretary Kissinger: That is impossible.

General Secretary Brezhnev: That introduces certain questions. It is not something I really wanted to mention but it is a fact. Let us act in good faith.

Secretary Kissinger: Mr. General Secretary, I have to check this, but we ordered it stopped, and if it is not stopped, it violates orders. But I wasn't accusing you of violating the agreement. That wasn't our point.

Here alternative story lines, involving dishonesty or cheating, are offered and rejected firmly, allowing for a strong reinforcement of the original three-fold positioning. The introduction of these alternatives offers a threat to the story line. Kissinger urgently dismisses it. As with discussions with the Chinese there may have been two sequences of social acts running contemporaneously. While the Russians may feel that merely by challenging Kissinger enough to put him on the defensive Brezhnev has managed to alter their pattern of dominance in his own favor, Kissinger himself may feel that he has effectively displaced the threat to the story line. The material to pursue this possibility further is not available in the Kissinger transcripts.

Both sides claim to value the "honest" man position and position themselves as honest and working within an honest framework. As we pointed out in our initial analysis, the inherent obligation is the need for both sides not only to be honest, but also to get things accomplished, to be committed to success. This is stressed as absolutely necessary in order to accomplish each side's greater goals, of avoiding nuclear war. Thus, following any agreements made, and behaving according to the rules of this world of diplomacy are of utmost importance to both sides and are connected to the idea of honesty. This behavior is central to their story line of trustworthy partners, of friends.

Secretary Kissinger: I want specifically to emphasize that we will observe and carry out to the best of our ability every understanding we have made, whether on trade or on specific geographic areas.

General Secretary Brezhnev: I certainly agree. If we reach agreement on certain issues, we should maintain them. Otherwise we are not honest partners.

General Secretary Brezhnev: I expect we should devote as little time as possible to protocol matters and get down to concrete things right away . . . Isn't that true . . . We should speak less on minor points and more on the really important policy issues . . . I cannot fail to say that in order to move further ahead we have to overcome a few difficulties and obstacles which are integrally linked to improving relations with us and improving the atmosphere in the world.

Secretary Kissinger: I believe we should proceed as follows, I will speak frankly, and I believe Dobrynin will confirm the correctness of what I say.

Secretary Kissinger: I believe we have worked seriously and that we have made good progress . . .

General Secretary Brezhnev: I endeavored to set out our position as clearly as possible, and I trust you will not disagree.

Secretary Kissinger: I agree. This is exactly my recollection of the conversation.

Secretary Kissinger: We have been following the policy we discussed then.

Vice Premier Deng: That is true. Both hands should be used.

Secretary Kissinger: Exactly!

Absent Friends

Many times honesty is directly involved in the threefold opposition of dualistic positions that is at the center of these talks—when the representative of one side or the other directly positions the third, the leader who is not present at the time. In addition to further inspiring confidence in the special friendship of the two people who are face-to-face against the third, these discussions allow for a positioning of superiority over the third member (and so of his nation) that is accepted so that this superior position might be shared. The story line here is that of conspiring friends, who feel so strong in their unity that the image of another's weakness helps the friends to feel strong.

Secretary Kissinger: My honest view is that the Soviet Union has suffered a major strategic defeat, and that's why they tried to bluff us last night.

Ambassador Huang: We have also said many times that very frankly our experience in dealing with the Russians is, to sum up in two sentences: first they will bully the weak and are afraid of the strong. And that their words are usually not trustworthy.

By bringing up the issue of honesty the United States and the Chinese position the Soviet Union as failing to follow an important rule of diplomacy. Their awareness of this failure affirms their own commitment to the rule.

Most harsh and revealing is a comment made by Kissinger to the British that suggests Kissinger's feelings of superiority are simply masked during his conversations with the Soviets, adding a small glimpse into what lies behind the overt story line:

Secretary Kissinger: As everybody knows, the Soviet leaders belong to the most unpleasant group one can deal with. Their capacity to lie on matters of common knowledge is stupendous.

This comment suggests that Kissinger's positioning during the talks with the Soviets is itself somewhat untrustworthy, for his interpretation here is contrary to what he claims in the talks. There is also a question of what lies behind the words of the Russians and the Chinese.

In discussion, other nations are also positioned as untrustworthy and therefore unlike (and inevitably not as successful as) those involved in the talks. Exposure of others is an opportunity to affirm one's own commitment to honesty in relations with the other party present.

Secretary Kissinger: The French have no strategy, only tactics. So in the Middle East they have been working to undermine us. This is of no advantage to anyone, not even to the French. So we decided that it would be useful to make it public—to bring it out in the open where the issues could be clarified.

Vice Premier Deng: That is good—if it does not continue in the open.

According to positioning theory, the social meaning of what someone says is determined by the relative positions of the speaker and the listener, at that moment, in that context, and the story line then unfolding. The relation between "position" and "social force" is very clear in these exchanges. By positioning each other as honest, the substantial statements each makes acquire a certain social force in that they obligate each side to follow a certain pathway, in short that of frankness. In this case they express truthfulness and are hearable as, and in this conversation evidently based on, acts of disclosure.

CONCLUDING COMMENT

Despite the continuing strength of theory building (Gaertner & Dovidio, 2000) and research (Brown, 2000) in intergroup relations, a number of important gaps remain. One such gap is dynamic situations in which a small group interact repeatedly over time, bringing into play social processes that allow for the sustaining of intergroup harmony. This is typically the situation when national leaders meet repeatedly to discuss important issues concerning their nation states. An example of such an ongoing and dynamic social process is depicted in the Kissinger papers.

The meetings of national leaders are vitally important for relationships between major world powers. If intergroup harmony is disrupted at this international level, the outcome could be another major or even world war, with dire consequences for all humankind. But the meetings of national leaders have received scant attention, and available intergroup theories are not well suited to examining the dynamic processes involved in such meetings.

Our assessment of the Kissinger papers was undertaken to test the power of the concepts and insights of positioning theory, to reveal aspects of small-scale interactions that are difficult to bring to light on the basis of any other intergroup theory. The most important advantage of using positioning theory in this context is the ability it gives the investigator to examine the unique pattern of obligations and rights implicit in each position. This insight allows for a more exact classification of the social acts that interactors perform and take others reciprocally positioned to have to be performed. This method of analysis allows an investigator to get some insight into the conditions that make for the stability of a certain pattern of relationships, including what might be the motives of the people involved. In our example positioning theory allows us to look behind the surface of political maneuvering to the social psychological forces beneath, revealing a "simple" need to keep the conversation going.

In some instances, the continuation of conversation proves to be fundamentally important for sustaining intergroup harmony and world peace. Our study through positioning theory has revealed, in a way that other available theories could not, that national leaders can invest heavily in "keeping the conversation going," in this case by positioning tactics that include presenting each other as "intimate friend," "honest man," and "trustworthy partner." We argue that the main goal here is to prevent a breakdown in talks, so that intergroup harmony can be more effectively maintained. When the stakes are so high—the threat of nuclear war and mass destruction—the "simple" act of keeping the conversation going becomes vital.

REFERENCES

Abrams, D., & Hogg, M. A. (Eds.) (1990). *Social identity theory: Constructive and critical advances.* London: Harvester Wheatsheaf.

Billig, M. G. (1976). *Social psychology and intergroup relations.* London: Academic Press.

Breakwell, M. B. (Ed.). (1991). *Social psychology of identity and the self concept.* London: Academic/Surrey University Press.

Brewer, M., & Miller, N. (1997). *Intergroup relations.* Pacific Grove, CA.: Brooks/Cole.

Brown, R. (2000). *Group processes.* 2nd ed. Oxford: Blackwell.

Bruner, J. (1990). Acts of meaning. Cambridge, MA.: Harvard University Press.

Bullock, A. (1992). *Hitler and Stalin: Parallel lives.* New York: Knopf.

Burr, W. (Ed.). (1999). *The Kissinger transcripts: The top secret talks with Beijing and Moscow.* New York: The New Press.

Davies, B. (1991). *Frogs and snails and feminist tales.* London and Sydney: Methuen.

Davies, B., & Harré, R. (1990). Positioning: the Discursive Production of Selves. *Journal for the Theory of Social Behaviour,* 20: 43–63.

Gaertner, S. L., & Dovidio, J. F. (Eds.) (2000). *Reducing intergroup bias: The common group identity model.* New York: Psychology Press.

Giles, H., & Coupland, N. (1991). *Language: Contexts and consequences.* Pacific Grove, CA.: Brooks/Cole.

Goffman, E. (1959). *The presentation of the self in everyday life.* New York: Doubleday/Anchor. Monterey, CA: Brooks Cole.

Harré, R., & Van Langenhove, L. (Eds.) (1999). *Positioning theory.* Oxford: Blackwell.

Sherif, M. (1966). *Group conflict and cooperation: Their social psychology.* London: Routledge & Kegan Paul.

Tajfel, H. (Ed.). (1982). *Social identity and intergroup relations.* Cambridge: Cambridge University Press.

Tan, S. L., & Moghaddam, F. M. (1999). Intergroup positioning. In R. Harré & L. Van Langenhove (Eds.), *Positioning theory* (pp. 74–86). Oxford: Blackwell.

Taylor, D. M., & Moghaddam, F. M. (1994). *Theories of intergroup relations: International social psychological perspectives.* Westport, CT.: Praeger.

Turner, J. C., Hogg, M. A., Oakes, P. J., Reicher, S. D., & Wetherell, M. S. (1987). *Rediscovering the social group: A self-categorization theory.* Oxford: Blackwell.

Worchel, S. (1999). *Written in blood: Ethnic identity and the struggle for human harmony.* New York: Worth.

Worchel, S., & Austin, W. G. (Eds.). (1986). *Psychology of intergroup relations.* Monterey, CA.: Brooks/Cole.

Zimbardo, P. (1972). Pathology of imprisonment. *Transactional/Society,* 4–8 (a).

CHAPTER 10

Constructing Identities: A Feminist Conversation Analytic Approach to Positioning in Action

Sue Wilkinson and Celia Kitzinger

"These Welsh people can be very funny"

"Handicapped instructors are usually harder markers"

"I mean, all men like boobs don't they"

Statements like these are commonplace. Social scientists often use them as evidence for the existence of the speaker's underlying stereotyped "attitudes," "cognitions," or "representations." According to most scholars, people make statements like these because they hold culturally shared sets of beliefs (Farr & Moscovici, 1984) or implicit theories (e.g., Tajfel, 1969, 1982) about the world, which result in attributional errors (e.g., Moghaddam, Taylor, Lambert, & Schmidt, 1995). Psychological explanations emphasize the roots of such beliefs or implicit theories in more general limitations of the human capacity to process information, while sociological explanations more often focus on the cultural and political construction of (for example) gender or disability, and the historical and cultural legacy of national identities; there have been repeated calls for a better integration of the psychological and social in explanations of stereotyping (e.g., Spears et al., 1997). Whether the emphasis is psychological or social, however, scholars move rapidly from the fact that such statements *are* made to an interest in the internal (psychological) or cultural (sociological) mechanisms that might have generated them. This means that research interest moves rapidly into the domain of the Likert scale or the laboratory, and away from actual occasions on which real people, in the context of live interactions with others, make statements like these. Our interest, by contrast, is in further exploring how and why speakers come to make statements like these in the course of their everyday lives. All three of the statements with which this chapter opens come from recorded data that we will analyse in the following pages.

In making statements like those above, a speaker is "positioning" an individual as a member of a group. Indeed, it is this feature of such statements that has led researchers to treat them as evidence for "stereotyping," because they ignore individual differences and treat people only as representatives of categories. In such statements, individuals' behavior is understood and explained in terms of what is culturally assumed to be typical for persons who share a particular category membership. Positioning theory emphasizes the social construction of the world through talk between people. Positioning is not simply the result of internal or cultural causes, with speakers as automata, either cultural dopes or unwitting victims of their cognitive failings. Rather, people actively elect, at particular times in specific encounters, to utter statements like these—and at other times they elect not to. In choosing to make such statements they are not simply "emptying out" their cognitions; rather, they are engaged in ongoing interaction, in the process of building or sustaining relationships with others through the medium of conversation. In speaking as they do, they are not simply reflecting a preexisting world in which (for example) the Welsh are always already known to be "funny"; rather, they are also actively constructing it.

Along with many other feminist researchers (e.g., Fenstermaker & West, 2002), we are concerned to develop a feminist understanding of everyday life drawn from a social constructionist or ethnomethodological perspective, which, like positioning theory, sees social order as grounded in contingent, embodied, ongoing interpretive work—in how people *do* social order rather than how they are animated by it. We see social facts such as power and oppression as *accomplishments*—they are processes continually created and sustained (and—sometimes—resisted) through the practices of cultural members in interaction. As feminist researchers we have an enduring interest in understanding how certain categories (of gender and sexuality, race and ethnicity, (dis)ability, and so on) are socially constructed, how individuals are produced as members of those categories and the consequences for them (and for the rest of us) of such positionings, and how the taken-for-granted world of social categorization is continually produced and reproduced in social interaction. As lesbian researchers we have been particularly interested in the ways in which we—and other lesbians—are continually positioned as heterosexual through an unquestioned set of mundane heterosexual assumptions that constitute and reconstitute heterosexist reality.

Positioning theorists have treated talk in interaction as key to the process whereby positioning is accomplished. The concept of positioning was developed precisely in order to "focus attention on dynamic aspects of encounters in contrast to the way in which the use of 'role' serves to highlight static, formal and ritualistic aspects" (Davies & Harré, 1990/2001, p. 261). Conversation analysis (CA) is the method par excellence for analysing talk in inter-action and for understanding the moment-by-moment construction of reality. Like speech act theory (more commonly used by positioning theorists) it treats talk as a form of action, sharing with speech act theory the understand-ing that utterances *do* things rather than *state* things (Austin, 1962; Searle, 1969). Unlike speech act theory, however, which, as Potter (2001, p. 46) points out, has had "more success with made-up talk than in applying the ideas to actual speech," CA is based on analysis of actual instances of live interaction. (For introductions to CA as a field see Heritage, 1984 and Drew, 1992; for a feminist approach to CA see Kitzinger, 2000a.)

Unlike some other approaches to positioning (e.g., Wetherell & Edley, 1999), then, our data are not derived from interviews or focus groups set up to elicit such positionings. The data upon which we draw in this chapter are an eclectic mix drawn from diverse domains including telephone and face-to-face conversations between friends and family members, and interactions in a group for women with breast cancer. They constitute fragments of recorded (not simply—as in Davies and Harré, 1990—recollected) conversation from data to which we happen to have access and in which something pertinent to "positioning" seems to us to be operating: none of the data were collected in order to elicit "positioning" talk, or with this particular project in mind (and only the last of these data sources consists of data we (SW) collected our-selves). For all of these data fragments, however, we have access to the original recordings as well as to the transcripts.

The substantial body of conversation analytic work on how persons are referred to talk-in-interaction (e.g., Schegloff, 1996; Sacks & Schegloff, 1979; Sacks, 1972) offers the most obvious purchase on issues of positioning, and this chapter uses that literature to focus initially on how individuals are re-ferred to as presumptive representatives of some category or other (including "Welsh people," "handicapped people," and "men"), exploring both the pro-cess whereby the shift from individual to category member is achieved, and the interactional uses of such shifts. But the equation of "person reference terms" with "positioning" is too simplistic, as there are obviously many in-stances in which individuals may be treated as category members without being explicitly referred to as such—we will see examples of this in the analysis that follows.

Our focus in this chapter is on ordinary, mundane, everyday positioning. This contrasts with research on positioning which has explored the often lengthy and extensive procedures by which individuals are formally produced as members of categories such as "mentally ill" (Smith, 1978), "learning dis-abled" (Mehan, 1996), or—in the case of infants born intersexed—"female" or "male" (Kessler, 1998). In contrast with the explicit deliberations and di-agnostics associated with such procedures, positioning in the talk we will be analysing is casual, fleeting, and performed in the service of some other ac-tivity altogether, in which the participants are otherwise engaged. Positioning in mundane encounters generally lacks the momentous (often institutional) consequences associated with (for example) officially positioning someone as "schizophrenic." What it does instead—equally momentous in its way—is to weave another thread into the fabric of everyday life, to contribute to the taken-for-granted definition of the world we live in. Through apparently trivial incidental person references, positioning those persons in terms of their category memberships, the world of such categories, and the inferences associated with them is produced, reproduced, and sometimes (as we will see) resisted. Indeed, it was this kind of mundane incidental positioning in the course of ordinary conversation that constituted the key piece of data for Davies's and Harré's (1990/2001) germinal paper.

"THESE WELSH PEOPLE CAN BE VERY FUNNY"

Let us first recontextualize the statement quoted at the beginning of this chapter that "these Welsh people can be very funny." It is taken from a telephone conversation between Deena and Mark, and the topic of conversation is Deena's daughter's forthcoming wedding, to which Mark has been invited. As Extract 1 opens, Deena is complaining to Mark that the whole cost of the wedding is being borne by the bride's parents alone. (Dierdre is Deena's daugher, and Mike her future son-in-law.) Note that the data extracts used in this chapter are transcribed so as to preserve as much as possible of the way in which the talk was originally produced—both in terms of the relationship of one turn to another (e.g., square brackets indicate overlap between speakers, an equals sign means no space between turns) and in terms of features such as emphasis (indicated by underlining), elongated sounds (colons), volume (loud talk is capitalised, soft talk enclosed by degree symbols) and laughter ("huh" is full laughter, (h) shows laughter tokens infiltrating talk). For a full key to this kind of data transcription, see the Appendix.

Extract 1: Holt: M88:2:4:40–41

```
01   Deena:   We're in the unfortunate p'sition I mean in this (.)
02            this day 'n age basically th'majority'v our friends
03            around he↓:re. the both (0.5) both sides a'the family:
04            (0.5) uh:m (.) you know chip i:n. you kno[w but u]h I =
05   Mark:                                             [eeYes. ]
06   Deena:   = mean from Mike's side we 'aven' even had a ↑ha'pny
07            offere[d. ]
08   Mark:          [Ha]ven't you? = hOh: [dear.]
09   Deena:                               [An' ] Dierdre's a bit sick about
10            it she said what (              ) they went- she'd been down
11            t'South Wales this weekend to his family (0.9) 'n came
12            back she said Mum they payin out four 'n a 'alf
13            thousand pounds she said to 'av all new- a:ll new .t.hh
```

```
14            all double glazing put in. =
15   Mark:     = Akh!
16   Deena:    She said but they won't offer you a thousand towards the
17             wedding [I said we]ll (1.0) this's a very- u-Dierdre said =
18   Mark:              [ nNo:.hh]
19   Deena:    = that u-he wouldn' ask his parents becuz um
20             (.)
21   Deena:    *he left home at eightee:n (0.3) an' 'ee
23             'asn't really been back since. 'N 'ee doesn't feel that
24             he ↑could. 'N I said well it's not up to him. I said it's*
25             up to them.
26   Mark:     mkhh[Hm:,h]
27   Deena:        ['N I   ] said these Welsh pih people c'n be very
28             funny I said p'raps it's not the tradition down #there
29             but apparently it is becuz (0.7) s'm other friends'v
30             theirs down there thei:r son's getting married (0.8)
             ((continues))
```
* Mark is making audible fidgeting noises between these symbols
# More fidgeting from Mark from here onward

Deena's statement that "these Welsh people can be very funny" is produced, then, in the context of a complaint against two specific people (presumably Welsh) who are the parents of her future son-in-law. In making this statement she is selecting a form of person reference that highlights their national identity, and she is doing so in order to suggest a reason for the behavior of which she is complaining: perhaps it's their Welshness that accounts for their not contributing to the cost of the wedding. The implication is that this would, to some extent, exonerate their behavior as a cultural variation. If paying for (sons') weddings is not part of their "tradition," this would militate against alternative possible explanations drawing on individual characteristics or motivations that would position her daughter's future in-laws as mean, miserly, tight-fisted, or Scrooge-like. Contrary to our first "hearing" of this data as exemplifying some kind of crude "stereotyping" of Welsh people, then, Deena seems here to bring off some display of sensitivity to the existence of cultural traditions different from her own, and the importance of understanding individual behavior in terms of the cultural traditions within which those individuals are located.

As conversation analysts we do not, however, want to make claims about Deena's "attitudes" to the Welsh, or about her degree of ethnocentrism more generally. Rather, in line with the focus on talk as action, we ask what she is *doing* interactionally. We have already said that she is making a complaint against her daughter's future in-laws, and we will turn now to how she makes her talk hearable as a complaint, while managing the delicate business of not being heard to launch direct personal criticisms against people who will soon be part of her extended family. The complaint is built first by describing her situation as unfortunate and counter-normative (lines 1–4), and then (line 6) by making what Schegloff (1988) calls a "negative observation," that is, an observation about something that *hasn't* happened, is *not* the case, or is *not* being done—which is a common format for "doing complaining." The complainable matter is elaborated using her daughter's reported words (rather than speaking of it in her own voice), and she uses Dierdre's reported speech to display her (first-hand evidential) knowledge that their failure to contribute cannot be attributed to financial insolvency: Dierdre's reported words render her future parents-in-law maximally culpable: they could easily afford to contribute to the cost of the wedding, they won't (rather than can't, line 16; note that this too is a negative observation) and she's "sick about it," lines 09–10. Through the design of her telling about the conversation with Dierdre, Deena displays herself as someone reluctant—despite her daughter's more forthright criticisms—to make negative personal attributions about her daughter's future in-laws (especially her future son-in-law, who is specifically exonerated at some length on lines 17–25). Positioning them as "Welsh people" offers a culturally-based explanation for their behavior—an explanation that has been carefully prepared for earlier in her talk, where she specifically states that it is normal for both sides of the family to contribute "around here" (line 3), thereby setting up a potential contrast with traditions in other geographical localities, such as South Wales (line 11), which specifically names the new in-laws' geographical location in preparation for the invocation of their Welshness.

The punch line, however, turns out to be that the future in-laws are acting, after all, as individuals and not as category members. Despite Deena's displayed willingness to understand the parents' actions as those of category members whose cultural tradition precludes contributing to the cost of (sons') weddings (and hence not to think ill of them as individuals), it turns out that members of the category "Welsh" are known in fact to make such contributions, such that the behavior of the future in-laws must be judged *as individuals* and not on the basis of their category membership. The positioning of the future in-laws as Welsh, and the invocation of possible inferences on the basis of that category membership, turns out to have been done in the service of rendering their failure to contribute to the cost of the wedding maximally complainable. Neither financial insolvency nor, it turns out, cultural tradition can excuse them. In effect, Mike's parents are positioned as "Welsh people" and then repositioned as "just people" after all, with this proposed possible positioning displayed as insufficient to explain their actions.

Over the course of the data extract we've quoted, then, Deena is managing the delicate business of complaining about her daughter's future in-laws. The activity in which she is centrally engaged is complaining about these people, while positioning herself as a reasonable, open-minded person, reluctant to think ill of them, and casting around for an alternative explanation for their behaviour (their membership in the category "Welsh"), before being forced to recognize their individual culpability for the unfortunate position in which she finds herself.

"HANDICAPPED INSTRUCTORS ARE USUALLY HARDER MARKERS"

In the previous example, the invocation of category membership was relatively unproblematic. On other occasions, however, the production of an individual as a member of a category can involve a great deal more work on the part of the speaker, as in the following instance taken from a telephone conversation in which two young women (former classmates) have been talking about problems with their teachers. In the fragment reproduced as Extract 2, Bee is totally preoccupied with effecting the transformation of an individual ("this man who I have for linguistics") into a member of the category "handicapped people"—while simultaneously deflecting the responsibility for this transformation from herself to "a woman in my class who's a nurse," and actively employing the inferences such a transformation has made possible. The linguistics teacher of lines 1–2 (referred to with the singular pronoun "he"/"him"/"his" in lines 2, 7, 9, 12, 14, 16, 17, and 20) becomes at line 24 a (possible) presumptive representative of the category "handicapped people" and is thereafter referred to with the plural "they" (lines 28, 30, 31, 37), indexing him only in terms of his category membership (see Sacks, 1995a, p. 335). This is what we mean in saying that Bee positions her linguistics teacher as a handicapped person. Using conversation analysis, we can explore in more detail exactly how this positioning is achieved and why (i.e., what action is accomplished through it).

Extract 2: TG:6:1–42

```
01  Bee:  [ . . . ]    This feller I have-(nn)/(iv-)"felluh"; this
02        ma:n. (0.2) t! ˙hhh He ha::(s)- uff-eh-who-who I have fer
03        Linguistics [is real    ]ly too much, ˙hh[h =        ]
04  Ava:            [Mm hm?]              [Mm [hm,]
05  Bee:                                      [ = I didn' notice it
06        b't there's a woman in my class who's a nurse 'n. ˙hh she
07        said to me she s'd didju notice he has a ha:ndicap en I
08        said wha:t. Youknow I said I don't see anything wrong
09        wi[th im, she says his ha:nds. =
10  Ava:    [Mm:.
11  Bee:  = ˙hhh So the nex' cla:ss hh! ˙hh fer en hour en f'fteen
12        minutes I sat there en I watched his ha:n(h)ds hh
13        hh[ ˙hhh =
14  Ava:     [ Why wha[t's the ma[tter   ] owith (his h'nds)/(him.)
15  Bee:             [ = She   [meh-]
16  Bee:  ˙hhh t! ˙hhh He keh- He doesn' haff uh-full use uff hiss
```

```
17        hh-fin::gers or something en he, tch! he ho:lds the chalk
18        funny = en, ˙hh =
19  Ava:   = Oh[:        ]
20  Bee:       [hhHe-] eh-his fingihs don't be:nd = en, [˙hhh-
21  Ava:                                    [Oh[::        ]
22  Bee:                                         [Yihknow] she
23        really eh-so she said you know, theh-ih- she's had
24        experience. ˙hh with handicap' people she said but ˙hh
25        ih-yihknow ih-theh- in the fie:ld.
26              (0.2)
27  Ava:  (Mm:.)
28  Bee:  thet they're i:n[::. =
29  Ava:                   [(Uh [huh)
30  Bee:                        [ = Yihknow theyd- they do b- (0.2)
31        t! ˙hhhh they try even harduh then uhr-yihknow a regular
32        instructor.
33  Ava:  Righ[t.
34  Bee:      [ ˙hhhh to uh ins(tr)- yihknow do the class'n
35        evr[ything.  ] An:d,
36  Ava:     [Uh huh.]
37  Bee:  She said they're usually harder markers 'n I said wo::wuhh
38        huhh! ˙hhh I said theh go, I said there's- there's three
39        courses a'ready thet uh(hh)hh[hff
40  Ava:                               [°Yeh
41  Bee:  I'm no(h)t gunnuh do well i(h)n,
42  Ava:  hhhh!
```

Some analysts might treat this as as a straightforward instance of stereotyped thinking (supported by spurious reference to a purported nurse-expert), and as indicative of Bee's "prejudiced attitudes" or her reliance on oppressive "cultural discourses" or "interpretive repertoires." But it is also evident that the action she is performing in invoking, or—more accurately—constructing, this stereotype is that of blaming her (handicapped) teacher for the poor mark she expects to get on this course. In that sense it's a case of ordinary, mundane prejudice in action. But Bee, unlike the speakers in many studies of prejudice (e.g., Wetherell & Edley, 1999; Wetherell and Potter, 1992), is not being interviewed by a researcher in order to elicit her attitudes, opinions, or discourses about members of this category (and might say entirely different things if she were). She is *using* the category in her ordinary life—positioning her teacher as "a handicapped person" in the course of telling a story to her friend. The story is one of a series of stories Ava and Bee tell each other about problematic teachers: one is a "pain in the ass," one was "really awful" and inconvenienced students by dying in the middle of the term, another is inaudible and won't use a microphone. So here again it is not enough simply to say that positioning is being done: it is also necessary to explore *how* that positioning is effected and the action that is thereby accomplished. Let us look at this in more detail.

In line 2, Bee aborts an initial reference to her teacher's "handicap," abandoning her sentence beginning "He has-" (the hyphen indicates that the sound is cut off) in favor of returning to further specify the individual about whom she is launching her telling. Given what we know about repair in conversation (e.g., Schegloff, Jefferson, & Sacks, 1977) it seems likely that what she was going to say, and doesn't, at line 2 is what she later, in line 7, puts into the mouth of her classmate: "He has a handicap." By leaving "He has-" incomplete, she backs off from producing this description under her own auspices in order to produce it instead in the form of reported speech from "a woman in my class who's a nurse."

This reported description of the teacher as someone who "has a handicap" (line 7) does not, of course, ascribe him category membership. Rather this is an adjectival phrase, which assigns to the individual ("he") a particular attribute (a handicap). In disability politics (though the development of these postdates this particular conversation, which was recorded in the 1960s), this has often been seen as a more respectful form of reference because it retains a focus on the individual qua individual, rather than subsuming individuality under categorical membership. So, for example, "people with disabilities" or "people living with AIDS" is preferred over "disabled people" or "AIDS victims" (Fine & Asch, 1998). We make this point in order to suggest that reference forms are not merely an academic concern: it can—and does—matter to social participants whether the terms applied to them are adjectival or categorical. The analysis that follows shows that this matters to Bee here too.

It is apparent that there is some delicacy for Bee in producing her teacher as a handicapped person. There are three moves in her telling: first she depicts herself as having been brought to the realization that he has a handicap; then she depicts herself as having been informed (by an expert with relevant "experience") about the inferences it is appropriate to make about members of the category "handicapped people," of which this teacher is now treated as (possibly) representative; finally, the positioning of this teacher as a handicapped person is sealed when, at lines 37–41, Bee treats the inferences now established as appropriate in relation to handicapped people as also appropriate in relation to her teacher, hence displaying her treatment of him as a member of that category.

Bee's first reference to "it" (although what the "it" is is not specified) comes at line 5, where she says "I didn't notice it." The "it" she claims not to have noticed is only subsequently specifiable as the teacher's "handicap" (technically, this is a "prospective indexical," Goodwin, 1996). Instead of simply reporting to Ava that her teacher has a handicap, Bee then tells a story about how she was brought to notice the handicap under expert guidance. It reportedly took a direct question from the expert nurse-classmate to bring Bee even to consider the possibility that there may have been something "wrong" with their teacher, and the question itself ("did you notice he has a handicap," line 7) is designed to incorporate the possibility that Bee might not have noticed this (thus supporting her prior claim to Ava not to have done so). Bee presents the nurse-classmate as having to locate the problem for her ("his hands," line 9) and herself as having watched his hands over the course of an entire class ("an hour and fifteen minutes") before she is able to see him as having a handicap ("he doesn't have full use of his fingers" etc., lines 16–20).

The naming of the category, "handicapped people" occurs in line 24, immediately after the existence of the teacher's handicap has been established. This promotes the inference—without explicitly stating it—that the teacher whose handicap has just been described is such a category member. Bee does not rely on the category "handicapped people" being sufficient for Ava to invoke the (allegedly category-typical) attributes of her linguistics teacher. Instead, in lines 22–37, she uses the reported speech of a professional with experience to warrant the category/attribute relationship and actively to construct the attributes of "handicapped people" ("trying even harder" and being "harder markers"). As in the previous examples we have looked at (although rather more laboriously here), a category is not simply invoked (e.g., as a pre-existing cultural stereotype) but, rather, it is actively constituted through its use in a specific local context.

The positioning of Bee's teacher as a handicapped person is sealed in lines 37–41. Here Bee treats the ascribed characteristics of handicapped people (specifically that they are "usually harder markers") as having implications for her own grade on her linguistics course, and thereby reflexively constituting her linguistics teacher as a presumptive category member. This is also the punch line of Bee's story. The story is designed to convey the impression that she didn't expect a poor mark on her linguistics course until the issue of her teacher's category membership, and its implications, was pointed out to her. Only when her teacher's membership of a category "known" to be hard markers is revealed, does the likelihood of a poor grade occur to her, and she reports her reaction with a noise ("wo::wuhhhuhh!") which dramatises her sudden revelation and mock-dismay (see Wilkinson & Kitzinger, forthcoming on reaction tokens). The justification for this reaction is then spelled out in the words that follows—linguistics is (yet another) course that she is "not gonna do well in" (line 41). Bee's "not doing well" is thereby set up as entirely the responsibility of the linguistics teacher, and his category membership, and as unrelated to her performance on this course. The success of her story line depends on *not* introducing her teacher at the outset as "the handicapped man I have for linguistics," but hinges on the revelation of his "handicap" and her realization of its consequences for her grade. The action performed by positioning her teacher as a handicapped person, then, is to anticipate—and preemptively to excuse—her (potentially poor) performance in her linguistics course.

"I MEAN, ALL MEN LIKE BOOBS DON'T THEY"

The previous extracts invoked categories of nationality and then disability; here, gender is the category of interest. This third data fragment is taken from a focus group discussion for women with breast cancer (all British, mostly working class, and predominantly over sixty: see Wilkinson 1998, 2000a, 2000b; Wilkinson & Kitzinger, 2000, for more information), moderated by one of us (SW). Our focus is on lines 24–26 where Eve treats her husband as a representative of the category "men" and articulates, as an inference associated with this category, a liking for "boobs." Shortly before this fragment opens, Sue has invited group members to talk about "how people around you reacted" to the news of a breast cancer diagnosis, particularly "people close to you: partners, family, friends." Two women have already responded to this invitation to talk: first May, who described how "my husband was very very upset [. . .] You know, 'n the whole family was really. They just worried for me because they love me"; and then, Jill, who described her husband as having been initially "just stunned." As Extract 3a opens, Jill is continuing with a description of her husband's subsequent reaction:

Extract 3a: SW: BCP5: 19: 21–33

```
01  Jill:   But um we talked about it 'n I said "Well-"
02          (0.5) um (1.0) as I say .hhh (0.2) he:: had a cry::: (0.5)
03          um (0.5) 'nd the:n >more or less pulled hisself together 'n<
04          .hh (0.8) he: uh (1.0) said "well never mind" so I said 'yeah
05          but- but sounds as though my breast's got to come off'
06          (0.8)
07          So he said "I'll still love you without one," I s- he said
08          "I didn't marry you for them."
09          (1.0)
10          He said u:h "that's- (.) that's nothing that."
11          (0.2)
12          You know (.) TO HIM.
13  Sue:    mm::.
14  Jill:   W- He said "All I want is (.) YOU to be sorted out 'n (0.2)
15  Eve:    be alr[ight]."
16  Jill:        [you ] know [Yeah ]
17  Eve:                     [ mmm]
18  Jill:   That's- that's all .hh his first thought was .hh "well
19          alright then- [.hhh (.) we'll GET rid of it ] 'n e:r =
20  Eve:                 [That's what Bill says no::w. ] =
21  Eve:    = as long as you're alright. =
22  Jill:   = 'n:: (.) as long as you're alright (.) that'll do for
23          me." You know.
24  Eve:    I mean he ain't sex-mad my 'usband but [I mean] a::ll me:n:
```

25   Jill   [No::::]
26   Eve: (0.2) like boobs don't they?
27   (0.5)

Eve's statement that "all men like boobs" is produced, then, as she launches a telling about her husband (Bill)'s reaction to her breast cancer diagnosis (and subsequent mastectomy). In the space of just a few seconds, she refers to him in three different ways: first (line 20) as "Bill" (naming him as an individual), then (line 24) as "my husband" (positioning him as "family" and herself as answering Sue's question), and finally (line 24) as a presumptive representative of the category "men" for whom, on this basis, the inference of "liking boobs" can be made. In making this statement, she is selecting a form of person reference that treats his gender as salient in accounting for his reaction. None of the previous speakers has done this: that is, although it is obvious that the people they are talking about *are* men (they are husbands, they have men's names, they are referred to as "he"), their maleness is not highlighted. Indeed, in May's account (quoted earlier) her husband is assimilated into and is positioned as one of "the whole family" (which includes her daughter and is a kinship rather than a gender category).

It is true, but only in the grossest and most uninteresting way, that Eve is making a stereotyped statement about an entire gender. What this characterization of her words misses out on is the *action* she is engaged in. In making a known-by-all-of-us-to-be-true statement about members of the category "men" (a category of which her husband is commonsensically known to be a member), Eve exonerates Bill from any personal culpability for his interest in "boobs," and hence from any blame or criticism for his difficulties with her post-mastectomy body. At this point in the conversation, the other women in the group have all presented their husbands as primarily concerned about their survival, in relation to which the loss of a breast is (as Jill quotes her husband as saying) "nothing" (line 10). None of them has even alluded to husbands' concerns about the implications of mastectomy for their sex lives. Eve is facing the difficulty of contrasting her own husband's reaction (at least, his initial reaction) with those of the previous two speakers, without presenting him in a negative light, or implying that her husband loves her less than do theirs. Let us trace how she does this.

Eve's assertion (at line 20) that her husband "now" says a similar thing to Jill's implies that earlier he did not. It is a delicate business to convey that her husband *was* initially very concerned about the loss of her breast, and for sexual reasons, without implying that he was not also concerned about her survival. She first preempts a possible hearing of what she hasn't yet said as implying that Bill is "sex mad" (line 24) and thereby introduces sex into the conversation as a topic of concern. "Liking boobs" is thus set up to be heard as sexual (and not, for example, as merely aesthetic). In treating men's liking for boobs as knowledge shared by all cultural members, Eve's statement is an instance of what conversation analysts have described as "idiomatic" or "formulaic" statements inviting affiliative responses (Drew & Holt, 1988; Kitzinger, 2000b). If she had received the chorus of "yes," "that's true," "they do don't they," and so on normatively consequent upon such formulaic offerings, she could have felt supported in developing her telling about her husband's sexual concerns. As we see at line 27, however, this is not forthcoming and, as we shall see when we return to this extract and what follows it in the following section of this chapter, Eve's telling is first (self-) interrupted, and then attenuated, as a result of other (interactionally-generated) positionings in the group.

Our key point, for now, however, is that Eve's "stereotyped" positioning of Bill as a representative of all men is done in the service of introducing sexuality into the conversation, and of talking about her own post-mastectomy sexual problems with Bill, while exonerating him of any individual culpability for his sexual interest in her breasts and, by extension, for his distress at the prospect of her mastectomy. We also want to draw attention to the ease with which Eve positions Bill as a "man." Her production of him as a category member is smooth and unproblematic: it is not prepared for, or worked at, in the way that (in Extract 1) the positioning of Mike's "family" as "Welsh people" does, because Eve can rely on the taken-for-granted knowledge of others in the group that "husbands" are, by definition, men (whereas future in-laws are not definitionally, or even very often, Welsh). Nor does it involve (as in Extract 2) the laborious invocation of a nurse-expert to diagnose "maleness" or to pronounce on its attributes. The very smoothness with which some positionings are brought off is something to which we want to draw attention in developing and extending our analysis of this last extract in the next section.

EXPLORING NORMATIVE POSITIONINGS: MAKING HETEROSEXISM VISIBLE

Let us now develop our analysis of Eve's statement that "all men like boobs don't they." We have already said that this is an instance of an idiomatic or formulaic statement, inviting an affiliative response. In this particular context, Eve is using it in order to launch a telling about her husband, inviting her recipients to agree with a self-evidently "true" statement about what men are like in order to describe this particular man's difficulties with her loss of a breast through mastectomy. As it turns out, there is a problem here, and a marked *absence* of affiliation follows Eve's claim about what "all men like" (the 0.5 second silence on line 27). Extract 3b (which starts by reproducing the last 4 lines of Extract 3a) reveals what happens next. Note that despite the absence of affiliation, Eve reasserts her claim at line 39 (where "men," including her husband Bill, are now indexed simply as "they").

Extract 3b: SW: BCP5: 19: 32–39

```
24  Eve:   I mean he ain't sex-mad my 'usband but [I mean] a::ll me:n:
25  Jill:                                            [No:::: ]
26  Eve:   (0.2) like boobs don't they?
27         (0.5)
28  Sue:   [°I believe so°     ]
29  Eve:   [So there you a:re.] = If 'he didn't-  = Wh::y? = Aren't you married¿
30         (0.5)
31  Eve:   hu::h! [hu:h    ]
32  Sue:          [Di£vo:r]ced£.
33  Eve:   [Di(h)vo(h)rced huh huh]
34  Jill:  [huh   huh            ]
35  Eve:   A::h we(h)ll.
36         (0.5)
37  Eve:   °Ah well.°   ((sadly))
38         (0.2)
39  Eve:   But m- they do.  = I mean it does affect 'em
40         a bi:t. = I think. °You know°.   But they get u:[sed to it.   ]
41  Ann:                                                   [.hhh Yeah I]
           ((continues))
```

As we have said, Eve's statement "all men like boobs" positions "men" as a group in order to launch a telling about her husband in particular. We might also now note, although there is no evidence that any of the participants is oriented to this, that "all men" are thereby presumed to be heterosexual. In the course of the action to which Eve is oriented (launching a telling about her husband's sexual interest in her breasts, exonerating him for his concern about their loss), she is, incidently, and without being in any way oriented to such an action, displaying her taken-for-granted assumption of normative male heterosexuality. For us as analysts, this tells us something about the social world of which Eve is a part, and which she here reflects and perpetuates.

The unproblematically invoked-as-normative nature of heterosexuality is apparent earlier in this interaction too (see Extract 3a). In the question to which Eve's talk is an answer, Sue has used the word "partners," thereby leaving open everyone's marital status, the gender of the partners, and their sexual identities. In response, May, Jill, and Eve all refer to their "husbands," thereby positioning themselves as married heterosexuals. It would not be accurate to say that they are "coming out" as, or positioning themselves as, heterosexuals—in the sense that someone might be "coming out" as lesbian if she replied to Sue's question by refering to "my partner . . . she . . . " (see Kitzinger, 2000a). Rather they, like other heterosexuals across our data, treat heterosexuality as the ordinary default way to be. The gender of their partners and their marital status is not treated as anything special: the *action* that they are engaged in is not "coming out" as, or positioning themselves as, heterosexual, but launching tellings about their husbands' reactions to their mastectomies. Other research and political activism has documented the extent to which we live in a world in which the macro-structure of society—laws about marriage, inheritance, tax, adoption, and so on—presumes and reinforces heterosexuality. What we see in this small data fragment (and it is replicated over many more; see also Peel, 2001) is that we also live in a world in which the *micro-structure* of ordinary, everyday interaction—who assumes what about whom, how those assumptions are built into talk—*also* positions everyone as normatively heterosexual. In a more mundane, routine—and perhaps for that reason more insidious—manner, the heterosexual social structure is built and rebuilt through talk by people who are not being overtly homophobic or anti-gay, but who are simply taking for granted a normative heterosexual world, and reconstituting it, moment by moment, in their interactions.

There is, however, as we have said, some interactional difficulty consequent upon Eve's statement that "all men like boobs." The interactional "slot" open at line 27 is a slot in which agreement or affiliation is relevant—and hence can be said to be relevantly missing. What we have instead is a 0.5 second silence and then a delayed, and quiet, response from Sue—who disclaims any direct epistemic access to whether or not men like boobs. In her response, "I believe so," she witholds affiliation. The relevance of knowing, as women, about what men "like" sexually, is at least potentially hearable, by a recipient to whom such things matter, as displaying an assumption that all the women present are heterosexual—as an invitation to bond over the presumed-shared knowledge of heterosexual women. In displaying herself *not* to have direct personal first-hand knowledge, Sue signals some difficulty with, or distance from, a taken-for-granted (traditional, feminine, married, heterosexual) perspective in a nonspecific, but subsequently buildable-upon, manner. Certainly Eve hears it this way and she self-interrupts (in line 29) to offer a candidate account for Sue's response: "Aren't you married." In displaying, through her question, that Sue's marital status is a possible explanation for her failure to affiliate, Eve thereby also displays her prior assumption that Sue *was* married and that it was by virtue of their being married women that she was inviting her recipients to affirm the truth of her statement about men. In other words, Eve's claim that "all men like boobs don't they" positions her coconversationalists as heterosexual (married) women—a positioning that becomes noticeable here because of some resistance from Sue.

Eve's question at line 29 arises not out of a dispassionate interest in Sue's marital status, but in order to solve the problem as to why Sue has just distanced herself from this bit of folk wisdom about what "all men" are like. The answer Sue gives, eventually—after a significant delay (of nearly a second)—"Divorced" (line 44), is an accurate answer to the "marital status" form of the question, but it does not engage with Eve's reason for asking the question. Some answer such as "No, I'm not married because I'm a lesbian and I neither know nor care about men's interest in boobs" *would* have done so, but would also, of course, by positioning Sue as lesbian, have caused major disruption to the otherwise ongoing activity of the group—activity for which Sue, as the researcher facilitating the group discussion, is responsible. So Sue's turn at line 28 ("I believe so") is a first "coming out" step in which she is oriented to her lesbianism in contrast with the group's displayed heterosexuality. Her turn at line 44 ("Divorced") is a reorientation to her position as researcher responsible for facilitating the group, stepping back from the "coming out" process she has initiated, and Eve has pursued, and hence "doing her job." The cost for lesbians and gay men of "doing our jobs" across a variety of contexts—that is, of ensuring that our social and professional interactions run off smoothly and unproblematically—is often to suppress our differences from the heterosexuals with whom we are engaging, to allow a heterosexual positioning to continue, so that the actions in which we and they are otherwise engaged can continue without disruption. This little fragment of data displays normative heterosexual positioning in action (see Kitzinger, 2003, for further analysis of this).

Positioning theorists have often focused on the shifting and ephemeral nature of positioning, and we have shown how positions are shifted in talk (e.g., Sue's shifting orientation to her position as lesbian, then to her position as group facilitator). We want also to point, however, to the *endurance* of some positions across interactions—positions that reflect and reinforce their speakers' taken-for-granted social worlds. The normativity of these positionings renders them generally invisible and they are not usually explicitly oriented to by participants. Heteronormativity became visible (at least to us as analysts) in Extract 3 only because Sue (briefly) resisted it—such that what had been submerged as taken-for-granted (the married heterosexual status of the co-participants) was named ("Aren't you married"). More usually (at least in our data), it is the nonnormative category that is named as part of providing an account for someone's actions, thereby making apparent that which is taken as normative: so culpable action (or inaction, or future possible action) is attributed to "Welsh people" (Extract 1) or "handicapped instructors" (Extract 2), thereby producing (without naming) Englishness and able-bodied status as normative. One of the challenges facing positioning theory (and conversation analysis) is to analyze more systematically the ways in which the endurance of a taken-for-granted social world of heterosexual, able-bodied, Caucasian, etc., normativity is produced through particular encounters in which the positioning of lesbians, the disabled, other ethnicities, and so on is routinely effected without anybody setting out to do anything particularly "prejudiced," and in the pursuit of some other agenda entirely.

FUTURE DIRECTIONS

Through our analysis of three short data extracts we have raised a range of issues and concerns on the basis of which we want to suggest four (somewhat overlapping) directions for the future development of positioning theory.

First, we have shown that positioning is done in pursuit of some local in-

teractional goal, such as building a complaint (Extract 1), deflecting responsibility (Extract 2), or launching a telling with an exoneration (Extract 3).
Although it is self-evidently the case in these data fragments that the speakers
are making inferences about the Welsh, or disabled people, or men, this is
not *all* they are doing, nor is it perhaps the best characterization of *what* they
are doing. Rather, as we have shown, their use of categorical reference terms
and their deployment of inferences about the categories invoked are in the
service of these other—more pressing—locally specific activities. From traditional (e.g., cognitive) psychological perspectives, it may be seen as a weakness of our research that participants refer only briefly to the categories they
invoke and that we were not able to interrogate them about their attitudes or
beliefs, or to make more substantial revelations about Deena's attitudes to the
Welsh, Bee's stereotypes about the disabled, or Eve's opinion of men. Our
research is very different, in that respect, from work on positioning that relies
on interviews or focus groups in which positioning is done as "topic talk,"
and in which researchers pursue the "identities," "interpretive repertoires,"
"discourses," or "psychodiscursive practices" through which their research
participants position themselves and others in relation to some (predefined)
category of interest to the researcher. For example, Wetherell and Edley
(1999) elicited topic talk about masculinity from their male research participants by asking questions like "Would you describe yourself as a masculine
man?" or "Are there moments in everyday life when you feel more masculine
than at other times?" (p. 335), and their data constitute attempts by inter-
viewees to answer questions about the category "man." While this approach
yields a great deal of talk *about* a category, it precludes any exploration of how
people *use* categories interactionally in everyday life. Yet the social world in
which we live is composed of these moment-by-moment positionings, these
fleeting invocations of particular categories for locally specific purposes, each
of which—almost incidently and without this being the speakers' intention—
further sediments major social divisions of ethnicity, disability, gender, sexual
orientation, and so on. For example, when Bee tells Ava about her linguistics
teacher, she is not oriented to talking about disability per se: rather she is
engaged in a telling that deflects responsibility from herself to her teacher for
a (projected) poor grade on her course. As such, this is an instance of mundane,
everyday positioning in the service of some *other* action. Nonetheless, the
active (re)construction of the category "handicapped people"—and the attribution to category members of behaviors implicated in student failure—contributes to the (re)construction of a world in which members of oppressed
groups continue to be stereotyped, in which disability continues to be seen as
a negative attribute, and in which disabled teachers present problems for their
students. Indeed, one way of characterizing this episode is to say that an able-
bodied person positions a disabled person in such a way as to occlude entirely
the discrimination suffered by people with disabilities—and, further, to effect
a reversal such that instead of the teacher's being oppressed by an able-bodied

world, the student is the victim of his disability. (In much the same way, as we have discussed elsewhere, heterosexuals sometimes accuse lesbians of "oppressing" them, or white people complain of racial discrimination against them: see Kitzinger & Wilkinson, 1994.) In that sense it's a case of ordinary, mundane prejudice in action. We would like to see the development of more work on positioning that contributes to an understanding of how social categories are reproduced and reinforced (and, sometimes, resisted) through the everyday actions of people going about their business in the world.

Second, the data we have discussed here reveal a number of distinctively different practices and actions, all of which are sometimes glossed by use of the term "positioning." We would like to draw attention to just three of these as a way of pointing to the value of unpacking, with more precision, what analysts mean in refering to "positioning" in their data. These are: (a) naming or indexing a category; (b) invoking categorical membership; and (c) invoking attributes.

Naming or Indexing a Category

The most straightforward practice of positioning is perhaps the one with which we started this chapter: positioning through the use of categorical reference terms such as "Welsh people," "handicapped instructors," "men," and so on. As it happens, such instances in our data all refer to third-party others, but obviously such terms can also be used to refer to the speaker (e.g., "speaking as a woman . . . "), or to a co-conversationalist (e.g., "as a woman you . . . "): see West and Fenstermaker (2002) for analysis of some instances of these. Whether done as first, second, or third party references, these forms have in common the subsuming of an individual into a category such that the individual is positioned as a presumptive representative (or, sometimes, as an exceptional member) of that category. This can, in fact, be achieved without the category of which the individual is taken to be a member ever being named, as in Extract 4 below, in which Leslie is complaining to her mother about a particular individual who has recently visited her:

Extract 4: Holt: 1:8:3
```
01  Les:    He still mumbles a lot I can't tell what he's sayin[g,
02  Mum:                                                        [Ah-ha
03          (.)
04  Mum:    u-We:ll (0.2)  'At's a'trouble with a lot of them, h[mh
05  Les:                                                         [Ye-:s,
```

Here the behavior (mumbling) of the individual ("he") of whom Leslie is complaining is treated by Mum as a typical (and regrettable) behavior of some unnamed category of persons ("them") whose referent is nowhere explicated. Based on the contextual information from this call, we might reasonably speculate that Mum intends to index some category such as "young people today." The point for our purposes here is that an individual becomes a representative of a category that is indexed but never named. Indexing, rather than naming, a categorical membership is a significant variant, presumably selected for what, by virtue of its nonspecificity, it renders possible interactionally—something we do not have space to pursue here.

Invoking Categorical Membership

The term "positioning" has also been used to describe how speakers invoke membership of particular categories (e.g., "married heterosexual women") for themselves and/or for their co-conversationalists through the assumptions they display in their talk. This was most apparent in Extract 3, in which we showed how May, Jill, and Eve, by referring to their husbands, positioned themselves as married heterosexuals, and how Eve through her invitation to bond over the presumed-shared knowledge of heterosexual women positioned all the women present (including Sue) as heterosexual. The category "heterosexual" is neither named nor indexed but is oriented to as an invoked category by Sue (through her disaffiliation from the idiom invoking heterosexual female knowledge) and by Eve (through her offer of "not married" as a candidate explanation for Sue's disaffiliation). It seems likely, and this would be worth exploring further, that normative categories (such as "heterosexual," "white," "able-bodied," etc.) are often assumed and invoked in talk but rarely named, whereas the parallel non-normative categories ("lesbian," "black," "disabled," etc.) are more often named explicitly—and that the difference between naming/indexing and invoking a category thus reflects (and perpetuates) profound sociopolitical divisions. It would be useful, then, for positioning theorists working with naturalistic data to develop sensitivity to the ways in which normative positions, reinforcing culturally taken-for-granted identities, are implicit in, and invoked by, talk in interaction.

Invoking Attributes

Like other positioning theorists, we have also used the term "positioning" to refer to practices whereby speakers display to their co-conversationalists the sort of person they are—that is, what kinds of attributes they possess as individuals (rather than what category they belong to). We have said, for example, that Deena (in Extract 1) positions herself a reasonable, open-minded person, reluctant to think ill of her daughter's future in-laws, and casting around for an alternative explanation for their behavior (their membership in the category "Welsh people"), before being forced to recognize their individual culpability. To position oneself, by implication, as "reasonable" is surely different from positioning oneself, by implication, as "not-Welsh/English," and both are different again from explicitly positioning others as members of a named category, "Welsh people." We would like to see positioning theorists develop more sophisticated analyses of whether and how these different kinds of positioning matter, and what they are used to do in the world.

In sum, then, our second recommendation for the future is the development of more precision in exploring the full range of different practices and actions currently glossed by the term "positioning."

Third, we have emphasized, through our analyses, the importance of showing not just *that* an individual is produced as member of a category, and certain inferences thereby made relevant, but *how* that is accomplished. We have begun to explore how an individual is produced as a member of a category and how inferences associated with that category are mobilized, and for what ends. People do not talk in logical syllogisms such as "All men like boobs; Bill is a man; therefore Bill likes boobs." Instead, as we have seen, some things are taken for granted and left unspoken (Bill being a man), others are treated as commonplace knowledge (men's liking for boobs), and the logical outcome may (as in this instance) be left for the listeners to infer for themselves. The appropriate contrast is not with an idealized logical form, however, but with other instances in which the processes of positioning and inference-drawing run off differently. So while men's interest in boobs (like the "funniness" of Welsh people) is treated as commonplace knowledge, the propensity for handicapped instructors to be harder markers is treated as a piece of specialized knowledge to be conveyed by an authorized expert. Speakers display, through their talk, what they take to be already known by members of their culture, and what constitutes potentially new information, and thereby show us, as analysts, their understanding of their culture. Not all categories, it seems, are equally inference-rich, nor can social members necessarily always rely on each other to draw the correct inferences on any given occasion: some inferences are spelled out in detail, and/or given expert warrant. Although categories preexist these occasions of use, they are also reflexively (re)constituted *through* their use in these specific local contexts.

Finally, in contrast to the emphasis from many positioning theorists (and from postmodern scholarship more generally) on the ephemeral, constantly shifting, unstable nature of positions in social encounters, we have tried to illustrate the way in which some positions, in particular those that reflect and reproduce heterosexuality, may be relatively stable across interactions. Normative positions (such as heterosexuality, whiteness, able-bodiedness) may be invisible in many interactions precisely because they *are* normative, so that they become visible only when there is some resistance to or challenge of them. Normative heterosexuality, we suggest, constitutes an ordinary, taken-for-granted, relatively unchanging backdrop against which shifts and changes in relation to other positions take place. Analysis of these less "visible" normative positions is, we have suggested, important both for the theoretical development of positioning theory (and conversation analysis) and for understanding how oppression works in ordinary, everyday interactions.

APPENDIX

Transcription Key for Data Extracts:

[ ]	square brackets	overlapping talk
=	equals sign	no space between turns
(0.5)	time in round brackets	intervals within or between talk (measured in tenths of a second)
(.)	period in round brackets	discernable pause or gap, too short to measure
:::	colons	extension of preceding sound (the more colons, the greater the extension)
.	period	closing intonation (not necessarily the end of a sentence)
,	comma	continuing intonation (not necessarily between clauses of sentences)
?	question mark	rising intonation (not necessarily a question)
¿	inverted question mark	rising intonation weaker than that indicated by a question mark
!	exclamation mark	animated tone (not necessarily an exclamation)
-	dash	abrupt cut off of sound
↑↓	up or down arrow	marked rise or fall in intonation, immediately following the arrow
here	underlining	emphasis
HERE	capitals	loudness, relative to surrounding talk
°here°	degree signs	softness, relative to surrounding talk
£	pound sign	smile voice
huh		full laugh
(h)		laughter particle inserted into talk

hhh		audible outbreath (no. of 'h's indicates length)
.hhh		audible inbreath (no. of 'h's indicates length)
( )	empty round brackets	transcriber unable to hear anything
(bring)	word(s) in round brackets	transcriber uncertain of hearing
(boy)/(buy)	slash separating word(s) in round brackets	alternate hearings by transcriber
((sniff))	word(s) in double round brackets	sounds or other material hard to transcribe; also transcriber's comments

Also:

[. . .]	3 periods in square brackets	material omitted for presentational purposes

ACKNOWLEDGMENTS

We would particularly like to thank Alison Thomas and Nigel Wells for their generous hospitality during the first month of our move to Vancouver. This chapter was substantially written surrounded by inquisitive chickens under the apple trees in their lovely home in Langley, BC. We also benefited from Alison's lively interest in and discussion of some of the data. An earlier version of our analysis of Extract 2 (from the "TG" telephone call) was originally produced by Sue during her study leave from Loughborough University UK, as part of her course work for Manny Schegloff at UCLA. Sue is grateful to Loughborough University for the study leave that enabled her to acquire conversation analytic skills, and we both thank Manny for giving so freely of his time, expertise, and careful teaching. All errors of analysis are of course ours alone.

REFERENCES

Austin, J. L. (1962). *How to do things with words.* Oxford: Clarendon Press.

Davies, B., & Harré, R. (1990/2001). Positioning: The discursive production of selves. *Journal for the Theory of Social Behavior.* Reprinted in M. Wetherell, S. Taylor, & S. J. Yates (Eds.), *Discourse theory and practice: A reader.* London: Sage.

Drew, P. (1992). Conversation analysis In E. F. Borgatta & M. L. Borgatta (Eds.), *Encyclopaedia of sociology* (pp. 303–309). Macmillan: New York.

Drew, P., & Holt, E. (1988). Complainable matters: The use of idiomatic expressions in making complaints. *Social Problems*, 35: 398–417.

Farr, R., & Moscovici, S. (Eds.). (1984). *Social representations.* Cambridge: Cambridge University Press.

Fenstermaker, S., & West, C. (Eds.). (2002). *Doing gender, doing difference: Inequality, power and institutional change.* New York: Routledge.

Fine, M., & Asch, A. (Eds.). (1988). *Women with disabilities: Essays in psychology, culture and politics.* Philadelphia: Temple University Press.

Goodwin, C. (1996). Transparent vision. In E. Ochs, E. A. Schegloff & S. A. Thompson (Eds.). *Interaction and grammar.* Cambridge: Cambridge University Press.

Heritage, J. (1984). Conversation analysis, chapter 8 (pp. 233–280) in *Garfinkel and ethnomethodology.* Cambridge: Polity Press.

Kessler, S. (1998). *Lessons from the intersexed.* New Brunswick, NJ: Rutgers University Press.

Kitzinger, C. (2000a). Doing feminist conversation analysis. *Feminism & Psychology, 10,* 163–193.

Kitzinger, C. (2000b). How to resist an idiom. *Research on Language and Social Interaction, 33*(2): 121–154.

Kitzinger, C. (2003). Feminist approaches to qualitative research: Voice, experience, action. In C. Seale, G. Giampietro, J. Gubrium & D. Silverman (Eds.), *Qualitative research practice.* London: Sage.

Kitzinger, C. & Wilkinson, S. (1994). Re-viewing heterosexuality. *Feminism & Psychology,* 4(2): 330–336.

Mehan, H. (1996). The construction of an LD student: A case study in the politics of representation. In M. Silverstein & G. Urban (Eds.), *Natural histories of discourses.* Chicago: University of Chicago Press. Reprinted (pp. 345—363) in M. Wetherell, S. Taylor, & S. J. Yates (Eds.), *Discourse theory and practice: A reader.* London: Sage.

Moghaddam, F. M., Taylor, D. M., Lambert, W. E., & Schmidt, A. E. (1995). Attributions and discrimination: A study of attributions to the self, the group, and external factors among whites, blacks, and Cubans in Miami, *Journal of Cross-Cultural Psychology,* 26: 209–220.

Peel, E. (2001). Mundane heterosexism: Understanding incidents of the everyday. *Women's Studies International Forum, 24,* 541–554.

Potter, J. A. (2001). Wittgenstein and Austin. In M. Wetherell, S. Taylor, & S. J. Yates (Eds.), *Discourse theory and practice: A reader.* London: Sage.

Sacks, H. (1972). On the analysability of stories by children, pp 329–345. In J. Gumperz & D. Hymes (Eds.), *Directions in sociolinguistics: The ethnography of communiation.* Holt, Reinhart and Winson.

Sacks, H. (1995). Lecture 8 (Part III, Spring 1996, pp. 333–340). *Lectures on conversation.* Oxford: Blackwell.

Sacks, H., & Schegloff, E. A. (1979). Two preferences in the organization of reference to persons in conversation and their interaction (pp. 15–21). In G. Psathas (Ed.), *Everyday language: Studies in ethnomethodology.* New York: Irvington Publishers.

Schegloff, E. A. (1988). Goffman and the analysis of conversation. In P. Drew & A. Wootton (Eds.), *Erving Goffman: Exploring the interaction order* (pp. 9–135). Cambridge: Polity Press.

Schegloff, E. A. (1996). Some practices for referring to persons in talk-in-interaction: A partial sketch of a systematics. In B. Fox (Ed.), *Studies in anaphora.* Amsterdam: John Benjamins.

Schegloff, E. A., Jefferson, G. & Sacks, H. (1977). The preference for self-correction in the organization of repair in conversation. *Language*, 53: 361–382.

Searle, J. R. (1969). *Speech acts: An essay in the philosophy of language.* Cambridge: Cambridge University Press.

Smith, D. (1978). K is mentally ill: The anatomy of a factual account. *Sociology*, 12: 23–53.

Spears, R., Oakes, P., Ellemers, N., & Haslam, S. A. (Eds.). (1997), *The social psychology of stereotyping and group life.* Oxford: Blackwell.

Tajfel, H. (1969). Cognitive aspects of prejudice. *Journal of Social Issues*, 25: 79–97.

Tajfel, H. (Ed.). (1982). *Social identity and intergroup relations.* London: Cambridge University Press.

West, C., & Fenstermaker, S. (2002). Accountability in action: The accomplishment of gender, race and class in a meeting of the University of California Board of Regents. *Discourse & Society*, 13(4): 537–563.

Wetherell, M., & Edley, N. (1999). Negotiating hegemonic masculinity: Imaginary positions and psycho-discursive practices, *Feminism & Psychology*. 9: 335–356.

Wetherell, M., & Potter, J. (1992). *Mapping the language of racism: Discourse and the legitimation of exploitation.* Hemel Hempstead: Harvester Wheatsheaf.

Wilkinson, S. (1998). Focus groups in health research: Exploring the meanings of health and illness. *Journal of Health Psychology*, 3(3): 329–348.

Wilkinson, S. (2000a). Feminist research traditions in health psychology: Breast cancer research. *Journal of Health Psychology*, 5(3): 353–366.

Wilkinson, S. (2000b). Women with breast cancer talking causes: Comparing content, biographical and discursive analyses. *Feminism & Psychology*, 10(4): 431–460.

Wilkinson, S., & Kitzinger, C. (2000), Thinking differently about "thinking positive": A discursive approach to cancer patients' talk. *Social Science & Medicine*, 50(6): 797–811.

Wilkinson, S., & Kitzinger, C. (forthcoming). Doing being amazed: Reaction tokens and the international construction of 'surprise' (under submission).

CHAPTER 11

Gender Positioning: A Sixteenth/Seventeenth-Century Example

Jennifer Lynn Adams and Rom Harré

Modern English has only one pronoun, "you," to address a person(s) in the second person. However in the past, English, like other European languages, had more than one form, including "thee," "thou" (T-form) and "ye," "you" (V-form). This duality of pronouns is similar to the "tu" (T-form) and "usted" (V-form) of Spanish and many other languages.

In the standard representation of the semantics of these forms we have two main uses:

1. To express social intimacy, reciprocal use of the "T" form, which we represent as "T–T," in contrast to social distance, reciprocal use of the "V" form, which we represent as "V–V."

2. To express social respect, when a high status speaker uses the "T" form to address someone of lower status and the interlocutor uses the "V" form in response. Equality of status can be expressed either by "T–T" or by "V–V," depending on the relative social distance of speaker and respondent.

Thus the duality of the second person pronoun was used to mark both status relationships and degree of intimacy. In the study here reported we use the distinction to explore the taken-for-granted relations between men and women in the late sixteenth and early seventeenth century, as these are represented in Shakespeare's *Love's Labours Lost*.

In sketching the history of the second person in European languages, Brown and Gillman (1960, p. 255) remark that there was at first no pronominal device for differentiating address among equals. However, very gradually, a distinction developed between the T (thee) of intimacy and the V (you) of formality" (Brown & Gilman, 1960, p. 257). They refer to this dimension of the use of "thee" and "you" as the solidarity semantic, because "thee" is "used between people who are like-minded" (Brown & Gilman, 1960, p. 258). Though further research (Mühlhäusler & Harré, 1992) has shown that this interpretation is not wholly adequate, the dimension picked out by Brown and Gillman does seem to be fairly robust.

This chapter uses the difference patterns in the semantics of "thee" and "you" in an analysis of their uses in Shakespeare's *Love's Labours Lost* to bring to light and explore assumptions about gender relations that are implicit in the text.

THE PLOT OF *LOVE'S LABOURS LOST*

Shakespeare writes a comical and ironic commentary on love in his play, *Love's Labours Lost*. He presents the women as seductresses and the men as mere pawns who have no willpower in the women's presence. The men plan on retreating to a country house to study seriously and without distractions for three years. They all sign a contract not to place themselves in the presence of women for this time. However, they end up having to meet with the princess and her ladies in waiting. Ultimately, all the men fall madly in love and end up breaking their contract. The rest of the play deals with their follies and comical dealings in love, and the ingenious plans the women think of to trick the men into being forsworn yet again. The psychological lesson is easily read: men are weak and women are strong.

THE GENERAL PATTERN OF SECOND PERSON GRAMMAR IN THE PLAY

"You"

In *Love's Labours Lost*, "you" has two main uses with regard to status: it is used between two people of equal status who stand in a formal relationship, and to persons of higher status when addressed by their inferiors.

To illustrate the first of the V–V usages, we note that the King and his Lords use "you" when addressing each other approximately 77 percent of the time. Similarly, this word is used between the Princess and her ladies in waiting in 78 percent of their exchanges. We take it that these are both examples of the use of "you" between people of equal but high status, dominating the intimacy we must presume between the members of each of the two groups.

To illustrate the T–V usages we see that persons of lower status address a person who is higher status than them with "you." Armando's page addresses him as "you" a significant 100 percent of the time. In addition, Dull, named for his stupidity, addresses those with more intelligence than he has with "you" 100 percent of the time. It is worth noting that markable status differences derive not only from conventional social relationships such as master and page, but also interpersonal differences of other kinds, for instance intelligence.

The second use of "you" is when a contrast is to be emphasized between moments of intimacy and of formality. The symmetrical pattern, "V–V" is employed. For the most part, "you" is used between the king and his lords and the princess and her ladies, not only because they are of equal status but also because there is a formal relationship between them. Ninety-one percent of the time, "you" is the pronoun of choice between all the members of the courtly groups, both male and female. It appears to be the default pronoun that is used whenever one is not talking to someone of lower status or about an intimate subject such as love or some other personal issue.

"Thee"

To illustrate the role of "thee" as the reciprocal of "you" in a V–T semantic with people of lower status we note that Armando addresses Boy, his page, exclusively with "thee." Boy responds to Armando's remarks and orders exclusively with "you." Another example of "thee" as an expression of unequal status occurs between Berowne, one of the prince's circle, and Costard. Berowne addresses Costard the clown as "thee." He says, "Stay, slave, I must employ thee" (Shakespeare, [1996], p. 75). Costard as a dependent to Berowne has a lower status, and when he is addressed as "thee" he replies with "you." Another character addressed with "thee" and "thou" is Dull, rightly named for his stupidity, reminding us that in Elizabethan England status is not only ascribed, but achieved.

"Thee" is also the pronoun of choice when there is an intimate relationship between two people, the T–T semantics. The most prominent uses of "thee" were in letters or in discussions of love. In letters, 100 percent of the time, "thee" was used to address the recipient. This usage marks off the letters involved in the plot as very intimate forms of communication. In addition, the majority of the letters in this play were love letters expressing the man's love and devotion towards a woman. Expression of one's love for another is obviously something very intimate that requires the use of the intimate pronoun "thee." This runs contrary to Brown and Gillman's "solidarity" exegesis. The usage in *Love's Labours Lost* is performative, a move in establishing a relationship, rather than expressing one that already exists.

It is also noteworthy that "thee" is frequently used instead of the "you" that would have usually been used by these speakers when the topic of discussion is love. Berowne proclaims his love for Rosaline and the King responds by saying, "What zeal, what fury, hath inspired thee now?" (Shakespeare, [1996], p. 125). The pronoun changes from "V" to "T" even when the talk is about the topic of love, rather than the performative speech of a suitor addressing his fancied lady. Thus topic is also an influence on choice of pronoun.

It is said that Russian officers use the formal "Vy" instead of the usual "Ty" when talking among friends about guns.

PRONOUNS AND POSITIONING

"Positioning" is the phenomenon in social psychology when implicitly or explicitly a person is restricted to a certain range of rights and obligations, particularly as to what speech acts are open to a speaker in a certain conversation. More generally, being positioned as an actor having a certain limited right to make use of certain speech forms, in a certain context, limits what that person can say and do. It limits not only the options of choice of speaking forms, but also of action and even of thought (Van Langenhove & Harré, 1999).

One of the more interesting aspects of the use of "thee" is as a positioning tool. Shakespeare's characters use a *change* of pronouns from the V-form to the T-form to put a person in his or her place. They can use this change in pronoun usage, made possible by the existence of the T and V forms, to change the degree of intimacy and/or to place a person in a lower status. Many times these changes in pronoun usage are transient and short term. Thus they express change in position, a momentary relationship, rather than change in role or status, long-term social relations. In positionings, the speakers deviate from the normal pronoun usage used between people in their long term relationships only momentarily. However, that would be enough to express a change in the intimacy of the relationship or a temporary change in status due to the situation. Brown and Gillman explain that "this kind of variation in language behavior expresses a contemporaneous feeling or attitude" (Brown & Gillman, 1960, p. 274). We think that these authors were using this rather clumsy phrase to try to express what is now called "positioning."

There are two main uses of a change in pronouns: to express an attitude of contempt in that the one addressed in the new way now stands lower in some social hierarchy, or to express a change in degree of intimacy.

To Establish a Change in Current Social Status, Vis-à-Vis the Speaker

When "thee" is used between two people who usually address each other as "you," this expresses an attitude of contempt for that person and places them in a lower rank or status. The king puts Berowne down after Berowne at first refuses to sign a contract not to see any women for three years but then finally succumbs and signs. The king says to Berowne, "How well this yielding rescues thee from shame" (Shakespeare, [1996], p. 15). An additional example of the use of "thee" is when the king addresses Berowne with contempt when he tears up a letter without letting the king read it (Shakespeare,

[1996], p. 123). Brown and Gilman explain that "the T (thee) of contempt and anger is usually introduced between persons who normally exchange V (you) but it can, of course, also be used by a subordinate to a superior. As the social distance is greater, the overthrow of the norm is more shocking and generally represents a greater extremity of passion" (Brown & Gillman, 1960, p. 275).

Most of the cases of the change in pronoun use made by Shakespeare were not in contempt or anger but were used instead in a sarcastic and comical manner. A good example of this use of "thee" is when Berowne uses "thee" towards the king and his fellow lords in Act IV, even though he normally addresses them as "you." There are two reasons why he addresses them as "thee." In this scene he overhears each of the men reading aloud a letter or poem each has written to his lover. Berowne sarcastically remarks about their poems and letters while hiding from them. So the first reason why he uses "thee" is because he feels that he is hearing the personal thoughts of his comrades, so it is necessary to use the intimate pronoun "thee." Secondly, the men have taken a step down in their status. They have shown their weakness and have given in to a woman, rather as the way a man drops on one knee when he proposes to a woman. Since each has fallen in love, they have committed perjury and broken their contract. Longaville exclaims, "Am I the first that have been perjured so" (Shakespeare, [1996], p. 111). Berowne responds with "I could put thee in comfort, not by two that I know." He uses "thee" for both because Longaville has communicated something intimate and because he has taken a step down in his status relative to steadfast Berowne by committing perjury. This change in pronoun use is merely transient and part of the moment and situation. After the king reproves both Longaville and Dumaine for falling in love, Berowne addresses the king using "thee" because the king has also fallen in love. He is now equally to be condescended to as both Longaville and Dumaine. This change in pronouns stresses the fact that the king is now no longer so positioned that he can reprove anyone for faithlessness to their oath. Berowne says, "Ah, good my liege, I pray thee pardon me. Good heart, what grace hast thou to reprove these worms for loving, that are most in love?" (Shakespeare, 1992, p. 119).

To Express Fine Shades of Feeling, Reciprocated and Not Reciprocated

The second use of "thee" as a positioning tool is in matters of love. If one person uses "thee" but the other responds with "you," the second speaker expresses the fact that he or she does feel that there is an intimate relationship between them, a relation to which the first speaker's "thee" tends to push them. Shakespeare uses this comically. Armando expresses his feelings and assessments of the relation by saying to Jaquenetta, "I love *thee*." She sarcastically responds "So I heard *you* say" (Shakespeare, 1992, p. 35). The continuous exchange of "you" and "thee" between Jaquenetta and Armando shows the difference in feelings of intimacy that they hold towards one another. There is one instance of a conversation between the king and the princess in which they consistently address each other as "you" (Shakespeare, 1992, pp. 51–53). However, at the end of the conversation the king changes his pronoun use to "thee," showing a change in his view of their relationship as now more intimate. Here one can see a shift in position proposed and refused.

One comical conversation occurs between Berowne and the princess posing as Rosaline. Berowne says, "White-handed mistress, one sweet word with thee," starting off the conversation in an intimate tone (Shakespeare, 1992, p. 167). She rebukes him by saying "Honey, milk, and sugar—there is three." Her cold and sarcastic rebuttal causes Berowne to change his use of pronouns to the formal "you," and he responds with, "Nay then, two treys, an if you grow so nice" (Shakespeare, 1992, p. 167). Again we have a short stretch of dialogue illustrative of the dynamics of positioning.

Within all these conversational exchanges, the women maintain their stand as beings of superior will. They do not lower themselves into a more intimate conversation with the men. Instead they caustically rebut the men's remarks and take the stand of independent women, a stand presented by contemporary feminists as both radical and contemporary. In this play, the males woo the women using "thee" a greater number of times than the women use "thee" in return. This inequality of exchange in pronouns also suggests that the women of the play are refusing to accept either intimacy or an inferior status, the two roles for which the "T" form of the second person singular was the standard expression. In terms of positioning theory they are simultaneously refusing both the positions of dependency that the men's use of "thee" invites them to collude in.

CONCLUSION

In conclusion, the analysis of the uses of "thee" and "you" has shown that the women in Shakespeare's play are taking a stand against the positioning immanent in the uses of the pronouns. "You" is used between both the men and the women expressing equality of status between persons of the opposite sex when they are of the same social position. Secondly, the women use the pronouns sarcastically to take a stand, resisting positioning. They use the "you" form to show that they do not have the same feelings of love for the men as the men have expressed by moving to the use of "thee" as the pronoun of intimacy.

However, since the seventeenth century "thee" has become virtually extinct, surviving only in some highly specialized religious language, and in the speech of some Quakers. The loss of these two forms of the second person suggests that one's status has become of less importance in modern society. Women have found equal status with men. But the loss of "thee" occurred in the seventeenth century. It cannot be that contemporary changes in the status of men and women explains the earlier change. Brown and Gilman (1960, p. 264) argue that "the reciprocal solidarity semantic has grown with social mobility and an equalitarian ideology." However there are other possible explanations (cf. Mühlhäusler & Harré, 1991).

Finally, this analysis of the uses of "thee" and "you" has supported Brown and Gilman's claim that "thee" is used for intimacy and lower status and "you" is used in instances of formality and the expression of status. We have shown that in addition to the uses Brown and Gillman have pointed out, "thee" and "you" had an important role in the tactics of resisting positioning and were so used by the women.

REFERENCES

Brown, R., & Gillman, A. (1960). "The pronouns of power and solidarity." In Thomas Sebiok (Ed.), *Style in language*. Cambridge, MA: M.I.T. Press.

Mühlhäusler, P., & Harré, R. (1991). *Pronouns and people*. Oxford: Blackwell.

Shakespeare, William. (1996). *Love's Labours Lost*. New York: Washington Square Press.

Van Langenhove, L., & Harré, R. (1999). *Positioning*. Oxford: Blackwell.

CHAPTER 12

Positioning and Postcolonial Apologizing In Australia

Lucinda Aberdeen

In 1999, I participated in a conference, *Unmasking Whiteness: Race Relations and Reconciliation*, in Brisbane, Australia. Formally the purpose of the conference was "to provide a national forum for the presentation and discussion of provocative new research findings and methodologies, and to promote a dialogue on the future directions of race relations and reconciliation" (Mackay, 1999, p. 3). Its particular focus was "on providing critical and analytical understandings on how whiteness is socially constructed and how it underpins racial inequality in Australian society" (Mackay, 1999, p. 4).

The conference's opening ceremony incorporated a welcome to the delegates by local indigenous elders as the traditional owners of the area where the conference was held. The plenary session that followed involved a panel of indigenous Australians[1] recalling their personal experiences of racist abuse. These were painful memories for those telling them and distressing to those listening as was evident by the visible distress amongst a number of speakers and delegates.

During the question time that followed, a Anglo-Australian[2] delegate rose to her feet from the audience where I was seated myself. As I recall, she indicated that she wanted to offer an apology to the panel members for the hardships to which they had been subjected at the hands of non-indigenous Australians. However, she asked first if she could be shown "the indigenous way of apologizing" in order, as she indicated, to offer an apology in a culturally appropriate manner. The indigenous Australian chairing the session, who was also one of the conference organizers, responded sharply "You want us to give you that too?" The delegate said nothing further and sat down. The chair elaborated her views that the delegate's request was evidence of the ongoing historical appropriation of indigenous culture by European colonizers, in this case from the privileged vantage point of academia.

Some of the delegates with whom I spoke after the session found this interchange disquieting, as did I. Others expressed outrage at what they perceived to be an injustice. Was not the delegate trying to observe the very conventions that colonization and its accomplice, racism, had ignored or otherwise violated? The question remained a troubling one for delegates ostensibly committed to reconciliation between indigenous and non-indigenous Australians.

The perplexing nature of this interchange led me to question further both the conditions that made it possible and how it might have been conducted otherwise. That is, how might a more productive postcolonial dialogue over justice and difference, between indigenous and non-indigenous Australians, possibly occur?

To theorize the conditions and discursive enactments of this particular interchange, I sought for a microsociological perspective enabling the detailed analysis of small-group interactions yet capable of articulating these with wider sociohistorical processes and significations. Two perspectives, namely the sociology of apology and reconciliation (Tavuchis, 1991) and positioning theory (Harré & Van Langenhove, 1999), seemed particularly appropriate for this purpose. It is the analysis of the aforementioned interchange in the light of these two approaches that constitutes the central focus of this discussion. However, before proceeding it is useful at this point to consider what these two perspectives offer to an analysis such as this.

Tavuchis' analysis defines apology as "essentially a speech act that seeks forgiveness, that is, recertification of bona fide membership and unquestioned inclusion within a moral order" (1991, p. 27). He argues that an apology is paradoxical in that it is primarily a discursive gesture that cannot undo that which has been wrongfully done to another or others. Yet it is powerful as it has the

capacity to effectively eradicate the consequences of the offense by evoking the unpredictable capacity of forgiveness . . . [and] is thus deeply implicated in the central human predicaments of transgression and reconciliation. (Tavuchis, 1991, p. viii)

Tavuchis conceptualizes the production of an apology as a three-phased moral equation. It commences with the naming of the offense as an identifiably apologizable action, followed by the apology, which expresses sorrow and regret and concludes with the response of the offended party (1991, p. 23). Failure in any of these phases results in failure to produce an apology. Moreover, any appeal by the speaker to forces beyond his or her influence effectively converts or subverts the apology to an account or excuse as it removes the moral dimension of accepting responsibility or answerability (1991, p. 19). Tavuchis concludes therefore that producing "a successful apology is a delicate and precarious transaction" (1991, p. vii). His analysis also highlights the vulnerability of those who attempt or offer an apology. When we apologize "we stand unarmed and exposed, relying in a manner of speaking on our moral nakedness to set things right" (1991, p. 18). In addition to analyzing interpersonal apologies, Tavuchis considers apologies of a collective nature where the speaker may represent a collectivity. One of these, the apology of one collectivity to another, which he terms the "Many to Many" (1991, p. 48) will be considered later.

In terms of positioning theory (Harré & Van Langenhove, 1999), the conference interchange can be seen as a social episode occurring within a local moral order within which the speakers are assigned rights, duties, and obligations to speak and act. In this perspective, people are positioned through conversation. Hence positioning is understood to be a discursive practice. Moreover, the process of assignment or positioning is dynamic and fluid in that speakers position and reposition themselves and others in diverse ways that may embrace, resist, subvert, or acquiesce to an assignment. Harré and Van Langenhove (1999) argue that the conceptual and methodological essence of positioning theory is found in the positioning triangle. This consists of a mutually determining triad comprising the speakers' positions, the speech acts consisting of what the speakers say and do, and the story line or "conversational history and the sequence of things already been said" (Harré & Van Langenhove, 1999, p. 6). Each of these will be considered in this analysis but in order to provide a sense of the context informing the conference interchange, it is convenient to consider the story line first here.

THE POSTCOLONIAL STORY LINE

Public discussions about the nature and purpose of institutional or collective apologies to indigenous Australians, two centuries after British colonialization, had already been prevalent for several years prior to the *Unmasking Whiteness: Race Relations and Reconciliation* conference. These discussions were largely triggered by events that unfolded at an inaugural national convention of the Council for Aboriginal Reconciliation held in Melbourne in May 1997. The Council had been formed in 1991 as a result of the bipartisan support of the Australian Federal Parliament to the final recommendation of the Royal Commission into Aboriginal Deaths in Custody in Australia (1991) to introduce a process of reconciliation between indigenous and non-indigenous Australians. This process was to be directed and guided by the Council for Aboriginal Reconciliation over a period of ten years concluding in 2001, the time of Australia's centenary of federation as a nation. Supporters of this state-sponsored reconciliation process came to see it as an opportunity to symbolically expunge the shame and guilt associated with the nation's racist foundations (Moran, 1998). The manner in which such a process was to occur, however, remained subject to differing interpretations. As Augoustinos and Penny have noted:

The introduction of a relatively unfamiliar and nebulous concept of "reconciliation" into Australian public discourse resulted in widespread debate regarding the precise ways in which reconciliation is to be defined and implemented as social policy. (2001, p. 4.2)

The Reconciliation Convention was attended by some 1800 delegates under the theme "Renewal of the Nation." It coincided with the release of the report of the National Inquiry by the Human Rights and Equal Opportunities Commission (HREOC) into the Separation of Aboriginal and Torres Strait Islander Children from their Families, *Bringing Them Home* (1997). Among the report's 54 recommendations was a call for a formal apology from those responsible for forced removals of indigenous children and the violation of their human rights, which constituted genocide and resulted in the "Stolen Generations." Those called upon to apologize were the federal and state Australian parliaments, churches, police forces, and nongovernment agencies.

In an address he made during the convention's opening ceremony, the Australian prime minister, John Howard, did not, however, offer a national apology to indigenous Australians for past injustices resulting from state policies and practices. He argued that this was not possible because current generations of Australians were not responsible for the practices of their forebears in Australia. This argument would have had considerable force had the issue been one of a personal apology for an individual wrongdoing, yet this was not the type of apology the occasion required. Nevertheless, the prime minister offered an expression of personal sorrow. His decision not to offer a collective apology for the nation was met with immediate disapproval and contempt by many of the assembled delegates, a response that I observed personally. Moreover, it "conflicted significantly with the views of indigenous leaders, who viewed an apology as *essential* to the reconciliation process" (Augoustinos & Penny, 2001, p. 4.3).[3] In a similar vein, Tavuchis notes that "the major structural requirement and ultimate task of collective apologetic speech is to put things on record, to document a prelude to reconciliation' (1991, p. 109).

Ensuing criticism of the Australian prime minister's position argued, in part, that he had conflated the nature of private and public apology (see Cunneen & Libesman, 2000; Grace, 2001; Gooder & Jacobs, 2000; and Power, 2000). Characteristically a private or interpersonal apology is offered by one individual to another in search of forgiveness for personal wrongdoing. Tavuchis (1991) argues that expression of sorrow is central to an interpersonal apology and its production by demonstrating convincingly that such an apology "realizes its potential through sorrow and remorse" (1991, p. 109). Prime Minister Howard did offer an expression of personal sorrow. However, he qualified this to argue that neither he nor the current generations of Australians whom he represented could accept responsibility for that which he expressed sorrow, as it was not caused by their personal wrongdoing. His utterance of regret therefore did not aim to seek forgiveness and could not of itself constitute a personal apology.

The position taken by John Howard meant that politically he chose not to accept responsibility nor answerability as head of the Australian government for previous state practices and policies, the actions of those who implemented them, nor their impacts on indigenous Australians. Other non-indigenous Australians, however, desired that he offer a national or public institutional apology to unburden the shame and guilt arising from the revelations of the injustices done to indigenous Australians (Gooder & Jacobs, 2000). They sought "an affirmation of moral responsibility, in the most public of forums" (Tavuchis 1991, p. 107). The force of such a collective apology, Tavuchis argues, "rests on its corroborative functions; in publicly acknowledging the fact of violation, accepting or fixing responsibility, and implicitly or explicitly promising that similar acts will not be repeated in future" (1991, p. 108). Gooder and Jacobs have named those Australians seeking an acceptance and fixing of responsibility through a collective apology, "the sorry people."

... the call for an apology, and the failure of the Federal Government to deliver a "proper" version of this apology, has also brought together a large number of settler Australians in a collective expression of sympathy towards Aborigines and Torres Strait Islanders. This is the group we dub the "sorry people." (2000, p. 232)

The concerns of the sorry people, fueled in part by debates regarding proposed amendments to federal native title legislation, were apparent when the first National Sorry Day, recommended by the *Bringing Them Home* report, was held in May 1998. This event saw the collective outpouring of personal apologies by non-indigenous Australians. Many thousands signed virtual and real Sorry Books to register their sorrow. The *Unmasking Whiteness* Conference was held almost twelve months after the first National Sorry Day.

AN ANALYSIS OF THE CONFERENCE INTERCHANGE

Having traced the story line so far, it is necessary to consider and analyze both the positions of the speakers and their speech acts in relation to the story line in order to understand the positioning triangle at work. In the language of positioning theory, first order positioning is the position in which a speaker situates him or herself or is situated by others in a conversation. Second order positioning refers to the repositioning of speakers through the challenges of other speakers involved who do not accept the first order positioning. The first speaker in this episode, the Anglo-Australian delegate, initially positioned herself as a "sorry person" whose duties and rights included apologizing to victims of Australian racism. This resonated implicitly with the position of sorry people in that it presupposed apology was both necessary as a "conventional expression of courtesy ... and an act of healing" (LeCouteur, 2001, p. 152) in the absence of an official apology from the Australian polity.

The speaker's pre-apology request, to be shown the "indigenous way of apologizing," can be seen as a performative utterance or speech act that positioned her as a serious and respectful student of indigenous social customs. This was consistent with her story line and served to position the speaker as someone who was culturally sensitive. By her initial positioning, the speaker also located herself as a member of a moral community committed to reconciliation between indigenous and other Australians and thereby affirmed her story line. In this manner her position, speech act, and story line are mutually determining.

However, in terms of Tavuchis's analysis of apology and reconciliation, the speaker's initial positioning and her speech act point to a number of potential flaws in her proposed apology. First, in her position as a sorry person she could not successfully produce an interpersonal apology or a collective apology. To successfully produce the former apology a speaker needs, in Tavuchis' analysis, to be able to unconditionally accept responsibility for the wrongdoing for which she wishes to apologize. The delegate, however, was not personally responsible for the racism that caused the conference panel members grief and hardship, and she could not therefore apologize personally for that which she had not personally caused. In short she could not offer the type of apology from the individual to the collectivity that Tavuchis terms as "One to Many" (1991, p. 48). Furthermore, as the speaker did not represent the institutions whose practices harmed the conference panel members she could not in her position offer them an effective collective or institutional apology from one collectivity to another: "Many to Many" (Tavuchis, 1991, p. 48). Put succinctly, she had no responsibility for the policies and practices of such institutions. At best she could only attempt to represent an "imagined community" (Anderson, 1991) of the beneficiaries of British settler-colonialism who wished to repudiate the actions of their governments and forebears. Therefore the expression of her own regret and sorrow for the suffering experienced by the panel members was not itself a sufficient condition to produce a successful apology.

Second, even if the speaker could have been held responsible for the racism recalled at the conference as an individual or institutional representative, her speech act seeking advice on the "indigenous way of apologizing" compromised any such responsibility. Rather than assuming vicarious responsibility for the wrongdoing she had inflicted on the panel members, the speaker called for the help of one of the victims of racism to assist her in producing what was to be an apology. In this sense, was asking the offended party to protect her from the vulnerability to which her assumed culpability exposed her. However, by appealing in this manner, the speaker diminished the moral dimension of her accepting responsibility and subverted a possible apology.

Returning to positioning theory, the response of the second speaker chairing the conference session indicates that the perlocutionary force of the first speaker's preapology request was to antagonize the second speaker. Her ensuing speech act precluded the right of the first speaker to offer an apology. The chair therefore challenged the first speaker's self-positioning as a sorry person in search of a reconciled postcolonial moral order of indigenous and non-indigenous peoples. Instead she was repositioned in the position of an exploitative Anglo-Australian academic and in Tavuchis's analysis could not then apologize as she had failed to convince the second speaker of her "worthiness" (Tavuchis, 1991, p. 22) to do so. In this process, the second speaker thereby positioned herself as indigenous Australian with a story line that recalls the dispossession of indigenous Australians resulting from colonization.

Tavuchis observes that in these kinds of "public confrontations that the negative implications of apologies are likely to manifest themselves" (1991, p. 123). Elucidating the dynamics of this social episode, through both positioning theory and Tavuchis's work, however, enables questions to be raised as to how it might have unfolded differently to result in a peaceable rather than antagonistic outcome. He notes "that until there is mutually understood response to a call (emanating from the offender, offended or interested third party), there is no occasion for an apology" (1991, p. 25). It was not established at the conference session whether the panel participants expected an apology. Nor was the more fundamental issue of what these participants expected, if anything, from sorry people. To this end, no mutual understanding had been established. Had the issue of whether an apology was sought after or desired by those positioned as members of marginalized minorities been determined, the social episode may not have unfolded as a confrontation. In terms of positioning theory the rights, duty, and obligations assigned to the position of a sorry person would not have been exercised without prior engagement.

Given the social episode analyzed here, it is no surprise that producing a successful apology remains an "extraordinary and unpredictable achievement" (Tavuchis, 1991, p. 27). Tavuchis himself identifies "the conditions under which in-groups and out-groups (or their members) apologize to each other as members of *different* moral communities" (1991, p. 123) as one of a number of areas in need of further inquiry. In this difficult and confusing area of postcolonial apologizing, positioning theory may serve as a useful tool in identifying, untangling, and anticipating the elements involved in such exchanges at the micro-social level.

NOTES

1. Terminology referring to the indigenous peoples of Australia is contested and problematic owing to its connections with British colonization. The term "indigenous Australian" has been used here to include Aboriginal and Torres Strait Islander peoples generally. At the same time, it is recognized that there is a preference among some indigenous people to use regional terms from indigenous languages or clan names for specific communities with which they identify. This may well have been the case with the panel members and others participating in the conference.

2. Terminology referring to Anglo-Australians is also problematic as it indiscriminately groups together descendants of convicts and settlers with more recent waves of European immigrants. The author is herself a fifth generation Australian of Scottish convict and English and Irish settler heritage.

3. Among indigenous Australians more generally, attitudes toward a national apology specifically and toward reconciliation remained varied (see, for example, Van den Berg, 2002).

REFERENCES

Anderson, B. (1991). *Imagined community: Reflections on the origins and spread of nationalism.* 2nd ed. Verso: London.

Augoustinos, M., LeCouteur, A., & Soyland, J. (2002). Self-sufficient arguments in political rhetoric: Constructing reconciliation and apologizing to the Stolen Generations, *Discourse and Society,* 13 (1): 105–142.

Augoustinos, M., & Penny, S. L. (2001). Reconciliation: The genesis of a new social representation. *Papers on social representation,* 10 4.1–4.18 [http://www.swp.uni-linz.ac.at/psr.htm]

Cunneen, C., & Libesman, T. (2000). An apology for expressing regret? *Meanjin.* 1: 145–154.

Gooder, H., & Jacobs, J. M. (2000). "On the border of the unsayable": The apology in postcolonizing Australia. *Interventions,* 2 (2): 229–247.

Grace, D. (2001). The question of an apology: Reconciliation and civility. *Australian Human Rights Journal,* 7 (1) 77–90.

Harré, R., & Van Langenhove, L. (1999). *Positioning theory: Moral context of intentional behaviour.* Blackwell: Oxford.

Human Rights and Equal Opportunities Commission. (1997). *Bringing them home: National inquiry into the separation of Aboriginal and Torres Strait Islander children from their families.* Canberra: Australian Government Publishing Service.

LeCouteur, A. (2001). On saying "sorry": Repertoires of apology to Australia's Stolen Generations. In A. McHoul & M. Rapley (Eds.), *How to analyze talk in institutional settings: A casebook of methods.* London: Continuum.

Mackay, B. (Ed.). (1999). *Unmasking whiteness: Race relations and reconciliation.* Nathan, Australia: Griffith University.

Moran, A. (1998). Aboriginal reconciliation: Transformations in settler nationalism. *The Reconciliation Issue, Melbourne Journal of Politics,* 25: 101–131.

Power, M. (2000). Reconciliation, restoration and guilt: The politics of apologies. *Media International Australia Incorporating Culture and Policy,* 95, May: 199–205.

Royal Commission into Aboriginal Deaths in Custody in Australia. (1991). *National Report,* 5 volumes. Canberra: Australian Government Publishing Service.

Tavuchis, N. (1991). *Mea culpa: A sociology of apology and reconciliation.* Stanford, California: Stanford University Press.

Van den Berg, R. (2002). *Nyoongar people of Australia: Perspectives on racism and multiculturalism.* Leiden: Brill.

CHAPTER 13

Applying Positioning Principles to a Theory of Collective Identity

Donald M. Taylor, Evelyne Bougie, and Julie Caouette

In this chapter we will outline a theory of the "self" (Taylor, 1997, 2002). One central tenant of the theory is that while personal identity is the experienced core of the self, collective identity is the necessary context that allows an individual to develop a healthy sense of self. By a healthy self we refer to one that orients the individual to have effective interaction with his or her social environment. The articulation of a personal identity requires commerce with one's collective identity whereby collective identity serves the role of a stable template against which the individual can articulate a personal identity. This process requires the individual to engage in some form of internal psychological dialogue, to borrow terminology from positioning theory (Harré & Van Langenhove, 1999a).

Our proposed theory of "self" has never adequately explicated the precise nature of this critical dialogue between the two levels of identity. Positioning theory may well be a vehicle that allows for a richer understanding of the process. That is, by viewing personal identity as involving a variety of positionings vis-à-vis collective identity, we may come to better understand the actual process the individual engages while formulating a healthy sense of personal identity.

We begin the chapter then with an overview of our theory of "self." Next we focus on those aspects of positioning theory that might usefully be applied to our theory. In the next section we describe how the identity process might operate from a positioning theory perspective. Finally, in the last section we apply our analysis to individuals who belong to groups that served as the springboard of our theory of "self" initially: society's most disadvantaged groups, including Aboriginal people, and African Americans.

TOWARD A THEORY OF "SELF"

The focus of the present theory of "self" is the relatively stable mental template that each of us has that forms the backdrop or self-context for having effective commerce with our social environment: the self-concept. Our view of the self-concept makes two fundamental distinctions. The first contrasts identity with esteem. This is a fundamental distinction made by many self theorists (e.g., Baumeister, 1997; Ervin & Stryker, 2001) and is indeed captured in the very definition of "self-concept." For example, in their basic social psychology textbook, Alcock, Carment and Sadava (2001, p. 68) define the self-concept as "the sum of *feelings, beliefs* and *impressions* that individuals have of themselves." Indeed so many theorists have made this distinction that a variety of interchangeable terms have evolved. For example, we employ the term "identity," Alcock and colleagues (2001) prefer the terms *beliefs* and *impressions*, and still others have used labels such as *description* and *cognition*. Similarly, our use of "esteem" is equivalent to terms such as *feelings, affect,* and *emotion*. In essence our concept of identity responds to the question, "who am I," whereas esteem deals with the question, "am I worthy"?

The second dimension contrasts personal aspects of the self with those that are collective. This distinction was first introduced by social identity theorists (Tajfel, 1978; Tajfel & Turner, 1979) and has gained widespread application. Applying these two dimensions to our theory we arrive at a two-dimensional diagram that generates four distinct components to the self (see Figure 13.1).

We need to underscore that our analysis of the self-concept depicted in Figure 13.1 does not in and of itself offer new insights into the self. The four components, distinguishing between identity and esteem on the one hand, and personal and collective identity on the other, are, as we have already noted, distinctions that have been made previously and more eloquently by a number of other self-theorists (see Baumeister, 1998, for a review). We review

Figure 13.1
Four Aspects of the Self-Concept

	Identity	**Esteem**
Personal	Personal Identity	Personal (Self) Esteem
Collective	Collective Identity	Collective Esteem

the four components here because they form the basic building blocks that will then allow us to make a series of novel predictions about the self-concept.

From Figure 13.1, then, we can see that by crossing the two dimensions of the self-concept (identity vs. esteem by personal vs. collective) we can distinguish four aspects of the self-concept. Each of these requires elaboration. The first quadrant points to the personal identity elements of the self-concept. Here we are referring to personal characteristics that do not evaluate, but rather describe who I am. So, I am an intelligent, warm, athletic, and somewhat irresponsible person. These are not merely characteristics but implied values, goals, or end-states that define who I am (Dweck, 1999; Hoyle, Kernis, Leary, & Baldwin, 1999b). That is, the personal self orients us to act on the environment so as to be consistent with values and goals defined by the personal self. So, by identifying myself as intelligent I see myself as someone whose goals in life, including the life's work I aspire to, will be an extension of the meaning associated with intelligence. The "intelligent" component of my personal identity does not specify precisely which goals I set for myself, nor does it guarantee me any success at achieving them. What it does do is provide me with a sense of general orientation and motivation to achieve them. Similarly, "warm" implies goals I have for my interpersonal relationships and "athletic" orients me to physical activity. Again, it may not specify which sport I take up, or if I will be any good at the sport, but it does orient and motivate me toward sporting activity.

The second quadrant refers to my self-esteem in terms of the personal aspects of my self-concept. Here the focus is not on what my personal characteristics are, but rather how I evaluate my characteristics. Again, in order to make an evaluation of myself I will need to compare myself with others in terms of the characteristic in question. My own group, or relevant subgroups of my own group, are the most likely available reference points for such an evaluation. That is, the most readily available persons for social comparison are members of one's own immediate in-group, and this is exacerbated by our tendency to compare with similar others (Festinger, 1954).

It is important here to underscore the genuine difference between personal identity and personal (self) esteem. My personal identity may include the characteristics "intelligent" and "athletic." It might be concluded that my personal (self) esteem must automatically be extremely positive. There are two important reasons for not immediately inferring esteem from identity. First, there is the question of the extent to which I am successfully actualizing the characteristic in question. Intelligence may be a positively valued attribute, but I might not be living up to the "intelligent" component of my personal identity. Secondly, and more subtly, even if I am successfully actualizing my personal identity, a positive personal esteem is not guaranteed. For example, while it is generally true that in North American culture intelligence and athleticism are valued, such is not necessarily the case. Suppose the reference group I use to check on how my personal identity is evaluated downgrades people with these characteristics. Certain sub-groups of high school students may judge me to be "nerdy," and "jocks" may have a negative reputation. The point is that knowing my personal identity does not automatically indicate my personal (self) esteem. I need to make a separate inquiry, or comparison with my reference group, to obtain evaluative feedback.

Quadrant three focuses on descriptive or identity aspects of my collective self-concept. Included here are characteristics I share with other members of my group. In the case of my ethnic group this might include a shared history, shared values, shared goals, and a shared set of behaviors including, for example, the language we speak. Personality characteristics may also be involved to the extent that they are ones deemed to be applicable to most, if not all, members of my group. My ethnic group may perceive itself to be hardworking or intelligent. In this case these personality characteristics would be included as part of my collective identity because these are characteristics that apply to all members of my group.

Finally, quadrant four refers to self-esteem that arises from group membership, collective self-esteem (Luhtanen & Crocker, 1992). In the case of personal self-esteem the individual compares his or herself to other ingroup members. In the case of collective self-esteem the individual compares his or her group with other groups. The result of the comparison indirectly determines its evaluative impact on the individual. I say indirectly because when I compare my own group to another group, the resulting comparison does not refer to me personally, but to my group as a whole. However, I am a member of my group; I am by extension and inclusion impacted by the intergroup comparison. When a sports team wins the championship it has a positive effect on the players, their fans, and indeed at times the entire nation. Didn't Canada win the gold medal for both men and women's ice hockey at the 2002 winter Olympic Games? We Canadians made it an intergroup comparison—our nation against the world—and we won, thereby allowing every Canadian to bask in reflected glory. Returning to our focus, members of a disadvantaged minority group may accumulate feedback that leads to low collective self-esteem every time they make comparisons of their group with advantaged outgroups. Indeed, one way members of disadvantaged groups protect their self-esteem is avoiding comparisons with high-status outgroups (see Crocker & Major, 1989). But when circumstances force an individual disadvantaged group member to make such an intergroup comparison, the result is a blow to collective esteem.

The self-concept, then, is comprised of four components that become integrated to form the individual's complete mental image of him or herself. The integration of the four components can provide insight into the psychological complexity the individual might have to cope with. For example, someone might have high personal self-esteem, but his or her membership in a disadvantaged minority group might mean that he or she also has a low collective self-esteem. In previewing the next section we speculate that it would be even more destructive for a person to have an *unclear*, as compared to a negative, collective identity. By unclear we refer to a collective identity that does not have a set of clearly defined values, goals, and norms, nor a clearly defined set of strategies for their achievement. We might wonder whether for a person with an unclear collective identity it would even be possible to have a healthy identity at the personal level.

THE PRIMACY OF COLLECTIVE IDENTITY

Having described the four basic building blocks of a self-concept, we are in a position to offer a theoretical proposition that forms the essence of our argument in terms of understanding society's most disadvantaged. We propose that a person's collective identity is the most important and psychologically primary component to the self-concept. Personal identity involves the individual comparing him or herself with members of his or her own group in order to determine what characteristics make him or her unique. Similarly, personal self-esteem requires that the individual make evaluative comparisons with his or her own group. How, then, can an individual possibly develop personal identity and personal self-esteem in the absence of a clearly defined group (collective) identity? Without a collective identity, the individual has no clearly established template against which to articulate a personal identity or personal self-esteem. Thus, while all four components of the self-concept are crucial, collective identity takes psychological precedence.

What we are proposing runs counter to most current thinking about the "self." The preponderance of theoretical analyses focus attention on the individual and her or his personal identity and esteem (see Baumeister, 1998, for a review). We are arguing explicitly that this emphasis is counterproductive. Logically, it is impossible to form a personal identity without a collective identity to serve as a reference point. This makes collective identity the key component to the self-concept. And this primacy has profound implications. By way of illustration we can refer to a simplistic example. A seven-foot man will no doubt have height as an important component of his personal identity. The focus on height is only relevant because it stands out relative to the majority of other men and to a built environment that is awkward for a seven-foot person.

More profound aspects of personal identity are similarly derived. Free will, the belief that individuals make choices and are responsible for those choices, is as central a belief as there is. Presumably, an individual's choices in life are extensions of personal identity. But personal identity can only be articulated against the backdrop of a clearly defined collective identity, which specifies values, goals, norms, and strategies for successful negotiation.

If collective identity is psychologically primary to personal identity, so too is personal identity a necessary precursor to personal esteem. It is impossible to develop personal esteem without a personal identity because without identity there would be no concrete characteristics upon which to obtain evaluative feedback.

Thus, collective identity is rationally and psychologically primary, and therefore is the most important component of the self-concept. For groups that have a well-defined collective identity, attention naturally turns to personal identity and esteem. But when collective identity is compromised in any way, the entire self-concept is jeopardized. For most white mainstream North Americans it is difficult to relate to threats to collective identity, since there are no external forces or groups that are powerful enough to disrupt or dislocate mainstream collective identity. Mainstreamers then cannot appreciate the feeling of alienation associated with a threatened and unclear collective identity. Mainstreamers can only appreciate their cultural collective identity at a superficial level. For example when mainstreamers travel to a very different culture it often provokes a new appreciation, and affirmation, of their own cultural collective identity.

The primacy of collective identity and its relationship to the other three components of the self-concept are captured schematically in the following diagram (see Figure 13.2).

THE RELATIVE IMPORTANCE OF IDENTITY AND ESTEEM

We have placed special emphasis on identity in general, and collective identity in particular. In so doing we seem to be at odds with the current theoretical climate that focuses on self-esteem (see Owens, Stryker, & Goodman, 2001).

Figure 13.2
Relationship Between Collective Identity and the Self-Concept

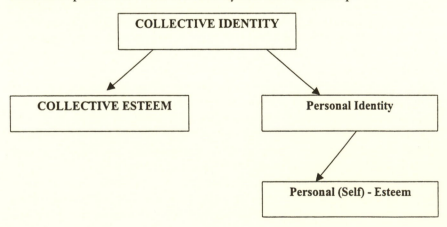

Indeed, virtually every difficulty that people face, be it academic under-achievement, problems with interpersonal relationships, or social violence, has been blamed on low self-esteem.

The following quote from a California state task force underscores the importance that society confers on the notion of high self-esteem: "Self-esteem might function as a social vaccine to inoculate individuals against the lures of crime, violence, substance abuse, teen pregnancy, child abuse, chronic welfare dependency and educational failure. The lack of self-esteem is central to most personal and social ills plaguing our state and nation" (1990, p. 4).

To be fair, social psychologists are coming to recognize that high self-esteem may have been an over simplistic antidote to all of society's ills. Indeed there is even some suggestion that certain forms of high self-esteem may be psychologically destructive (see Baumeister, 1998, for a review). Where an individual has an inflated self-esteem that is coupled with an esteem that is unstable or vulnerable, the psychological effects may be maladaptive with a particular penchant for violence. Coping with a less than extremely positive self-image may be a challenge, but it may be worse to entertain an extremely high opinion of yourself only to have the image shattered by any life event that challenges such a lofty view of the self.

Without wishing to discount the importance of self-esteem, we would like to redress the balance by developing a thorough appreciation for the second important dimension of the self-concept, identity.

CULTURAL COLLECTIVE IDENTITY

Since collective identity is so central to our analysis, an important clarification is necessary. We all belong to a variety of groups, ranging from our nation and cultural group to our occupational and leisure groups. As such we have a variety of collective identities we can, and do, call upon in the process of articulating a self-concept. But the one collective identity that takes on special significance when it comes to forming our self-concept is our cultural group. What makes our cultural collective identity so special is its pervasiveness. Culture specifies for its members the goals, values, norms, and behaviors for all of its members in all circumstances. My occupational collective identity may be operative in my work environment, and my leisure group may serve as the reference when I am playing ice hockey. But my cultural collective identity relates to every facet of my life, including work and leisure. My occupational and leisure collective identities have their specific demands, but they will be consistent with and subsumed under cultural demands. Simply, then, cultural collective identity is special because it is the one collective identity that pertains to all of life's domains.

The only other collective identity that may be as pervasive as culture is religious collective identity. For some people religion does serve as the template for every facet of their life. Indeed, for some, religion and culture are synonymous. Beyond culture, then, religion is the only collective identity that in some circumstances can have the breadth and depth of a cultural collective identity.

Summarizing our theoretical argument, then, we propose that cultural collective identity is the necessary backdrop for the self-concept to develop. Specifically, a clear cultural collective identity is necessary for the formation of personal identity, and a clear personal identity is needed for the development of personal (self) esteem.

A BRIEF REVIEW OF POSITIONING THEORY: FOCUS ON REFLEXIVE POSITIONING AND THE DIALOGICAL SELF

Before exploring how positioning theory can expand an analysis of identity processes as outlined in our theory of the "self," we need to briefly review the key elements of positioning theory (Harré & Van Langenhove, 1999a). We will place special emphasis on those aspects of positioning theory that are especially suited to our analysis of the "self."

At its most general level, positioning theory needs to be understood within a social constructionist perspective (Harré & Van Langenhove, 1999a). According to such a viewpoint, we can appreciate that our social world is not a fixed reality that needs to be uncovered, but rather is more fluid in that it is based on a set of shared meanings between individuals. Specifically, positioning theory provides a framework that allows for the exploration of how people negotiate such shared meanings. The appropriate level of analysis according to a positioning framework needs to take place at the level of discourse. Through social interactions and conversations, people unveil who they are and what their social world is, and negotiate discursively these meanings.

The main underlying premise in positioning theory, then, is that people negotiate meanings about their selves and social world by strategically positioning themselves throughout a dialogue (Van Langenhove & Harré, 1999). Specifically, a position provides one with a set of rights and duties that supply meaning to one's act. Importantly for our analysis of the self, such positioning also reveals the nature of one's identity. A position closely resembles the concept of role, in that a role gives direction and meaning to the type of actions that one engages in (Harré & Slocum, ch. 8 in this book). However, the concept of position is different in that positions are ever shifting within a conversation, constantly and rapidly being renegotiated. A position is dynamic, whereas a role is static. For example, being a student or a professor entitles one to a variety of duties and rights that remain somewhat consistent from day to day. If I am a student, I will sit attentively in class, expect my professor to be more knowledgeable on certain topics than I am, and I will take notes. If I am a professor, I will engage in research and further my knowledge on topics relevant to the subject I teach and I will prepare my classes.

Knowing one's own roles helps to provide direction and meaning to one's actions. This becomes an important part of my identity, and others also have the ability to perceive who I am. Once roles are defined, one's actions can be placed in context and understood within a shared set of meanings. Roles, then, are a central feature of identity, but they tend to be relatively stable and static once their norms have been established.

In contrast, a position can shift throughout a conversation, where one person's position can be questioned or not by the other. One's identity and social world is being dynamically constructed through positioning. For example, this same student can come after class and ask the professor a thoughtful question, thus positioning him or herself as more knowledgeable. Depending on the evolution of the conversation, the professor might deny or accept such positioning of the student, and position him or herself vis-à-vis this student. Throughout the day, one will position oneself within such different attributes (as knowledgeable) under many different occasions.

Undeniably, one of the most important contributions of positioning theory to psychology is its focus on rapidly changing social interactions. As pointed out by Harré and Van Langenhove (1999b) psychologists unfortunately too rarely study the dynamic flux of social life. Positioning theory aims to address this shortcoming by exploring rapid and evolving social episodes, by analyzing the active negotiation of meanings people give to their actions through their positioning within their conversation.

We find this focus on the dynamics of social life to be intuitively appealing and consistent with recent trends in the conceptualization of the self (for a review, see Hoyle et al., 1999a). The self is now perceived as being dynamic and complex. One's identity is being actively constructed and is not composed of a single entity but has many facets that can interplay within different social episodes. As meanings are dynamically negotiated throughout conversation via positioning, one's identity is not fixed, but is constantly reconstructed.

By using the concept of "position" instead of "role" as the central organizing construct of social analysis, the focus of attention shifts from the more ritualistic and formal to the more dynamic and negotiable aspects of *interpersonal* as well as *intergroup* encounters (Tan & Moghaddam, 1999). Positioning not only involves the ongoing construction of "selves" as individuals, but also of "selves" as members or representatives of groups. For instance, in interacting with teammates, one can attempt to position him or herself as the leader of the team (interpersonal positioning), or one can attempt to position his or her team as being better than the other teams (intergroup positioning).

However, positioning also occurs in the *intrapersonal* domain: The term "reflexive positioning" has been proposed to refer to the process by which people position themselves privately in their, presumably subvocal, private discourse (Moghaddam, 1999). By private discourse we mean the private dialogues one has with oneself, both as the speaker and the conversant. One's appraisal of one's leadership qualities, one's private response to having been depicted by someone else as being a member of a denigrated team, or one's formulation of the event that one plans to tell a friend, are examples of reflexive positioning, or the ways in which people privately position themselves to themselves throughout the course of a day (Moghaddam, 1999).

The reflexive and dynamic nature of the self is what allows a person to be both the positioner and the one positioned at the same time. To borrow from James' (1948/1892) classic distinction between the I and the Me, it is the I (or the self as subject) that positions the Me (or the self as object) through observing and reporting on the actions of the Me. Furthermore, the I-self has access to many vantage points, allowing multiple interpretations of the same thoughts, behaviors, and events. It can thus be said that an internal dialogue is constantly taking place between the multiple positions that the I-self can take. Thus, a person who has just been promoted to the position of team captain overhears a myriad of voices as she anticipates how she will relay the event to her friends and family and imagines their individual responses. This is what is meant by "dialogical self," in which the I-self not only takes up different vantage points but also speaks with voices emanating from these various positions (Moghaddam, 1999).

The self is thus positioned interpersonally through the story lines that evolve in imaginary dialogues and conversations based on the multiple vantage points of oneself as well as a host of imaginary others. People are pervasively involved in imaginary social relationships with various imaginary beings, such as political leaders, film stars, sports heroes, spouses, and parents, to name a few (Moghaddam, 1999). Accordingly, our view of the self implies that one could very well be involved in this internal dialogue with the different aspects of one's self-concept. The next section will explore the idea that an intrapersonal dialogue could be taking place between the key elements of selfhood, that is, between collective and personal identities.

POSITIONING AND IDENTITY

Our theory of self posits that "personal identity" is what the individual experiences as the integrated and stable "me" that instigates commerce with the environment. We argue that articulating a personal identity requires a clearly defined collective identity, and thus the process by which a personal identity relates to collective identity is pivotal. Thus far, the relationship between the two levels of identity has been implicitly depicted as a fixed comparison process. Positioning theory provokes us to address the relationship in a more in-depth manner that allows for an appreciation of the complexity and fluidity of the relationship.

The fixed comparison process implied by our theory of self revolves around the individual using her or his cultural collective identity as a template against which to compare unique personal qualities and thereby formulating a clear personal identity. Knowing what dimensions are important, and where one is situated on that dimension, can only come from a cultural template that specifies what individual members of the culture should strive for. Viewed this way, the implication is that a cultural collective identity is a relatively fixed schema, and that straightforward comparisons are made between one's personal identity and the fixed collective identity. Clearly, the process is more fluid and dynamic than the relatively static process implied here, and this is precisely the emphasis that positioning theory offers.

Positioning theory would have us envisage a form of ongoing subvocal, private dialogue between a person's collective and personal identity. We would still argue that one's collective identity will remain relatively fixed and stable. We say relatively because cultures constantly evolve. However, more striking is the endurance of cultures, their stability over time, and their apparent resistance to change (Strauss, 1997). Indeed, members of any cultural group have been heard to voice amazement at how their own culture seems rooted in the past and seemingly in need of a make-over. Young people are especially prone to question and at times ridicule what they perceive to be outmoded cultural demands. "Get with the new millennium" is their urging. We would argue that it is precisely because cultural collective identity serves as the psychological backdrop against which the individual crafts a personal identity that the collective identity must remain relatively stable and clearly defined.

As much as collective identity requires stability, personal identity must be fluid and adaptive while remaining integrated throughout. It is at this juncture that positioning theory offers potential insights into the process of identity formation. Again we need to underscore that in order to allow for a more fluid personal identity it is important to have a stable collective identity. Imagine a collective identity vacuum, that is a collective identity that is devoid of human priorities or one that offers a confusing array of priorities. There would be little opportunity for a meaningful internal dialogue between personal and collective identity. The personal identity as one subvocal interlocutor would not even know how to orient, much less how to position the personal identity for an internal dialogue. Cultural collective identities provide the cues as to which dimensions should be addressed.

While cultures differ widely, there seems to be some consensus that there are at least two universal needs that motivate human behavior. In their simplest form they are to get along and to get ahead. More formally they have been referred to as communion and agency, love and status, intimacy and power, or social inclusion and social dominance (for a review see Wiggins, 1991). At the very least, then, every culture will spell out the appropriate goals and norms for achieving goals in these two fundamental domains. As such we might focus on cultural collective identities in the domains of intimacy and achievement as a means of exploring the role of positioning.

Family relations, friendships, and partners are important relationships when it comes to intimacy. Cultures differ widely with respect to the intimacy role for not merely the family, but indeed every member of the appropriate family. Even cultures within Western society vary widely in terms of the precise role of father, mother, son, and daughter, not to mention the variance in expectations associated with grandparents, aunts, uncles, and godparents. Each culture then has a template for the prototypic relationship, a model that all members socialized into the culture should strive for.

The child will be socialized into this template and come to internalize it as the collective identity template. Of course, the template will be more or less clearly articulated depending upon the clarity and consensus of standards within the culture itself, the extent to which the socializing agents themselves model the template, and the extent to which the child is socialized into the subtle double standards and informal versus formal standards that accompany the stated template.

It is against this internalized collective identity that an individual engages the process of developing a personal identity, the identity that guides his or her interface with the surrounding world. The obvious manner in which this vital identity process evolves leads us directly to social comparisons that the individual makes between his or her own thoughts, feelings, and behaviors, and those prescribed by the collective identity. Positioning theory offers a conceptual framework for understanding this fundamental identity process. We might imagine that the individual adopts an "if–then" (to borrow a terminology from Baldwin & Sinclair, 1996) form of internal dialogue where different imagined or "if" positions of the personal self are reflected upon cultural collective identity in order to rehearse the "then" consequences for the personal self. For example, a young person might take various positions with regard to marriage and imagine a variety of "if" positions and then, in dialogue against the collective identity template, work through the "then" implications for the personal self. What if I never get married and have no children; what if I marry early and begin a family immediately?

Without positioning theory we would be left to imagine that a young person would engage in a series of static comparisons of the personal self with the collective template and adjust the personal self to match the cultural template. However, much as the driver of an automobile constantly makes small wheel adjustments to follow even a seemingly straight road, so too the individual, through positioning, can make continual comparisons with the template in order to stay on the straight and narrow. Using a positioning theory perspective in the form of an "if–then" dialogue, we gain a better sense of the dynamic and more fluid nature of the identity process.

Let us by way of example consider a young person contemplating a relationship with a member of the opposite sex. A North American collective identity does not offer a single, inflexible template. Perhaps prior to the 1960s the template was relatively clear. Young people were encouraged to begin by "playing the field," where it was the cultural norm to engage in a variety of not very intimate relationships and thereby formulate some sense of what type of person one was comfortable with. "Going steady" might follow, where an exclusive relationship would emerge, but even here there was no sense that the person would end up marrying their "steady." Next, a life-long partner would be sought, and following a formal engagement the relationship would be culminated in marriage and, supposedly, the beginning of sexual relationships. Each of these stages was bounded by specified age ranges and economic security. Of course, there were informal cultural norms, especially surrounding levels of sexual intimacy, with an array of double standards to add subtlety to even this apparently clear cultural template.

Today's North American template is far more variable, offering numerous options with respect to intimate relations, thereby making the formation of a personal identity, all the more potentially fluid. In order to form a personal identity, an ongoing "if–then" dialogue will be essential. What is the feedback and rationale that various representatives of my culture will give me if I date two women at the same time? And if I do, is this the kind of person I want to be? By positioning myself in a variety of dating scenarios with respect to different subcultures within my broader culture I can contemplate my own reaction in terms of feelings and identity. Thus, I make full use of my cultural template to come to know myself better, that is, have a clearer sense of who I am.

The application of positioning theory is even more striking if we use as an example a newcomer to North America from, for example, Southeast Asia. Such a person has two, often competing, cultural templates; the heritage culture and mainstream culture. Our newcomer, who might be a young woman, does not have to literally engage in every interpersonal alternative to form a personal identity in the face of competing cultural demands. An ongoing "if–then" internal dialogue will be essential. What will happen if I date someone who is not from my culture, if I shun any thoughts of an arranged marriage, if I live with my boyfriend, are all fundamental questions that involve not merely social engineering but basic personal identity values. Each time our young woman positions herself with respect to each cultural template, she will be able to imagine the consequences and her own personal feelings about those consequences. How will my parents and extended family react? What would they say and how will it differ if I position myself in terms of the same issues with respect to my mainstream friends at school? Engaging in such a dialogue over a period of time, she may not always arrive at the same feeling and so the capacity to position repeatedly over time, and continually reposition, will ultimately allow our young woman to carve out a clearly defined personal identity for herself.

An important aspect of positioning for identity is purposely taking positions that are not options for the personal identity that the individual is seriously contemplating. That is, since the individual is engaging in a private dialogue, contemplating a position that would never be considered realistically has no real-life consequences. The exercise does, however, permit the individual to affirm what they are *not* in terms of personal identity. Knowing what one is not can be helpful in defining what one is.

Collective identities that serve as the positioning template for personal identity formation do more than specify end goals and values. In addition they spell out the appropriate route for achieving these end points, and they articulate the routes in some detail. By way of illustration we can turn our attention to the second basic human need that all cultures address, achievement. North American culture specifies what forms of achievement are valued, and there is general consensus around the status of various jobs and professions. Usually the achievement hierarchy is associated with corresponding social and monetary status. Indeed, as we see in the case of highly paid professional athletes, when there is a lack of correspondence between cultural status and monetary status, there is a public disgust.

North American culture not only spells out the end goals but also points to formal education and training as the routes to achieving those ends. Here is where positioning of the "if–then" form is essential for the definition of personal self. Choice of school, program, and subgroup of students to "hang" with, all involve an ongoing private dialogue as the individual attempts to define the self. For example, a student might position him or herself with respect to going to a very prestigious but expensive and demanding school as compared to one that is smaller, less prestigious, less expensive, and less demanding. By engaging this positioning process the individual comes to understand him or herself better in terms of personal identity by his or her internal reactions to the different positionings. Similarly, once at the chosen school our student might take a variety of internal and private positions with respect to a number of student subgroups, each with very different academic and social expectations. Again the private positioning process involving collective identity as the stable backdrop allows the student to internalize a clear personal identity.

The positioning process is also multilayered. For example, a student may position her or himself with respect to academic interest and from an interest perspective decide that personality and abnormal psychology are courses that should be chosen. And these choices would be entirely consistent with the person's personal identity. However, the same student addressing the same issue, but from a slightly different position, may lead to the recognition that, at a more fundamental level, courses such as statistics and research design are not to be dismissed. That is, while not seemingly central to personal identity, such courses may tap into a personal identity that is consistent with ultimately pursuing graduate studies at a prestigious university. The information about the role of research courses may not be immediately self-evident but would be a consistent informal message from those in the discipline. Thus, the individual may select these courses, not knowing their immediate relevance, but feeling the choice to be consistent with a personal identity that has at its core the pursuit of advanced study for a professional position.

POSITIONING AND PERSONAL (SELF) ESTEEM

To the extent that an individual has a clearly defined cultural collective identity, she or he can use positioning to carve a personal identity. But if cultural collective identity specifies a single cultural ideal then most people will feel less than adequate as they engage the personal identity process. That is, if there is but a single objective specified by a cultural template, then only the individual who has come closest to achieving the cultural ideal will feel personally satisfied. Everyone else will feel less than adequate. If intelligence is a simple cultural value, then only the smartest will have a fulfilling personal identity. But this presupposes that the cultural collective identity specifies one, and only one, route to achieving the desired end state. Fortunately, cultural collective identities specify varieties of ways to achieve a desirous end state in terms of relationships and achievement. Thus, any individual has at his or her disposal an array of cultural possibilities. Most individuals will gravitate to those routes that offer them the best chance of achieving their goal, thereby developing a personal identity that offers some opportunity to be relatively successful and as such form a relatively positive personal (self) esteem.

This proposition has been most clearly delineated by social identity theorists (Tajfel, 1978; Tajfel & Turner, 1979). They argue that, at a group level, individuals want to belong to a group that is distinctive from other groups. Moreover, they want the distinctive or unique characteristics of their group to be positively valued. We would argue that the same process operates at the individual level. Specifically, we would argue that the individual faces a constant tension between wanting to be unique on the one hand while being like others on the other. This tension has been captured at the group level by Brewer's concept of optimal distinctiveness (see 2001 for a review).

The result of this tension is that individuals will position their personal identities with respect to their cultural collective identity in a variety of ways. The positioning exercise will always be with a view to searching for the most rewarding position, the one that brings positive reinforcement and helps define the individual as unique and special. At the same time, however, the various positionings must be those that are allowable within the framework that is defined by the cultural collective identity.

POSITIONING AND SOCIETY'S MOST DISADVANTAGED GROUPS

There are two important steps to our theoretical analysis for the development of a healthy self. In our terms, a healthy self is one that is clearly defined so that it can effectively orient and guide the individual in her or his interaction with the social environment. Equally important is a level of esteem that motivates effective commerce with some confidence. The first necessary step for achieving such a healthy self is a clearly defined stable cultural collective identity. The second step involves capitalizing on a clear cultural collective identity so that an individual can engage in positioning in order to articulate a clear personal identity.

What about a group that does not have a cultural collective identity that is clear? No amount of positioning will allow an individual to engage the self-concept process if there is no interlocutor to provide feedback once a position has been taken. We focus here on the consequences of an unclear cultural collective identity because we believe that to be the problem that confronts society' most disadvantaged groups. Theorists who evoke a self-fulfilling prophecy (Merton, 1948; Rosenthal & Jacobson, 1968) depict disadvantaged group members as suffering from low self-esteem brought about by being socialized to believe that they are to blame for their disadvantage. While this process of internalizing negatively based stereotypes is psychologically debilitating, we believe that confronting a less than clearly defined cultural collective identity is far more damaging.

We take as our example the plight of Aboriginal people in North America. As a result of internal colonization, many Aboriginal communities confront a litany of social problems ranging from widespread academic underachievement and economic disadvantage to alcoholism, substance misuse, family violence, and a high rate of suicide among young people (Frideres, 1988). Aboriginal people face the challenge of juggling two cultures, mainstream culture on the one hand, and their heritage culture on the other. Until recently, the heritage culture of Aboriginal people was disrespected and systematically undermined. Recently, policies of empowerment have at least paid lip-service to the idea that Aboriginal people should have some control over their institutions with a view to having the heritage culture respected and represented through them.

Empowerment policies presuppose that Aboriginal people have an intact cultural collective identity that they can turn to if given the opportunity. But Aboriginal cultures have been absolutely decimated by European colonization such that there is very little left upon which to build a cultural identity. Indeed, the extent of the damage to heritage cultures is such that the cultural revival of aboriginal peoples has forced them to return to practices, values, symbols, and a way of life that were in operation prior to the arrival of Europeans. The reason for returning so far in the past in search of reclamation is that that was the last time that Aboriginal people had a clear cultural collective identity. Since then there has been no clear cultural template to turn to. Indeed, the heritage languages of most aboriginal groups in North America have been lost forever. Those that are still in use, such as Innuttitut, Cree, and Ojibway are struggling for survival (Foster, 1982; Priest, 1985).

Minority groups that constitute much of North American cultural diversity do not suffer from the same unclear cultural collective identity. Japanese, Korean, Italian, and Greek North Americans have to integrate their heritage culture with North American mainstream culture, and that is challenge enough. But at least their heritage culture is one that is intact and clearly defined. But for groups such as Aboriginal people who have had their cultural collective identity destroyed through internal colonization, or groups such as African Americans whose heritage cultural identity has been obliterated by slavery, there is no clear cultural collective identity to use as a point for positioning in order to articulate a personal identity.

Recovering a stolen cultural collective identity is not an easy task. Aboriginal people are attempting to recover their identity by harkening back to values and a way of life that predates European contact. Similarly, African Americans are reclaiming their African heritage, connecting to a place they have never been, but a place that, in the preslavery time, provided a clear cultural collective identity. The problem with restoring a historically based collective identity is that it is less than fully functional for the present. The role of cultural collective identity is not merely for group members to have a shared cultural history. As we have argued, it is a stable reference group against which the individual engages positioning processes on an ongoing basis in order to develop a healthy personal identity.

The major obstacle to articulating a functional cultural collective identity is that the forces that destroyed the heritage cultures of society's most disadvantaged continue to operate despite a more enlightened mainstream North American society. While overt discrimination is no longer normative, systemic discrimination continues unabated for two reasons. First, heritage cultures have been destroyed to the point that there remain no solid building blocks from which to build. The social fabric of nomadic Aboriginal life has been destroyed forever, as has the family and community structure of the descendents of African slaves. Second, mainstream North American culture is so powerful that it makes it virtually impossible to ignore it in the crafting of a unique collective identity. That is, it is difficult enough for members of disadvantaged groups to avoid becoming assimilated to North American mainstream culture. To imagine crafting a unique and modern cultural collective identity that is truly respected in the context of North American mainstream culture is a daunting challenge.

But this is precisely the challenge that needs to be met in order for the essential positioning processes to operate effectively. Assimilation robs people of their cultural identity, so it is not a psychologically realistic option. Carving a new cultural collective identity might be an overwhelming challenge, but at least we may have helped define the challenge.

REFERENCES

Alcock, J. E., Carment, D. W., & Sadava, S. W. (2001). *A textbook of social psychology* (5th ed.). Toronto: Prentice Hall.

Baldwin, M. W. & Sinclair, L. (1996). Self-esteem and "if. . .then" contingencies of interpersonal acceptance. *Journal of Personality and Social Psychology, 71*(6), 1130–1141.

Baumeister, R. F. (1997). Identity, self-concept, and self-esteem: The self lost and found. In R. Hogan, J. A. Johnson, & S. Briggs (Eds.). *Handbook of personality psychology* (pp. 681–710). San Diego: Academic Press.

Baumeister, R. F. (1998). The self. In D. T. Gilbert, S. T. Fiske, & G. Lindzey (Eds.), *The handbook of social psychology*, vol. 1 (4th ed., pp. 680–740). New York: McGraw-Hill.

Brewer, M. B. (2001). The social self: On being the same and different at the same time. In M. A. Hogg & D. Abrams (Eds.), *Intergroup relations: Essential readings* (pp. 245–253). Philadelphia: Psychology Press.

California task force to promote self-esteem and social responsibility. (1990). *Toward a state of self-esteem*. Sacramento: California State Department of Education.

Crocker, J., & Major, B. (1989). Social stigma and self-esteem: The self-protective properties of stigma. *Psychological Review*, 96(4), 608–630.

Dweck, C. S. (1999). *Self-theories: Their role in motivation, personality, and development.* Philadelphia: Psychology Press.

Ervin, L. H., & Stryker, S. (2001). Theorizing the relationship between self-esteem and identity. In T. J. Owens, S. Stryker, et al. (Eds.). *Extending self-esteem theory and research: Sociological and psychological currents* (pp. 29–55). New York: Cambridge University Press.

Festinger, L. (1954). A theory of social comparison processes. *Human Relations*, 7, 117–140.

Foster, M. (1982). Indigenous languages: Present and future. *Language and Society*, 7, 7–14.

Frideres, J. S. (1988). *Native people in Canada: Contemporary conflicts* (3rd ed.). Scarborough: Prentice-Hall.

Harré, R., & Van Langenhove, L. (Eds.) (1999a). *Positioning theory: Moral contexts of intentional action.* Boston: Blackwell.

Harré, R., & Van Langenhove, L. (1999b). The dynamics of social episodes. In R. Harré & L. Van Langenhove (Eds.), *Positioning theory: Moral contexts of intentional action* (pp. 1–13). Boston: Blackwell.

Harré, R., & Slocum, N. (2003). Disputes as complex social events: On the uses of positioning theory. In R. Harré & F. M. Moghaddam (Eds.), *The Self and Others* (pp. 123–136). Westport CT: Praeger.

Hoyle, R. H., Kernis, M. H., Leary, M. R., & Baldwin, M. W. (1999a). *Selfhood: Identity, esteem, regulation.* Boulder: Westview Press.

Hoyle, R. H., Kernis, M. H., Leary, M. R., & Baldwin, M. W. (1999b). The self-system. In R. H. Hoyle et al. *Selfhood: Identity, esteem, regulation* (pp. 11–28). Boulder: Westview Press.

James, W. (1948/1892). *Psychology.* Cleveland: World Publishing.

Luhtanen, R., & Crocker, J. (1992). A collective self-esteem scale: Self-evaluation of one's social identity. *Personality and Social Psychology Bulletin*, 18 (3), 302–318.

Merton, R. (1948). Self-fulfilling prophecy. *Antioch Review*, 8, 193–210.

Moghaddam, F. M. (1999). Reflexive positioning: Culture and private discourse. In R. Harré & L. Van Langenhove (Eds.), *Positioning theory: Moral contexts of intentional action* (pp. 74–86). Boston: Blackwell.

Owens, T. J., Stryker, S., & Goodman, N. (Eds.). (2001). *Extending self-esteem theory and research: Sociological and psychological currents.* New York: Cambridge University Press.

Priest, G. E. (1985). Aboriginal languages in Canada. *Language and Society*, 15, 13–19.

Rosenthal, R., & Jacobson, L. (1968). *Pygmalion in the classroom: Teacher expectation and pupils' intellectual development*. New York: Holt, Rinehart, and Winston.

Strauss, C. (1997). *A cognitive theory of cultural meaning*. Cambridge: Cambridge University Press.

Tajfel, H. (1978). *Differentiation between social groups: Studies in the social psychology of intergroup relations*. London: Academic Press.

Tajfel, H., & Turner, J. C. (1979). An integrative theory of intergroup conflict. In W. G. Austin & S. Worchel (Eds.), *The social psychology of intergroup relations* (pp. 33–47). Monterey, CA: Brooks/Cole.

Tan, S. L., & Moghaddam, F. M. (1999). Positioning in intergoup relations. In R. Harré & L. Van Langenhove (Eds.), *Positioning theory: Moral contexts of intentional action* (pp. 178–194). Boston: Blackwell.

Taylor, D. M. (1997). The quest for collective identity: The plight of disadvantaged ethnic minorities. *Canadian Psychology*, 38 (3), 174–190.

Taylor, D. M. (2002). *The quest for identity: From ethnic minorities to generation Xers*. New York: Praeger.

Van Langenhove, L., & Harré, R. (1999). Introducing positioning theory. In R. Harré & L. Van Langenhove (Eds.), *Positioning theory: Moral contexts of intentional action* (pp. 14–31). Boston: Blackwell.

Wiggins, J. S. (1991). Agency and communion as conceptual coordinates for the understanding and measurement of interpersonal behavior. In W. M. Grove & D. Cicchetti (Eds.), *Thinking clearly about psychology* (pp. 89–113). Minneapolis: University of Minnesota Press.

PART III

The Self and Context

CHAPTER 14

Integration Speak: Introducing Positioning Theory in Regional Integration Studies

Nikki Slocum and Luk Van Langenhove

INTRODUCTION[1]

This chapter deals with issues such as cooperation between states, the formation of transnational regions as actors in governance, and identity and social cohesion. The main upshot is that, based upon the concepts of regionhood and integration speak, a positioning theory approach to integration studies can be developed that is of theoretical and practical use. A positioning theory perspective highlights the social functions served, and the social tasks accomplished, in social interactions and how people accomplish these social tasks through the use of symbols in their communications. When applied to regional integration, positioning theory emphasizes the meaning (including the duties and rights) that people attribute to (geographic) spaces (e.g., states, micro-regions, macro-regions) and to persons seen as representing those spaces, as well as to the interactions between them.

A LINGUISTIC AND CONSTRUCTIVIST TURN IN INTEGRATION STUDIES

Regional integration has traditionally fallen under the umbrella of studies in international relations. The study of international relations is an academic field that deals with the relationships of people who do not share a common political, economic, social, or cultural heritage. More specifically, it focuses on the behavior of states in their complex relationships with each other. For many years, the dominant theoretical views in international relations (IR) have been realism, liberalism, and their neo-versions (cf. Baldwin, 1993). From a methodological point of view, it has to be noted that IR presents itself not as a social science discipline, but as a field of study that requires the insight and methods of a number of disciplines.

Within the field of international relations, regional integration has become one of the most prominent issues of study due to its global proliferation. Integration, in some instances, has been an economic strategy to increase the development of a region; in other cases it has been a means aimed at solving (potential) conflicts or problems of governance that have been amplified by processes and effects concomitant to globalization. Social constructionist approaches, including positioning theory, can be useful tools in studying processes of international relations, such as regional integration. Applying positioning theory to integration speak allows us to advance in developing a theoretical framework to study the "logic" of integration (Mattli, 1999), the complex relationships between regional integration processes and the political, economic, cultural, and social contexts in which they are embedded, and the discourses by which these are constituted.

The social constructionist and linguistic approaches emphasize the impact of intersubjectivity and social context on the continuing process of, for example, European integration. If the social and linguistic contexts of integration processes are taken as the primary topics of study, then social constructionist approaches can contribute to formulating a coherent framework to study integration that incorporates (cf. Christiansen et al., 1999, p. 538)

i. studying the *rules and norms* and *rights and duties* related to integration processes;

ii. studying the *formation* and *functions* of discursive tools (such as the concept of identity) that are employed in talk about integration; and

iii. studying the relationship between discursive aspects of integration processes and related actions.

In developing such a linguistic turn to regional integration studies, we want to introduce the concept of *"integration speak."* This term refers to all of the ways in which issues of regional integration are presented, be it in written or spoken form. We are using the term in much the same way as Harré, Brockmeier, and Mühlhäuser (1999) have used the concept of "green speak" in their seminal study of environmental discourse. Integration speak is about how the different issues of regional integration are constructed, represented, and negotiated in different sorts of discourses by different actors. For example, one specific form of integration speak is "Euro-speak" (Diez, 1999): the purposebuilt vocabulary of terms to describe—and shape—the reality of the European Union. Such Euro-speak includes concepts such as "subsidiarity," "democratic deficit," "the third pillar," "the deepening and widening," and so forth. Thus, rather than attempting to provide a set of necessary and sufficient conditions that define integration speak terms, such as "regions," "integration," or "identity," we examine what these discursive tools are used to *do* in various contexts (Wittgenstein, 1953; Austin, 1961).

When speaking about integration, one can *do* many things, such as make a promise or express gratitude. For example, Jean-Marie Le Pen *warns* his audience when he speaks of the EU in the following:

The same people who are in favor of quickie divorces are trying to weld together the ancient nations of Europe in a perpetual marriage. What are they going to do if we want to leave the EU? Send in the Wehrmacht? The Germans suffered a lot at the end of the war. It was their own fault, of course. But now they want to take their revenge, and so Europe will be dominated by Germany, America's most obedient ally.[2]

By issuing this warning Le Pen gives the impression that he is protecting the people from the EU. In other words, in issuing this locution, he herewith *positions* himself as protector and the EU as a danger or threat.

The concept of a speaking *position* refers to the set of rights, duties, and obligations with respect to the kind of (speech) acts that an actor occupying a position can, or is expected to, legitimately and properly execute. Positioning theory provides a theoretical framework that highlights what people are *doing* when they talk about integration and related concepts. It illuminates the functions that integration discourses serve. The *positioning triad* is an analytical tool that highlights the relationships between the building blocks of meaning, which are constituted by:

1. Positioned actors → Positions
2. Acts → Social forces (e.g. illocutionary, perlocutionary forces), and
3. Contexts → Story lines

While positioning theory was initially conceived to analyze social relations between persons, it can be applied to international relations and integration studies as well. First, states and regions can be attributed "actorness" in much the same way that persons are. This is reflected in utterances such as, "the United States have reacted angrily to. . .", "Europe is behaving . . .", "Russia warned. . ." or "Israel invaded. . .". Insofar as they are attributed actorness, states and regions can be said to occupy *positions* in the international relations system. Second, international relations are always constituted of conversations between persons. This can be the president of the United States addressing Congress or an informal talk with Mubarak at Camp David, as well as a citizen expressing her beliefs about European Union foreign policy (or lack thereof) in a conversation with a neighbor.

The rest of this chapter elaborates on the three components of the positioning triad and applies them to integration studies, illustrating with instances from integration speak.

POSITIONED ACTORS AND ACTORNESS

There are two main sources of positioned actors:

First, some actors are directly *referred to* or *implied* in the text of a speech act. These are accomplished through the use of indexers, such as (personal) pronouns. Examples of direct references are "I," "me," "you," "my friend, Cris," "the Belgian soccer team," "Zambia," and "Africa." When referring directly to "Belgium" in the context of a meeting of the member states of the European Union (EU), an *implied* reference would be the other member states, such as "Germany," "France," and so forth. However, in the context of a meeting of the main regions of Europe, a direct reference to "Flanders" would have concomitant indirect references to other regions, like "Wallonia." For example, the statement, "Flanders is a wealthy region," can accomplish several positionings, including (but not excluded to):

1. It (directly) positions the region "Flanders" as an actor;
2. It can (indirectly) position the region "Wallonia" as an actor;
3. It (directly) positions "Flanders" as wealthy;
4. It can (indirectly) position "Wallonia" as poor (or at least not wealthy).

The second main source of positioned actors is the social force of an act, which can position the author and his or her (given or implied) interlocutors. For example, in issuing a warning (social force of a speech act), Le Pen positions himself as a protector of "the French," the "EU" as a threatening enemy, and "the French" as vulnerable. In both the first and second cases, the positioned "actors" can be animate ("my friend, Cris"), or inanimate ("the EU"). Thus, states (Belgium), micro-regions (Flanders), macro-regions (Europe), multifarious institutions (the Commission), and other groups (the anti-globalists) can be positioned as actors.

In this manner, regions can be positioned as actors in the international system. This means that they can be positioned as constituting a complex stratified system of intentional acts, such as making treaties, joining international organizations, condemning the behavior of states, and so forth. While on the one hand every area on Earth can be a "region," given suitable historical, economic, cultural, and social conditions, regions will only exist as the result of certain acts (cf. The Maastricht Treaty). But such acts only make sense in a dialogical social context, which means that there need to be other relevant actors who take up a certain story line and thereby position the other actor in a certain way. Consider the following analogy: human beings do not become persons because they have a birth certificate and a given name but because other persons treat them as if they were persons (Vygotsky, 1978). It is this process of *personification*, a process of reciprocal achievements, that enables a baby to learn the skills necessary to accomplish acts in a given society. In much the same way, a region can be regarded as the result of a process of reciprocal achievements that can be labeled *"regionification."*

This means that to treat a certain geographic area in this way, that is as constitutive of being a region, concomitantly ascribes that status to the region. In other words: regions are the products of processes of "regionification"; regions exist only if they are recognized as such by persons (who are sometimes positioned as representing other entities, such as organizations, states or other regions). It is in this way that regions can be positioned as having *"actorness"* properties. They are thus positioned as entities in the system of I.R. that (i) have a certain degree of autonomy and that (ii) have powers to engage in some sort of purposive action. Bretherton and Vogler (1999) identify the following as properties of actorness:

- A shared commitment to a set of overarching values and principles;
- The ability to identify policy priorities and to formulate coherent policies;
- The ability to negotiate effectively with other actors in the international system;
- The availability of, and capacity to utilize, policy instruments; and
- A domestic legitimacy of decision processes and priorities, relating to external policy.

Because positioning theory allows us to analyze how "actorness" is engendered, we can modify the above to be more precise and avoid reification. In our view, it should be said that regions that are *positioned* as actors (or as having "actorness") are *sometimes:*

- *positioned as* having a shared commitment to a set of overarching values and principles;
- *positioned as* having the ability to identify policy priorities and to formulate coherent policies;
- *positioned as* having the ability to negotiate effectively with other actors in the international system;
- *positioned as* having the availability of, and capacity to utilize, policy instruments; and
- *positioned as* having a domestic legitimacy of decision processes and priorities relating to external policy.

It should be noted that, while these qualities are sometimes attributed to regions, regions can also be positioned as *not* possessing these qualities. For example, the EU has been positioned as having domestic legitimacy, but it has also been positioned as lacking cohesion and legitimacy. In fact, the latter positioning act functions to undermine the positioning of the EU as an actor. James Madison recognized the importance of being positioned as a global actor, when he emphasized the primary importance of a unified foreign policy for the United States of America in *The Federalist Papers* of 1788, saying, "If we are to be one nation in any respect, it clearly ought to be in respect to other nations."

According to public international law, only states qualify as actors, because only states can make treaties, join international organizations, and so on. (This is called possessing a "legal personality.") On the other hand, international organizations such as the UN and the EU have a recognized legal status as well. The classic realist approach in international relations is more or less the same: states are actors, and although other entities, such as regional organizations, may have some actorness properties, their role is subordinate to those of states. In our view, like states, macro-regions (EU) and micro-regions (Flanders) can be positioned as rational systems (with "statehood properties").

Two main implications for "actorness" follow from these insights. First, the "actorness" varies according to the perspective of the assessor: Actorness depends upon the power (that is, the rights) of the actor to act at various levels, in various realms (issues), toward various ends (goals). These are the actor's positions. Important to note is that the assessor's assessment of the actorness of another actor will depend upon the assessor's own goals. The assessor will determine the extent to which the powers (the rights and duties) of the other actors are perceived as (ir)relevant to achieving these goals. For example, if I am interested in lobbying the UN to forbid an American attack on Iraq, I will consider Russia, China, and France as appropriate actors to address for this goal; in other words, I will grant them considerable "actorness." In contrast, in this context I will not attribute much actorness to Wallonia, because it does not have the right to act toward this end.

A second implication is that a geographical region such as Europe can appear as several actors: in such a case, Europe is not the same actor during the course of every act. Nor is there a set of necessary and sufficient criteria to identify which acts constitute "Europe." It can be said that acts assessed as being executed by the actor "Europe" are seen or positioned as sharing a set of "family resemblance" (Wittgenstein, 1953). A given act must be attributed to an actor (e.g., Cris, Flanders, Belgium, Europe, the UN, and so forth). This attribution will depend (at least in part) on the attributed motivations of the actor in doing the act. Such attributed motivations take the form of a story line, such as: "Tony Blair gave money to Africa, because he wants to improve his image," or "the UK donated money to Africa, because it is trying to make up for its suppression of Africans during the colonial period." Within the context of such a story line, both the actor (Tony; the UK) and the act itself ("buying an image"; "remuneration") are defined.

In summary, regions are not a given part of reality, but are the result of a process of social construction. For a given geographical area to be (positioned) as region, at least three necessary conditions need to be fulfilled:

i. A geographical area must be positioned by other actors as a region (regionification process) [That is, a "region" exists];

ii. People must position this "region" as an actor [That is, the "region" is an actor]; and

iii. People must be positioned as acting and generating meaning on behalf of a region. [That is, the "region" acts.]

These three conditions form the basis of *regionhood*, which distinguishes regions from nonregions.

ACTS OR SOCIAL FORCES

Acts are the *meaning-full* counterparts of actions. The act is what is accomplished socially through a particular action, which can be constituted by linguistic and/or nonlinguistic discourse. For example, the shaking of hands (nonlinguistic action) can have the meaning that a bet is sealed (act), or it can be a greeting (act). A greeting can also be accomplished by a different action: a man can tip his hat (action) to greet a colleague. An example more relevant to regional integration is the action of allowing an Arab to hold a seat in the Knesset, which was interpreted by some people as an act of compromise to promote democracy and peace, and by others as an act of treason.

As a linguistic example, in the above passage from Le Pen, one of the speech acts accomplished is a *warning*. In the same interview, Le Pen accomplishes an *accusation* in saying, "It's not me who has become extreme Right. It's the whole of society which has become extreme Left." With the same utterance, Le Pen is also *defending* himself against an (implicit) accusation, which exemplifies how an utterance (a linguistic action) can have multiple social forces; that is, it can accomplish multiple acts. Here, it is important to note that Le Pen is not simply describing reality or "stating the facts." Rather, he is *doing* something socially. Language is a discursive tool that has a social, or illocutionary, force. As noted by Diez (1999, p. 600), "language is performative in that it does not only take note of, say, the founding of the EC. Instead, it is *through* language that this founding is performed."

STORY LINES

Essential to how an action is interpreted as an act is the context. The contexts of acts and positions are story lines. Story lines are temporal and (hence) a teleological series of customary events, or plots, that are familiar to a society. In other words, story lines implicitly or explicitly link the past with the present and future. An example from integration speak is the EU story line of "an ever-closer union," in which individual (nation-) states are interpreted as coming together in some kind of union. These teleological elements in integration speak are embedded in complex cultural and historical accounts of history. An important aspect of this teleological character is that it offers an arena to make progress possible, an aspect upon which we will elaborate later.

As the concept of integration implies a process, any instance of it will entail the interpretation of a string of actions as a set of acts with an identified pattern or trend. Varied interpretations of acts in regional integration processes are numerous. Let us take, for example, the proposed action of Denmark joining Europe's Economic and Monetary Union (EMU). In the debates on this issue that preceded the referendum in the year 2000, various Danes interpreted this proposed action as an act in quite different story lines (Slocum, 2001). Pia Kjaersgaard, leader of the Danish People's Party, interpreted the proposed action as an act in the storyline that "the EU is invading and eroding Danish identity," as exemplified in the following passage:

The essential issue is the preservation of our sovereignty. The euro will erode our national authority and identity at a time when Denmark is already becoming more and more multiethnic and globalized. Do we want to lose control of our lives with more and more decisions made by the European Central Bank in Frankfurt or in Brussels? Do we want this multiculturalism, this multiethnicity, about which the country was never consulted? I say we don't want either.[3]

In another storyline, Danes interpreted the EU and EMU as increasing the power of Denmark, saving it from obscurity and economic ruin. This story line is evident in Maja Lillelund's answer to how she would vote in the referendum and why:

I will vote yes. I haven't followed the debate that closely, but I simply can't see Denmark outside the European community. Having become a part of the community we need to move forward with it, to stay part of the mainstream. We are not like Norway. They have their oil and can manage on their own. We in Denmark are not strong enough to be outside.[4]

Both of these story lines entail certain presumptions about how events will (or would, given the outcome of the referendum) unfold in the future, as well as evaluations of such a turn of events. The teleological elements of the former "invasion" story line are that Danes would lose control of their lives, given EMU membership, but will maintain such control by voting no. In the latter "increased power" storyline, it is predicted that, without EMU membership, Denmark will fall behind and deteriorate to further weakness, but Denmark would gain strength by being a member of the EMU. These teleological elements of the story lines provide the rationales for the speakers' conclusions regarding what actions should be undertaken—in this case, voting yes or no in the referendum (Slocum, 2001).

In positioning a region as a rational system, story lines are used to make sense out of sequences of actions. These story lines, when efficaciously applied to specific cases, give meaning to certain actions (that is, they define them as acts) and tie them together in a manner that gives them a particular sense or rational appearance. Such a story line often entails an explanation as to why various goals and means for their realization are selected. For example, China claims (uses the story line) that it suppresses the Falun Gong movement in order to protect (act) the Chinese society. These storylines, or explanations, frequently employ the use of discursive concepts such as "having certain beliefs." An example of this is the story line often heard in the United States that *China abuses* (act) human rights because *China believes* that a community is more important than the individual. These examples also illustrate how the same actions can be defined as different acts (here abusing versus protecting) within the contexts of different story lines.

A variety of story lines are particularly common in contemporary integration speak. These include the following:

1. Integration will bring increased economic prosperity to the region.
2. Integration will ensure peace (e.g. prevent violent war) in a region.
3. Integration will increase the power of a region and hence allow it to balance U.S. (cultural, political, social, economic, military . . .) hegemony.
4. Integration will enable a region to become a global actor (to better compete with other powerful countries and regions).
5. Integration will provide a new common identity for a region.
6. Increased regionalism will provide more democracy (the principle of subsidiarity).
7. States that do not integrate will maintain greater sovereignty; those that do will lose their sovereignty.
8. States that do not integrate will preserve their identity; those that do will lose it.
9. Globalism and increased integration are harming the environment.
10. Those promoting globalism and increased integration are taking advantage of the poor; these are the manipulative tools of capitalists.
11. Globalism and integration serve only the elite; the average person suffers under them.

TRIADIC INTERACTION

In positioning theory, positioned actors, acts, and story lines are portrayed as part of a triad in order to emphasize their mutually influential relationship. As stated earlier, story lines are constituted by patterns of acts that are recognized as such by the members of a culture. Simultaneously, the story lines provide the context within which an action is interpreted as an act, or given meaning. For example, within the context of the "E.U. invasion" story line, the action of voting "yes" in the Danish euro referendum was interpreted as an act of *treason*. In contrast, the same action in the context of the "increased power" story line was interpreted as an act of *saving* Denmark.

It is through acts (which have a social force), within the contexts of story lines, that the players are positioned. At the same time, the positions of the actors influence how an action is interpreted as an act. Take for example, Pierre, a Frenchman, who is sitting in a Parisian café and sharing a French baguette with some friends. Pierre says, "These baguettes are really the best!" In this context, Pierre's locution (action) is likely to be interpreted as a compliment (act) to the baker. Pierre is here positioned as an individual in the story line "relaxing with friends." Now, let us imagine Pierre on vacation in California. Pierre is sitting with some American friends in a café, orders a French baguette, and makes the same remark. Here, (as correct as he may be about the bread) Pierre's comment may be interpreted as snobbery or condescension, as he is more likely to be positioned as "the Frenchman" in the story line of "displaying national pride."

It is also the case that not everyone possesses the same rights and duties—or abilities to assume various positions—and hence, not everyone is equally able to perform the same acts. Thus, while Pierre can make a claim about the superiority of French baguettes, he will not be permitted to act on behalf of France in signing a treaty with José Maria Aznar. In contrast, Jacques Chirac can act as "France," or as an individual (Jacques), or even as "Europe" if he is negotiating with the Japanese (or, more precisely, someone positioned as acting on behalf of "the Japanese"). The position attributed to an actor in a given episode will also influence the act he is seen to be performing.

DISCURSIVE TOOLS

Engendering social forces, positioning actors, and building story lines are accomplished through the employment of discursive tools, such as concepts, metaphors, simile, tropes, and so forth. The compilation of the discursive tools available for addressing a given issue is a topical lexicon. As such, integration speak, the talking and writing about regional integration processes, involves the use of a particular lexicon.

In "integration speak," one common discursive tool is the concept of identity. This discursive resource is generally found within the story line that people "have" (a metaphor that portrays possession of a static object) a certain identity that is tied to a specific space (e.g., a national identity), and that this identity causes them to act in various ways. Positioning theory is a useful tool to examine how various identity concepts serve various social functions in specific contexts. For example, in the Danish euro referendum that we referred to earlier, identity concepts were often employed to argue for or against Denmark becoming a member of the EMU.

While many Danes expressed fear of a loss of identity in joining the EU, it is important to remember that identity is not literally an object that one can lose (and perhaps find again). Identity is a dynamic concept, the meaning of which is constructed in discourses. The meaning of identity (and other concepts) is derived from how it is used in the discourse, the functions that it serves, the acts it is used to accomplish, the illocutionary force it bears when used in a specific episode. In general, different identity concepts are used to position actors in various ways.

In relation to regions, the identity concept is employed in two main ways. First, when positioned as an actor, a region can be positioned by being attributed a particular identity; in fact, the attribution of an identity to a region is one way to position it as an actor. As with persons, when a region is positioned in a specific context (story line), it is attributed a set of rights, duties, and characteristics that determine how and with which other actors (e.g., regions) it may or may not act. However, as regions themselves are inanimate, acts attributed to them are always executed by persons who are positioned as acting on behalf of a region. People are often (implicitly) presumed to be acting on behalf of an institution. Perhaps because (nation-) states are the strongest institutions of the post-Westphalia system, people are often positioned as acting on behalf of their state. It is interesting to note that the new emphasis on *regions*, in addition to states, creates new actors that are capable of new kinds of acts.

The second main way in which the identity concept is used in relation to regions is by positioning individuals within the context of a story line that links the individual to a certain region. For example, the story line often (implicitly) presumes that a national identity *causes* or motivates people to act in a particular way. Again, the new story line that people can be motivated by identities other than those linked to (nation-) states, such as a regional identity, opens up new possibilities for action. Thus, new possibilities for types of actors (ways of being) and ways of acting emerge within new story lines.

The concept of a region as an actor is a discursive tool that is relatively new to contemporary discourse. By virtue of the fact that a new region is a new actor, at a unique position in a web of interrelationships, greater possibilities become available for meaning—that is, for acting and being (identity). Because of the fact that (by definition) a new region (or any other actor) has no or little history, the meanings given to it and its actions are more flexible than the often entrenched patterns of (usually unreflected) attributions associated with older actors. Through proactive positioning of a region and the actions attributed to it (as acts), people can generate and communicate such new meanings. Here it becomes clearer why new institutions generate new possibilities for action (acts)! For example, within the European Commission, a German's actions (such as a proposal for a certain foreign policy) are more likely to be interpreted as improving or helping Europe (act) than as fighting for German interests (and, tacitly, as being in competition with other European states' interests). It is often the unspoken but implicit contexts—or story lines—that make evident the differences in these acts. The action of "helping Europe" is often embedded in a storyline that the EU is in competition with other large powers, particularly the United States and Japan. The act of serving German interests, in contrast, is embedded in a story line that the European countries are competing with each other.

The contents of topical lexicons, such as integration speak, are likely to vary among different communities. For example, integration speak is found among communities such as:

- The community of officials involved in formalized integration initiatives (cf. civil servant of the European Commission and their colleagues in national administrations dealing with European affairs)
- The scientific communities of international law, international relations, geography, and so on
- The political community
- The media

There are complex relations between these different communities that can be studied from a positioning theory perspective. Of particular interest is the relationship between academic and nonacademic integration speak. Integration speak (or talk about integration) includes, but is not limited to, first-order positioning (Harré & Van Langenhove, 1992). Integration theory, on the other hand, is talk about integration speak—or talk about talk about integration. If one takes this a step higher, you have talk about talk of integration speak—or talk about the theories of integration speak. Scientific work that is done from a social constructionist perspective can be second- or third-order positioning. However, it is important to note that in second- and third-order positioning, first-order positioning always occurs as well. The variations in the lexicons are likely to have important implications for practice that are well worth studying.

Lexicons, or sets of discursive tools, can be studied and evaluated from two perspectives: (i) the adequacy of the lexical resources for some discursive tasks and (ii) the role of the lexicon in focusing attention on otherwise "invisible" aspects of material reality. The *lexical adequacy* of integration speak refers to the question of whether the lexical resources of language X are suited to the discussion of the phenomena referred to as regional integration. Harré et al. (1999) distinguish three types of adequacy:

i. *Referential* adequacy is the availability of lexical resources to discuss a given topic in sufficient detail (sufficiency being relative to the task in hand);

ii. *Systematic* adequacy refers to the quality of being structured so as to approach maximum rule economy and efficiency;

iii. *Social* adequacy is the extent to which a language is acceptable to a maximum number of speakers in a target community, promotes social unity and intercommunication, and caters to present as well as anticipated future social needs.

Integration-speak will be adequate if the language used is referentially, systematically, and socially adequate.

The adequacy of a lexicon and the specific story lines and positions generated in a situation have significant implications for what is considered desirable or even possible to do. The lexical resources of integration speak that are employed in a given instance influence not only whether cooperation or integration is considered to be formal or informal but also whether it is considered possible. For example, in April 2002, a conference took place between members of the Southern Caucasus states (Georgia, Armenia, and Azerbaijan) to discuss possibilities for informal cooperation between them that would not set political resolution of problems as a requisite. Some of the Azerbaijanis claimed that cooperation between their country and Armenia would be impossible. Due to Armenian occupation of Azerbaijani territory, they considered themselves to be at war with Armenia and saw this fact as incompatible with efforts to cooperate in any fashion. In these statements, the potential cooperators are positioned as representatives of their respective countries. Simultaneously, and in contrast, at the so-called Red Bridge, a marketplace located at the confluence of the borders of the three countries, members of each of these states trade readily on an informal basis. Thus, what was claimed to be impossible when people were positioned as Azerbaijanis and Armenians actually takes place at the Red Bridge. It would be a useful research endeavor to examine the positioning that occurs in this context and other instances of informal cooperation, as well as the story lines that make such cooperation possible.

CREATING NEW POSSIBILITIES FOR CONCEPTUALIZATION AND ACTION

The topic of social adequacy of a lexicon highlights the importance of language for conceptualization, communication, and action. As exemplified in the quotations provided from the discourse surrounding the Danish euro referendum, the same action can be conceptualized (that is, defined as acts that are embedded in story lines) in different ways. Furthermore, as discussed earlier, the story line suggests how the future will develop, and thus also suggests what appear to be rational options for action as well as what options appear to be irrational. For example, if joining the EU is conceived as treason, one should best decline membership.

While clear patterns can be discerned in narratives, discourse, and action, it is important that these not be reified or seen as deterministic. Story lines do not make people act in a given way; rather, people use discursive tools to create meaningful experiences. People are the makers and users of these tools; in this way, they are the craft masters of their reality. We earlier touched upon the idea that the creation of new types of actors and story lines also engenders new possibilities for experience and action. It is to the realm of creativity and its implications for that we turn now.

Positioning theory emphasizes the active nature of people in engendering their social realities. By highlighting the social/illocutionary forces of acts, positioning theory helps one to focus on the functions served by one's actions. Thus, one can query whether one's actions are accomplishing the social tasks that one desires. From this point of view, social events appear less mechanical; one can more consciously choose one's goals and then pose the question as to how these can best be reached. Future studies could usefully focus on how new story lines, positions, and acts can be engendered in the context of practical situations in a way that bridges the present into a desired future.

Concomitant to these theoretical insights is a need for research methods that are consistent with them. An increasingly popular venue for this kind of future-oriented inquiry is that of "foresight studies." Foresight is a method for the systematic gathering of future-oriented intelligence toward the aim of medium- to long-term vision-building (STRATA, 2001). Foresight can be used to inform policy, build networks, and enhance capacity for handling long-term issues. It is a so-called participatory research method in that researchers do not impose (implicitly or otherwise) goals upon society. Rather, various stakeholders of the issue(s) being explored participate in exploring potential developments and the relationships between various possible means and outcomes. Positioning theory, and the social constructionist view more generally, are particularly useful in such exercises, because they illuminate and facilitate the questioning of both means and ends in society.

Foresight exercises are a possible method for applying the insights provided by positioning theory to issues relevant to regional integration. One example of such an exercise is to investigate the possibilities for new forms of governance and how to overcome the challenges presented. For example, in the European context, supranational governance was proposed as a solution to the war-torn continent. However, contemporary conceptions of identity presented a barrier to supranational governance. In foresight exercises, participants can address the question, "How can we construct our identities in a way that facilitates peace?" Such discussions also lead to the questioning of whether or not (only) a supranational form of governance is the best means to a peaceful society. In turn, additional alternatives might be (and have been) suggested, such as micro-regional governance. And again in turn, the types of identities that would facilitate this solution can be explored. With this approach, complex social issues can be tackled in a manner that does not oversimplify them and promotes creative practical solutions.

This approach also facilitates democracy through the creation of discursive space where citizens can develop story lines and take positions regarding many local and global problems that face humanity. Heretofore the mainstream idea has been that global problems cannot be discussed or negotiated by the billions of people that inhabit the earth, so governments or regions must do so on their behalf. As a result, citizens are hardly involved in the system of international relations. For example, the antiglobalization movement shows that there is a civic movement emerging that combines grass-roots movements with high-tech tools (such as the Internet) in order to challenge international policymaking. The question is not if the antiglobalists are wrong or right. Rather, the point is to acknowledge that the protestors have no room to voice their concerns other than the streets and the Internet. In accordance with the presently endorsed approach, it should be clear that European governance, or governance of any region, does not need to be "translated" but constructed through a democratic process in which all story lines are permitted to be expressed. Through foresight and other participatory exercises, the functions served by various story lines can be illuminated, in order to inform decisions. Whether one thinks we need more or less integration (for example, in Europe, where this issue is a hot potato), the debates will profit from more integration speak!

NOTES

1. UNU/CRIS: United Nations University, Comparative Regional Integration Studies. The views expressed in this chapter are those of the authors alone and do not necessarily represent those of the United Nations University. For correspondence, please contact nslocum@cris.unu.edu.

2. *The Telegraph.* 25 April 2002. Inside the world of Jean-Marie Le Pen.

3. Roger Cohen. A Danish Identity Crisis: Are We Europeans? *The New York Times.* 10 September 2000.

4. CNN.com In-Depth Specials. Denmark Decides. Vox pop. http://europe.cnn.com/SPECIALS/2000/denmark

REFERENCES

Austin, J. (1961). *How to do things with words.* Oxford: Clarendon Press.

Baldwin, R. (1993). A domino theory of regionalism. CEPR discussion paper series 857. London: CEPR.

Bretherton, C., & Vogler, J. (1999). *The European Union as a global actor.* London: Routledge.

Christiansen, T., Jorgensen, K., & Wiener, A. (1999). The social construction of Europe, *Journal of European Public Policy*, 6(4), 528–544.

Diez, T. (1999). Speaking "Europe": The politics of integration discourse. *Journal of European Public Policy*, 6(4), 598–613.

Harré, R., & Van Langenhove, L. (1992). Varieties of positioning. *Journal for the Theory of Social Behaviour*, 20, 393–407.

Harré, R., & Van Langenhove, L. (1999). Epilogue: Further opportunities. In R. Harré & L. Van Langenhove (Eds.), *Positioning theory: Moral contexts of intentional action.* Oxford: Basil Blackwell.

Harré, R., Brockmeier, J., & Mühlhäuser, P. (1999). *Greenspeak: A study of environmental discourse.* London: Sage Publications.

Mattli, W. (1999). *The Logic of Regional Integration. Europe and Beyond.* Cambridge: Cambridge University Press.

Slocum, N. (2001). *Positioning analyses of discursive expressions of conflicts.* Unpublished dissertation. Georgetown University.
STRATA (2001). A practical guide to regional foresight.
Vygotsky, L. (1978). *Mind in society: The development of higher psychological processes.* Cambridge: Harvard University Press.
Wittgenstein, L. (1953). *Philosophical investigations.* Oxford: Blackwell.

CHAPTER 15

Culture Clash and Patents: Positioning and Intellectual Property Rights

Fathali Moghaddam and Shayna Ginsburg

> Let me tell you next of stones that burn like logs. It is a fact that through-out the province of Cathay there is a sort of black stone, which is dug out of veins in the hillside and burns like logs. These stones keep a fire going better than wood. I assure you that, if you put them in the fire in the evening and see that they are well alight, they will continue to burn all night, so that you will find them still glowing in the morning.
>
> Marco Polo

The thirteenth-century travels of Marco Polo in the Mongol Empire and in other parts of the East are part of a long tradition of international communications and trade. During his travels Marco Polo came across many new products and wrote about them for Western audiences. During the age of exploration that followed the Renaissance, merchants, explorers, and travelers helped to bring back to the West many ideas and products originating from the non-Western societies. Until fairly recently in human history, there was very little that could be done to prevent outsiders from adopting and using the ideas and products they discovered in other societies. It is only since the 1980s that serious and effective steps have been taken to enforce intellectual property patents at the international level.

A patent is an instrument through which a central authority (the federal government in U.S. law, the sovereign in English law, the World Trade Organization in international law) grants some privilege, property, or authority to one or more individuals (see *Black's Law Dictionary*). The individual(s) granted patents gain the right to charge other people fees for the use of whatever they have patented, for the lifetime of the patent. Thus, underlying the system of patents are fundamental cultural assumptions. For example, if an international patent is granted to person P for product X, it is assumed that X is something that can be privately owned, that authorities can place particular time limits to such ownership, that authorities can decide on ownership of X, and that something P has done is a valid basis to give him or her the patent on X.

Put another way, the cultural assumptions underlying relationships between the authorities who give patents, patent holders, and potential users of the patented product constitute a story line. The general plot is the acquisition of personal property and its commercial uses. Central to this story line are rights, demands placed on others by the person who possesses it (Moghaddam, 2000) and duties, a demand placed by others on the person who owes it (Moghaddam, Slocum, Finkel, More, & Harré, 2000). The patent story line arises out of the meaning system of modern industrial societies, a story line that is dominant and fast spreading around the world—but it is not the only story line. The objective of this chapter is to explore some aspects of the clash of cultures that is taking place in the arena of international patents, and with illustrative examples show what can happen when the patent story line clashes with story lines from non-Western cultures and non-Western people who refuse to accept the positions of patent granting authority, patent holder and so on.

Ultimately, international patents are about ownership rights and duties. What sort of person can be owner? What can be owned? What rights do owners have? What duties do users have? These are bottom line financial issues, and a review of the history of economic progress in industrialized societies reveals that patents have played a fundamentally important role in the rise of Western powers, first in England and the rest of Europe (MacLeod, 1989) and then the United States (Walterscheid, 1998). The enormously important wealth-generating role of the patent system (Kaufer, 1989) perhaps inevitably has attracted increasingly critical attention from non-Western societies (Shiva, 2002). Our discussion is about aspects of these conflicting story lines.

PATENTS AND THE WESTERN TRADITION

The idea of patents is first recorded in Aristotle's fourth century B.C. *Politics*, in which he refers to an idea by Hippodamus, who calls for a system of rewards to those who discover things useful in the state. Some historians have mentioned isolated instances of patents, as in Byzantium and Bordeaux; however, the regular mention of patents did not again arise until the Renaissance. The text of the oldest patent law in the world was created by the Venetian Senate in 1474, officially announced as Inventor Bylaws. Patent law then moved to Great Britain in the mid-sixteenth century under the Tudor monarchy, spawned by foreign international trade policy and a desire to stimulate local manufacture. In 1624 the Monopoly Act was created and enacted into law.

One of the many legal concepts that traveled to America from England, the history and evolution of the English patent system is inextricably linked to the foundation of America's patent system, especially since the very idea of a patent system was introduced into the United States through immigrants from England to the American colonies between 1640 and 1776. The importance of patenting stemmed from the confusion over the invention of the steamboat, which was granted to two different people in different states. From this confusion the Founding Fathers of this nation noted the importance of protecting a citizen's right to intellectual property, as evident from the inclusion of a national patenting system in the drafting of the Constitution.

Article 1, Section 8, Clause 8, more commonly referred to as the Intellectual Property Clause, states, "Congress shall have the power. . .To promote the progress of science and useful arts, by securing for limited times to authors and inventors the exclusive right to their respective writings and discoveries" (U.S. Const. Art 1, sect. 8, cl. 8). Although the language is rather vague, the more relevant detail is that the foundation for the protection of personal rights was laid early in the history of this nation. Yet, the ambiguity of the intellectual property clause has contributed to a long and controversial debate surrounding patents and has led Congress to pass a series of additions and amendments to the rule. It is important to note that the additions made are rather arbitrary. For instance, the Patent Act of 1790 set out a 14-year limit on patents without the possibility of extension. There is no real reason why 14 was chosen, only that congressman believed it sounded reasonable. That particular number choice is completely a cultural element, not technical at all. In 1793 another act formally created a Patent Board, granting the responsibility of the issuance of patents to the Department of State. As greater demands were placed on the system, the system developed new rules. The 1836 Patent Act established the Patent Office and added on the possibility for additional seven-year extensions with proper approval. This too is a cultural creation.

The popularity of patent law in America has tended to vacillate with the times. The system has been viewed by some as a strategic device to manipulate the economy. For instance, as the economy declined, the number of patents issued increased. The excitement over patents waned in the 1920s and 1930s, which has come to be known as the trust-busting era. Patents were closely associated with big business and thereby viewed as its weapon. This sentiment immediately subsided with the attack on Pearl Harbor, an event that called on both private and public inventors to submit ideas with great alacrity. That same year the Patent Act went into effect, followed in 1982 by the establishment of the Court of Appeals for the Federal Circuit (CAFC), which handles patent cases to the present day.

In Japan, the only non-Western society with a strong patent system, it became clearly apparent that a patent system must be created in order to speed up modernization efforts, which began after the start of the Meiji Reform. As such, the Patent Monopoly Act was publicly proclaimed in Japan on April 18, 1885, the eighteenth year of the Meiji Era.

PATENTS IN GLOBAL CONTEXT

Currently, patenting is widespread throughout the world, although some differences do exist. The greatest difference between the United States patent system and those of the rest of the world concerns the novelty date and statutory bars. In the United States the date of invention is considered to be that time after filing, when the proposed invention has gone through a process of "interference" (meaning that its claims do not infringe on existing patents) and has been accepted. The date of filing is separately known as the statutory bars. In Europe, Japan, and almost all countries with a patent system, the date of filing for a patent becomes the date of invention. As such, these countries' systems combine the U.S. systems of novelty date and statutory bars.

The primary condition for patents in the European countries set forward by the European Patent Convention (EPC) is that the inventor demonstrate an "inventive step," in which the problem and solution are highly considered. The European patent system considers forms of medical treatment or therapy unpatentable. Just as in the United States, however, useful chemical structures and pharmaceutical products can be patented. If a new use for the same product is discovered, given the broad patent protection of the first use discovery, a second attempt at patenting is considered an infringement.

Japanese patent law is likewise similar to the two systems previously discussed. One rule of thumb is that inventions which could be easily made by a worker of ordinary skill in the art are not patentable. The main focus in Japan's patent law concerns the merits of the invention. Another unique aspect of the system is the meritorious effect, or *yoshi/koka*, meaning that the applicant must demonstrate some commendable effect not previously shown. Despite the subtle differences between the major patent systems of the globe, there are many similarities, which has allowed for the creation of an comprehensive international patent system.

INTERNATIONALIZING THE PATENT

The first attempt at an international agreement occurred on March 20, 1883 at the Paris Convention for the Protection of Industrial Property. Since its origination, it has been revised six times between 1900 and 1967 and amended in 1979 (WIPO Database of Intellectual Property, 2002). The Patent Cooperation Treaty (PCT) done at Washington on June 19, 1970, establishes a union of contracting states to be known as the International Patent Cooperation Union with the objective of "cooperation in the filing, searching, and examination, of applications for the protection of inventions, and for rendering special technical services" (Lovell, Comp. b).

The General Agreement on Tariffs and Trade (GATT), first signed in 1947, is a segment of the World Trade Organization (WTO). The agreement was designed to provide an international forum to encourage free trade between member states by regulating and reducing tariffs on traded goods and by providing a common mechanism for resolving trade disputes. GATT membership now includes more than 110 countries. The GATT as an international organization no longer exists, and this function of the old system has been incorporated into the present-day WTO (World Trade Organization). The WTO Agreements encompass the areas of goods, services, and intellectual property. While the trade of goods has been around for ages, the trade of ideas has recently sprung into the forefront with the advent of great advances in technology, which has allowed for invention and research.

The Convention on Biodiversity adopted in 1992 at the Earth Summit in Rio de Janeiro provides a legal framework for the conservation of global biodiversity, the sustainable use of biological resources, and the fair and equitable sharing of genetic resources. It calls on governments to "respect, preserve and maintain the knowledge, innovations and practices of indigenous peoples and other traditional, land-based communities" (Convention on Biological Diversity, 2002). We note, here, the radical and immensely important shift from personal to collective ownership of knowledge, and the novel idea of collective innovation. Although over 150 countries have signed the treaty, the United States did not, citing concerns about inadequacies in the protection of human rights as well as provisions on financial assistance to developing countries. Yet critics have argued that the United States selfishly did not sign the treaty because the government has a commercial interest in exploiting natural resources. At present, the United States remains isolated in its position as the only developed nation not signing the treaty; however, it is currently pending in the 104th Congress.

Accompanying the 1986–94 Uruguay Round the WTO, as part of the Marrakesh Agreement, produced an Agreement on Trade-Related Aspects of Intellectual Property Rights (TRIPS), which went into effect on January 1, 1995, and which basically works as an institution to "reduce distortions and impediments to international trade. . . to promote effective and adequate protection of intellectual property rights, and to ensure that measures and procedures to enforce intellectual property rights do not themselves become barriers to legitimate trade" (GATT: Uruguay Round). TRIPS is the most comprehensive multilateral agreement on intellectual property to date. The basic tenants of the agreement are that (1) patent availability runs a minimum of 20 years; (2) patent protection exists for products and processes; (3) governments can deny a patent for commercial use if it is expected to disrupt public order and/ or morality; (4) things such as therapeutic or surgical methods for the treatment of humans or animals, and inventions of plants and animals or essentially biological processes, can be excluded from patentability.

IDEAS OF OWNERSHIP

The current TRIPS Agreement is based on Western capitalist understandings of knowledge and ownership and reflects the needs of Western industries. Scholarship in the arena of comparative legal cultures has highlighted major differences around the world in terms of how rights, duties, and ownership are treated in different legal systems (for example, see the numerous studies in Varga, 1992). TRIPS does not reflect the ownership conceptions of many indigenous people in South America, for example, whose intellectual property tends to belong to the whole community and is often part of their culture and spirituality. More generally, arising out of a tradition of individual private property rights, patent law was not created to protect traditional or collective rights. In some indigenous South American tribes, local healers are usually considered by the community to be custodians of hereditary knowledge, not private owners with exclusive personal rights in the Western sense.

But there is a complication in the picture, because the forces for and against international agreements on patents does not divide up neatly into Western versus non-Western interests. There are deep rifts within non-Western societies, which tend to be characterized by dualism, " . . . the existence of two sectors, one modern and the other traditional, that coexist in the same society" (Moghaddam & Taylor, 1985). The modern sector is occupied by an elite who are typically educated in Western institutions, fluent in Western languages, economically invested in commerce with the West, and supportive of international patents and globalization generally. These people share the Western conception of personal property owned by an individual.

With increasing globalization, increasing tourism has spread throughout the world. Supporters of ecotourism have described it as purposeful travel that helps improve appreciation for cultural and natural history, while helping in conservation efforts as well as producing economic benefits that encourage further environmental improvement. Ecotourism has been a major factor in generating jobs, stimulating incomes, diversifying the economy, and enhancing the standard of living. These opportunities allow for the developing countries and developed countries to sustain a livable environment. Yet the expanding global tourism industry also brings with it a number of threats through biopiracy, namely to indigenous communities throughout the world. While ecotourism does have many economic advantages, there are concerns about numerous ecotourism trips where scientists, tourists, students, and researchers enter into forests to collect information about local plants and ecosystems. This has sometimes involved the theft of knowledge from indigenous collectives, knowledge developed over centuries and based on local biodiversity. Some visitors have gone further and attempted to patent the knowledge they have collected. The result is the appropriation and patenting of traditional plants, medicines, and related knowledge by outside researchers and corporations. Critics contend that indigenous worldviews are not taken into consideration nor consulted as scientific knowledge when policies and decision making regarding bioprospecting are made.

In the area of biotechnology there is further debate on the right to patent living organisms, especially resources and seeds that have been developed or passed on as traditional and public knowledge. This capitalization on public knowledge often comes into conflict with indigenous knowledge and the rights of indigenous people, sustainability of local ecosystems, and even the ability of nations to provide food security and protection of the global environment.

Biopiracy

The South is home to around two-thirds of the world's plant species, 35,000 of which are believed to have medicinal value. Some 25 percent of the drugs prescribed by European and North American physicians are derived from plants found in the forests of the South. Supporters of the rights of indigenous people in low-income countries claim that in almost all cases these plants have been "discovered" through information derived about their use in traditional medicine. The unauthorized and uncompensated yet lucrative business of taking biological resources has come to be referred to as "biopiracy," or the theft of intellectual property, such as traditional plant medicines, from poor communities by multinational corporations and research institutions.

The Neem Tree: A Case Study

The neem tree is a fast-growing evergreen of up to 20 meters in height. Native to east India and Burma, the Neem tree also grows in much of southeast Asia and west Africa. Long revered for its many healing properties, neem has been regarded as a national treasure. Neem's many virtues are attributable to its chemical compounds contained in the bark, leaves, flowers, seeds, and fruit pulp. Specific compounds in the neem enhance the immune system's response to pathogens, helping to prevent infections and eliminating them before they can cause disease. The plant has been used to treat a wide variety of diseases and complaints that run the gamut from leprosy and diabetes to ulcers and skin disorders. It is for these reasons that the neem has been called "the curer of the ailments" or "the blessed tree."

For centuries, the healing properties of the neem were ignored by the West. Apparently, scientists and researchers were condescending to Indian peasants and plant doctors, until official reports of its beneficial effects were made known. In 1985 the plant patent was sold to the multinational chemical corporation, W.R. Grace and Co. The patent on this plant has provoked widespread objections from many indigenous people of India that have been using this plant for centuries.

PATENT, RIGHTS, AND DUTIES

A patent, then, is a form of personal property that provides its owner with the right to exclude others from making, using, selling, or importing the invention described in the patent claims, for a period of time. Corporate ownership in capitalism is collective, but not in the sense that tribal ownership is. In the United States, patents are granted through the U.S. Patent and Trademark Office (PTO). There are three hallmark qualities that an invention must possess in order to be considered for patentability: novelty, utility, and nonobviousness. Novelty, although a seemingly straightforward concept, is a bit more complicated. Most importantly, it means that a patent must follow the "first-to- invent" rule. It can not have been described in a printed publication anywhere in the world prior to a person's invention and it cannot have been in public use, or known or used by others *in the U.S.* before the date of invention. Finally, the claimed invention cannot have been described in a printed publication anywhere the world or put on sale or in public use *in the U.S.* more than one year prior to the date one files for a patent. Utility is a simpler term, although some problems arise because one's idea of what is or is not useful can be highly subjective and arbitrary. It could vary greatly between cultures. The nonobviousness requirement was developed in order to limit the number of patents that were being issued; it is limited to persons of ordinary skill in that particular field or art. One again, what is obvious in one particular culture may be completely foreign to another. The best example of this is the patent system. Because it is a Western institution, indigenous cultures throughout the world have no exposure to the patent system's rules and regulations and cannot or should not be held accountable to adhere to its discipline. In a sense, patents are negotiable; there is no exact or definitive criteria for what is new, unique, or nonobvious, that could possible apply to all cultures throughout the world.

Patents inherently position patent holders and potential users in terms of rights and duties. However, because patents are based on somewhat arbitrary criteria and are negotiable, even after the granting of patents the rights and duties, and ultimately the positions of the parties, can be renegotiated. As an illustrative example, consider the conflict surrounding HIV/AIDS medication.

Since 1996, people with HIV and AIDS who live in countries like the United States and the rest of the developed world have been able to benefit from a combination of HIV antiretroviral drugs (HAART), resulting in an enormous decrease in sickness and number of deaths. These drugs cost the average American approximately $15,000 per year, an utterly unaffordable amount for a poverty-stricken individual in a third world country with no heath care policy. Beginning in 1998, concern over the effects of international trade laws that restrict access to HIV-related medicines has grown. A court case was brought up by the 39 leading pharmaceutical companies in the United States, including Bristol-Myers Squibb and GlaxoSmithKline, against the government of South Africa. These companies viewed the South African Health Minister's powers to override patents in the interest of public health as a breach of the TRIPS agreement. The agreement on Trade Related Intellectual Property Rights has sought to impose international standards for patent protection, requiring countries to grant patent protection to pharmaceutical companies and their products for a minimum of 20 years.

About 11.5 million people have died of AIDS in sub-Saharan Africa, which accounts for 83 percent of the world's total HIV/AIDS related deaths. Although HIV infects 11 percent of the country's 43 million people, the government has not declared the crisis a national emergency. As such, the court case was drawn out for approximately three years before an agreement was reached on April 23, 2001, on a note of rickety cooperation. South Africa agreed to comply with TRIPS and the pharmaceutical companies agreed to supply HIV and AIDS drugs at drastically reduced prices. Both groups had important interests at stake, thus causing them to work together toward a solution. South Africa's interests clearly involve access to medications for its people, whereas the interests of the pharmaceutical companies involve avoiding negative media attention for what has been interpreted as profits before patients. Various humanitarian aid organizations became frustrated with the pharmaceutical companies and decided to import such medications anyhow, without complying with international rules. Similarly, negative attention emerged from various domestic quarters of the U.S. administration, requiring the government to take a big step in a new direction, that is, not to show strong support for the pharmaceutical industry.

Two other concepts are inextricably linked to the idea of patenting drugs. First, parallel importing involves the buying of a product from a middleman, rather than from the original manufacturer or the one who holds the patent. Sometimes, pharmaceutical companies sell products to countries at different prices. If Brazil obtains a medication from the United States at a significantly lower price than South Africa, it seems only rational that South Africa would attempt to obtain the same drug from Brazil rather than from the United States. The problem resides in the international property rules as set out in TRIPS. The second related concept is called compulsory licensing, which involves using a generic drug to replace a medication without obtaining permission from the patent holder. Such generic medications for AIDS and HIV drugs include nevirapine, AZT, and 3TC. Countries like Brazil and India have learned how to make these cheaper generic versions of HIV and AIDS medications, subsequently importing them to South Africa. South Africa buys these drugs, breaking the TRIPS agreement, because the government cannot afford to purchase them in compliance with international laws. Clearly, two different interests are at stake in the scenario described above. It is common for different conceptions of rights and duties in distinct cultures to cause friction between groups.

A CASE STUDY: AYAHUASCA

So far we have highlighted three main points. First, patents evolved out of a Western cultural context, and their globalization is supported by various interests, including non-Western elite, who share Western ideas of property rights. Second, the criteria for issuing patents varies somewhat, even across industrialized societies. The arbitrary nature of the criteria for issuing patents include the number of years of duration, and the definition of terms such as "novelty" and "utility." Third, the patent story line involves certain rights and duties that can be challenged, as illustrated by the example of African governments challenging AIDS drug patents. We now turn to consider a more specific case involving a clash of Western and non-Western cultures over the issue of patents.

The patent in question can be seen as arising from legitimate "pharmaceutical research and development investment" or it can be seen as part of a growing trend toward biopiracy. Pharmaceutical corporations invest in hundreds, sometimes thousands, of different research projects, out of which may arise a very small number of profitable drugs. Some of their investments are in projects to extract promising substances from plants native to non-Western countries, particularly in South America. Such research and development using native plants can potentially benefit all humankind. On the other hand, local plants could be seen as belonging to indigenous populations, particularly in cases where the plants in question have a long history of communal use by local people. The following are story lines that evolve from such different perspectives.

Miller's Story Line

In the 1980s Loren Miller, a graduate student of pharmacology, brought a variety of the ayahuasca plant home from a domestic garden in Ecuador to the United States (Fecteau, 2002). He then founded the International Plant Medicine Corporation in California and applied for a U.S. patent since he believed he had discovered a unique and distinct variety of the plant, which he named "Da Vine" (Lambrecht, 1999). His belief that this was a new variety of the plant rested on characteristics such as leaf size, shape, texture, flower color, and size, and lack of nuts. He demonstrated utility in his suspicions that the plant might possess effective properties for psychotherapy, cardiovascular medicines, and even treating cancer. Miller and the Plant Medicine Corporation were subsequently awarded the patent on June 17, 1986, as U.S. patent PP05751. The patent granted exclusive rights to sell and develop new varieties of the plant (Miller, 1986).

Amazonia Story Line

In indigenous cultures all over the world the people often experience an extremely close relationship to their natural environment and the spiritual world. Ayahuasca is venerated throughout the Amazon region of South America. Throughout Amazonia the plant has been used for cleansing and healing purposes in order to achieve a holistic purification of the body, mind, and spirit. Ayahuasca is used in religious and healing ceremonies and has been said to produce a rare phenomenon and ecstatic experience. There are at least 72 groups that use a similar preparation of the brew and over 40 different names for the sacred medicine. The name for this medicinal and healing plant comes from the Quechua words "aya" which means soul or spirit and "huasca" which means vine. Essentially, the name translates to "The Vine of the Soul." Those who partake in the ceremonial consummation of this plant brew believe it can cure a wide range of physical, psychological, and spiritual maladies. Despite the inevitable criticisms of the placebo effect, ayahuasca is proven to be a powerful drug with an indisputable chemical effect.

According to indigenous traditions, ayahuasca is only taken under the supervision of an experienced healer, or shaman, who considers him or herself the guardian of the cosmos (Wright, 1998). Both the healer and the patient partake in the brew together. The shaman is the great master of ecstasy. He or she is trained in arriving at this ecstatic state in which a person stands outside of or transcends his or herself and the physical world. This distinguishing characteristic of shamanism with its focus on an ecstatic trance state or out-of-body experience is accompanied by the belief that the soul of the shaman either ascends to the sky and reaches heaven or descends through the earth into the underworld. Special healing techniques are utilized by a shaman to help identify the nature of a specific illness or trouble from which the person is suffering and then cleanse the person of the evil magic within. It is common for participants to undergo an intense hallucinogenic experience.

This tradition has been around for centuries and certain rituals are always observed. A special ayahuasca ceremonial cup, hewn out of stone and with engraved ornamentation, is used in the ceremony. Additionally, a healer will institute certain ritual traditions such as whistling, singing, praying, and reciting orations (Dobkin de Rios, 2002). It is the combination of the magical potion and the rituals that accompany it that comprises the sacred practice.

The Clash

It was not until 1994 that the Amazonian tribes learned of the U.S. patent. They were outraged for what they viewed as a cultural attack on their heritage. To emphasize their outrage, two shamans from Ecuador and Colombia adorned in exotic headdresses of parrot feathers and necklaces of rare shells and wild boar teeth visited the United States Patent and Trademark Office in suburban Washington on March 30, 1999, chanting a religious ceremony and sipping potion (Lambrecht, 1999). These medicine men presented a challenge to the patent's validity, stating "Commercializing an ingredient of our religious and healing ceremonies is a profound affront to more than 400 cultures that populate the Amazon basin." Antonio Jacanamijoy, a native leader of the Inga from Colombia and head of the Coordinating Body of Indigenous Organizations of the Amazon Basin (COICA), explained that "Ayahuasca gives shamans the power to heal our sick, meet with spirits and divine the future." He went on to assert their claim that "Our ancestors learned the knowledge of this medicine and we are the owners of this knowledge." This situation contains a close parallel to the interactions that occurred with Native American tribes and early English settlers of "the new world." When Columbus reached America and claimed the land for the monarchy, he disregarded the current inhabitants of the region. Property was literally stolen from countless Indian tribes by people who believed themselves to be more intelligent and more civilized. Yet the very act of stealing made these men the barbarians, rather than the Indians. It is by the same standards that the indigenous peoples of the Amazon hold Miller and other patent holders of biological resources to be the crude and boorish ones.

In March 1999, on behalf of the COICA and the Coalition for Amazonian Peoples and the Environment (Amazon Coalition), the Center for International Environmental Law (CIEL) filed a legal challenge with the PTO to the U.S. patent claimed on the ayahuasca vine. The claim essentially requested reexamination of the ayahuasca patent.

On November 3, 1999, the U.S. Patent and Trademark Office (PTO) cancelled the patent issued to Miller for the ayahuasca vine in an office action. On April 14, 2000, the PTO even went so far as to claim that the patent never should have been issued in the first place. According to patent law, no invention can be patented if described in printed publications more than one year prior to the date of the patent application. The PTO's rejection of the patent was based on the fact that publications describing Banisteriopsis caapi were "known and available" prior to the patent application filing date. Similarly, evidence revealed that what was patented in 1986 as an ostensibly new, distinct variety of ayahuasca was later found to be the wild uncultivated type and is neither new nor distinctive, thus not warranting a patent after all.

For over a year that followed Miller appealed to the patent and trademark office asking them to reconsider their decision to cancel the patent on "Da Vine." As each filing deadline drew nearer, however, Miller was repeatedly granted extensions of time. Finally a brief was drawn up highlighting four main issues he had with the patent rejection. CIEL, COICA, and the Amazon Alliance were all shut out of the reconsideration, in accordance with the law that existed in 1986 when the patent was granted in the first place.

On January 26, 2001, the PTO issued a notice that terminated the proceeding on "Da Vine" and reversed the decision to reject the patent claim.

CIEL and the people it represented claimed that the court misread the law and confused the issue of plant patent protection in general with the issue of whether plant variety is patentable at all. Essentially, the decision rested on a misunderstanding between infringement and patentability, two Western legal concepts. This issue was resolved in a Western court of law. Despite the unfamiliarity of the concept of patents to the indigenous people of the region, in the end the minority had to conform to the majority narrative.

Countries like the United States have instituted a system to maximize the number of patents that are granted to individuals or institutions or pseudo-individuals, in order to likewise maximize economic gain. Intellectual property has become one of this country's largest exports; it comprises an enormous industry on its own. With increasing globalization has come an increased amount of Westernization. Countries of South America feel they are being forced to comply with the U.S. system of patents since the United States has the upper hand in terms of wealth and power. Although the United States may substantiate its actions on a legal basis, peoples of the Amazon perceive a great injustice being done to them culturally. The indigenous peoples believe they have been robbed of their ancestral knowledge through the U.S. patent of the plant. The case raises ethical and moral questions concerning intellectual property rights involving the traditional knowledge and materials guarded by native cultures.

Shamans from the Amazon have raised questions of how a man could claim ownership over a naturally occurring plant. The very concept of patenting is foreign to these indigenous tribes. Their ideas of ownership and property are different from those of Western culture. Although an era of globalization is upon us, the homogenous nature of the elite in the United States who make up such rules and laws is far beyond the conception of masses of inhabitants of the Amazon basin. Furthermore, even if indigenous peoples could understand our patent system, it seems illogical that a man could claim ownership over a specimen when he does not even live where the plant grows.

CONCLUDING COMMENT

From the perspective of indigenous populations of low-income societies, at least, the major representatives of Western and particularly U.S. capital have shown no reservations to commercially exploiting sacred plants integral to non-Western cultures. Outraged leaders of low-income societies find it culturally inappropriate and irresponsible that Miller has claimed and has been granted a patent on the most sacred plant of the indigenous peoples of the Amazon. Critics see this as equivalent to non-Christians applying and getting a patent to the Christian cross. This case should alert us to the need for more attention to the rights of indigenous people, as well as the duties of representatives of high-income societies as the global village becomes realized and local cultures become exposed to both the costs and benefits of modern patent law.

At the heart of these issues are clashes between groups with fundamentally different moral orders, associated with different conceptions of what constitutes ownership, who can be an owner, and what can be owned. To position oneself as an owner and others as users of one's property is to ascribe to oneself certain rights, and to others certain duties. Both within and outside the Western world, critics contend that patents are being used unfairly, to legally position some as owners and others as users. In this process, the real rights of indigenous people are being overlooked, while their newly found "duties" as "users" are increasingly (and unfairly) being enforced through international trade agreements.

REFERENCES

Convention on Biological Diversity. (2002, March 11). Retrieved April 17, 2002, from http://www.biodiv.org/convention/articles.asp.

Dobkin de Rios, M. Ayahuasca & Its Mechanisms of Healing. In *Visionary Vine: Hallucinogenic Healing in the Peruvian Amazon.* Retrieved February 2, 2002, from http://diseyes.lycaeum.org/fresh/mechheal.htm.

Fecteau, L. M. *The Ayahuasca patent revocation: Raising questions about current U.S. patent policy.* Retrieved February 10, 2002, from http://www.bc.edu/bc_org/avp/law/lwsch/journals/bctwj/21_103_TXT.htm.

Gaertner, S. L., & Davidis, J. F. (2000). *Reducing intergroup bias: The common ingroup identity model.* New York: Psychology Press.

Kaufer, E. (1989). *Economics of the patent system.* London: Routledge.

Lambrecht, B. (1999, March 31). Amazon tribe protests at US patent office in Washington over "biopiracy" theft of traditional sacred drug. *St. Louis Post.* Retrieved February 10, 2002, from http://www.organicconsumers.org/Patent/amazon.cfm.

Lovell, W. S. (Comp. a). The General Agreement on Tariffs and Trade: The Uruguay Round. Retrieved February 23, 2002, from http://www.cerebalaw.com/gatttext.htm.

Lovell, W. S. (Comp. b). The Patent Cooperation Treaty. Retrieved April 4, 2002, from http://www.cerebalaw.com/pctext.htm.

MacLeod, C. (1989). *Inventing the industrial revolution: The English patent system, 1660–1800.* Cambridge: Cambridge University Press.

Miller, L. (1986). *U.S. Patent No. PP05751.* Washington, DC. U.S. Patent and Trademark Office.

Moghaddam, F. M. (2000). Toward a cultural theory of human rights. *Theory & Psychology,* 10, 291–312.

Moghaddam, F. M., Slocum, N. R., Finkel, N., Mor, T., & Harré, R. (2000). Toward a cultural theory of duties. *Culture & Psychology,* 6, 275–302.

Moghaddam, F. M., & Taylor, D. M. (1985). Psychology in the developing world: An evaluation through the concepts of "dual perception" and "parallel growth." *American Psychologist,* 40, 1144–1146.

Paris Convention for the Protection of Industrial Property. Retrieved April 17, 2002, from http://clea.wipo.int/lpbin/lpext.dll/clea/LipEN/46e4b/47db8?f=file [document.htm]#JD_73619.

Polo, M. (1958). *The travels*. (Translated by R. Latham). Harmondsworth, UK: Penguin.

Shiva, V. (2002). *Protest or plunder? Understanding intellectual property rights*. London: Zed Books.

Varga, C. (Ed.). (1992). *Comparative legal cultures*. New York: New York University Press.

Walterscheid, E. C. (1998). *To promote the progress of useful arts: American patent law and administration. 1787–1836*. Fred B. Rothman & Co.

WIPO database of intellectual property. Retrieved April 17, 2002, from http://clea.wipo.int/lpbin/lpext.dll/clea/LipEN/46e4b/47db8?f = file[document.htm] #JD_73619.

Wright, R. M. (1998). *Cosmos, self, and history in Baniwa religion* (1st ed.). Austin: University of Texas Press.

CHAPTER 16

Assessment of Quality Systems with Positioning Theory

Lionel Boxer

INTRODUCTION

Despite the best planning and intentions, sociopsychological issues can undermine operational effectiveness. This chapter explores how positioning theory can be used to understand such sociopsychological barriers and perhaps neutralize their impact.

Dynamics resulting from the interaction of both the social constructionist model introduced in this chapter and tripolar discursive action affect every social exchange. With each encounter there is a different dynamic formed and positioning unfolds in a different way. As such people assume a variety of positions depending on what they can achieve in socializing and how others react to their self-positioning. Furthermore, their positioning of others is likewise accepted or challenged.

The value to business managers of understanding how positioning occurs will be illustrated through the assessment of a quality system in the social scene of work using discourse analysis of narratives. What follows is a case study of a company whose corporate board does not understand how positioning disrupts their ability to realize they obstruct the effective operation of their quality system. A positioning framework defined here will be applied to analyze the social situations causing the quality management system to be dysfunctional.

The effectiveness of a quality system is assessed from the perspective of how people create themselves and others in their dealings (Davies & Harré, 1990). Selves are discursively produced. That is, when people talk to others and engage in personal reflection, they adopt positions for themselves and impose positions on others.

Self as a Function of the Social Situation

It will be seen that a position is a dynamic notion of self that differs from role, which is a static notion. To make this clear, Figure 16.1 demonstrates conditions within which the self can vary. At risk of confusing the qualitative with quantitativeness, the dynamic nature of positioning is here represented by considering the algebraic definition of a line ($y = mx + b$). While a linear relationship is not intended by this analogy, a person's self (or position) at any one time (y) is equal to the positioning (m) that occurs during a particular social situation (x) added to their appointed role (b). Figure 16.1 represents the equation, Self = (Positioning $\times$ Social Situation) + Role. For example, the CEO has a different position when with the board of directors than when with union representatives, and a different self when dealing with personal staff.

Role is a static component of self that is conferred upon an incumbent by one's organization. Position, on the other hand is the variable component of self that is affected by each social situation. That effect is referred to as positioning and, while the algebraic equation $y = mx + b$ might imply it is a number, positioning is more appropriately defined through qualitative terms. It is in light of the variation of how people's selves are produced that the effectiveness of quality systems can be determined. Rather than procedural appropriateness and conformance, discursive suitability—discourse that enables or obstructs—will be the central issue of this analysis.

Quality and Quality Systems

Positioning theory will be returned to later in this chapter. At this stage, quality management will be discussed in the context of ISO9000-certified quality systems. A quality system consists of all the policies, procedures, forms, and records that an organization puts in place to manage quality. In very simple terms, managing quality includes determining what will be done, ensuring that what was planned is done, and demonstrating that this planning and checking takes place.

In the past ten years, commercial arrangements have evolved to require that sound quality management be practiced by most businesses. Typically, this

Figure 16.1
Representation of Various Selves

has meant that certification (in some places the term registration is used in place of certification) to the ISO9000 system of standards must be achieved. ISO9000 has been explained extensively elsewhere and will not be discussed here. In brief, it is an internationally accepted framework for quality systems (Boxer, 1993; Sadgrove, 1994) that has been developed by national standards bodies in over 50 countries (ISO, 2002). Such certification is awarded following successful assessment of an organization's quality system, and to retain certification, periodic assessments are conducted annually or at some other imposed interval.

While formal procedures can be established in a quality system that can be certified as appropriate for the business, it is anecdotally accepted that problems can still occur. It is suggested here that procedural issues of a quality system are only part of what certification should assess. Sociopsychological issues also need to be assessed as appropriate for the business. Here it is demonstrated that positioning theory can be used to assess quality systems for effective sociopsychological practices. Such effectiveness could be defined for the purpose at hand as having

- a culture where quality is taken seriously,
- a collective approach that supports implementation of the quality system, and
- individual behaviour that is congruent with these social attributes.

Opinion of the Quality Profession

Not withstanding Crosby's (1979) assertion that "quality is free," both managers and directors of companies question the investment required to establish, certify, and maintain a quality system. The author's experience has been that there is ill-informed criticism of the certification process; the amount of paperwork and the effort required to perform the duties specified by a quality system is misperceived to be caused by the activities leading to and retaining certification. Done properly a certified quality system does produce savings many times greater than the cost of the system (Deming, 1982; Crosby, 1979). Hence, if you break out of the crisis mode then these systems deliver benefit and quality *is* free. However, to derive these benefits some activities need to be directed at reviewing the effectiveness of the quality system.

While ISO9000 requires a quality system to be reviewed by management on a regular basis, it is assumed here that this review is rarely performed with determination or diligence commensurate with the seriousness intended by the quality profession. This is reflected in Crosby's (1984) comment on *The Quality Man* video. In this video, Philip Crosby chats casually about his career—culminating as a corporate vice president and quality consultant—while playing a round of golf at St. Andrews in Scotland. He offers vignettes from the understanding gained during his career to describe his golf game as it unfolds.

As long as you don't have to suffer the consequences of your actions you don't get serious about it . . . The quality manager . . . is powerless . . .; all the quality manager can do is sort the good from the bad (and) complain about it . . . When it is all done it is all over . . . the accountants are controllers and they sit on the board of directors . . . quality is the same thing . . . it is a senior management responsibility . . . they take finance seriously . . . take business of delivery seriously . . . we need to take quality seriously.

In terms of positioning theory, Crosby could be interpreted as saying that financial controllers have assumed a superior position with respect to quality managers and the board of directors has accepted that positioning. He suggests that quality managers have been denied a parallel preferment. In this same breath, Crosby could be seen to imply that quality professionals should engage in second-order positioning to resolve this imbalance of influence. First, second, and third-order positioning will become more clear as this chapter unfolds.

Asking Whether or not Quality is Taken Seriously

In the form of a case study, this chapter outlines a proposed approach for assessing the effectiveness of a quality system, enabling us to ask ourselves "are we taking quality seriously?" The approach harnesses positioning theory (Ling, 1998; Harré & Van Langenhove, 1999) to understand how people interact within the organization, with an objective of identifying systemic and behavioral issues to be resolved.

The next section provides a brief explanation of positioning theory, followed by the development of a positioning-based analytical framework, and then a case study involving Consolidated Based Painters (CBP). Having been given the task of determining the cause of the dysfunctional processes in place, the author was able to apply an experimental approach to his analysis of his client's integrated quality system. The approach is based on Harré's positioning theory, various principles identified by Foucault, and the author's development of an approach that had previously been applied in sociology and education. This application provides a demonstration that the theory and approach has practical applications in management studies.

FOUCAULTIAN AND FEMINIST INSIGHT INTO POSITIONING THEORY

At this stage in this chapter, a tangential discussion is provided to give a theoretical basis for the methodology used in this research. It is suggested that this section on Foucaultian and feminist insight be read carefully before proceeding to the section on methodology. It is important to have this understanding of the workings of positioning theory, as it will be used in the analysis of the case study.

Moghaddam (1997) provides a perspective of the realities of change with regard to the resilient effects of informal aspects of social relationships. He shows that despite the formal aspects put in place, informal aspects sustain normality. Through Foucauldian insight, it will be apparent that people can enable or obstruct effective operation of quality systems through the selves that they dialogically negotiate and assume themselves and those they impose on others.

Davies and Harré (1990), the seminal work of positioning theory, is traced back through what the author perceives to be its feminist pedigree to the work of Michel Foucault. While Foucault's gaze is shown to be an important component in positioning, it is suggested that his gaze is insufficient to fully explain the dynamics at work. This shortfall is resolved by developing a concept of social flux that results from social dynamics in a way that is analogous to electromagnetic flux being an outcome of electromagnetic dynamics.

Feminist Pedigree of Positioning Theory Provides a Framework

Cheney (1995) shows how many feminists drew on Foucault's discourse and power concepts. Building on the work of Foucauldian-influenced feminists, Davies and Harré (1990) put forth the idea that positioning is an ever-negotiable definition of self. They argue that *position* is a *dynamic* alternative to the *static* concept of *role* (see chapter 1 in this volume.) Power and parity are at work in positioning. Harré and Van Langenhove (1999) includes ideas from Davies and Harré (1990) and other seminal works on positioning theory. These works contribute to Figures 16.1, 16.2, 16.3, and 16.4 that the author has developed here.

To position is to negotiate power and parity through a tripolar process of discursive action that is the result of people speaking from established positions, with respect to a story line, and making use of rhetorical speech acts. This is demonstrated by Figure 16.2, which shows discursive action at the intersection of three components.

Later in this section, it will be shown that a force—social flux—influences this discursive action. The three components influencing discursive action are suggested to be in a sort of tension, which implies power is involved. In suggesting that power is in relations, Foucault (1980) implies that power is only evident in a dynamic. In other words, he denies that power can be noticed in static situations.

Grounded in Foucault

Fairclough (1992, pp. 37–38) notes the contribution of Foucault's work to understanding the "relationship of discourse and power" and the "discursive production of social subjects." As suggested in the previous section, Foucault

Figure 16.2
Tripolar Discursive Action Results in Position of Self and Other with Second-Order Positioning

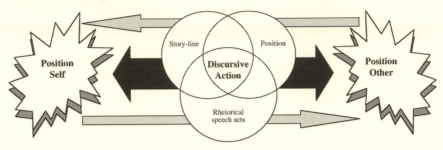

has influenced feminist theorists who provide the inspiration for the seminal work on positioning theory by Davies and Harré (1990). Foucault's (1972) innovation of the analysis of self was in how he combined its dynamic and static aspects in one whole. To Foucault (1972, p.15), this may have corresponded with the dynamic of substantial insight (*savoir*) versus the static of superficial knowledge (*connaissance*). Positioning is a dynamic and ongoing process that is a reflection of each social encounter that takes place. Each encounter involves an underlying social force in the organization, but positions at the beginning of the encounter will be affected by the people involved, the story lines that unfold, and the rhetorical speech acts that are employed. Each encounter has the potential to affect positioning through reinforcement or alteration of the recollection of previous encounters.

When two people meet, they negotiate their relative power and parity and come to an agreement about where each of them stands. Beyond that, entire social groups—women for example—can be positioned. Feminists, such as Weedon (1987, pp. 22–23) have complained that women are victims of "specific discursive relations and social practices" and a "male gaze," that have created "subject positions which (women) are encouraged to assume" (p. 34). West and Zimmerman (1987) refer to "doing gender" as complying with these culturally determined subject positions. While the feminist interpretation of Foucault may be questionable to some, Weedon has coined "male gaze" to denote the oppression they perceive society imposes on them. In a similar way, I coin "management gaze" to describe phenomena generated by the macro-community of managers (or more simply "doing management"). Following on from a discussion about "dominant culture discourses," Chan and Clegg (2001, p. 8) have referred to a "cultural gaze" within which "problem frameworks are set." The "cultural gaze" affects the "set of solutions . . . that appear to flow naturally from the problem." However, is the metaphor of gaze insufficient to explain residual or predisposed preference? Where does such a predisposition come from? Weedon (1987) and Clegg (1998) both draw on

Foucault's concept of gaze. From this, it could be suggested that gaze is a component of the author's construct of social flux that is created in the social constructionist model.

The complexity of human interaction requires sensitivity for effective analysis. While positioning theory provides a robust framework, introducing a concept like gaze will provide a broader base of sensors to perceive the richness of discursive data.

Foucault's Gaze

Foucault's gaze has two implications that are important to this discussion. First, gaze describes the power to watch and judge or arrive at a prognosis. Second, it explains how members of the community that comprises the gaze are able to make statements that are taken as truth by those outside the community.

Gaze describes the power derived from being a member of a social collective, be it a profession, gender, or other association. Foucault (1994) was interested in knowledge and studied that phenomenon through discourse, or sets "of linguistic facts linked together by syntactic rules of construction." He saw the strategic practice of controversial discussions and strategic ordering of discourse as revealing. Continental philosophers—Foucault was French—differ from their Anglo-American counterparts in part by their interest in discursive concepts such as this Foucauldian gaze. Said (2000) suggests that these insights are proving to be increasingly useful in explaining contemporary social happenings. Foucault (1973, 1977) developed concepts of both medical gaze and judicial gaze that he used to describe power relationships particularly between the members of minority and majority groups. He saw such gestures not as those of an individual, or even a collective, but an anonymity. Hence it is not a doctor or prison officer who has a gaze. Rather, it is the anonymous medical fraternity that has a gaze, as does the anonymous legal fraternity, and—as will be put forward in this chapter—perhaps so does the anonymous management fraternity. Anecdotal evidence of such a management gaze could be found in Crosby's (1984) light-hearted comment: "I guess I worked for ten or twelve years before I ever found out that management was supposed to help you. I always thought that management was kind of a punishment from God."

In his *Birth of the Clinic*, Foucault (1973) made use of gaze to describe the power that a doctor derives from the medical profession to observe a patient, diagnose the patient's condition, and prescribe a cure. Later in *Discipline and Punish: The Birth of the Prison*, Foucault (1977) uses gaze to explain the sanction that enables the judicial system to relentlessly observe, scrutinize, and impose punishment, and the anonymity that enabled justice to be dispensed. Self-discipline is shown to result from people's perception that they are continuously being watched by an unknown entity. It can be seen that Foucault's notion of gaze has evolved to suit the situation under analysis. Hence, it is presumed that gaze is context dependent.

A foundation to the concept of gaze is Foucault's (1972, pp. 50–54) idea that "sites of . . . discourse" lead to "positions of the subject" and that there are various "positions that the subject can occupy" (p. 52). Sites of discourse (hospitals for medicos and prisons for judiciary) are the place "from which the doctor makes his discourse, and from which this discourse derives its legitimate source and point of application" (p. 51). Foucault's "sites of discourse" could equate to Harré and Van Langenhove's representational place at which positioning happens (Figure 16.3). Feminists appear to be the first to pick up on this notion, and it is shown in the next paragraph that this is the seed that led to positioning theory.

Weedon's objective in referring to positioning affected by "male gaze" appears to be the encouragement for women to offer "a resistance to that subject position" (1987, p. 112) and a demonstration that each woman "exists as a thinking, feeling subject and social agent, capable of resistance and innovations produced out of the clash between contradictory subject positions and practices" (p. 125). Davies and Harré (1990) drew on Weedon (1987) and other similar thinkers to develop the idea of positioning theory. Their title "The Discursive Production of Selves" captures what happens when people position themselves and others, but their sources in Foucault's ideas were indirect. Through returning to first principles in Foucault, it could be said that the force affecting how discourse unfolds is in part impacted by Foucault's concept of gaze, and people's response to discourse will vary depending on how they react to the dynamics created.

Social Flux

As explained previously, gaze is insufficient to explain residual behavior and position, but something like gaze contributes to understanding why people differ and need to deliberate to resolve differences of opinion. Gaze serves as a foundation for a construct that explains residual or predisposed preference, the construct of social flux.

It is proposed here that positioning is affected by a *social flux* generated by the social order in a society. This is different from common usage of flux, where the term refers to erratic undirected movement. Here, what is implied is specific and directional force caused by a definable source. Flux is used in established electromagnetic theory to describe the rate of flow of force out of magnetic fields. Dynamics between moving components of an electric generator (magnets and coils of wire) can cause magnetic fields (Davis, 2000). Drawing on this analogy, a social flux is proposed to result from the dynamics between moving components of social scenes.

To demonstrate the production of social flux, I have developed a social constructionist model (Figure 16.3). Social flux happens at the intersection of these four issues: duties and obligations, local system of rights, local moral order, and public and private acts. Figure 16.3 shows that intersection and the resulting cylinder of social flux. Just as moving physical bodies can result in electromagnetic flux, social dynamics could produce a social flux. As shown in Figure 16.4, it is within the influence of that exudation where tripolar discursive action takes place.

To understand the nature of residual social flux, consider the highly standardized and regulated process of army officer training. Standard problems are posed to candidates, previously indoctrinated through the mild brainwashing of recruit training. Further regulation is provided through ritualized problem solving, monitoring by course-directing staff and standard solutions to each problem. Commissioned officers become part of military leadership; hence consistency and intensity of gaze is perpetuated from generation to generation. There is anecdotal evidence in traditional regiments to suggest such continuity occurs. This continuity might well stem from processes represented in the social constructionist model and a *residual social flux* could be seen to be the force that leads to this continuity. What sustains this apparent perpetual motion is the promise of promotion and exaltation at the center of the military system, an appropriate reward system, with incentives tied to the objectives of the organization. It is in cases where the reward system is not congruent with the objectives of the organization that residual social flux can have a counterproductive effect.

There appear to be limitations to Foucault's gaze, especially when attempting to understand how managers can enable or obstruct appropriate deliberation of sensitive issues. A concept such as social flux could be sufficient to influence the evolution of culture and replication of social practices as described by Dawkins (1976). Through introducing Dawkins's evolutionary construct, social flux could be seen to be able to replicate itself and obstruct competing flux. In keeping with the electromagnet flux analogy, a residual force is invisible, can inhibit other objects, establishes partition of space to

Figures 16.3 and 16.4
Social Constructionist Model and Tripolar Discursive Action

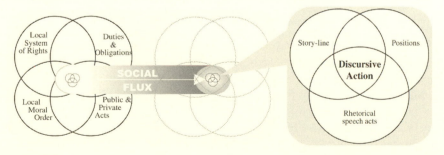

conform to and sustain itself, networks with other forces, *enables* and *obstructs*, and establishes conditions for other phenomena to occur (Nippes, 1994). Furthermore, it is common usage that people talk about being "charged up" by a situation.

With a construct of social flux it is possible to envisage how subcategories of effects can be derived—organizational flux, to denote the flux imposed by an organization; and financial flux, to denote the flux imposed by the financial community. All of these sorts of flux describe the subsets of force that affect the set of solutions to issues requiring resolution. Perhaps social flux is the cause of Chan and Clegg's (2001) "cultural gaze." Furthermore, unlike the single-dimensional forces implied in force field analysis (Lewin, 1951), flux can be defined more precisely through the components of the social constructionist model if it is assumed that they have a directional affect on social flux. Such an analysis will be demonstrated in the conclusion of this chapter.

The Space in Which Positioning Takes Place

Positioning is a dynamic and ongoing process that depends on each encounter that takes place. Each encounter involves the underlying social flux in the organization, but positions at the beginning of the encounter will be affected by the people involved, the story lines that unfold, and the rhetorical speech acts that are employed. Each encounter has the potential to affect positioning through reinforcement or alteration of the recollection of previous encounters.

The space in which positioning occurs is at the intersection of the four components of the social constructionist model shown in figure 16.3. Recalling that each situation is different and positioning is said to be the result of the social dynamics of all situations, social flux could be seen to be a cylinder that is constantly being exuded by the evolving social order. This cylinder of social flux is the space in which positioning occurs. Hence, if the positioning is to change, the social flux must change. To change the social flux it is necessary to alter one or more of the components of the social constructionist model.

First-, Second-, and Third-Order Positioning

Positioning is dynamic. Consider tennis players exchanging blows or medieval knights in a jousting match. In fencing, this is referred to as parry and riposte.

Figure 16.2 shows that first-order positioning (black lines) occurs with initial contact and, depending on whether or not the subjects involved accept or reject this idea, second-order positioning (gray lines) takes place to alter the first-order positioning. Second-order positioning may or may not take place;

if a person is satisfied with how they have been positioned they may not resist—that is, engage in second-order positioning.

Third-order positioning occurs when someone who is outside of the social relationship being described engages in positioning. Consider how a sports commentator describes a boxing match or a football game.

Using the Positioning Analytical Framework

The analytical framework described in this section suggests that, as positioning is caused by the social order, the social constructionist model shown in Figure 16.3 can be used as a diagnostic tool in social situations. The cause of dysfunction can be determined by tracing observed positioning described in Figure 16.4 through understanding the social flux. This involves deconstructing the various components of the social order and defining the cause of observed positioning in terms of the four components of social order as shown in Figure 16.3.

First, positioning observed in discursive action needs to be understood as being either of oneself or of another. Then the result of that positioning can be determined as summarized in the framework illustrated in Figure 16.5.

METHODOLOGY—A POSITIONING ANALYTICAL FRAMEWORK

In considering the implications of social flux with respect to a quality system, it is suggested that managers engage in deliberate positioning when they take steps to enable or obstruct quality issues from being dealt with in a certain way. For example, if a manager confronts staff in a positive way regarding the adoption of a certain procedure, that manager is positioning him or herself as enabling. In such an action, the manager is also positioning staff to enthusiastically continue their compliance with new procedures. On the other hand, if a manager approaches a quality system with indifference, he or she is self-positioning as obstructing. Similarly, the manager is also positioning staff as unlikely to continue viewing new procedures as being important. In each case,

Figure 16.5
Discursive Action Resulting in Positioning

	Deliberative Positioning	Deliberate Positioning	Forced Positioning
Self-Positioning	Deliberative Self-Positioning **Deliberative Intent**	Deliberate Self-Positioning **Deliberate Intent**	Forced Self-Positioning **Forced Intent**
Other-Positioning	Deliberative Positioning of Other **Parity**	Deliberate Positioning of Other **Personal Power**	Forced Positioning of Other **Institutional Power**

Consensus Democratic Parity } ◄————————— Continuum ————————►{ No Consensus Institutional Power staff can oppose this positioning through second-order positioning. Beyond the issue of specific procedures, managers can position themselves or others to the benefit or detriment of the direction intended by the most innocent comments.

It is suggested that even when managers do not intend—that is, when they behave habitually—to enable or obstruct quality issues from being dealt with, their actions remain influential. Here it is suggested that the social flux can cause managers to enable and obstruct. In demonstrating this, social flux might provide insight into behavior that is incongruent with intentions. That is, if a business is committed to adopting and implementing its quality system and managers obstruct the implementation, tracing back through the social flux would be expected to offer an explanation for why such irrational behavior occurs. By doing so, the four components of the social constructionist model in Figure 16.3 can suggest causes of systemic nonconformance or dysfunction.

Through collecting examples of discourse regarding the operation of a quality system and assessing how people are positioned and how they position themselves and others, this analysis provides insight into how effective that quality system will be. Such discourse needs to involve participants relating their encounters with their subordinates; peers and superiors are all subject to positioning during every social encounter.

Grounded theory procedures of open, axial, and selective coding have been used to guide data collection and analysis. Conflicting forms of positioning— inappropriate hierarchies, oppositions, and dichotomies—are suggested to provide evidence of a dysfunctional approach to the quality system.

CASE STUDY—CONSOLIDATED BASED PAINTERS

Having previously established an integrated quality system and contributed to their quality system certification, I was familiar with Consolidated Based Painters (CBP). I began working in Melbourne with this Australia-wide organization in the late 1990s and their ISO9000 certification was achieved in 1998. However, I had never dealt with employees of the *owners* of the business, nor was I familiar with their processes. Yet, I had questioned the reliability and robustness of the CBP business model.

Realizing the need for centralized marketing, three painting businesses formed CBP, of which they shared ownership/directorship. CBP's charter was to sell wider facility-management services to property managers and other commercial customers. Sales incentives resulted in CBP being sales driven; the rest of the business reacted to situations created by sales. Once sold, orders were processed, customers billed, and work orders distributed to one of the owners. CBP was a simple business that sold services, established service delivery contracts, and subcontracted product delivery. It faced high turnover, uncertain policy, and significant repetitive costly errors and oversights.

CBP is owned by three painting firms: Indispray, Flexoroll, and Latexply.

These three businesses had attempted to work together on several occasions in the past but never were able to agree on operating procedures. They also realized that their methods of operation would not meet the quality requirements of the corporate customers they were seeking. They devised a plan to establish an umbrella organization to front their service-delivery operations. If this were done simply to develop efficiencies of scale the establishment of CBP would have been commendable and most successful. However, their intention was to create a buffer or shield to hide behind and avoid the realities of the marketplace. CBP was devised to accept the shock of business reality, which would enable the three owner firms to carry on their somewhat antiquated practices as suppliers to CBP.

While CBP had an independent management structure, the board of the business was composed of the chief executives of each of the three painting companies, which all owned equal shares in the business. Hence, the suppliers to the business owned the business. This structure enabled the suppliers to dictate purchasing policy of CBP. Despite the development of a professional quality system, which had achieved certification by an accredited third party certification referee, the convoluted business model in place strained the quality intentions defined in CBP policy. As an extension of my role in developing the system, I was retained to conduct a review of its effectiveness.

Interviews—Selected Raw Data

Narrative data was collected through ten semi-structured interviews with staff and managers of the service delivery units within the three owners of the personal service delivery business (the owners were each independent companies with a core business of service delivery). Those interviewed were not intended to be representative, but to provide key narratives central to life in this particular context. These data were subjected to narrative analysis, drawing on grounded theory procedures (Strauss & Corbin, 1990) to analyze data. This led to coding data and establishing categories to develop an understanding of the effectiveness of the quality system. Symbolic discourse in the form of metaphor was extracted from the data and various subject positions of the participants and those they referred to were identified.

Participants related meaning through rich, meaningful stories. Semi-structured interviews are somewhat freewheeling and enable questions to be regulated to suit how participants respond (Burgess, 1982; Flick, 1998). Having consulted to senior managers over 20 years I was able to facilitate this process. Ten participants were selected based on the work of Eisenhardt (1989) and the availability of people willing and able to provide insight into the operation of the quality system.

Interview data were subjected to open, axial, and selective coding (Strauss & Corbin, 1990) and from this an understanding of the sociopsychological practices was attempted. From the understanding that was developed, findings were formulated and presented to the management of the business.

Extracts from data presented in the following subsections demonstrate the positioning that interview data has enabled me to observe. Of primary concern has been the positions taken by managers and how these have influenced the effectiveness of the quality system. Also of interest was the positioning imposed on staff and the ways they have responded to that positioning. These reactions can be seen to be second-order positioning. It will be seen that managers can enable or obstruct compliance with procedures and that dysfunctional processes can be attributed to the social order created by managers.

Participants have been arranged in sequence to first provide the perspective of CBP managers and then the reactions of the various staff, employed by the service delivery alliance partners (which are also owners of CBP). While these staff members are not employees of CBP, the unique relationship of their employers with CBP makes their roles subordinate to the managers in CBP. This positioning, which is highlighted in the following subsections, is then used to demonstrate the causes of dysfunctional processes.

Representations of interviews have been consolidated here. Pseudonyms have been used and, for brevity only selected participants and comments are included.

Charlott—Service Delivery Director at CBP

Charlott is proud of her qualifications and related situations to her MBA studies at times during our meeting. She had been with CBP since inception and struck me as a very professional manager with extraordinary capabilities. She was certain about her facts and displayed a determination to see things developed as required. Charlott accomplished this though a well-led team but faced high levels of turnover due to the frustrations confronting most people.

Her reaction to the quality system effectiveness provoked an outburst. She smiled as she expressed her dismay.

They don't care about the quality manual! You have to understand, these people (Indispray, Flexoroll, and Latexply) want to leave things as they are and they are not prepared to come midway. They think they can hide behind our facade. They know they don't have to come to the party. They are a bunch of frustrating nitwits.

Charlott had come from an industry where customers and suppliers were clearly defined. She expressed frustration about the situation she was put into.

They think they own us. That is ridiculous. You can't have the sales clerk (referring to Mary) owning the supplier. It just doesn't work this way, but they have this idea and you cannot talk to them about it. And, there is nothing you can do about it. The Board set it up this way so they would not have to change (develop quality systems within

Indispray, Flexoroll, and Latexply)! It is a different story with Eric. Have you spoken to Eric yet?

I asked Charlott whether or not things could be improved. For example, the supplier development clause in the purchasing component of the quality system could be invoked. This invited a strong reaction.

If I try to approach them as their customer they laugh at me. I go to their managers to talk to them about how services can be enhanced and they say, "you can't tell us how to run our business . . . you have no authority here" and then they throw me out! Imagine that.

However, Charlott demonstrated her resourcefulness as she explained how she gets around this.

Every two months, we are able to review procedures at each of Indispray, Flexoroll, and Latexply. At these meetings we have a proforma of questions we can ask, as laid out in the CBP business model. The results of these are passed on to the board meetings that take place the following week. During these meetings, I remind the managers at these companies that my report will be going to the Board. That actually gives me a bit of leverage and they are more cooperative—for the moment. But after the review it's back to normal.

Joe—Sales Director at CBP

Joe could be described as a typical salesperson, who views his job as getting sales and moving on. Once the sales have been passed on to service delivery Joe—an archetypical salesperson—does not want to know about it. He was the second employee of the business and previously worked for Flexoroll as a salesman for about ten years. Of all those interviewed, Joe's was the shortest as he "has no time for quality," but his brief comments were most enlightening.

I do not see what the problem is. We have customers and it is our job to deliver services they pay for.

When I asked him what he thought of the capabilities of Indispray, Flexoroll, and Latexply he was abrupt and precise in his rely.

They are a pack of idiots. How hard can it be to do this stuff anyway.

Joe's contempt for the "suppliers" is further elaborated by his reluctance to let customers meet representatives of Indispray, Flexoroll, and Latexply.

I do not want customers to see them. Prospects wouldn't deal with us if they had to listen to their crap. The first thing they say—and I have made the mistake once—is we can't do that. Customers don't want to hear negative crap like that! You have to understand that sales is the answer to the company's success; no one has a job until sales sells something.

Well how can one argue with that! Joe confirms his neglect for quality as well as how he positions others in CBP and suppliers as subordinate to him.

I don't care about quality, that is Service Delivery's job. They get the jobs from us and make sure that the work happens. And the Board supports that. The Board don't pay me to hear that we can't do things. We are on the cutting edge of this industry and have to deliver what the customer wants . . . it is not rocket science you know. Do I look like I care? I tell my people "don't waste time fixing problems, just get the order processed." The Board expects this of us; you want it changed then take it up with them.

Mary—CBP Coordination Manager at Indispray

Having worked for Indispray for twelve years, Mary was aware of the mechanisms within her own business and well versed in the company's procedures. She led a team of five who reviewed and distributed the orders sold into the various work teams in Indispray.

Mary expressed distress with the treatment she received from her contacts at CBP. She felt that they did not treat her with the respect she would expect from them.

We own CBP. They have no right to come in here and tell us what to do. They rely on us to deliver the services they sell and they need to understand our businesses better. They should be doing what we say!

In expanding on this, she related an experience with the sales manager of CBP regarding a customer complaint. One of her people had initially received the call from CBP and, due to the sensitivity of the issue, passed it on to Mary.

How do I feel about it? Frustrated. I received this telephone call from the service delivery clerk at CBP about a mix-up and you could hear him screaming in the background. I could hear him clearly saying, "Those Indispray people are incompetent and screw up everything they touch." I was really upset about this. Here I was trying to solve the problem and both the person on the other end and I could hear this carrying on by you know who. He is always like that.

Her reaction to requirements imposed on Indispray by the quality system demonstrated a reluctance to adopt the sort of commercial practices required by customers. She found working with CBP frustrating and was annoyed at their lack of concern for their limitations.

They do not know anything about our business. We invited them to come and work with us for a day when they start there, and some do, but they go back and treat us the same way as everyone else. It is really frustrating. They do not want to know about what we can and cannot do. We tell them, but we never know about these things until after the deal is sold to the customers.

When I asked Mary to explain how it was that jobs could be sold that were beyond the capability of their business to deliver, she explained more about the constraints. She found that without her manager's support she was unable to take steps to improve her situation.

That's right. How can they sell a job they know we cannot do, but they do not want to know. I have asked them to include us in the proposal development process, but they don't want to know us. In fact, when we have been around their customers they are very rude to us. They don't let us talk to them. My manager tells me to just do my job and not do what I cannot do.

On being confronted by questions regarding her CBP ownership perception, Mary replied with an outburst.

Of course we own them. Indispray is a shareholder and our CEO is on the Board!

When I asked her to elaborate on her level of discomfort, she broadened the reluctance of her managers to take steps to enhance the business. Mary related the difficulty she has in obtaining approval to enhance Indispray's delivery capabilities.

Our managers don't want us to spend time changing our system. They want CBP to sell jobs that we can do and for us to get the work done. The thing is, many of these changes are so small and easy to accomplish that it wouldn't take much time at all. But my boss won't support us.

Alf—Call Center Manager at Indispray

Alf has been with Flexoroll for three years and did not work in the pre-CBP environment. His previous employment has been in similar work and he seemed content with the call centre environment he worked in.

They are a right pack of. . . . You know, I call them ten times a day and I am lucky if they get back to me by the afternoon. When I finally get through to them it is a challenge to get things done. All they say is that they will look at it. I get the feeling that they are just brushing me off. Sometimes they answer and say, "I don't do that anymore, talk to . . .," but they don't give us any warning.

Providing examples led to Alf eventually discussing procedural documentation. He found format and updates to be two issues that caused specific problems.

I don't know what they think we need, but they provide the manuals that make no sense.

This was news to me, as I had been told by CBP that they had spent considerable time identifying the appropriate formats and updating procedures, which apparently consumed considerable time at CBP. On asking Alf it turns out that this was not the case.

Each order contains different information. I think it has something to do with their turnover (at CBP). The terminology varies—they have different words and they end up meaning the same thing. It confuses our workers to no end. When they come out, updates are generally (photocopies with) hand written in the edge of the pages.

Of a more serious nature, Alf related a breakdown in the contract review requirement of ISO9000. This was connected with his comments about the disrepair of the procedural documentation provided by CBP to Indispray, Flexoroll, and Latexply.

They sell stuff that is not in the manual and likely will never be. Why? Why . . . because you can't do some of the stuff they promise to customers. Sometimes what they sell doesn't even comply with legislation. They lie to get the work and then we are expected to find some way to get the job done.

Jane—CBP Liaison at Flexoroll

Jane has been with Flexoroll for fifteen years and has considerable understanding of the processes. She has worked for no other company. Her approach to dealing with CBP appears to involve expecting the worst and psyching herself up to act out her fears.

What really bothers me about CBP is that you can call them ten times and they never return your call. The only way to get something done is to be lucky enough to catch them at their desk. I think they just leave their phones on voice mail all the time.

When Jane was asked why she thought that happened, she replied that it was what she came to expect.

It is typical of the way they (CBP) behave. They are rude and abrupt. They don't want to help us.

On exploring this further, Jane discussed the distress she felt and the preparation involved each time she had to call CBP.

I find it stressful. Sure I do. Each time I have to call them, I need to prepare for a stressful telephone call. That is what is so frustrating about getting that (awful) answering machine all the time.

When asked why she felt stressful, Jane explained what it was like dealing with CBP. Interestingly, when she eventually got through to them Jane did not find speaking with CBP people pleasant either.

All they ever do is talk down to us. They do not respect us and expect us to pick up the pieces. And that is how I feel when I am dealing with them. They throw us mixed-up pieces and leave us to figure out how to put things together.

Eric—CBP Liaison at Latexply

Eric has been with Latexply for one year and did not work in the pre-CBP environment. Previously he has worked in the finance industry. Eric provides a fresh perspective and attitude.

I am glad we are having these discussions (the quality system assessment). There are many things here that disturb me.

When he was asked to relate some examples of things that disturbed him, he focused on providing specific issues and ideas for solutions. Unlike most other employees, he offered to contribute to resolving problems.

When I came to work here this was all new to me. But after a while—after I learned all the jargon and such—after a while it all became a sort of déjà vu. When problems arise, I find out what caused them and then write up a short explanation of the problem and the steps I am going to take to solve things short-term and email them to CBP. In that email, I also put my ideas in for long-term resolutions. We did this in the bank and it works here too.

His approach, appearing unique, led to asking if other people at Latexply did the same sort of thing when problems arose.

I would be surprised if anyone in Latexply would know what problem solving is. And for the others (Flexoroll and Indispray), well—I think they just like getting into a fight with CBP. You know, they don't realize it but it is their habits over the years.

Given these comments, it is not surprising to learn that Eric has better experiences with CBP. Furthermore, he views the quality system as helpful and essential to his business.

The other liaison people (at Flexoroll and Indispray) seem to have problems with CBP. We all talk—once a week we get on our own conference call and exchange gossip. I have my share of problems, but not to the extent that these folk do—I can understand why CBP does not call them back. I got this a bit when I started, but I let them know how I stood and, in one case I called our CEO and told him the problems I was having and how I wanted to work with CBP. CBP gave me a chance and I proved myself to them. You know CBP are mostly sales people and they are not interested in realities or whether or not it can be done; we have to help them.

Interpretation of Interviews—Analysis Using Framework

A common theme of frustration occurs in all interviews. Traditional feminist and critical theories might be helpful in explaining this. Davies and Harré (1990) draw on these foundations to consolidate their formulation of positioning theory. Yet, there is another side to these theories; they site power in language and allow for situated and competing ideologies and so are more apt for the rich and messy data provided by a naturalistic inquiry such as this one.

Charlott—Service Director at CBP

Charlott shows her resourcefulness is dealing with what she describes as "frustrating nitwits." The ownership issue is paramount in her comments, as is the refusal of Indispray's managers to acknowledge that they are suppliers to CBP. In effect they delegitimize the quality system.

Charlott refuses to acknowledge the positioning enacted by Mary and uses stealth to engage in second-order positioning. While Mary does not realize she is being repositioned, she does acknowledge the terms of the agreement between CBP and Indispray. Thus, Charlott is able to negotiate arrangements. However, this repositioning lasts as long as the duration of the contractually scheduled review. Thereafter, positioning reverts to "normal."

It is anecdotally accepted by quality professionals that a healthy customer-supplier relationship, and thus a healthy quality system, depends on a deferential acknowledgement that the "customer is king," despite who owns whom. As there is no opportunity for supplier development by CBP, compliance with ISO9000 fails and certification is threatened.

Where appropriate, Charlotte harnesses personal power to alter positioning to her benefit. However, in general she is a victim of institutional power. She would like to achieve, but she perceives forces—regardless of whether or not they are real—that prevent this from occurring. It appears that Charlotte does not have a right to alter her position. Her duty requires her to conform to dysfunction.

Joe—Sales Director at CBP

Perhaps the primary cause of frustration—apart from the ownership structure—is Joe's attitude to all others in CBP and the three businesses that own CBP. He views his role in sales as "primadonna" in the business.

His self-positioning is forced, as his rule is that "sales is the answer to the company's success" and the Board appears to have told him so. He leaves no opportunity for deliberative positioning to occur. He appears to be happy with imposing deliberative positioning on others but would certainly not permit the reverse. There is nothing deliberative in this man.

It appears that he has been empowered by the board of CBP to sell services at all costs. He does not appear to have a quality caveat to regulate his actions. He has been given a role that is unanswerable to regarding quality and he can impose the most unworkable situations on the business.

Joe achieves his position through deliberate intent and exerts personal power to demand that others comply with his perception of orderliness. The social order—while a construct of his perception—governs his view of himself and how others should be. It appears that the local moral order is in favor of sales. Joe is able to make public acts that contribute to dysfunction.

Mary—CBP Liaison at Indispray

Mary displays a great deal of frustration about working within the constraints of the quality system. She knows that that she must comply but is faced with incapable processes that her managers do not appear to want to know about. Her comments are reflected in those of other participants.

While her employer is part owner of CBP, Mary has difficulty in accepting obligations as a supplier to that business. She carries on as though she has a sort of sovereign title over CBP and infuriates everyone in that business (as is reflected in the next subsection). Here she is confronted with dichotomous concepts of dominance, contrast, and difference; in her mind she is the monarch, yet peasants who expect her to behave like a pawn vex her. Perhaps this is a symptom of delusions of grandeur. This infuriates her, but the status she has been led to believe is hers is caused by misinformation that the corporate public relations has created and dispersed throughout that business. Perhaps it is not misinformation, but the message has been misdirected, or perhaps she has read shareholder literature. Clearly, a lower-level supervisor does not have an ownership stake in the business, but she is convinced that she does.

Reluctance of Indispray's managers to engage with CBP in a customer-supplier relationship contributes to Mary's frustration. She wants to improve processes but is not given resources to do so.

Having been positioned, albeit in her fantasies, as an owner, she inflicts herself on CBP. This obstructs her from perceiving that she has an obligation to deal with CBP as a supplier, her management does not enforce the customer-supplier relationship that logic suggests is real, and the quality system collapses, as will be seen in CBP's reaction to this irrational behaviour.

Mary is a victim of the personal power of others and her distorted perception of the social order. Misunderstanding how things are, the forced intent of her aberrations appears to cause her aggressive behavior and inability to achieve parity. It appears that the local moral order is unclear or based on misinformation. Mary has few rights but is able to be difficult and obstruct efforts to resolve dysfunction.

Alf—Call Center Manager at Indispray

Alf is not happy with the way he is treated by CBP in general. This is largely caused by Joe's primadonna behavior and the way unworkable assignments are dumped on him. He is a most sensitive "absurdity detector" and tells it like it is.

CBP's sales-at-all-cost focus appears to have gotten the best of Alf; he has been positioned as a servant. He does not appear to take steps to challenge this positioning. Realizing that CBP has the upper hand, Alf positions himself as victim of circumstances, perhaps as though he is trapped in a tragic role in serfdom.

Alf's frustration leads him to assume a confrontational position through deliberate intent. He positions others through personal power; they are incompetent and unhelpful in his mind. Parity is beyond his comprehension. It appears that Alf perceives that he has no rights to resolve problems and does not perceive an obligation to prevent dysfunction.

Jane—CBP Liaison at Flexoroll

Jane appears to perceive herself at the bottom of a power hierarchy and senses the inequity. She accepts that they are hiding from her by putting their answering machines on all the time.

Similar to the way Alf accepts his lot with CBP, Jane views her situation as unavoidable. However, she worsens things by playing out how bad things will be in her mind before she has even spoken to people at CBP.

That she lets CBP throw inappropriate or incomplete material to her and expect her to fix things implies that Jane accepts the positioning imposed on her. Not only does Jane accept the positioning, but she also reinforces it on herself through what could be explained as West and Zimmerman's (1987, p. 146) "routine accomplishment embedded in everyday action."

Jane is a victim of being positioned by forced intent due to the way things are. Her inability to effect change causes her to be frustrated and that appears to prevent her from being able to perceive an alternative. It appears that Jane perceives she has no rights and does not understand her duty to make things work or facilitate improvements.

Eric—CBP Liaison at Latexply

Eric is in control of his situation and, while he was positioned the same as his peers at Flexoroll and Indispray, he took steps to alter that. Eric repositioned himself through direct discourse with CBP and by invoking support from his CEO.

Insightful comments made by Eric about Indispray and Flexoroll's habits of arguing with CBP might be simply written off as habits. However, West and Zimmerman (1987, p. 146) suggest that through repeating these habits, people "render legitimate . . . institutional arrangements." It appears that the CBP Board has indeed established some inappropriate arrangements that position people inappropriately for effective quality system operation. Yet, Eric—in his own case—is able to rise above this.

Given an opportunity, Eric demonstrated his ability to work closely with

CBP and successfully repositioned himself. Perhaps, his forcefulness and de-termination was something lacking in Alf and Jane. Perhaps, instead he had not been in his role long enough to be affected by the positioning, which introduces a temporal parameter to positioning.

Eric appears to want an opportunity to achieve parity, but he realizes the institutional forces are preventing him from assuming an appropriate position. Despite this, he exerts his personal power to resolve the situation, and his positive approach may move the organization towards parity if he is permitted to use his initiative. It appears that Eric ignores the local moral order and makes things work "despite the system." Whereas this resolves short-term issues, it does nothing to prevent recurrence of issues that are systemic. Hence, dysfunction is permitted to remain the norm.

FINDINGS

In the next sections high-level processes are overviewed in relation to the data, to provide an understanding of the problems interfering with the quality system. What has been identified are dysfunctional relationships and con-founding social processes.

West and Zimmerman (1987, p. 147), in referring to limitations of gender perception, conclude that social change requires both institutional and cul-tural change. While they acknowledge that this is not novel, they suggest that it is necessary to reconceptualize challenging issues (such as dealing with qual-ity systems) not as simple individual human parameters, but as integral in the dynamics of social orders.

In CBP there is a complacency and reluctance to do the right thing. Lev-eraging on West and Zimmerman's (1987, p. 126) notion of "doing gender," doing this complacency and reluctance is undertaken by people at all levels whose competence as members of a potentially productive enterprise is hostile to it production. As such the residual/outcome of doing complacency and reluctance halts efforts to be competent and cooperative. Doing complacency and reluctance involves a complex of socially guided perceptual interactional and micro-political activities that cause or locate particular pursuits as ex-pressions of *action* and *un-action*.

Sales Process—Conducted by People Called *Sales*

Sales were rewarded based on the volume of their "product" moved and, for a considerable time, there was no contract review. Contract review mis-interpretation (they took the word *contract* to imply that the financial arrange-ments would be reviewed) prevented operational personnel from making capability or capacity of inquiry. A financial flux within the organization looked upon operational people as disenfranchised from contractual arrange-ments. Reluctance of *sales* to deal with nonconformities within CBP processes appeared to be based on positioning that could be expressed by "don't waste time fixing problems, just get the order processed."

Contract Establishment—Conducted by People Called Delivery

Closed sales were abruptly handed over by *sales*, who abdicate their responsibility and desert operations. Dealing with discontinuities, unresolved issues, and unworkable situations was standard operating procedure for operations. Services could be initiated, but *delivery* was positioned "inefficient and careless." *Delivery* felt positioned as "oppressed and frustrated"; former employees met regularly for drinks; their being thus positioned molded them into an informal club. It could be assumed that the financial flux was obstructive to effective business operation and oppressive to all other aspects of the business.

Subcontract—Conducted by People in Indispray, Flexoroll, and Latexply Called Owners

With services being provided by *owners* there was an unfortunate situation, in which junior managers of the subcontractors positioned CBP "we own (CBP), they should be doing what we say." When their interpretation was questioned, they replied "of course we own them . . . (our business) is a shareholder." Their reading of the situation and positioning provided understanding of the local moral order and system of rights that some people perceived to exist. This explained the inability of CBP managers to treat their "subcontractors" (*owners*) as suppliers in what should be a simple customer-supplier relationship. *Owners* subsequently refused to be accountable to any form of CBP authority, even at the expense of customer satisfaction. *Owners* assumed their own authority and deployed a social flux, oppressing operations of CBP in reaction to the social flux of the sales force.

CONCLUSIONS AND REFLECTION

In this chapter, positioning theory has been shown to be a powerful tool that can demonstrate what happens within organizations. One can examine the causes of problems by tracing back through the conversations, story lines and rhetorical speech acts, back to the social constructionist model (Figure 16.3). The root causes of systemic problems affecting the quality system at CBP can be found at the four elements that result in the exudation referred to here as social flux. These root causes are expressed below:

- **Local moral order** permitted decisions that put the integrity of services at risk
- **Duties and obligations** made some people in the organization subordinate to others

- **Local system of rights** permitted some people to create and enforce unworkable situations

- **Public and private acts** reflected predictable story lines, rhetorical speech acts, and conversations in which people perpetuated dysfunction and this led them to frustration and resignation.

These components of the social constructionist model demonstrate a residual damaging social flux. In simple terms, the reward system in place is counterproductive. It rewards people for doing dysfunctional things. The quality system is confounded by some people's actions, which are rewarded by the Board. The Board has established a social order where forced positioning affects the various players in this social scene. In some cases players are able to engage in second-order positioning, but in others certain players are provided with such an asymmetry of power such that they can only be the receivers of deliberate positioning. It is only in isolated cases that consensus-based deliberative positioning can take place, and this is generally on the periphery, away from the real centers of power.

Observations were taken in real workplaces, filled with employees doing their work and dealing with people. The discursive action incorporated in this research represents one view of what happens in a place of work. Due to the range of situations in offices and factories, analysis in other places will result in a variety of outcomes. Perhaps with a number of broader surveys a conclusive general theory may be developed, but in this case findings can only relate to the local social scene occurring in the CBP business model. To that end, I propose conducting similar studies of quality systems in other organizations.

In this case, the cause of dysfunctional processes was inaccurate Board-level assumptions and subsequent decisions not being effectively articulated and disseminated throughout the owners' service delivery processes. Reporting this to the Board was challenging and they were reluctant to accept responsibility. That they asked me to leave while they discussed my report says something about their positioning of themselves, me, and everyone else involved. Their intent to control the knowledge that I had provided them with suggests that more could be derived from considering Foucault (1980). The ongoing challenge remains how to deal with the necessary corrective action at board level in CBP and in general. People need to believe that that must face the consequences of their actions; "we need to take quality seriously."

REFERENCES

Boxer, L. J. (1993). Understanding AS3900/ISO9000. *Corporate Review*, vol. 4, No. 2, pp. 11–14.

Burgess, R. G. (1982). *Field research: A sourcebook and field manual*. Boston: Allen and Unwin.

Chan, A., & Clegg, S. (2001). "Gamekeeping": Genealogy and culture in organization studies. Unpublished paper, February 2001.

Cheney, L. V. (1995). *Telling the truth: Why our culture and our country have stopped making sense, and what we can do about it.* New York: Simon and Schuster.

Clegg, S. (1998). Foucault, Power and Organizations. In A. McKinlay & K. Starkey, (Eds.), *Foucault, management and organization theory: From panopticon to technologies of self.* London: Sage.

Crosby, P. B. (1979). *Quality is free.* New York: McGraw-Hill.

Crosby, P. B. (1984). *The quality man.* video. BBC Enterprises, London.

Davies, B., & Harré, R. (1990). Positioning: The discursive production of selves. *Journal for the Theory of Social Behaviour,* 20 (1), 44–63. http://www.massey.ac.nz/~alock//position/position.htm.

Davis, D. (2000). Magnetic Flux. Ch. 21 in *College physics,* Saunders College Publishing, Burlington, MA, http://oldsci.eiu.edu/physics/DDavis/1160/Ch21Ind/Flux.html, accessed 6 May 2002.

Dawkins, R. (1976). *The selfish gene.* New York: Oxford University Press.

Deming, W. E. (1982). *Out of the crisis.* Cambridge: Massachusetts Institute of Technology.

Eisenhardt, K. M. (1989). Building theories from case study research. *Academy of Management Review,* 14 (4), 532–550.

Fairclough, N. (1992). *Discourse and social change.* Cambridge: Polity.

Flick, U. (1998). *An introduction to qualitative research.* London: Sage.

Foucault, M. (1972). *The archaeology of knowledge.* A. M. Sheridan Smith (Trans.). London: Routledge.

Foucault, M. (1973). *The birth of the clinic: An archaeology of medical perception.* A. M. Sheridan Smith (Trans.). New York: Random House.

Foucault M. (1977). *Discipline and punish: The birth of the prison.* A. M. Sheridan (Trans.). New York: Pantheon Books.

Foucault, M. (1980). *Power/knowledge: Selected interviews and other writings,* Gordon, C. (Ed.), Gordon, C., Marshall, L., Mepham, J., & Soper, K. (Trans.). New York: Pantheon.

Foucault, M. (1994). *Power, essential works of Foucault, 1954–1984.* Faubion, J. D. (Ed.). Hurley, R. (Trans.). Paris: Editions Gallimard. http://www.nytimes.com/books/first/f/foucault-power.html, accessed 4 March 2002.

Harré, R., & Van Langenhove, L. (Eds.). (1999). *Positioning theory: Moral contexts of intentional action.* Oxford: Blackwell Publishers.

ISO 2002. Where ISO9000 came from and who is behind it. http://www.iso.ch/iso/en/iso9000–14000/tour/wherfrom.html, accessed 1 July 2002.

Lewin, K. (1951). *Field theory in social science.* New York: Harper and Row.

Ling, I. (1998). The role of the curriculum coordinator: An exploration through discursive practice. Unpublished Ph.D. thesis, University of Melbourne.

Moghaddam, A. (1997). Change and continuity in organizations—assessing intergroup relations. In C. Granrose & S. Oskamp, (Eds.), *Change and continuity in cross-cultural work groups.* London: Sage.

Nippes, P. I. (1994). Principles of magnetism and stray currents in rotating machinery. *P/M Technology,* 7 (3), 14–20.

Sadgrove, K. (1994). *ISO9000 BS5750 made easy: A practical guide to quality,* London: Kogan Page.

Said, E. W. (2000). Deconstructing the tyranny of reason: Edward W. Said pays tribute to the original mind of philosopher Michel Foucault. *The Australian Financial Review*, 22–6. Dec (2000). pp. Review 4–5.

Strauss, A., & Corbin, J. (1990). *Basics of qualitative research: Grounded theory procedures and techniques*. London: Sage.

Weedon, C. (1987). *Feminist practice and poststructuralist theory*. Oxford: Blackwell.

West, C., & Zimmerman, D. H. (1987). Doing gender. *Gender and Society*, 1, (2), 125–151.

CHAPTER 17

Positioning the Subject in Body/Landscape Relations

Bronwyn Davies

The focus of this chapter is on the ways in which subjects position themselves and are positioned as embodied beings in relation to landscape. In what follows I will make a deconstructive move on the body–landscape binary through the development of a different approach to body/landscape relations. This new approach is achieved through the development of metaphors and through unexpected juxtapositions of ideas and observations. The chapter thus works as a poetic performance, and at the same time it makes observations and arguments from the material, political, and discursively constructed world.

In this chapter I will look at the ways in which discursive practices constitute embodied subjects in relation to landscape, and on the ways speaking subjects negotiate their positions in relation to landscape. I will at the same time deconstruct usual ways of situating the body as distinct and separate from landscape. The positions created in and through talk as speakers and hearers take themselves up as persons in relation to landscape are examined as political acts, and at the same time as necessary discursive acts for the achievement of self as recognizably a person and in particular as a competent person. Through development of the metaphors of (in)scription, (be)longing, incorporation, and folding I examine the longing for and belonging in landscape that takes place as we are (in)scribed and incorporated as human in the folds of one discursive landscape or another, and in the folds of one physical landscape or another.

Awareness of being embodied, and in particular, being embodied in relation to landscape, is something we have little practice in observing or articulating. The body is generally understood as natural, and as such is taken for granted. It is not made observable, generally, until it ceases functioning in ways that various authoritative discourses such as health or fitness or religious discourses say that it should, or until we find ourselves in an entirely different discursive or physical landscape.

Elizabeth Grosz talks about the inscription of bodies as a permanent and *unnatural* feature of human embodiment. She makes clear how the overt, violent practices of controlling and shaping bodies are only one aspect of how bodies are inscribed. Equally relevant is the covert shaping that takes place through the bodily inscription of "norms and values" and of patterns of desire. But there are important ways in which the analysis I develop here parts company with Grosz, in particular, her claim that such bodily inscription is as permanent as scarification of the body surface, and also in her construction of "the natural" as that which is, by definition, unscarred and unshaped (Davies, 2000a).

Grosz constructs the body as inscribed with fictions that are written on a natural surface. I also see the body, in all its forms, as powerfully inscribed. That inscription, however, does not make the body any less "natural" than anything else that we might like to (in)scribe as nature. Nature is as much a discursive construction as anything we might (in)scribe as "unnatural." To (in)scribe the embodied subject does not scarify, in the sense of limiting or achieving finality in the ways it can be read or reinscribed. I bracket (in)scription here to draw attention to the constitutive acts of reading and writing—the scription. In doing so, I want to draw attention to both the constitutive power and the potentially shifting nature of what we might scribe on our bodies. Bodies (and landscapes) are not impervious to language and are shaped through our acts of reading and writing them. We inscribe and reinscribe our embodied selves in physical, emotional, and political ways, both in ways we are aware of and in ways we are not. Those inscriptions are not only the result of conscious acts of scribing, nor only of acts of scribing over which we might be said to have choice or control. The patterns of inscription, the texts that we create, both singly and collectively, might themselves be described as having a life, as having effects, "as capable of action, capable of rupture and disruption, even of themselves" (Grosz, 1995, p. 127). Grosz elaborates a Deleuzian theory of texts as volatile, liable to change and movement, capable of action, and capable of rupture and disruption, even of themselves (Grosz, 1995, pp. 126–127):

. . . texts could, more in keeping with Deleuze, be read, used, as modes of effectivity and action which, at their best, scatter thoughts and images into different linkages or new alignments without necessarily destroying their materiality. . . . Instead of the eternal status of truth, or the more provisional status of knowledge, texts have short-term effects, though they may continue to be read for generations. They only remain effective and alive if they have effects, produce realignments, shake things up. In Deleuzian terms, such a text, such thought, could be described as fundamentally moving, "nomadological" or "rhizomatic."

Thinking of our bodies as (in)scribed Deleuzian texts, the possibility of change is written into the body. It is also true that some (in)scriptions make

deep and knotty folds that may make the body-text less fluid, and less amenable to change. And there are some (in)scriptions that are so significant to
us in constituting who we understand ourselves to be that we choose not to
change them—indeed change might be taken to herald a crumbling of the
self. It is also true that bodies can become exhausted and debilitated through
too much change.

Taking up a language, or a particular way of speaking within a language,
does not necessarily *induct* the speaker into the assumptions and beliefs of that
language, let alone *fix* the speaker in them (Davies, 2000b). Ways of speaking
do not necessarily include an awareness of "their assumptions nor the power
of the images to invoke particular ways of being" (Davies & Harré, 1990,
p. 49). Further, we are, many of us, multilingual and multidiscursive; that is,
we have more than one way of speaking ourselves into being and thus more
than one way of inscribing our embodied selves. Unlike the scarification of
tattooing, for example, the possibilities of being one or another person may
open up and shut down as we speak now one language or another, or move
from one discursive landscape to another. An example of this might be found
in the recent shameful reviling of refugees by the ultra-conservative Australian
government. In such situations as that which came to be known as the Tampa
crisis or the "children overboard" story, we might imagine a woman with a
self-respect and dignity and love of her child that are inscribed in her body.
In becoming a refugee and fleeing her own homeland, that self-respecting,
dignified woman may become invisible, even to herself. Cut adrift from her
own landscapes and language, she can be repositioned, reinscribed, by the
people in the country she has fled to, as an incompetent, selfish, and manipulative being who will even harm (or might as well have harmed) her own
child to achieve her selfish ends. Or alternatively she may be positioned as
innocent victim of the selfish government of the country she has fled to. In
the tussle between these positionings, there is no room for the original perception of a person with self-respect and dignity and with integrity and courage who may be so desperate that she might reasonably and rationally take
such a calculated risk. Nor is there room to imagine that that same intelligent
and competent woman might see her boat sinking and seek life vests for her
children to ensure their survival. There is thus, in this squabble, both a profound reduction of the person she might be said to be, *and* a devastating failure
to comprehend the experience of being deprived of one's land, of floating,
trapped on the sea, with no land to take oneself and one's children to.

We can see a different kind of multiplicity of relations between embodied
selves, discourse, and landscape in a portrait that Janette Turner Hospital
draws of Ethel, an indigenous Australian woman sitting in the desert, longing for the language she has been deprived of through the practices of colonization. Ethel speaks in English, but she attends closely to the landscape
where she believes the words of her ancestors have been inscribed for thousands of years:

Consider Ethel. She sits there, cross-legged in the red dust at the edge of the bora rings, smiling to herself, rocking gently backwards and forwards as though she hears singing and the rhythmic stamping of feet in the gidgee boughs. She has been putting the scattered rocks back where they belong, filling gaps in the circles and centuries. They have been there, the bora rings, for over twenty thousand years, it is believed; it is only in the past hundred, a hiccup in time, that indifferent graziers and the treads of their four-wheel drives have scattered the stones and have imprinted zippered scars across their sacred clay skin.

From time to time Ethel grins at me, and her teeth flash in her black face like stark white lightning.

"My mob chuckling up their sleeves," she tells me. "My mob been here all along. They been waiting for this."

"I wouldn't have thought your mob were wearing sleeves."

"Fuck off Jess," she grins. "Whitefella Maroo been and gone once, and been and gone twice, and we're still here, my mob and me."

She is waiting for a lost language to come back to her. She believes it will rise out of the stones. It will drift into her, into the place where words are made, with the smoke from the gidgee leaves. She pokes at her smoldering branches with a stick. She is waiting for a name other than Ethel to rise out of them, for the name she was never given, but should have been, for the name history took from her. She is waiting to meet her other self. She is waiting for her name to settle into her cupped hands, knowing that it might not come from the smoke because there is no predicting the ways of the Old People. It might fall from a passing bird. The *Wandjinas* might bring it. It might slither over her arm. *She, the rock python* might set it down beside her. She waits. (Turner Hospital, 1996, p. 40)

In this story, the indigenous language has been withheld from Ethel. She nonetheless understands the language to be inscribed in the landscape. The landscape will speak to her if she listens carefully enough, through the smoke of the fire she has lit, or through a bird, or the *Wandjinas*, or a rock python. Though she cannot hear the precise words, what she does know of the language binds her to the land in a complex set of duties and obligations that override the whitefella language that she also speaks. The whitefella presence, with all its destructive power, with its capacity to reinscribe the landscape with zippered scars, and fences, and the scattering of sacred stones, comes and goes: it is a minor power compared to that of the Old People. Their language (in)scribes her and her relationship with the land. Ethel positions Jess as one with far less powerful knowledge than she has. Jess's knowledge comes from a new, and what seems in comparison to the ancient language inscribed in the landscape, superficial language. Like the zippered scars of the tire tracks, it will disappear, as it has before. Even though the language eludes Ethel, she takes it on trust that it is there in the landscape, and that it has given and will go on giving her and her people particular powers, and particular rights and obligations in relation to the landscape. Her (in)scription of herself in relation to landscape may be less visible to some than the tire tracks, but in this moment it is no less powerful in constituting her as an indigenous person who knows what Jess cannot know.

In Deleuzian terms, Ethel sees herself in relation to landscape not only as multiply inscribed, but she reads the text of the landscape through her lost language as *having effects, producing realignments, and shaking things up*. This is not a passive landscape waiting to be inscribed, but a landscape that can be described as fundamentally active with its past (in)scriptions (Grosz, 1995, pp. 126–127). I use this example to show Ethel's multiple inscriptions of herself in relation to landscape, but also to introduce a discursive construction of landscape as alive, as text, and as deeply implicated in the construction of the human subject. I do not invite a viewing of this particular construction as exotic, but to open up the discursive space in which to think body/landscape relations against the grain of their usual separation from bodies and their construction within binaries such as animate–inanimate, body–ground, active–inert, and culture–nature.

In non-indigenous discursive practices, landscapes are often defined in terms of that which is "natural" (as opposed to "unnatural" or "manufactured"). In contrast I want to make a discursive move in which *all landscapes are natural*, in the sense that anything might be inscribed as natural, once it is placed in a binary opposition with the unnatural, or the manufactured, or the discursively constituted. The "natural," just like the unnatural, is a discursive construction. All landscapes are transformable, over time, or through the advent of a different presence in them, or through the conceptual/linguistic frame through which they are (in)scribed. This activity of (in)scription should not be understood as an activity solely undertaken by "unnatural humans" in contrast to "natural animals." (Nonhuman animals also inscribe landscape in multiple ways.) They (in)scribe territories and social relations with scent, urine, and sound, both to keep others out of their marked territory and to attract others to it. They arrange the landscape in visual displays to attract or repel particular others. They also modify landscapes for specific utilitarian purposes. Ants build roads and houses, for example, and seals make holes in ice to breathe). Another way to deconstruct the body–landscape binary is to imagine ourselves as landscape.

The first landscape we encounter, as animals who are born as sentient beings, is the internal landscape of our mother's body folded around us. This experience of first knowing inside a fold of the mother's body is an experience not only of humans and other placental mammals such as whales and rodents, but also of monotremes whose eggs are hatched in a temporary pouch where the baby suckles until it is fully formed, and of marsupials who give birth to fetal young which also suckle in the pouch. It is also the experience of gastric brooding frogs who lay eggs that are externally fertilized and then swallowed, growing to fully formed frogs in the mother's stomach. All these give birth to sentient beings, of whom it could be said their first landscape is a fold in their mother's body, whether that fold is a womb, a stomach, or a pouch. The fold creates an interior, a holding place, a deep surface on which the baby lives and from which, or in which, it finds its sustenance.

The body is not separate from landscape, in this example, but is itself, in the case of the mother, a landscape with/in which another being dwells. In the case of the baby, it is connected to or held within the landscape and either draws sustenance directly from the substance of the mother's body, or from the yolk created from the mother's body, or in some rare cases, from the other unhatched eggs inside the mother's body[1] This original body–landscape relation troubles the easy assumptions of separation and the distinctions between where bodies begin and end and where landscapes take up. Bodies and landscapes might be said to live in such complex patterns of interdependence that landscape should be understood as much more than a mere context in which embodied beings live out their lives. I use this image of mother as landscape as my beginning point to trouble the human–animal binary and with it the assumption that humans are separate from and dominant over landscape in a way that other animals are not. I am at the same time troubling the body–landscape binary, which is a central plank in the construction of humanist subjects whose rational controlling "nature" makes them separate from the contexts in which they find themselves.

To dwell a little longer on that prior-to-birth-landscape that some of us experience, it can also be thought of as one in which language, or systems of communication, have already been experienced and made relevant as the vibrations of sound pass through the physical matter of the mother's body. We hear/feel the patterns of sound that our mother makes, and we hear/feel the sounds around her whether we are in a womb or a pouch or a stomach. When we take up our existence in folds other than the fold of the mother's body, the patterns of sound take on a new importance. Discourse and other patterns of communication provide the basis for knowing how to read landscape, and for knowing how to manage our embodied existence within it. And in becoming competent subjects we are, in that same process, inscribed as that which the discourse takes us to be. As Butler says "Discourse is not merely spoken words, but a notion of signification which concerns not merely how it is that certain signifiers come to mean what they mean, but how certain discursive forms articulate objects and subjects in their intelligibility" (Butler, 1995a). Discourse (in the case of the human species and probably many other species) constitutes landscape in order to form the conditions of our existence within it and in relation to it. "Whitefella" discourses, as I said above, construct us, at the same time, as fundamentally separate from it.

In what follows I will focus on *(be)longing* in landscape. I bracket (be)longing in this way to give special weight to *longing*. In the process of constructing ourselves appropriately in landscape, we long for a secure relationship, for an affinity, for a sense of being in our proper or usual place. This longing is intricately tied up with becoming the appropriate(d) body, which is *of* that landscape, which *belongs to* that landscape. I will begin with the stories of three individuals, two fictional and one autobiographical.

In the first story Janette Turner Hospital creates a character who is not indigenous but who identifies herself in relation to the landscape of her child-hood. The story tells of a moment of being enfolded in and *becoming* the landscape. Again, I introduce this image, not as an exotically different image, but to shift and open the discursive spaces in which I am writing. The story is set in a rain forest similar to those no more than an hour's drive up the mountains from Townsville where I live. Charade does not know who her parents are. But she does not choose separation or the absence of the father as her point of beginning. Instead she chooses as her first memory a moment of complete and ecstatic immersion in the rain forest. It is one of many possible beginnings, but this is the one in which she (be)longs in the landscape:

. . . where, Charade wonders, is the beginning? And how does she cut her own story free from the middle of the history of so many others? In a sense she is the epilogue to several lives.

Well then . . .

Here's one beginning, she suggests, in the rainforest where time comes and goes like a bird.

The birds. To the tag end of trillions of years of decay and growth come the birds: bellbirds, lyrebirds, lorikeets, parakeets. Shadow and rotting sweetnesses lure them. On their wings is such a weight of colour that they float dazed on the green air, slowly losing height, drifting down where Charade sits crushing the mosses and ferns. Oh, she gasps. Oh.

She is five, perhaps six years old, rapt, knees hugged up under her chin. The fallen tree trunk behind her back, given over to creepers, is collapsing softly, and along its jellied spine where a flock of new saplings has a toehold—there is walnut, silky oak, mahogany—the jostling and clamoring for light is constant and silent and deadly earnest. If she sits still long enough, the philodendron will loop itself around her ankles and kingfishers will nest in her hair.

That is my earliest memory, Charade says. (Turner Hospital, 1988, pp. 46–47)

Charade sits and waits, hugging her knees. She sees in intense detail the color and movement of the forest, and in doing so, weaves herself, in her imagination, into the rain forest. She names the birds and the trees; she grows in among the philodendrons that weave themselves around her; she *becomes a place* on which the philodendron will grow, in which kingfishers can make their nests. Like the birds, she has come to this landscape at "the tag end of trillions of years of decay and growth" and like the new saplings she grows strongly there, clamoring silently for light.

The second story is of a moment of (be)longing which is troubled by a dispute over whether or not the storyteller can (be)long in the way her story suggests. This story is told by Roberta Sykes, who grew up in Townsville. Her autobiography also tells of a child whose parentage is obscure, since her mother is white and she is black. Her mother refuses to talk to her about who her father is, or she makes up stories about a black American serviceman and then denies them. Her mother is adamant that her daughters will not grow up identifying as Aboriginal. To be Aboriginal at that time in Queensland entailed a serious denial of normal rights of citizenship. But not knowing whether she is of Aboriginal descent is a gap, an absence, that haunts Roberta's life and fills her with longing. She tells the story of when she was old enough to be able to explore the town on her own. She went to a sports field each weekend where she watched Aboriginal children playing. She tells of an old man who eventually began to talk to her, teaching her how to see them, by closely observing the ways that they looked or moved, telling her how to see which totem they belonged to. In effect, he teaches her to see the (in)scription of their bodies in relation to landscape in some of the ways that Ethel knew about. Roberta asks him, then, to locate her in relation to that same landscape:

"Who am I?" I asked the old man . . . He gazed away as if trying to decide whether to answer me or not, then he picked up the stick in his toes and drew in the dirt.

"You fella snake." He spoke towards the ground as we both leaned against the fence and watched his foot drawing, as though it had a life of its own. "Baby one, eh," he added after a pause, a twinkle in his cloudy eyes.

I watched the coiled snake taking shape in the soil. (Sykes, 1997, p. 110)

In this powerful moment, she knows how she (be)longs in the landscape. It is a precious gift, a statement of (be)longing: the small girl sees in the image traced on the ground an image of who she is. The first book of her autobiographical trilogy is called *Snake Cradle*. The snake drawn on the ground, and the later live snakes she befriended, are claimed as even more primary than the landscape of her mother's body or the language of her father's name: the snake is her cradle, the place that holds her safe. But this gift, the image of the snake has become a dangerous and politically fraught image. The old man's action suggested he recognized the child as indigenous and that he gifted her with the detail of that recognition: a recognition that gives her very specific rights and obligations in relation to the landscape. Nearly half a century after this remembered event, her autobiographical words have led to a strong protest from those indigenous people who think she has no right to such a story. They position her as an interloper, as one whose story cannot be true. Pat O'Shane (1998, p. 29), for example, writes in an open letter to Roberta claiming that she does not have moral rights to the story she has told:

. . . you import the idea of the old man and the snake. That story, Bobbi, is a dead giveaway. Anyone who had an idea she was Aboriginal would want to do some research about the people from whom she believed she was born. She would have done as author Sally Morgan did: lift the covers, peel back the layers, and not be put off with half-truths and other deceits. But more than that: you would have known that in Aboriginal custom, no old man would have stopped to talk to a "lonely little girl" (a complete stranger at that) and tell her the snake story in the way that you recount it. . . .

The letter, titled "Sins of omission," takes up half a page in the weekend national newspaper. Roberta's autobiographical writing elaborates in careful detail how "the facts" and "identity," or clear belonging in any binary category constantly elude her restless searching. Pat O'Shane, a magistrate of undisputed Aboriginal descent, respected by Aboriginal and non-Aboriginal groups alike, an elected Chancellor of a University, authoritatively redraws the boundaries that Roberta's story troubles, and powerfully positions Roberta outside the tightly drawn lines. She does so with a legalistic evidence-based argument—Roberta has not behaved as "anyone" would behave with uncertain parentage—therefore she has no right to tell her story in such a way that it suggests she may be Aboriginal. While Roberta's life is exemplary in terms of behaving as one who has deep obligations to fight on behalf of indigenous people in Australia, any rights she has to this particular indigenous knowledge of (be)longing in landscape is denied her.

In contrast to O'Shane's adoption of the patriarchal metaphor of the father as central to identity, the stories of Charade and of Roberta disrupt the notion that the primary identification of the individual is through the father. As I have argued elsewhere (Davies, 2000c), the idea that the name of the father confers identity (and that identity may be lost without the name of the father) is very local and specific to particular patriarchal cultures. Althusser says, for example, of the unborn child, "it is certain in advance that it will bear its Father's Name, and will therefore have an identity and be irreplaceable" (1971, p. 176). These stories do not bear out that certainty. They are stories, rather, that show not a longing for the absent father, but a longing and belonging in landscape, and they open up the pain and emotion of connection to specific landscapes denied. The struggle in the second story is carried out through Roberta's body—the dispute is organized around the question of whether it is an indigenous body, or whether it is a non-indigenous (privileged) body. If it is an indigenous body, it has rights to speak in certain ways, and specific rights and obligations in relation to the Australian landscape. As Nast observes: "In effect, bodies are physical field sites upon which the world inscribes itself—places to which others come and make their difference, places like any other place—localized and with continuously negotiated boundaries and subregions" (Nast, 1998, p. 95).

A different set of metaphors for understanding this dispute between Roberta Sykes and Pat O'Shane can be drawn from the Australian Aranda modes of dance and song in which *incorporation* and *folding* are central. If we think of the image of the hunter moving through the folded landscape (folded differently over different geological ages, and folded differently in his viewing of it as he moves over hills and valleys in pursuit of his prey) then we can imagine many ways of seeing, each way necessitated by the particular fold in the landscape one is caught in at any one point in time. As he moves, and the land unfolds differently to his eye, the other ways of seeing, from within each different fold, are not erased—they were there before and will be there again.

The Aranda words of the songs and the movements of the dancer's body incorporate the folding and unfolding of the landscape that is moved through, and merge the body, the land, the hunter, and the hunted. Carter (1996, p. 61) refers to the "flexibly incorporative, or folded nature of Aranda song." The singer of the song and the dancer of the dance fold and unfold in a "reverent mime of the land" (p. 92). The elastic hunter/singer dispatches "on its shallowly-curving arc" the spear that "is the foot of the hunter elongated. It is the ground puckered up and drawn tight as the throat of a purse. The thin projectile sings and quivers over the glinting space, its tone being its vectorial signature" (p. 88). The Aranda language is "poetically and grammatically 'additive', like undulating or cave-pocked country which bunches up planes, thus incorporating more ground" (p. 60). "[W]hat distinguishes the culture of the Aranda might be its capacity simultaneously to hold in place multiple views and meanings, to think, not in terms of paradoxes and contradictions, but in terms of a lesser or greater folding of the land" (p. 103).

Roberta Sykes and Pat O'Shane might be said to stand, during this dispute, in a different fold in the landscape. What is possible, desirable, even obvious from one fold, makes no sense in the other. From where Pat O'Shane stands, Roberta has not displayed the appropriate forms of action and knowing for one who would claim indignity. The folds of the landscape from where she stands are deeply knotted with colonial history and with the appropriation and destruction of indigenous knowledge. Her strong stand makes sense from that fold in the landscape. Roberta's story of (be)longing makes the sense she wants in a quite different fold in the emotional and political and conceptual landscape. Pat O'Shane works with "whitefella" reasoning (which has great power in many of the folds in the landscape she inhabits) to disconnect or *disincorporate* Roberta from the Australian landscape, to argue that she cannot experience herself, as indigenous people may do, as coextensive *in that way* with landscape. She draws the strings of discourse in tight excluding folds.

The third example is set in New Zealand in a novel by Patricia Grace. It takes place at a time when the indigenous people still speak their own language but have agreed to schools being built on their land so the pakeha teachers might teach pakeha knowledge to their children. In school the indigenous language is forbidden. In this particular story, the narrator, Kura, is eight years old and she is charged with caring for her sister, her *teina*, Riripeti, on her first days and weeks at school. She says:

The teacher didn't notice Riripeti marching into school with me, and was busy writing on the blackboard when I stood Riripeti by Tihi at the little children's table. I was the one who told her to stand there. I straightened her, put her feet together, put her shoulders back and went to stand by my own desk. We said our good mornings to the teacher before we all sat down.

"Who is this?" the teacher said when she saw Riripeti sitting on the form. I put my hand up because that was the right thing to do, but the teacher didn't look at my hand. "Who are you and where are your manners, coming in and sitting down as though you own the place?" she said to Riripeti, but Riripeti didn't know what the teacher was saying. "Stand up when you're spoken to," the teacher said. I wanted to whisper in our language so this teina of mine would know what to do, but I knew I wasn't allowed to speak our language so I made a little movement with my hands trying to tell her to stand. She didn't understand and sat there smiling, swinging her shoulders, swinging her eyes—to me, then back again to the teacher. (Grace, 1998, p. 31)

The teacher pushes and pokes Riripeti, who does not understand the words being spoken to her, and who is forbidden access to her own language to find out. She pushes her into the corner, and infuriated by her eyes turning around to Kura, instead of facing the corner, she "jolted her head round and gave her a smacking on the legs, then Riripeti stood stiff and still without moving, facing the corner" (Grace, 1998, p. 32). The child, Riripeti, can find no way to read the landscape of this classroom. The teacher positions her as deliberately wrong, as bad, as someone in need of constant punishment, and the days are filled with silent misery. Then:

One morning Riripeti sat down by the track and said she couldn't go to school any more. Usually when she did that we could manage to persuade her, but that day I believed her. It was true she couldn't go to school. Her spirit was out of her, gone roaming. Her hair was as dry as a horse's tail, rough and hard, her eyes were like flat shadows, not at all like eyes. I had seen a dying dog look like that, which made me think it might be true what the teacher said, that my teina was turning into an animal. (Grace, 1998, p. 34)

So Riripeti went each day to play in the trees, like an animal or bird, and after a while she seemed to Kura not to be so sick any more. The children told the teacher each day that she was sick. But Riripeti, or Betty, as the teacher insists on calling her, did eventually die. She could not find her footing in this alien landscape.

Let me turn now, to the stories told in a collective biography workshop on Magnetic Island just off the coast from Townsville. The workshop was focused on body/landscape relations and the participants were non-indigenous—whitefellas. In telling these stories, however, I will draw on the discursive space opened up in Ethel's, Charade's, Roberta's, and Riripeti's stories. I divide the collective biography stories that follow into three kinds. The first consists of stories in which landscape is the desired space in which the body is immersed in a harmonious blending of embodied being and landscape—stories similar to that told about Charade and by Roberta Sykes. These are stories of longing and belonging, of (be)longing and of incorporation in landscape. The second group of stories tell of being out of place, of losing one's footing in the landscape, of being lost and at a loss as Riripeti was. These are very painful stories and they highlight and lie in sharp contrast to the stories of (be)longing. The third kind tell of individual struggles to become embodied appropriately, to develop ways of moving, thinking, and understanding that enable the storyteller to become the competent subject, the subjected being, who will not lose her footing in the landscape—who will be incorporated in landscape.

STORIES OF ECSTATIC IMMERSION—LANDSCAPE SATURATED WITH DESIRE

The incorporation of selves in landscapes of other selves begins before birth. At that time, we are literally held and grow in the landscape of our mothers' bodies in a plural I: mother and child. After birth, the landscape of the mother may continue to be longed for. The first story tells of the first awareness of (be)longing in the landscape of the mother's body:

The young mother sits with her first born baby daughter on a cane lounge in a sparsely furnished room. She holds her baby on her foot, balancing her by holding her hands outstretched. She swings her foot up and down, then slowly, sensuously swings her backwards and forwards, smiling as she sings.

The baby girl laughs in pleasure at the game, and in the glow of her mother's gaze. Looking up into her mother's face, she sees the soft waves framing her face, her head surrounded by a roll of hair. She basks in the warmth of her mother's happiness, her smile and her singing. The solid smooth curve of her mother's knee rises above her, while she sits, precarious and excited, but balanced and secure—smoothly, lazily swinging, held by her mother's hands, the focus of all her mother's love, careful attention and intense pleasure.

The child's embodiment in this moment is first located in the sensation of swinging, but that swinging is inextricably linked with held hands, the mother's sensuous movement, the mother's smile and her singing voice. Her eyes see her mother's face, her hair, her knee. The body sitting astride the foot is not described in detail: the intensity of her awareness is primarily in the landscape that holds her, that incorporates her; what the story tells us about the child's embodied self is that it hears singing, it is held, it is laughing, and it is basking in the warm gaze. This is probably a rare memory of intense delight. There is nothing that alarms the child in this moment "with its violence and its strangeness" (Cixous, in Cixous & Calle-Gruber, 1997, p. 43).

The next story is of fusion in landscape in her grandmother's garden. Here it is the detail of the taste of nectar on the tip of the child's small tongue, the feel of her skin brushed by the air, and the feel of her grandmother's hand that brings to life the embodied being in this garden landscape:

In the summer when the rest of the grandmother's garden is warm and dry and sunny, the "jungle" behind the garage is a dark cool place.

Nanna Ida takes me there when I am very small by the hand when she waters the special damp-loving plants that need watering in the evenings. She takes me with her when she picks the figs she makes into grey jam. She's a bit like a witch when we're in the jungle together. She's tall and sharp and bony not like my other round and cuddly Nanna. Her hand is cool and damp and her fingers are sinewy and grip tightly my own small hand.

I like to go there alone and everyone knows they can find me hiding there. It's so quiet and still. My skin is always cool and moist and open to the air in there in the darkness. I sit still on the mossy wet stump and breathe the fresh green dark air. The tiny flowers that grow at the base of the fig tree are purple cups of nectar. I pick them one at a time and poke my tongue gently inside to lick out the sweetness. I'm so still and quiet and I wait there hoping that fairies will come.

This is a landscape deeply (in)scribed with (be)longing. It is heavy with desire. It is a place the child can be alone, yet known by others to be there. It is also a hybrid place, a place of mixed ancestry, a place in which the feel of the air and the taste of the flowers may well be the same as it was thousands of years ago, and at the same time it is a place made by witches who came from across the world, bringing their ancient language and longings with them. The child's immersion in the garden has similarities to Charade's image of immersion, of incorporation, in the rain forest. Each is connected to the lives of others, and each securely finds, alone, a sense of themselves in place. Each child finds in the cool damp space a form of embodiment, of solitude and ease, of (be)longing. Charade's imagined embodiment is such that the forest grows into and around her, it enfolds and incorporates her, and her boundaries dissolve. In the garden, the child's embodiment is made up of fresh green dark air drawn into her body, of her skin cooled and made moist by the air, of body held by the mossy wet stump, of drinking the sweet nectar from purple cups. She imagines, she longs for, the presence of fairies, the imagining of whom is made possible by the language of her mother and her grandmother and all the mothers before her.

Embodiment in landscape is made and remade. It is made out of the possibilities found through language and through the particular materiality of place and the possibilities for embodiment held there. The threads of history shift and change and overlap. Continuous being is not passed down from generation to generation intact, but made again and again out of what is possible for this child, these children, in the spaces in which they find themselves.

STORIES OF ALARM, OF SEPARATION, OF BEING OUT OF PLACE

Stories of being out of place, pulled out of one's place in the landscape, are held in strong contrast to immersion, to being in place. In the next story alarm and separation are talked about inside a story of being enfolded and cared for.

Small pink body. Naked. Blonde hair—soft like baby's breath. And blue bubblegum ATTACHED TO the tiny folds of my labia. How did it get there? There is only the knowledge of me as naughty child—ANNOYED parent—tut tutting—and place of body where this sticky substance was not supposed to be. Dark laundry—light glistening on dusty louvered windows—stone laundry trough and cold grey water, Solyptol added to help dissolve the gum AND mother picking at my blue sticky lips—

Then being left

Alone
To detach this substance from my body.
Small hand
dipping in and out of Solyptol smelling water.
Cold dark grey trough
little fingers pulling at strings of blue
Rolling strands into little balls
and dropping them onto the floor
sensing shame
Then awareness
of the "new" but unacceptable part of myself.
Separate = me? but not me
Then mother—tutting again—less angry now
Soft warm arms lifting—towel rubbing briskly at tender lips.
Then her lips dropping a kiss—
transparent enveloping love.

The child is intensely aware of the detail of the strange landscape in which she finds herself: in cold grey water, in the Solyptol-smelling laundry tub with light glimmering through the dark dusty louvered windows of the laundry. She finds herself acutely aware of her small embodied being in this strange landscape, but uncertain now about what is to be included in the region of her legitimate embodied self. In her disapproval and abandonment and then re-embracing love, the mother traces (she inscribes) the child with a new knowledge, a knowledge of the landscape of her body as having regions and subregions, some of them loaded with emotion, unacceptable, alarming, acknowledged only in strange dank landscapes.

In each of these stories the child's body is traced with words and with actions, and with perceptions that give it new substance, that inscribe and incorporate it into different landscapes, that enfold it now one way and now another.

STORIES OF BODILY COMPETENCE, OF WORKING TO BE APPROPRIATELY EMBODIED IN PLACE

Given the shock to the body of being out of place, of having no landscape in which it can belong, and given the ecstatic well-being contained in the stories of (be)longing, it is no surprise that many of the body–landscape stories told in the workshop were of heroic struggles to become appropriately embodied. Being born into a particular landscape gives no guarantee of belonging there. The stories tell of a struggle towards appropriate(d) embodiment, through which the child can be recognized, even if only momentarily, as belonging as a masterful subject to whom subject status will be accorded. Butler, elaborating on Althusser's definition of subjection, writes of this process:

The more a practice is mastered, the more fully subjection is achieved. Submission and mastery take place simultaneously, and it is this paradoxical simultaneity that constitutes the ambivalence of subjection. Where one might expect submission to consist in a yielding to an externally imposed dominant order, and to be marked by a loss of control and mastery, it is paradoxically marked by mastery itself . . . neither submission nor mastery is *performed by a subject;* the lived simultaneity of submission as mastery, and mastery as submission, is the condition of possibility for the subject itself. (Butler, 1995b, pp. 14–15)

Kura, the narrator of Riripeti's story, reveals some of her own mastery, and mastery as subjection in her knowledge of how to be a good girl in her classroom. The child's (be)longing is thus often labored over as in the final story to be told here. The child struggles all day to learn to swim in the cool dark water of the river. She works to embody herself in the landscape in a way that she knows will mean that she (be)longs, not only as one positioned in the warm approving gaze of her family, but as one who already knows how bodies should be(have) in this watery landscape. Her autonomy is labored over, she works to differentiate herself from that child who cannot swim, who is not entitled to (the illusion of) autonomy. She separates herself off from her family (though not too far that she can't see them if she wants) so that she can (in)scribe her body, her musculature, with the correct forms of (be)longing in the Australian landscape:

The water is river-dark, cool in the late afternoon, satiny smooth on her skin. All day she has thrashed her arms and legs, trying to keep her head out of the water. Not afraid of the invasion of this clear un-salty water into her eyes, nose and mouth, but wanting to master this sought-after skill—she is teaching herself to swim.
    The family on the green grass beside the river fade into the background of her consciousness, enough to know they are there if needed. The white trunks of the gums with branches drooping into the water flash into her vision every time she urgently lifts her head for a breath. Face into the water, mouth closed, don't breathe, see the browny-yellowy underneath of the smooth water surface, thrash arms and legs, try to get the rhythm. Without warning, all the movements work together, not smoothly, but enough to lift her head, take a gasped breath—water as well as air, but enough— then do it again, again. She stands up in the waist high water, balancing her feet on the smooth stones underfoot, turns to the watching parents and calls out triumphantly "I can swim! I'm swimming!"

The child announces herself triumphantly as an appropriately embodied subject, as one who can be (re)cognized as an autonomous subject, capable of mastering invaluable skills of survival and pleasure in water.

What these explorations make visible is the complex and sometimes fraught work of (in)scription. The body in landscape, the body as landscape, landscape as an essential extension of the body, is worked and reworked, scribed and reinscribed. The physical, discursive, emotional, political, and social landscapes in which we are subjected and become speaking subjects are both solid and coercive, *and* fluid and shifting. We work hard at our subjection, we take enormous pleasure in our subjection, we suffer extreme pain through our subjection—and through being subjected, we become appropriate(d) beings in the landscape, and in that same process, beings who can (re)appropriate its meanings and patterns, (re)constitute bodies in relation to landscapes, (re)signify what we find we have become. What the collective biography, the fictional, and the autobiographical stories collected together here show is the *lived* complexity of that relation between the powerful (in)scribing effects of discourse in the shaping of body–landscapes. They reveal as well the fluid multidimensional, political and social nature of that (in)scription.

What I have also done here, in this writing, is to play at the boundaries of body–landscape, working to dissolve the inscription that marks the outer surface of human existence as the skin surrounding the body. Bodies I read as continuous with landscape, and landscape, in turn, I read as alive, active, a volatile text that, like bodies, and continuous with bodies, can change, and can be read in multiple ways, shifting between one (in)scription and another, though at the same time, inscriptions may last for thousands of years and act powerfully in relation not only to the inscribers, but to generations after them. This play at the borders of body–landscape is an attempt to enable us to see place not in terms of context, but as multiply inscribed text that, like bodies, has life, a life that is in large part a product of those ongoing (in)scriptions. The chapter is thus engaging in a discursive shift, which enables us to talk about bodies and place and the relation between them differently. It is not simply an analytic chapter that stands back and engages in the *production* of a new language—it is also and at the same time, a *performance* of that new language, exploring what it is that it can do and where it can imaginatively lead us. Reconceptualising the subject in and of landscape in this way has multiple implications. It may enable new readings of the experiences of refugees in losing their familiar landscapes and in being positioned as alien and dangerous by those who have power over the landscapes they attempt to move into. It may enable a new reading of the ways indigenous and non-indigenous people position each other, in particular in terms of identifying the different discourses through which body–landscape relations are constituted, and the rights and obligations that are entailed in these deeply embodied, deeply felt connections, and the detailed rights and obligations that are implicated in those connections. The concepts of longing and belonging, and of folding and incorporation, in particular, may enable a different reading of the ways teachers interact with children they read as different. But it also helps us to make sense of the hard work we engage in to constitute ourselves as continuous with the political, discursive, and physical texts in which we are embedded, one way and another.

NOTE

1. For some readers this image potentially falls back into an old binary divide in which women = nature and men = culture. This binary I have deconstructed in Davies and Whitehouse (1997) using data from male environmentalists who experience their bodies as merged with nature.

REFERENCES

Althusser, L. (1971). *Lenin and philosophy and other essays*. London: New Left Books.

Butler, J. (1995a). For a careful reading. In S. Benhabib, J. Butler, D. Cornell, & N. Fraser (Eds.), *Feminist contentions: A philosophical exchange* (pp. 127–143). New York: Routledge.

Butler, J. (1995b).Conscience doth make subjects of us all. *Yale French Studies*, 88, 6–26.

Carter, P. (1966). *The lie of the land*. London: Faber and Faber.

Cixous, H., & Calle-Gruber, M. (1997). *Hélène Cixous rootprints: Memory and life writing* (E. Prenowitz, Trans.). London: Routledge.

Davies, B. (2000a). *(In)scribing body/landscape relations*. Walnut Creek: AltaMira Press.

Davies, B. (2000b). The subject of poststructuralism. In Davies, B. *A body of writing 1990–1999* (pp. 133–114). Walnut Creek: AltaMira Press.

Davies, B. (2000c). Women's subjectivity and feminist stories. In Davies, B. *A body of writing 1990–1999* (pp. 133–144). Walnut Creek: AltaMira Press.

Davies, B., & Harré, R. (1990). Positioning: Conversation and the production of selves. *Journal for the Theory of Social Behaviour*, 20(1) 43–63.

Davies, B., & Whitehouse, H. (1997). Men on the boundaries: Landscapes and seascapes. *Journal of Gender Studies*, 6(3) 237–254.

Grace, P. (1998). *Baby No-eyes*. Auckland: Penguin Books.

Grosz, E. (1995). *Space, time and perversion*. Sydney: Allen and Unwin.

Nast, H. (1998). The body as "place". Reflexivity and fieldwork in Kano, Nigeria. In H. J. Nast & S. Pile (Eds.), *Places through the body* (pp. 93–116). London: Routledge.

O'Shane, P. (1998, November 7–8). Sin of omission. *The Weekend Australian* p. 29.

Sykes, R. (1997). *Snake cradle*. Sydney: Allen and Unwin.

Turner Hospital, J.(1988). *Charades*. St. Lucia: University of Queensland Press.

Turner Hospital, J. (1996). *Oyster*. Sydney: Knopf.

CHAPTER 18

Reflexive Vigilance: Engagement, Illumination, and Development

Tim May

To understand social relations from a relatively new vantage point is not only a contribution to knowledge for its own sake but also offers the possibility to think about the alternative organizations of those relations. The former consideration is often built upon justifications that are particular to a community of scholars. While not exhausting the scope of justification, those insights will be tempered by its potential applications. If the latter approach to insight prevails, an instrumentalism results such that what is true is seen to be what works. Those with the power to exercise their will over others and determine how the outcome will be evaluated will then find the justification for their actions in a "science" that is presumed to be the "truth" beyond individual will.

To guard against these tendencies there are checks both within communities of scholars and within those who are the subjects of its research. Differences in interpretation are inevitable. Scientists have spent enormous energy on seeking to understand the place of science in society based upon this simple observation. The very absence of consensus within a community of scholars may be taken to undermine its insights, for the forms of justification are themselves open to contestation. On the other hand, a community of scholars, finding themselves in broad agreement concerning particular lenses through which to view social reality including, it should be added, its social construction, exhibit classic Kuhnian paradigmatic tendencies. A set of background assumptions then provides for the conditions that permit engagement for the purposes of understanding the social world in the first instance. However, a community of scientists needs to exhibit more than a habitual form of action. Not only do they have to be attentive to the interactions between theory and data, but also increasingly to an anticipation of potential applications, the conditions in which they work, and how process relates to product.

As simple distinctions between politics and practice are challenged, a reflexive vigilance is required in order to guard against these conditions becoming complacence. Without that in place, those lenses that provided for engagement can easily become complacence that, by default, are presumed to speak in the name of things as they "are," or as they should be "known."

In terms of the above issues, to which I wish to return in the final section of this chapter, it is not necessary to give up on "epistemic gain" (Taylor, 1992). This does not just derive from comparing the explanatory power of two theories and concluding that one explains more than another. Nor does it come from a refusal to engage, or through bypassing the history of explanation within different disciplines. Gain comes in terms of how one explanation deals with another in terms of its historical context. Taking X as a previous position and Y as a new one, it may be expressed in the following terms: "It may be that from the standpoint of Y, not just the phenomena in dispute, but also the history of X and its particular pattern of anomalies, difficulties, makeshifts, and breakdown can be greatly illuminated. In adopting Y, we made better sense not just of the world, but of our history of trying to explain the world, part of which has been played out in terms of X" (Taylor, 1995, p. 43).

With this in mind, it is with the issues raised in this volume and how those relate to other issues and explanations of society and social relations that I am concerned in the next section. At one level this brings out both differences and similarities with other traditions of social thought. At another level it is suggestive in opening up potential areas of development in which further work might be considered through engagement with these traditions. Of course this cannot claim to be exhaustive, but I hope it is sufficiently indicative to raise a few productive possibilities in the service of illumination.

ENGAGEMENT IN THE SERVICE OF ILLUMINATION

Positioning theory enjoys a particular history and one constituted in opposition to the tenets of so-called classical psychology. Traced, as Rom Harré and Ali Moghaddam note in their Introduction, in Wundt's recognition that certain phenomena were not amenable to explanation in laboratory-based experiment and design methods, we see the beginnings of a cultural science. Wilhelm Dilthey (1833–1911) was also seeking to discover an epistemological basis for the human sciences through their being rooted in "inner" experience, rather than a natural-scientific "outer" experience. This concentration on understanding social life and the meanings for the individuals who comprise it led him to develop a "descriptive psychology." A center stage for historicism in the unfolding history of the social sciences via a focus upon the "lived experience" of people then became apparent.

Max Weber was also concerned with these issues. For Weber (1949), the practice of science had to replicate the same qualities that Emmanuel Kant found within the human mind. This could not simply be the collection of social facts, but a reflexive practice in terms of being an "idea of ideas" (Albrow, 1990, p. 149). More generally, the social sciences reflect the ways in which history and culture are changed by human actions. They work within dynamic environments and so must exhibit a conceptual and methodological dynamism through the application of reflexive practices. Max Weber's methodological writings combine Dilthey's emphasis on the meaningful "inner" experiences of people (understanding), together with an analysis of the observed regularities of human behavior in terms of cause and effect (Weber, 1949). He sought to fuse the intentionality of conduct with an analysis of cause and effect in order to understand and explain meaning through reference to the social conditions of action.

If the natural sciences explain an event by considering it as *"the effect of a cause"* (Strasser, 1985, p. 2. Original italics), to study human relations requires "understanding what makes someone tick" or how they "feel or act as a human being" (Taylor, 1981, p. 30). Despite Weber's attempts, cause and meaning depart in an unfolding history of the social sciences, and this directly informs the development of positioning theory. However, in an understanding of motivation as orientation and an examination of the differences between positioning and reversal theory, causes and reasons can combine (chapter 2). People choose "metamotivational" states and deploy causes in their narrative accounts. The possibility for combining the internal and external points of view (positioning theory and reversal theory) is then open to exploration in how motivational meanings can be incorporated into the discursive dominance of positioning theory.

Another source of inspiration for the history of cultural psychology is found in the work of William James (1842–1910). James, after all, sought to critique the idea of consciousness as a resolution to the subject–object dilemma. For James, consciousness "is the name of a nonentity, and has no right to a place among first principles." As Bertrand Russell continues: "he is not denying that our thoughts perform a function which is that of knowing . . . What he is denying might be put crudely as the view that consciousness is a "thing" (Russell, 1955, p. 840).

A similar argument is to be found in the work of John Dewey (1859–1952). For Dewey, ideas and actions should be judged according to the social situations that give rise to them. In contrast to the "top-down" approach of metaphysical speculation, the social sciences should now concern themselves with the concrete social conditions under which actions take place. The Cartesian solitary ego then became replaced by a "cooperative search for truth for the purpose of coping with real problems encountered in the course of action" (Joas, 1993, p. 19).

How the traditions of pragmatism relate to positioning theory is a fruitful area of investigation. As Rom Harré and Grant Gillett, for example, note in their discussion on perception and consciousness, the idea that a psyche has an independent existence separate from the subject who represents it is a "distortion." To signify an aspect of our identity is also to have an effect (I use the term deliberately) upon that identity because "access to that signification therefore alters my mental life. It does not merely provide a novel means for a redescription of it" (1994, p. 179).

The role of feelings in social life has often been downplayed in the history of social thought. That positioning theory seeks to correct for this tendency is apparent in this volume (chapters 3,4, and 5). The idea that feelings are invoked as reasons for changing courses of action is intelligible within a person's place within a moral discourse. The giving of accounts for action is not only a mode of description, but also a justification that positions a person within a moral order. In this sense, accounts work at the level of reflexive positioning and constitute personhood in terms of responsibility (also see Ricoeur, 1994).

Accounts may also seek to neutralize the role of the person in taking responsibility for one's actions. This is what Sykes and Matza (1957) called "techniques of neutralization." What is involved is a distancing from the consequences of one's actions (see chapters 3 and 9). The success of such a strategy depends on the extent to which a person is held accountable, and this links back to the previous conversation on reasons and causes. Accounts need to have a legitimacy among an audience. Actions are regarded as having taken place within what Goffman referred to as the interaction order "within which two or more persons find themselves in visual and aural range of one another" (Goffman, 1981, p. 84). Importantly, however, actions also take place at a distance, or in different arenas, the result of which means that people are not held to account for their actions and the consistency of their utterances.

Effective denials of involvement are given according to space, time, and a culturally generated outrage according to perceived consequences. The consequences of "denial talk" (Cohen, 2001) have different ramifications according to how people are positioned in the first place. They are, for example, apparent at a global scale when discussing the plight of those in the majority world (usually referred to as the "developing" world), as well as the castigation of whole groups of people as "other" when seeking to legitimate actions leading up to declarations of war. It is here that systems underpinning and informing the reproduction of the free market—a system that denies its own immorality by assuming itself to be natural and without value—can work to generate cultures of denial. As Stanley Cohen puts it in his study entitled "States of Denial," the result is that "More people are made superfluous and marginal: the deskilled, unskilled, and sinking poor; the old, who no longer work; the young who cannot find work; the massive shifting populations of migrants, asylum seekers and refugees. The 'solution' to these problems now physically reproduces the conditions of denial" (Cohen, 2001, p. 293).

Who is positioned to have power to seek to determine outcomes at this scale and who is excluded, how and with what consequences? To understand these effects, a link between language use and social conditions is required. In the work of Pierre Bourdieu, the power of a linguistic utterance is seen to reside in the institutional conditions for its production. The analyst may then ask with what power or authority utterances are invested by examining the access that the speaker has: "to the official, orthodox and legitimate speech" (1992, p. 109). Institutions are not just schools, prisons, factories, and so forth, but relatively stable sets of social relations that provide their members with certain resources. It is under particular conditions constituted by past practices that utterances are both produced and heard. Therefore, "efforts to find, in the specifically linguistic logic of different forms of argumentation, rhetoric and style, the source of their symbolic efficacy are destined to fail as long as they do not establish the relationship between the properties of discourses, the properties of the person who pronounces them and the properties of the institution which authorizes him to pronounce them" (1992, p. 111).

Although exclusion and violence may serve to *stabilize* identities—for example, in the case of slavery—we might argue that it is within dialogic conditions that the *formation* of identities is enabled (Joas, 1998, p. 15). This is examined in several chapters (4, 5, 6, 10, 11, and 12) These discussions center on the relations between emotions and masculinity; how honor and murder may be bound up in tight cultural bundles with tragic consequences; Alzheimer's as a neuropathological condition that may be improved by a reversal of "malignant positioning"; gender and sexuality, and postcolonial apologies.

To return to the above issues, one must not omit to ask, when studying particular social dynamics using the positioning triangle, a fundamental question: how do micro-actors macro-structure reality (Callon & Latour, 1981)? Issues that relate to how we understand positioning (chapters 7 and 8) as not only a dynamic process in which conflict plays a key role, but also one in which people end up being defined in terms of having a particular character, enable one to blend an understanding of subjectivity without collapsing into a continual intersubjectivity. It is, therefore, to an understanding of the relationship between positioning, belonging and character that we need to turn (May, 2000).

Without these dynamics in place, how could we understand the exceptional moral courage shown by those whose acts transcend the cultural pressures of a given context? Equally, we should recognize that those who are "strong evaluators" (Taylor, 1992) may not be "deeply reflective, and their actions can sometimes be determined by role, group, somatic, or temperamental traits rather than by their idea identities" (Rorty & Wong, 1993, p. 31). Bringing these elements together is a challenge to positioning theory and an important contribution to what are so often missing elements in socio-theoretical developments. How we understand the ways in which character relates to social environment and position but is also sensitive enough to comprehend subjectivity and difference, as well as how some actors are positioned to gain from objective social conditions, while others are not, are core to contemporary understandings.

Two features worthy of further reflection in addressing these issues are the unintended consequences and unacknowledged conditions of social action. In the former we see the limits to intentionality as an explanation of conduct, as well as the ways in which micro-actions both produce *and* reproduce systemic properties. For instance, when dealing with aggregate data it is often the case that patterns that were not discernable at a micro-level become apparent to the analyst. Minimally, one would expect this to result in a return to a number of those micro-episodes to check out prior interpretations. At this level, however, these patterns are not readily apparent. They are still "real" in their consequences but may require different tools of social inquiry.

In the criminal justice system, there is a tendency to treat black populations differently from white populations. This has long been argued to be the result of systemic inequality and/or bias as opposed to differences rooted in some imaginary fixed traits. Each person might appear before the institutions of criminal justice with a developed sense of personal identity, but to what extent is that then translated according to culturally biased notions of collective identity? The fluidity emphasized by positioning theory then becomes a fixity in the eyes of those who are positioned with the power to judge and effect life chances.

What comes first? Is it personal or collective identity (chapter 13)? To return to the idea of action-at-a-distance, the "if-then" dialogic process of identity formation can equally become an "if-then" process of identity fixing, thereby relieving another party of engagement through understanding. Returning to issues raised by those such as James and George Herbert Mead (1863–1931), identity formation takes place against a cultural background that forms not only a template from which to draw, but also defines, as the sociologist Robert Merton noted (1968), the appropriate means for the attainability of given ends. The ambivalence that exists in self-formation is then apparent at a group level: that is, seeking to define oneself as unique while also seeking to belong. The role of tradition in the latter is of importance as identity formation takes place within a context and sets of values and beliefs transmitted from the past. Patterns informing sense-making of the world around us, together with a sense of identity in terms of belonging in a world, are parts of the legacy of those transmissions and inform "struggles for recognition" (Fraser, 1997; Honneth, 1996).

To sufficiently capture this process may mean to move beyond face-to-face interactions. The process of disembedding and reembedding traditions within particular locals resides not just within oral traditions, but also "mediated interactions" and "mediated quasi-interaction." The former includes telephone conversations, e-mails, and letter writing, while the latter relates to mass communications such as newspapers, radio, televisions, computer games, and so on (Thompson, 1996). Positioning theory needs to take account of these, often unacknowledged, influences within the triangle that forms its tool of analysis.

These new forms of media may actually work to relieve the need for the constitution of collective identity in face-to-face work. This is not to impute permanence without interactional effort. It is, however, to say that the work of belonging may also lie elsewhere where space, place, ritual, and commercialization all play their part (chapters 14 and 15). Action-at-a-distance can take place depending on the relative power of the parties, or in the case of the discussion on intellectual property rights, states. Here we see the idea of belonging among Amazonian tribes being part of a certain locality clashing with the Western idea of patent being the right of an owner to exclude others from using, selling, making, or importing without sensitivity to its origin. That same mediated world of global capitalism that is indifferent to its effects comes up against a context-sensitive cultural formation concerned with the one thing it is not: sustainability and a respect for difference and diversity.

Michel Foucault's idea of discourse (chapter 16) differs in important respects to that of positioning theory, not least because of his ideas on subject-formation. However, one key element of his influential work that is missing, particularly within the areas of management and organizational studies, is how to analyze the limits to appropriation of discourse (May, 1999a)? Within the domain of everyday life both the ability and capability to conform and think and act differently arises. A study of this domain deploying positioning theory enables us to answer why "To the same situation, people react in different ways" (Foucault, 1988b, p. 14)? The idea of Foucault's agonism between freedom and power, such that the exercise of power presupposes a free subject, only makes sense "if someone has several courses of action open but chooses the one congruent with the wishes of another. The capacity to choose in any meaningful sense requires the existence of a human will that is not merely an effect of discourse" (Flax, 1991, p. 231).

Positioning theory has a great deal to offer in terms of the micro-management of policies, strategies, initiatives, and whatever other old term is appropriated into contemporary management-speak as "new," which will be invented tomorrow. As Zygmunt Bauman (1997) has noted, it is the art of forgetting that is often more celebrated and rewarded than memory. Nevertheless, that part of positioning theory's triangle that is cultural transmission should also be looked at in terms of cultural switching in order to reposition people according to some other set of ends. Continual restructuring within organizations, for example, destabilizes and allows power to operate without apparent responsibility via allusions to those things out of the sphere of control (May, 2001). This is, not, however, without the continuation of differential rewards!

Representations are those mediated forms that do not rely upon face-to-face interaction (chapter 17). As throughout this collection, the importance of embodiment in relation to space and place is central. At the same time, drawing upon the work of Gilles Deleuze, we see activity, not passivity, and the idea of the body as natural in opposition to the unnatural as a discursive construction. Introducing Deleuze at this point is interesting as it represents, for the book as a whole, an avenue of investigation in which the subject of positioning theory and its triangular tool of inquiry comes up against an interchangeability with its emphasis upon fluidity. As Deleuze wrote in relation to Foucault's philosophy, a "dispositif" is "an analysis of concrete social apparatuses." It is, he continues, "composed of lines, each having a different nature. And the lines in the apparatus do not outline or surround systems which are each homogeneous in their own right, object, subject, language, and so on, but follow directions, trace balances which are always off balance, now drawing together and then distancing themselves from one another. Each line is broken and subject to *changes in direction*, bifurcating and forked, and subject to *drifting*. Visible objects, affirmations which can be formulated, forces exercised and subject in position are like vectors and tensors" (Deleuze, 1992, p. 159. Original italics).

This is flux. This is possibility. It is uncertainty and also a process of permanent becoming. At one level it opens up hope and at another plays on ambivalence. It also has a different sense of the "self" from other contributions in this volume. A clarification of positioning theory in relation to this and other traditions and issues noted in this section would assist greatly in seeing its place and distinctiveness among our ways of seeing the social world.

REFLEXIVE VIGILANCE

In this final section I wish to return to the points raised in relation to reflexive vigilance, noted in the first part of the chapter. This, among other issues, concerns the position of the analyst of social relations. Turning this into a topic as a resource upon which to base an understanding of social relations allows it to work as an instrument for sensitizing researchers to the consequences of practices and assumptions. However, when does such activity become counter-productive from the point of view of research practice and understanding itself? When does it cease to inform in order to change practice and instead undermines it and thereby leads to paralysis and inactivity?

Take some methodological translations of the works of Jacques Derrida (1978). These have led to reflexive accounts that reproduce the very ego-identity that is the subject of his critical interventions. Manifest in confessions of failed attempts to discover an unproblematic reality, what has emerged is a whole new industry for textual reflections on the futility of this enterprise (May, 1998). The overall result is that representations can be rendered so incoherent that engagement is difficult, if not impossible, for the purposes of illuminating the dynamics of social issues. These accounts end up reproducing the very targets of Derrida's critiques: that is, the closure of texts and the centrality of the subject in the production of those texts.

At the same time, the presuppositions that are embedded within ways of thinking are now open to routine scrutiny. Ideas of neutrality, such as the maintenance of objectivity through positioning the researcher as nothing but a passive instrument of data collection, are now exposed as falsehoods that seek to mask the realities of the research process. The knower (as researcher) is now implicated in the construction of the known (the dynamics and content of society and social relations). Feminists, social constructionists, critical theorists, those influenced by varieties of realism, postmodernists, and post-structuralists have all added their voices to a challenge of this simple distinction. Over forty years ago C. Wright Mills (1957) noted how social science had inherited terms that, although outdated, remained rooted in practice. He argued that these "standard categories of thought," if generalized to contemporary situations, "become unwieldy, irrelevant, not convincing . . . so now The Modern Age is being succeeded by a *post-modern period*. Perhaps we may call it: The Fourth Epoch" (1970, p. 184. Italics added).

If the epoch that has given us these critiques is concerned with the search for new values, identities, and ways of life, perhaps it is not surprising that we can range, in reaction to these criticisms, from those who argue that nothing has changed to those for whom anything less than total embrace is an act of betrayal. Those napping in the cozy slumbers of past scientific "pretensions" can then find their practices being characterized as branches of literary criticism. These movements, however, detract from the productive potential that comes with engagement and over-extend in the process the reach and role of science in society. Polarizations between an unproblematic scientism and the idea that science is but a branch of literary criticism do little to aid understanding.

It was this concern that underpinned the ethos in which the first section was written. There is a powerful pull in constituting subjectivity as either an apparent distance from necessity, or by a connection enabled through the unthought categories of scholastic reason that provide clarity through an absence of uncertainty, the latter being what Pierre Bourdieu (1998) called the "oxymoron of epistemic doxa." Reflexive calls fail when they do not take account of the institutional conditions of knowledge production and in so doing replicate a false separation between production and reception. An examination of the connection between context, knowledge production, process, and consequences, gives way to an assumed homogeneity of the subject or a fatalism that turns contingency into necessity, allowing it to play out on those within the field in different ways according to the positions that they occupy and the pressures under which they find themselves.

The constitution of the social world through social science requires a conjunction of particular ways of seeing, along with an attention to the constitution of fields of scientific practice. In the social sciences it is central to any reflexive program to take account of this relationship in order to refine our understandings of social scientific knowledge and social life. These are not separate endeavors, but part of the same drive for understanding. The gap in scientific reflexive thinking thus relates to the absence of an understanding of the social conditions of social scientific knowledge production and its relation to knowledge reception and context and thus its capacity for action. This is often accompanied by a dismissive attitude in relation to the empirical (often conflating that with empiricism) that is accompanied by a claim to speak of how the world "is." To what extent, however, does justification then become no more than a retreat to an unfounded belief in the right to speak from a position that has long since ceased to be a matter for contemplation—and this we call post positivism! Or, the claim that the author is but one voice among many others in a relativistic universe—even though it was their voice that was published! And this we call postmodernism!

Despite these claims, instrumental positivism still marches on, hence the routine demands for relevant knowledge scripted for narrowly conceived ends. What we then witness are increasing turns to those who offer ways out of these dilemmas who come from different disciplinary trajectories. In filling this gap there is a bypassing of the importance of the contexts of production and reception: the very issues that were bypassed in the discussion on patents, hence the point about historical sensitivity in seeking epistemic gains. This is not a defense of disciplinary homogeneity, for there is an evident need for interdisciplinary work in the face of the changes that are informing knowledge production.

When we look at these changes, we not only need tools of analysis to examine the relationship between utterance and institutional context, but also the changing nature of institutional conditions of knowledge production. What are the medium-term implications, for example, of the argument that we have moved from a situation in which disciplinary control of knowledge content has led to a focus upon what I have termed endogenous reflexivity, to a more heterogeneous form of knowledge production in which referential reflexivity comes more to the fore (1998, 1999b, 2000)?

In two studies on the changing modes of knowledge production, the authors argue that there has been a transition from what they call Mode 1 to Mode 2 knowledge production. Mode 1 knowledge production takes place within a bounded environment in which scientists, via peer review, exert control. Mode 2 knowledge production, on the other hand, acknowledges that other professionals are now involved in this process and so accommodates a demand for more accountability and reflexivity, as well as a set of bureaucratic intermediaries to whom it is necessary to respond and thus incorporate change. The environment is characterized as one of increasing complexity and uncertainty (Gibbons et al., 1994; Nowotny et al., 2001). Positioning theory, along with other traditions, can examine the production and reception of knowledge in novel ways. This is not only a contribution to how knowledge works in society, but also a refinement to its own understandings.

To this we must add another ingredient: the expectations that people bring with them into the practices of the social sciences. As Agnes Heller notes in her discussion on truth and true knowledge: "Weber clearly warned his students not to seek insight into the meaning of life in their pursuit of the social sciences: the search for true knowledge must be chosen as a vocation and not as a path leading to Truth. To offer insight into Truth through the pursuit of true knowledge is to make a false promise, one which the social sciences have not the authority to keep" (Original Italics. Heller, 1989, p. 294).

Instead of understandings that can be borne in practice, we find an oscillation between the revenge of positivism and the denial of the position of the researchers and how that relates to their practice. Neither is capable of sustaining social scientific practice in contemporary times. In one we have the denouncement of doubt in the name of order and certainty and in the other, the abandonment of understanding leaving the terrain to those who are not so reserved when it comes to speaking in the name of organizational order. Both commit the fallacy of universal certainty but from totally different points of view. We should not seek the unattainable, nor deny the importance of what is attainable, but seek to understand the "socio-historically variable degrees of attainable certainty" (Wagner, 2001a, p. 30).

The idea that researchers can claim to speak in the name of a separate and unproblematic reality should be exposed to scrutiny—as should the claim to speak in the name of different realities as mediated by alternative modes of representation. The same tendency to legislate over the constitution and nature of social reality is evident in both. In the process scientism—defined as the belief that science is the *only* form of legitimate knowledge—becomes confused with science. The latter, if mixed with a sensitivity to context and a willingness to engage in an understanding of the relationship between justification and application that is not taken to be beyond question, can be molded by considerations that lie beyond the confines of its boundaries. These include the desirability of various courses of actions, as well as recognition of different forms of life and how well one form of explanation deals with another are all central features of this ethos, as is a due modesty informed by the maxim: the world is a far richer place than we can fully know.

SUMMARY

What can be taken from the above discussions and comparisons between explanations? It is about engagement in the service of illumination and a check upon the idea that any one tradition can exhaust an understanding of the social world. It also tells us that the social sciences are not just about falsification, for that would be to misunderstand their role and place in society. Social scientific practices embody a process of interpretation–reinterpretation according to the conditions of the age. Moving away from the quest for timeless knowledge does not commit us to relativism. Instead, knowledge is produced according to particular contexts in which problems arise. This is not to commit knowledge to an instrumental view, for problems themselves arise from a process that is contested. The movements I have charted, which upon first glance appear to go in opposite directions, but may end up in the same place, detract from the productive potential that comes with such engagement. Polarizations do little to aid this understanding. While claiming to speak in the name of an unproblematic reality should be questioned, so too should the claim to speak of different realities mediated by alternative modes of representation. What we see are the same tendencies in both: legislation over the constitution of social reality and an absence of engagement with the social problems of the time.

If the social sciences are to remains vibrant and relevant to their day, they must attend to the dynamics that inform everyday lives and to the changing pressures, in terms of the past, that inform their current and potential form and character (Wagner, 2001b). A skeptical attitude is therefore a necessary condition for an engaged position. Necessary, but not sufficient. When it is assumed to be sufficient, consciously or by default, it undermines the former and becomes, from a disciplinary point of view, the equivalent of speaking to oneself and believing that one is saying something of importance to others.

Reflexive vigilance acts as a check on the claim to speak of the world as it "is" or should be "known." Such a move enables not only a better understanding of the conditions that inform knowledge production and reception, but also how the social sciences can achieve an improved understanding of social conditions. Positioning theory is an important contribution to this process. The potential that exists in the insights it generates into social life is apparent in the contributions to this volume. The challenge is to deploy and further develop its tools of understanding through future engagement with issues that are central to contemporary social relations.

REFERENCES

Albrow, M. (1990). *Max Weber's construction of social theory*. London: Macmillan.

Bauman, Z. (1997). *Postmodernity and its discontents*. Cambridge, UK: Polity.

Bourdieu, P. (1992). *Language and symbolic power*. Edited and Introduced by J. B. Thompson, Translated by G. Raymond & M. Adamson. Cambridge: Polity.

Bourdieu, P. (1998). *Practical reason: On the theory of action*. Cambridge: Polity.

Callon, M., & Latour, B. (1981). Unscrewing the big leviathan: How actors macro-structure reality and how sociologists help them to do so. In K. Knorr-Cetina & A. Cicourel (Eds.), *Advances in social theory and methodology: Towards an integration of micro and macro theories*. London: Routledge and Kegan Paul.

Cohen, S. (2001). *States of denial: Knowing about atrocities and suffering*. Cambridge: Polity.

Deleuze, G. (1992). *What is* a dispositif? In Armstrong, T. J. (Ed.). *Michel Foucault: philosopher*. Translated by T. J. Armstrong. London: Harvester Wheatsheaf.

Derrida, J. (1978). *Writing and difference*. London: Routledge.

Flax, J. (1991). *Thinking fragments: Psychoanalysis, feminism, and postmodernism in the contemporary west*. Berkeley: University of California Press.

Foucault, M. (1988b). Technologies of the self. In L. H. Martin, H. Gutman, & P. H. Hutton, (Eds.). *Technologies of the self: A seminar with Michel Foucault*. London: Tavistock.

Fraser, N. (1997). *Justice interruptus*. London: Routledge.

Gibbons, M., Limoges, C., Nowotny, H., Schwartaman, S., Scott, P., & Trow, M. (1994). *The new production of knowledge: The dynamics of science and research in contemporary societies*. London: Sage.

Goffman, E. (1981). *Forms of talk*. Philadelphia: University of Pennsylvania Press.

Harré, R., & Gillett, G. (1994). *The discursive mind*. London: Sage.

Heller, A. (1989). From hermeneutics in social science toward a hermeneutics of social science. *Theory and Society*, 18, 291–322.

Honneth, A. (1996). *The struggle for recognition: The moral grammar of social conflicts*. Translated by J. Anderson. Cambridge, MA: MIT Press.

Joas, H. (1993). *Pragmatism and social theory*. Chicago: University of Chicago Press.

Joas, H. (1998). The autonomy of the self: The median heritage and its postmodern challenge. *European Journal of Social Theory*, 1 (1), 7–18.

May, T. (1998). Reflexivity in the age of reconstructive social science. *International Journal of Methodology: Theory and Practice*, 1 (1), 7–24.

May, T. (1999a). From banana time to just-in-time: Power and resistance at work. *Sociology*, 33 (4), 767–783.

May, T. (1999b). Reflexivity and sociological practice. *Sociological Research Online*. Special Section on "The Future of Sociology," 4 (3). http://www.socresonline.org.uk/socresonline/4/3/may.html.

May, T. (2000). The future of critique: Positioning, belonging and reflexivity. *European Journal of Social Theory*, 3 (2), 157–173.

May, T. (2001). Power, knowledge and organizational transformation: Administration as depoliticisation. Special Issue: "Social Epistemology and Knowledge Management." *Social Epistemology*, 15 (3), 171–186.

Merton, R. (1968). *Social theory and social structure*. New York: Free Press.

Mills, C. W. (1970). *The sociological imagination*. Originally Published in 1959. Harmondsworth: Penguin.

Nowotny, H., Scott, P., & Gibbons, M. (2001). *Re-thinking science: Knowledge and the public in an age of uncertainty*. Cambridge: Polity.

Ricoeur, P. (1994). *Oneself as another*. Translated by K. Blamey. Chicago: University of Chicago Press.

Rorty, A. O., & Wong, D. (1993). Aspects of Identity and Agency. In O. Flanagan & A. O. Rorty (Eds.). *Identity, character and morality: Essays in moral psychology*. Cambridge, MA: MIT Press.

Russell, B. (1955). *History of western philosophy and its connection with political and social circumstances from the earliest times to the present day*. 5th impression. London: George, Allen and Unwin.

Strasser, S. (1985). *Understanding and explanation: Basic ideas concerning the humanity of the human sciences*. Pittsburgh, PA: Duquesne University Press.

Taylor, C. (1981). Understanding in human science. *Review of Metaphysics*, 34, 25–38.

Taylor, C. (1992). *Sources of the self: The making of the modern identity*. Cambridge: Cambridge University Press.

Taylor, C. (1995). *Philosophical arguments*. Cambridge, MA: Harvard University Press.

Thompson, J. B. (1996). Tradition and self in a mediated world. In P. Heelas, S. Lash, & P. Morris. (Eds.), *Detraditionalization: Critical reflections on authority and identity*. Oxford: Blackwell.

Wagner, P. (2001a). *Theorizing modernity: Inescapability and attainability in social theory*. London: Sage.

Wagner, P. (2001b). *A history and theory of the social sciences*. London: Sage.

Weber, M. (1949). *The methodology of the social sciences*. Edited by E. Shils, & H. Finch, Glencoe, IL: The Free Press.

Author Index

Subject Index

About the Contributors

LUCINDA ABERDEEN has worked as a sociologist in local, state, and federal government settings in areas encompassing road accident research, social and environmental impact assessment, policy evaluation, disability, human rights, and racism in regional Australia. Currently she teaches courses in sociology, social research, and indigenous and ethnic diversity in Australia in the Social and Community Studies area of studies in the Faculty of Arts and Social Sciences at the University of the Sunshine Coast. Her current research interests are in discursive analysis of racism and reconciliation in Australia and research ethics in the social sciences.

JENNIFER ADAMS is a graduate of Georgetown University, with particular research interests in the psychological insights offered by literary authors.

MICHAEL J. APTER is a psychologist who has spent much of his career on the faculty of the University of Wales, although he has been a visiting professor at many other universities worldwide. He is the author or editor of fourteen books and numerous journal papers. Most of these deal with his "Reversal Theory." He now lives and works in America where he is a Director of Apter International Inc. and affiliated with the Center for Professional Development at Georgetown University.

CIARÁN BENSON is professor of psychology and former chair of the Department of Psychology, University College Dublin. He is also a member of the new Humanities Institute of Ireland. From 1993–1998 he was the government-appointed chairman of the Irish Arts Council with responsibility for funding the contemporary arts in Ireland. His most recent book is *The Cultural Psychology of Self: Place, Morality and Art in Human Worlds* (2001).

EVELYNE BOUGIE is completing a Ph.D. in social psychology at McGill University, Canada. Her research focuses on the collective identity of minority and majority groups.

LIONEL BOXER has been consulting to business and government since 1981 in a range of operations management issues ranging from quality management to leadership. He has worked in Canada, Australasia, and Southeast Asia. In 1993, he was listed in the International Who's Who of Quality and made a Fellow of the Quality Society of Australasia. Since 1986, he has lectured at several tertiary institutions, currently lecturing to masters of engineering students at royal Melbourne Institute of Technology, where he has completed M.B.A. and Ph.D. studies. His undergraduate industrial engineering studies were completed at The Royal Military College of Canada and Ryerson Polytechnic University.

JULIE CAOUETTE is a Ph.D. student at McGill University, Canada. Her research explores how privileged group members might experience collective guilt upon perceiving how their own group might have treated unfairly/exploited less powerful groups.

ADRIAN COYLE is a senior lecturer in the Department of Psychology at the University of Surrey. His writing and research have focused on various issues in social psychology, lesbian and gay psychology (especially identity, well-being, and therapy), and qualitative research methods.

BRONWYN DAVIES is professor of education and in 2003 has moved to the University of Western Sydney. Her most cited works are *Frogs and Snails and Feminist Tales: Preschool Children and Gender* (coming out in second edition in 2003) and her work with Rom Harré on positioning. *Frogs and Snails* is also about to be followed up in her new book, written with Kasama Hiroyuki, *Frogs and Snails in Japan: Preschool Children and Gender.* Her work on writing and bodies in landscape is published as *(In)scribing Body/Landscape Relations,* and her theoretical work is published as *A Body of Writing.*

SHAYNA GINSBURG graduated from Georgetown University in 2002 and is pursuing further studies in psychology and health. Her special focus is on the delivery of mental health services to minority communities.

ELIZABETH HANLEY graduated with a degree in psychology from Georgetown University. Having been cowinner of the psychology prize, she became involved in development projects in Africa. She is currently involved in literacy projects and is particularly interested in issues of social and cultural change in Africa.

ROM HARRÉ has been a longtime University Lecturer on the Philosophy of Science at Oxford University. He is also an Emeritus Fellow of Linacre College, Oxford, and has been visiting professor at universities around the world. He has authored or coauthored nearly 60 books.

CELIA KITZINGER is Professor of Conversation Analysis, Gender and Sexuality at the University of York, UK. Her main research interest is in using conversation analytic methods to study everyday oppression, with current projects on kinship and the family, and calls to a 'birth crisis' helpline. Her books include *Changing Our Minds: Lesbian Feminism and Psychology* (1993, with Rachel Perkins); *Feminism and Discourse* (1995, with Sue Wilkinson); and *Lesbian and Gay Psychology* (2002, with Adrian Coyle). She is currently writing a book on feminism and conversation analysis.

EVANTHIA LYONS is a senior lecturer in social psychology at SPERI, University of Surrey. Her research interests lie in the field of processes of identity construction and evaluation in particular sociohistorical contexts. Her work includes studies of identity processes in people with learning disabilities and mental illness, the development of national identities in children, and the role of social memories in maintaining inter-group conflicts.

TIM MAY is professor of sociology at Salford, Manchester, UK, and director of the Centre for Sustainable Urban and Regional Futures (www.surf. salford.ac.uk). He has written on social theory, methodology, philosophy of social science, and organizational transformation and is series editor of *Issues in Society*. He is presently conducting research into urban futures and the role of universities in the knowledge economy.

FATHALI MOGHADDAM is professor of psychology at Georgetown University. His most recent books are *The Individual and Society: A Cultural Integration* (2003), and *Understanding Terrorism: Psychosocial Roots, Consequences and Interventions* (with A. Marsella, 2003). His research focuses on justice and culture, an area to which he has made empirical and theoretical contributions.

W. GERROD PARROTT obtained his Ph.D. in Psychology from the University of Pennsylvania in 1985 and is presently a professor of psychology at Georgetown University. He is the author of *Emotions in Social Psychology* (2001) and, with Rom Harré, of *The Emotions: Social, Cultural and Biological Dimensions* (1996). His research interests focus on the social foundations, functions, and self-regulation of human emotions.

STEVEN R. SABAT is professor of psychology at Georgetown University, where he has twice received the Edward B. Bunn Award for Excellence in Teaching. The main focus of his research over the past two decades has been the intact cognitive and social abilities of people with Alzheimer's disease in the moderate to severe stages of the disease, the experience of having the disease from the sufferer's point of view, the ways in which communication between people with Alzheimer's disease and their carers may be enhanced, and how the expectations, assumptions, and behavior of healthy others can influence the behavior and experience of people with Alzheimer's disease. In addition, his interests include issues surrounding the epistemological basis of our understanding of the effects of brain injury on human beings. He has explored all of these issues in depth in numerous articles in scientific journals and in his recent book, *The Experience of Alzheimer's Disease: Life Through a Tangled Veil* (2001).

NIKKI SLOCUM is a researcher at the United Nations University research and training program on Comparative Regional Integration Studies (UNU/ CRIS) in Bruges, Belgium. She teaches qualitative methodology at the University of Brussels (VUB) and was previously a lecturer in psychology at Georgetown University.

DONALD M. TAYLOR is professor of psychology at McGill University, Canada, and has published prolifically in professional journals. He is coauthor of *Social Psychology in Cross-Cultural Perspective* (with F. M. Moghaddam and S. C. Wright), *Theories of Intergroup Relations* (with F. M. Moghaddam), *Coping with Cultural and Racial Diversity* (with W. E. Lambert) and most recently *The Quest for Identity*.

LUK VAN LANGENHOVE is director of the United Nations University research and training program on Comparative Regional Integration Studies (UNU/CRIS) in Burges, Belgium, and teaches qualitative methodology at the Vrije Universiteit Brussel. Previous publications include *Positioning Theory*. (1998)

CHRIS WALTON is a doctoral student at SPERI, University of Surrey. His thesis is concerned with the relationships between emotion discourses and discourses of gender and the negotiation of masculine subject positions.

MARGARET WETHERELL is professor of social psychology at the Open University and coeditor of the *British Journal of Social Psychology*. She is the author (with Jonathan Potter) of *Discourse and Social Psychology* (1987) and editor (with Stephanie Taylor and Simeon Yates) of *Discourse Theory and Practice* and *Discourse as Data* (2001). Her research interests include masculine identities and racism, and her current project is investigating political participation in deliberative assemblies and citizens' councils.

SUE WILKINSON is the Ruth Wynn Woodward Endowed Professor in the Department of Women's Studies, Simon Fraser University, Vancouver, Canada. Her recent research is on gender, sexuality and health—especially breast cancer, lesbian health, and identity construction—using feminist and conversation analytic methods. Her books include *Women and Health* (1994); *Representing the Other* (1996), (both with Celia Kitzinger); and *Feminist Social Psychologies: International Perspectives* (1996). She is the founding and current editor of the journal *Feminism & Psychology*.